W9-BMN-358

"I have read a lot of books about anxiety, and I can say without a doubt that *What Happened to Make You Anxious?* is the only book on the topic that I couldn't put down. Jaime explains the many realities of anxiety plus what you can do about it in a relatable, interesting, and applicable way. If you struggle with anxiety, don't skip this one."

—**Elizabeth Earnshaw, LMFT**, author of *I Want This to Work*, clinical fellow of the AAMFT, creator of @lizlistens on Instagram, and cofounder of A Better Life Therapy

"*What Happened to Make You Anxious* by Jaime Castillo is truly an incredible resource for folks struggling with anxiety and underlying little 't' traumas! This book will help you to change your relationship to anxiety and live life according to your true values. Jaime helps you to explore not just your anxiety symptoms, but also the underlying function of your anxiety. I HIGHLY recommend this book to anyone who is feeling consumed by their anxiety and looking to improve their relationship with it!"

—**Jennifer Rollin, LCSW-C**, therapist, founder of The Eating Disorder Center, and coauthor of *The Inside Scoop on Eating Disorder Recovery*

"In a world where we are more anxious than ever, *What Happened to Make You Anxious?* is the smart and compassionate book we all need right now. In this warm and supportive guide, readers learn science-backed tools so that they can stop fighting their anxiety (and themselves) and start healing. This book is going to help so many!"

—**Amanda E. White, LPC**, founder of @therapyforwomen, and author of *Not Drinking Tonight*

"If you've ever asked yourself, 'Why am I so anxious?,' this is the book that will finally give you a clear answer. Jaime's compassionate tone and easy-to-use strategies are guaranteed to help you understand, manage, and use your anxiety to help you in powerful ways."

—**Whitney Goodman, LMFT**, licensed psychotherapist, and author of *Toxic Positivity*

"This is a useful guide in helping readers approach their anxiety from a place of curiosity and understanding. Jaime offers direct and succinct tools that promote action and self-reflection. This is a must-read for the person who is ready to put the shame and self-criticism to the side and take steps to transform their relationship with anxiety!"

—**Alyssa Mancao, LCSW**, licensed clinical social worker; writer; and owner of Alyssa Marie Wellness Inc. located in Los Angeles, CA

"*What Happened to Make You Anxious* is more than a book; it is an insightful, practical guide—full of tools and resources for people who struggle not just with anxiety, but with finding ways to respond to their fears, doubts, and feelings of overwhelm in a manageable way. Jaime Castillo's work is beautifully written and full of professional wisdom. I highly recommend this read!"

—**Minaa B., LMSW**, writer, speaker, and therapist

"This book is fantastic, vulnerable, relatable, and versatile! It aims to help you understand the origins of anxiety, establish a relationship with worry, and cultivate connection with them to honor their purpose—as they serve as messengers. The activities within the book are creative and to the point. Jaime's beautiful and authentic anecdotes make you feel like you are chatting with a friend who really gets you."

—**Kelly O'Horo, LPC**, approved consultant, and founder of Infinite Healing and Wellness, an EMDR Center for Excellence; and contributing author of *Is Therapy Right for Me?*

What happened to make you anxious?

how to uncover the little "t" traumas that drive your anxiety, worry & fear

JAIME CASTILLO, LCSW

New Harbinger Publications, Inc.

Publisher's Note

Distributed in Canada by Raincoast Books

NEW HARBINGER PUBLICATIONS is a registered trademark of New Harbinger Publications, Inc.

Copyright © 2022 by Jaime Castillo
New Harbinger Publications, Inc.
5674 Shattuck Avenue
Oakland, CA 94609
www.newharbinger.com

Cover design by Amy Daniel; Acquired by Georgia Kolias; Edited by Krist Hein

Library of Congress Cataloging-in-Publication Data

Names: Castillo, Jaime (Psychologist) author.
Title: What happened to make you anxious? : how to uncover the little "t" traumas that drive your anxiety, worry, and fear / Jaime Castillo.
Description: Oakland, CA : New Harbinger Publications, 2022. | Includes bibliographical references.
Identifiers: LCCN 2022000692 | ISBN 9781684038756 (trade paperback)
Subjects: LCSH: Anxiety. | Fear. | Acceptance and commitment therapy.
Classification: LCC BF575.A6 C376 2022 | DDC 152.4/6--dc23/eng/20220125
LC record available at https://lccn.loc.gov/2022000692

Printed in the United States of America

24   23   22

10   9   8   7   6   5   4   3   2   1   First Printing

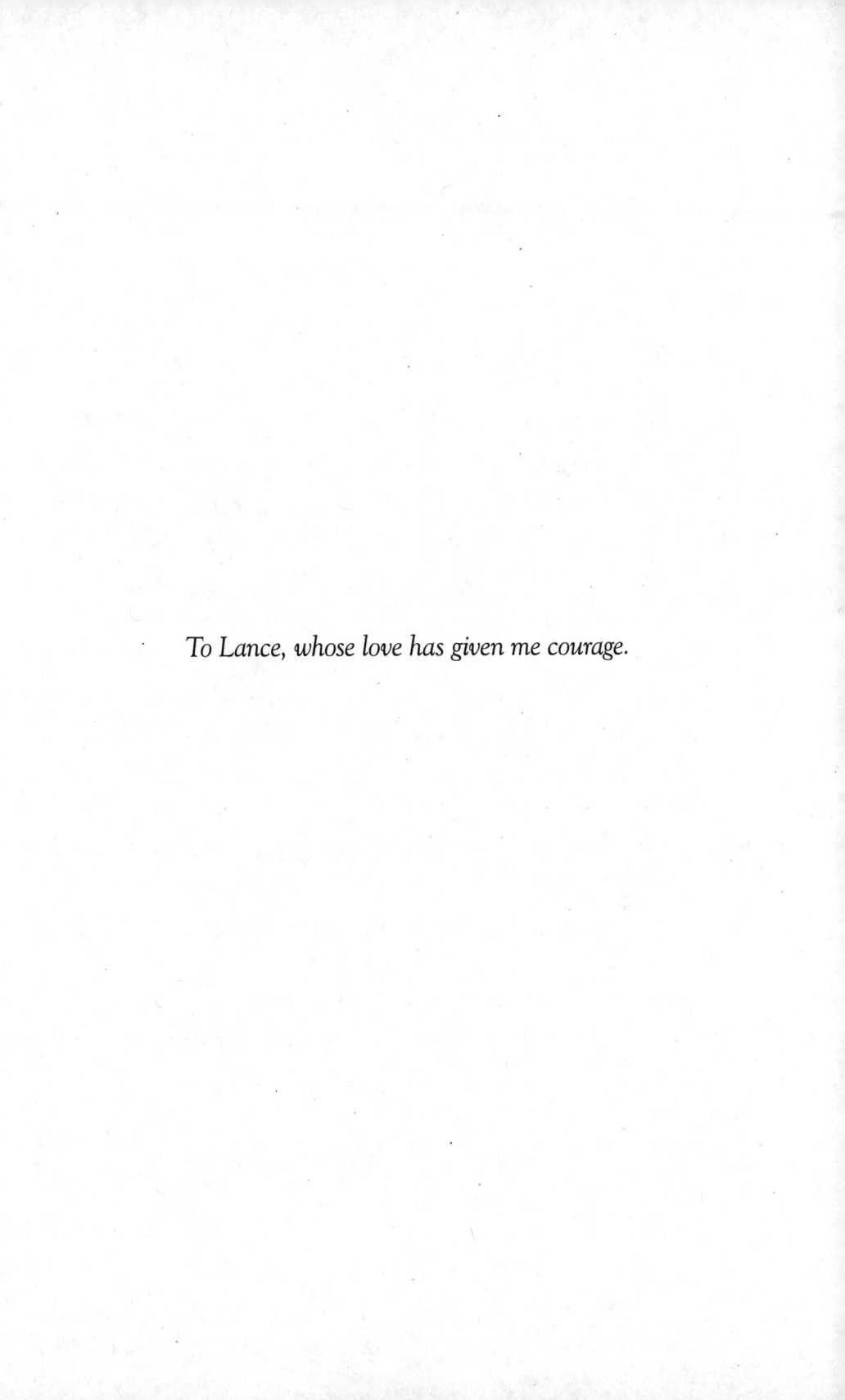

To Lance, whose love has given me courage.

contents

acknowledgments

To my husband, Lance, who has shown me unwavering love, support, and encouragement. To my parents, who taught me I can do anything I put my mind to, and to repeat the phrase *I think I can* when doing something hard (that came in handy several times while writing this book). To my brothers, whom I have looked up to and admired for forever; you are my heart. To my best friend, Chelsea, who convinced me that my voice was worthy of being heard. To my mentor, Sarah, who showed me the way as a budding therapist. To the Find Your Shine Therapy team, who bring me joy and inspiration every day. To my clients, who have trusted me with their stories. Thank you is not enough.

introduction

What if I told you that the way we have been taught to manage anxiety has actually made it worse? If our efforts to outrun or extinguish anxiety have actually fanned its flames? Anxiety is a necessary and adaptive human emotion that communicates important messages to us. It helps us to avoid danger and live a life in accordance with our values. So why does it cause so many problems in our lives? If anxiety is meant to be helpful, how is it that forty million people in the United States suffer from a clinical anxiety disorder?

Anxiety itself is not actually the culprit for the problems it seems to cause. Rather, our *response* to anxiety makes all the difference in how problematic it becomes. What we do when anxiety arises is a determining factor in whether we experience it as an occasional, helpful nudge toward our values or an unshakable force that robs us of life's pleasures.

Most of us have been conditioned to avoid anxiety whenever we notice its nudges. But because anxiety is actually there as an adaptive force to help keep us alive and well, it feels like the stakes are desperately high. Anxiety has a message that it will go to great lengths to deliver. When it's silenced, it raises its voice. When it's ignored, it tries another way to get our attention. It refuses to be outrun. It remains under the surface, waiting to be acknowledged. And it will be acknowledged at any cost to us.

If you have been at war with your anxiety for some time, it has likely started to cause problems in your work, social life, and/or intimate relationships. Anxiety is not just unpleasant to experience in the moment; over time, it can rob you of your sense of safety, connection, and overall well-being.

But there's another way. You don't have to be at odds with your anxiety any longer. When you can lean into your anxiety, understand the message it's trying to deliver and what is keeping it stuck, and then come to a mutual agreement about how to best solve the problem it is interpreting and insisting that you do something about, you find freedom.

I am going to show you exactly how to do this. Step by step, I will guide you through the process of turning toward your anxiety, allowing it to show you what it fears and where that fear originated, and then together uncovering and revisiting the past wounds that are the source of your anxiety. You will learn to befriend your anxiety rather than detaching from it and in so doing, detaching from yourself. This process will change your relationship to anxiety forever and allow you to start to live a more values-driven life.

I know this is possible for a couple of reasons. As a licensed therapist who specializes in treating anxiety, I have had the honor of guiding hundreds of people with anxiety through this journey to freedom. As a human with anxiety, I have walked through the process of uncovering my own unresolved past wounds that continued to fuel and strengthen my anxiety throughout my life. In the process, I was able to see my anxiety transform from a weekly anticipated and dreaded experience to an important insider with helpful information to share.

This book is informed by various behavioral theories and evidence-based therapeutic modalities, including the adaptive information processing (AIP) model, which informs eye movement desensitization and reprocessing (EMDR) therapy, internal family systems (IFS) therapy, and acceptance and commitment therapy (ACT). In this book I will use the most helpful and effective techniques from these interventions, combined with my years of experience in working with people on anxiety recovery, to guide you along this path to healing. There are also online free tools—audio files of the visualization exercises—available for download at the website for this book: http://www.newharbinger.com/48756. (See the very back of this book for more details.)

Most of us who live with anxiety have unresolved past wounds that either caused or contribute to it. However, anxiety can have many other causes. I recommend that you have medical causes of anxiety ruled out prior to engaging in this therapeutic work. Conditions like thyroid dysfunction, respiratory disorders, gastrointestinal problems, and the side effects of certain medications have been linked to anxiety. If you have an underlying medical condition that causes anxiety, it doesn't mean that this book is not appropriate for you; it just means you should have the medical issue treated first.

Anxiety occurs disproportionately in members of marginalized groups, likely a result of the effects of systemic oppression and stigma. Many studies have found associations between discrimination and anxiety, as well as other mental health conditions. The very real threats to safety that exist for members of oppressed groups cannot be overlooked. If you are a member of a marginalized group experiencing anxiety caused by discrimination, please note that it will not be possible to completely alleviate anxiety until systemic change occurs and the world becomes a safer place for you to be. That said, this book will be helpful for changing your relationship to your anxiety and for healing anxiety caused by past unresolved wounds, regardless of the type of wound.

Any threat to basic safety and/or survival is likely to cause anxiety for good reason. For example, most every one of us has experienced some level of anxiety related to the COVID-19 pandemic, which threatens our basic needs for safety and survival. If your basic needs are threatened by other issues—such as poverty, violence, food scarcity, or lack of access to health care—it may not be necessary to go searching for past unresolved wounds that are contributing to your anxiety, because your anxiety about these issues is clear, valid, and warranted.

In the chapters that follow, I'll help you distinguish between anxiety that fits the facts of the situation you're in, and anxiety that doesn't. We'll do therapeutic work together on the latter.

This book is not therapy, however. It is missing the most fundamental component of the therapeutic process: the relationship between client and therapist. It is also not meant to be a substitute for therapy. If you have been diagnosed with a mental health condition such as complex post-traumatic stress disorder (C-PTSD), a dissociative disorder, or obsessive-compulsive disorder (OCD) or are experiencing an active substance use or eating disorder, it is likely that this book will not provide the level of support you need.

The goal of this book is not to just help you manage symptoms of anxiety. It is more than breathing techniques and grounding skills. It is designed to take you on a journey into your past to explore where anxiety is "stuck," which will help you uncover why it is misfiring now. It is designed to get to the root of the problem so you can experience long-lasting change rather than continually searching for another method of coping with it. It will make the difference between avoiding anxiety and the parts of your life that come with it, and living fully.

understanding anxiety

For most of my adult life I've lived with a fear of appearing ignorant, ill-prepared, inexperienced, unqualified—or to use that childhood insult, *dumb*—in front of respectable people. This fear manifested as an anxiety that accompanied me through my young adulthood and the beginnings of my professional life. As a budding therapist, I knew it made sense to experience *some* doubt or insecurity, but this anxiety was disproportionate. It sometimes felt almost disabling.

I can remember sitting in meetings at my first professional internship, surrounded by people much more experienced than I was, physically shaking when I knew it was almost my turn to present a client case. There was nothing that felt more threatening to me in those moments than the possibility of saying something stupid and discovering that I didn't have what it took to be a good therapist. I was terrified to show vulnerability in other ways; for example, I strategically neglected to tell anyone when my licensing exam was scheduled. If I failed, I couldn't tolerate the prospect of having to disclose that to my colleagues. In my mind, this would have revealed to them that I was actually not as smart and respectable as they might have thought. At that point in my life, this felt worse than death.

The thing is, my anxiety had very little basis in reality. Not only was I qualified to be at the table, but at the agency where I interned, my supervisors, mentors, and even my fellow interns genuinely embodied a culture of support, compassion, and the encouragement of growth. I had never been publicly shamed or made to feel stupid. So in fact, it was irrational to be thinking I would reveal myself as an imposter who didn't actually deserve to be there if I said the wrong thing. But to my anxiety, none of that really mattered. It was convinced that I was in danger, and it put my nervous system on high alert.

As you can imagine, my anxiety felt really uncomfortable to experience. So naturally I did what I could to avoid or suppress it. That's what we do as humans, right? We try to avoid pain, and when we can't, we try to ease it. This includes emotional pain. When I was trembling inside, I would do anything I could think of to make it stop: taking sips of ice water, naming things around the room I could see, and even using my newly minted cognitive behavioral therapy (CBT) skill of challenging my own thinking. While these tools helped some, the biggest relief came when the meeting was over. It was as if my nervous system exclaimed *Crisis averted!* and finally backed down just enough to allow me to take a full, deep breath. The relief I felt would stick around until the next weekly meeting was held. It became a predictable and seemingly unending cycle of anxiety and relief.

When Anxiety Doesn't Make Sense

Anxiety—the strong, persistent fear or apprehension that something bad is going to happen—doesn't need to make sense to be real. Often, anxiety does fit with the facts of the situation that prompts it—it's rational. With this type of anxiety, anyone might look at the situation and think, *I would feel anxious about that*. For example, if you lose your job and experience anxiety about how you are going to pay your bills, your anxiety fits the facts of what's happened. In this case, anxiety may actually be useful, because it may prompt you to engage in a job search and get creative about scaling back expenses. While the experience may be stressful, once you obtain a new job and can pay your bills, it's likely your anxiety will naturally reduce. Other examples of anxiety that fit the facts of the situation might relate to an important presentation or exam, a newly diagnosed medical condition, a first date, and so on.

Another kind of anxiety, the kind that we'll be working with in the chapters that follow, is the kind that doesn't fit the facts of the situation. It is irrational, sometimes distressingly so. For example:

- Feeling panic all of a sudden just before you meet up with friends whom you adore

- Feeling fear after having a random thought that your partner is pulling away from the relationship

- Having a rather calm and worry-free day and then starting to have anxiety because you *don't* currently have anxiety and don't want to be caught off guard

This type of anxiety can add layers of frustration and confusion to a situation. It can feel unpredictable. It may even leave you dumbfounded. With this type of anxiety, it's hard to imagine someone else looking at your situation with compassion, saying "I'd feel anxious about that too." If you communicate this type of anxiety, it may get the opposite of compassion: invalidation. You might hear things like "Just stop worrying about that," "Let it go," or (my personal favorite) "Chill out!"

You probably *want* to be able to stop worrying, let it go, chill out, and get on with your life. But when your anxiety feels irrational and unsolvable, you may feel like your only option is to ignore it, or detach from it, or numb it. After all, you have places to go, people to see, relationships to foster and maintain. And there's no way around it: anxiety gets in the way of all of these.

As if your desire to live without the discomfort of anxiety wasn't enough, your efforts to avoid anxiety may be further encouraged and reinforced by society in a number of ways. Our news and social media feeds have a hundred ways every day to remind us that our anxiety makes us unlikable. We are made to feel that we're doing something wrong when we live with anxiety and are simultaneously exposed over and over to perfectly curated Instagram feeds and people who appear to have it all together. The cultural pressure to measure up to our peers gives us even more incentive to suppress our signs of anxiety.

It makes good sense to want to get rid of our anxiety. It's incredibly uncomfortable to live with that feeling in the pit of your stomach or that can't-seem-to-get-a-full-breath sensation that anxiety often brings. It makes us feel out of control and helpless. And society says we won't fare very well as a partner, employee, or friend if our anxiety isn't well managed. The result? Most of us don't need convincing that we should want to reduce our anxiety.

Many people have tried everything under the sun to stop their anxiety from happening. People actually die from desperate attempts to control anxiety, such as numbing it with substances or other self-harming behaviors. Attempts to block, avoid, or numb anxiety might create some relief in the short term. But they often lead to dire consequences over time—at a minimum, a reinforcement and perpetuation of anxiety, and at worst, your life.

But what if there were another way to approach our anxiety?

Anxiety Can Be a Friend

When anxiety fits the facts of the situation you're in (that is, it's rational), there is nothing you need to do other than learn and use some basic anxiety-management techniques to cope the best you can in the moment. Then, if possible, problem solve the situation so that you can reduce its real dangers or discomforts. But if you frequently experience the kind of anxiety that doesn't fit the facts, or if you're not sure whether it does, or if anxiety seems to be causing problems in your life, this book is for you.

First, you will learn tools for temporarily calming anxiety because, let's be honest, talking about anxiety probably gives you anxiety. I want to make sure you're as equipped as possible to manage the emotions that might bubble to the surface as you start to do this work.

Most people who live with anxiety devote a great deal of energy to trying to suppress rather than understand it. This makes sense, in a way. When we're committed to putting out a fire and using all of our resources to do so, we can't simultaneously get to know why the fire started in the first place. As long as we are actively suppressing anxiety, our ability to understand it fully will be compromised. For that reason, I recommend choosing to engage with this text at times when your anxiety feels relatively managed, perhaps a 5 out of 10 or lower. The self-regulating tools will help you get there.

Next, you'll learn the role of avoidance in increasing and perpetuating anxiety and the need for moving toward rather than away from it to find true healing. You'll be guided through exercises designed to give you a better understanding of your unique anxiety—how it manifests currently and where it all started. Everyone's anxiety is personal to them, and it's important to spend some time learning what yours is like. This makes it easier to see and to remember that *your anxiety* is not the same thing as *you.*

Once you're able to accept your anxiety as an entity separate from yourself, it becomes something you can be curious about and have a relationship with. You'll become able to repair your relationship with anxiety, seeing it in its true light as a protective part of yourself that wants the same things for you as *you* want for you. You'll learn to work *with* your anxiety rather than fighting against it and will be given opportunities for healing old wounds that are causing your brain to register threats that don't actually exist.

Finally, you'll establish a pact with your anxiety that will honor its purpose and function, while giving you enough space and distance from it that you will be able to live a meaningful, fulfilled, value-driven life that is no longer hijacked by fear.

REFLECTION: Your Coping Behaviors—A Journal Exercise

What efforts do you make to stop anxiety? Give this some reflection, and in your journal, write some of the tactics you regularly rely on. Maybe you avoid certain people or places. Maybe you have a glass of wine at the end of the day. Maybe you go for a run. Coping behaviors aren't always bad, but it's important to be able to get to know them and recognize them in real time for what they are: efforts to stop anxiety.

I know this process of befriending your own anxiety is possible, because I've done it myself. In the years since I was an intern trembling before speaking at my weekly staff meetings, I have learned and applied the skills I will teach you in the chapters that follow. I have transformed my relationship with my own anxiety, and I have helped hundreds of my clients do the same.

The Brain's Threat Meter

In my professional work as a therapist, as I continued gathering training and experience I started to better understand how and why the cycle of anxiety starts and perpetuates. When we live with anxiety, our threat meter becomes hijacked and causes us to feel the same level of threat— for example, in a professional meeting—as we would if we were out in the wild and saw a mountain lion approaching us. When the part of our brain that is designed to perceive and respond to threats is activated, it compromises the other part of our brain—the one designed to help us think logically, problem solve, and rationalize.

From an evolutionary perspective this is actually very useful, because if we encounter a lion in the wild we need to be able to act fast rather than pull out a piece of scratch paper and start listing our options in order of likelihood to help us survive. However, this mechanism creates challenges when our brain is perceiving a threat that doesn't actually exist (or exists on a *much* smaller, less threatening scale than we're perceiving). We need to be able to problem solve and rationalize, but the part of our brain that helps us do that isn't functioning well. This is why, when we're struggling with anxiety, advice from well-intentioned people like "Just stop worrying" or "Think happy thoughts!" feels invalidating. We would gladly do those things if we could, but our brain thinks we're about to be a lion's meal, so it's a little averse to putting that on the back burner and thinking about cute puppies instead. It's this same mechanism that makes efforts to reason with our anxiety feel futile.

When Anxiety Generalizes

Further complicating matters, the part of our brain that perceives threats isn't always discerning about what *part* of the experience was threatening. When a threat happens, our survival brain casts a really wide net. That's why if you are walking in a park on a rainy summer day and a tree you're passing is struck by lightning, your brain will register not only that lightning is dangerous, but perhaps also that rain, summer days, and that particular park are dangerous too. You may have a hard time revisiting that park after that experience, even though your logic would tell you that the park itself is not dangerous. Similarly, you may find it difficult to walk outside on rainy summer days, even if you know there is almost no likelihood that you would ever experience a close lightning strike again. This tendency to draw causation isn't limited to actual dangerous events, but also rings true for *perceived* danger, like the professional meetings I've described. For example, it would not have been surprising if my brain started to associate that particular meeting room with danger, causing anxiety when I was in that room even if for a completely different occasion.

REFLECTION: Your Threat Meter—A Journal Exercise

In what ways has your own anxiety generalized to things outside of the actual threat? Perhaps you had an anxiety attack in a certain location, and now you

find that location provokes anxiety despite there being no real threat associated with it. Maybe your anxiety started in a social context but has become
generalized over time to health anxiety, anxiety while driving, or some other
unrelated form of anxiety. If you have a hard time linking your anxiety back to
an actual threat, that's okay. While it may not be obvious now, my hope is that
in doing this work, you will begin to get a clear picture of both the root of your
anxiety and the ways it's generalized.

Just as our brains try to make sense of threats, they like to understand safety too. In the story I told at the beginning of this chapter, I
mentioned that when a staff meeting was over, I felt instant relief. Our
brains have a tendency to interpret that as *I felt relief because I got out of
that meeting.* This reinforces the idea that meetings are dangerous and is
likely to increase my anxiety the next time I'm in the meeting. It's as if
our survival brain says to us, *See, I knew that meeting was life threatening.
That's why you felt so much calmer when it ended. Best to avoid those meetings altogether going forward.* This is accurate when we experience anxiety
that fits the facts, like if we were to encounter a lion in the wild. Once
we escape the lion, it makes sense that our anxiety would lessen and we
would take from that experience the message that we should avoid lions
in the future. However, it doesn't make sense in the context of
meetings.

So how do you break this cycle? The first step in this work is to
better understand why the anxiety is there in the first place. After all, we
can't change it if we don't know why it exists to begin with. Sometimes
it's obvious, as in the lightning strike example. If we experience a close
lightning strike in a park and subsequently experience fear of lightning
and parks, we don't have to do a ton of investigative work to get to the
bottom of why that's happening. Other times, though, there isn't such a
clear and obvious cause, like when I experienced anxiety in my professional meetings. That's why it was so frustrating—I knew it was irrational and couldn't pinpoint why it was happening.

Anxiety as a Messenger

What I learned was that rather than trying to problem solve anxiety, rationalize myself out of it, or extinguish it, I needed to treat anxiety as a messenger that had important information for me about danger. It was working to protect me, even though its efforts were actually counterproductive. Once I shifted out of attempting to solve it and got curious about what it actually wanted from me, that is when healing happened.

Think of anxiety as a four-year-old child who randomly starts throwing a temper tantrum, screaming and flailing about. Imagine saying "Johnnie, it makes no sense that you're crying right now. This is ridiculous. Would you stop it?" If you have spent any amount of time around four-year-olds, you know what outcome this rationalizing approach would lead to: Johnnie is going to cry harder until his needs are met. It would be more effective to get down to his eye level with Johnnie and say, "What is it? Tell me. I'm here and I'm listening."

Anxiety wants the same thing from us. It's trying to tell us something, and as long as we try to rationalize or push it away, it's going to escalate, until we can sit with it and say, *What is it, anxiety? Show me.* Once you can change your relationship with anxiety in this way, you will start to notice a decrease in tension. Your anxiety will finally start to feel heard—because it is actually *being* heard.

And the communication goes both ways. It wasn't until I was at a professional training a couple of years ago that I finally opened up to my anxiety about feeling dumb. I was working in a professional dyad with a colleague, and my fear of sounding dumb came up in whatever we were discussing. My partner said, "Why don't you just close your eyes and explore that a bit?" She asked me to connect to the part of my body that felt anxious. It showed up immediately—it felt like the shape and weight of a ten-pound dumbbell sitting on my chest. She asked me to notice how I felt about it. Annoyed. Unwelcoming. She encouraged me to just notice it rather than try to push it away.

I sat there with my eyes closed, wondering *How much longer until this training is over?* Hadn't I just told her this anxiety was unwelcome? I didn't exactly want to sit with it, especially in the middle of a professional training. What if it got bigger or more powerful? What if it completely overtook me? I voiced these concerns, and she clearly had been paying attention to the training material, because she struck the perfect balance of validating my fears and encouraging me to continue this exercise despite them.

After some time, I agreed to sit with my anxiety without trying to detach from it. With the help of her prompts, I asked it what it feared. I listened for the answer. It told me it didn't want me to sound dumb or else I would be the laughingstock of whatever group I was in. Although I wasn't totally on board with its role yet, I was able to acknowledge that we shared a common goal. I didn't want that either. Actually, the thought of that terrified me. Over the next couple of days, my colleague continued to lead me through this inner work, and as she did, I started gleaning more and more important insights, which led to substantial mental shifts.

As you navigate this work, you too will gain a better understanding of how your anxiety is trying to help you. You will learn that you and your anxiety share a common goal for yourself but likely have different ideas about how best to achieve that goal.

Giving Anxiety a Voice

When I began this work, it was as if for the first time ever I paused on my fierce ascent up the mountain of life. In my peripheral vision I saw my friend anxiety flailing its arms and silently shouting in a desperate attempt to get my attention. I said, *Oh hi there. You must be trying to help me.* Just this step alone allowed my anxiety to breathe a huge sigh of relief. I had finally acknowledged it rather than trying to distance myself from it and power through. I noticed my anxiety already easing up. It was the equivalent of sitting down on the floor with a completely dysregulated four-year-old.

This felt like a giant leap in my own healing journey, but as I continued to do the work, I realized that it was only the beginning. As my own inner work deepened, I realized that my anxiety and I had some real qualms about one another that we needed to hash out. Thirty years' worth of qualms, to be exact. My anxiety wanted to know why, for so long, I had been ignoring it and all of the ways in which it was trying to help me. For my part, I wanted to know why it thought it deserved to take up space in my chest and hinder me and cause extra problems in my life in so many different ways.

For the first time, I gave my anxiety a voice. I learned that it was separate from me. We had a conversation. And it actually didn't feel so bad to listen to it rather than try to outrun it. I apologized for trying to silence it without listening to it first.

In later chapters, you will address your own qualms about your anxiety, which will be the impetus to changing your relationship with it. You will gain a greater understanding of the ways in which anxiety is actually trying to help you. You will learn to partner with it rather than feeling at odds with it. You will experience greater freedom in your life because you will no longer be at war with yourself.

REFLECTION: Resolving Qualms—A Journal Exercise

What do you anticipate needing to share with your anxiety about the way it has impacted you? Can you start to imagine what grievances your anxiety might have to share with you? How do you anticipate that having this conversation might impact your relationship with anxiety?

Once I trusted that my anxiety was really trying to help me, and that there was a real path to healing, I agreed to let my colleague guide me through what's called a *float back exercise* (a concept from EMDR). This allowed my anxiety to show me some boulders I had become tethered to earlier in my life. The roles reversed; I stopped climbing the mountain of life and let anxiety lead me on a descent into the canyon that was my past experiences. This took a tremendous amount of trust and willingness to stop along the way to take breaks. After all, I hadn't taken this route before; it was overwhelming and scary, and it felt contrary to my goal of reaching the top of the mountain. I had to acknowledge my discomfort often; I had to ask anxiety to give me grace in the rate at which I was comfortable descending. Surprisingly, it obliged me, despite my not having reciprocated with that same grace in the preceding years.

Then a memory from when I was five years old hit me like a ton of bricks. *This must have been the biggest boulder that I've been tethered to*, I thought to myself. In this memory, I was sitting at the dinner table with my two older brothers and our mom and dad. My brothers were taking turns quoting lines from a cartoon. I wanted to quote a line that included the phrase "corny details." I got my words mixed up and said "horny details." My brothers, being immature eight- and ten-year-olds, erupted in laughter, and my mom's face turned bright red as she fought back her own giggles. I was dumbfounded. I didn't even know what horny meant. All I knew was I had gotten it wrong. Because everyone was so embarrassed on my behalf, nobody explained to me the error I had made, which would turn out to be the precipitating event for my anxiety decades later when I sat in professional meetings. I had great parents who would have never suggested that I was stupid, but from this experience this is the message that I internalized, along with a firm belief that I shouldn't speak up anymore. I carried this belief within me for nearly thirty years.

Now, in the float back exercise, I kept my eyes closed and allowed myself to really sink into this memory. I was periodically interrupted by my own thoughts, like *Get outta here. This is painful. Why are you doing this?* My colleague had prepared me for the exercise, explaining how to handle my natural responses; accordingly, I noticed these thoughts and returned my attention to the memory. I surrendered to the anxiety and allowed it to show me what it needed to. I remembered all that I could of the memory, which didn't need to be much. It was more about the felt sense of it. And boy, was I feeling it. As I continued the exercise, I felt my throat tightening and moisture welling up in my eyes. *Here we go*, I thought. I leaned into the feeling, and I freely shed tears for that little girl, who felt so rejected at that dinner table. Then, following my colleague's prompts, I imagined my adult self entering this memory with my five-year-old self and giving her what she had needed so badly then but didn't receive: a trusted adult to sit down with her and say "The word *horny* means that you want to have sex. Your brothers are laughing because it's an adult word and they are still kids, which means they are still a little immature. It's actually not even that funny, and you have nothing to worry about. Now let's go do something fun!" I breathed a huge sigh of relief as I pictured my five-year-old self smiling and hugging me, then the two of us running off to play with dolls. It was everything she needed and never got. And now I was in a position to give it to her, and I did. I'd never experienced anything more powerful in my healing journey than that exercise.

After spending some time with the feelings brought on by this exercise, I opened my eyes and turned my attention back to my colleague, who was looking at me, beaming, with tears in her eyes.

"What the heck did you just do to me?" I asked her.

She laughed. I laughed. And I became a staunch believer in this work.

The experience I had with my younger self that day became foundational to the work I do with my clients. I will teach you the principles and guide you through the same process in later chapters.

Prior to this healing work, I wouldn't have considered that dinner table memory a traumatic one. I had been in therapy before, and this memory was never addressed. I wouldn't have bet that it was traumatic enough to be causing problems in my life all of these years later. But that's the thing about what I call *little t traumas*: they aren't always big, impactful events; rather, they are smaller, less significant ones that produce big feelings that we unknowingly carry with us—feelings that get reinforced over time.

If there's one thing this experience taught me, it was that these kinds of memories matter. It was why, decades later—when I sat in that professional internship meeting and had the thought *What if I sound dumb?*—it felt like my life was ending. It's why, when I tried to rationalize and name things in my environment and challenge my thinking, the anxiety only grew over time. It was the reason my brain was misperceiving threats now. It was a huge boulder in my past that was unresolved and keeping me stuck. That feeling of being dumb, laughed at, and alone was what my anxiety had been trying to protect me from all along.

As you become aware of your own unresolved past experiences, you will gain insight into the ways in which your anxiety is trying to protect you, perhaps from other feelings that are far more painful than anxiety itself. You will acknowledge that you and your anxiety share a common goal, and you don't actually want it to stop doing its job. Rather than trying to terminate it, you can work with your anxiety to modify its job description in a way that makes life easier for you both.

The next couple of chapters will guide you through what I refer to as "the work before the work." You will learn basic anxiety management techniques that will help take the edge off your anxiety temporarily when it's getting in the way of your basic functioning. You will understand the role that avoidance of your anxiety has in preserving it and keeping you stuck. You will also get clear on why the work to come is the best solution for long-term anxiety management.

Next, you will be guided through the work. In chapters 4 through 6 you will engage in exercises that orient you to your anxiety, and you will allow your anxiety to guide you back to the boulders that are keeping you stuck. You will make connections with the younger version of yourself who first experienced these anxiety-provoking experiences. Together you will explore what your younger self needed at that time, and I will guide you through how to provide that now. You will become the source of healing that the younger you has always needed but never gotten until now. You will find that your most powerful resource in healing the source of your anxiety is your current, adult self.

Finally, you will engage in future-oriented work that will help you maintain a working relationship with your anxiety moving forward. You'll establish a communication plan with it so that when it registers a future threat, you can discuss it together and come up with a plan for how to respond. You'll understand what to do if you have an "anxiety relapse," or a time when anxiety does become debilitating again.

I know this is possible because I have experienced these shifts in doing my own work. My anxiety is not gone, but now I don't want it to be. I can see how it works to help me, and it's clear to me that no matter what it's fussing about, we share a common goal of self-preservation of some sort. We both want safety, acceptance, belonging, and respect, and when anxiety shows up, it's usually because it feels like one of these things is being threatened. I have become more aware of when it's trying to grab my attention and can engage in dialogue with it that feels productive and helpful to us both. In the context of professional meetings, I am able to soothe my anxiety by imagining soothing that five-year-old little girl. I'm able to safely explore what anxiety needs from me and then work to meet those needs. I can also communicate when I need anxiety to loosen its grip and give me some space, which it now trusts me to do. Since doing this work, we have come up with a mutual agreement for the future: I will listen to and respect it, and it will back off and allow me to engage in professional settings the way I want to be able to—without a crippling fear of rejection. The results have been amazing—and led me to be able to say yes to writing this book.

My hope for you in doing this work is that you will gain the perspective to reframe your anxiety as a helpful force in your life. I understand that at this point it is probably hard to see anything about your anxiety as helpful. Befriending your anxiety might feel like the opposite of what you're used to doing. But stick with me on this journey, and you will find that the willingness to lean into your anxiety rather than avoid it will give you a quality of freedom you've only dreamed of.

A Note for Trauma Survivors

If you have a significant trauma history, are currently experiencing ongoing trauma or threats to your safety, or have diagnosed PTSD or dissociative disorder, it is likely that what will come up in the course of doing this work is outside of the scope of self-help material and will require the support and oversight of a licensed therapist. You may still find the process of befriending your anxiety to be helpful and even transformative, but the guidance of a professional, trauma-informed therapist is essential to keep you safe as you learn and heal. If you're unsure about whether it's safe to proceed, a therapist may be able to do an assessment to help you determine your level of readiness to engage in these types of exercises on your own.

CHAPTER 2

finding your healing window

If you're feeling some combination of hopeful and terrified about learning to befriend your anxiety, you're probably on the right track. Contemplating this work might bring up thoughts like *If I go there, what if I can't make the anxiety stop?* or *What if I remember things from my past that are too much for me to handle?* If you are experiencing such thoughts, you are not alone. And this work *will* inevitably bring up discomfort; if it doesn't, there will be no benefit. The saying "The only way out is through" applies to what we will do together.

That said, the discomfort you experience in the process of working with your anxiety should remain manageable. As I mentioned at the end of the last chapter, if trauma is a significant part of your past or present, you'll need help from a therapist. Diving into past experiences before your nervous system trusts that it's safe to do so can actually cause more harm than benefit. For example, it may be that your brain learned to detach from reality when reality was too overwhelming, and you still experience some dissociation. If so, trying to revisit the experiences that caused dissociation in the first place without proper safety and oversight may cause your brain to want to further detach. Similarly, if you experienced a "freeze" response during a traumatic experience and then you revisit past experiences without an adequate sense of safety, it is highly likely you'll "freeze" again. This is harmful: it reinforces the trauma response rather than fostering its healing.

You will know it is safe to continue this work when you can achieve two things:

- *State change.* This is a term that comes from EMDR therapy. It means you are capable of going from an anxious state to a less anxious state by practicing the tools and techniques outlined in this chapter. You will feel more confident when your anxiety increases if you know you can use a tool like deep breathing to bring it back down again.

- *Dual awareness.* Another term from EMDR therapy, it suggests that when revisiting a trauma memory, you should be able to pay attention to the memory, while not losing sight of the fact that you are in the here and now, where the danger is not currently happening. If you can maintain this perspective, you will likely not experience dissociation or "reliving" the memory. A necessary component of practicing dual awareness is that the here and now is *actually* safe.

This chapter will provide the tools you need to achieve an anxiety state change and maintain dual awareness while doing the work. The skills taught in this chapter are not designed to be problem-solvers. In other words, these skills do not address the root of your anxiety and are not "the work"; rather, they are the work *before* the work. They will not eradicate anxiety or keep you feeling calm over the long term; they are designed to bring you some sense of felt safety in the present moment. Think of these skills as helping you dial down your anxiety.

The work you'll do in this book requires finding the amount of discomfort that is right for you. It is important that you have *some* exposure to anxiety-provoking past experiences, but this should never reach a level that causes you to *relive* past experiences rather than *revisit* them. This concept was described as the "window of tolerance" by Dr. Dan Siegel (1999), and this term is used to describe the optimal zone where healing is possible.

One way to determine if you are within your window of tolerance while doing this work is to assess your concept of time. The goal is to remain cognitively in the present, with an embodied understanding that you are in a time and space that is free of imminent danger, while you are revisiting a memory in which that was not the case. This is dual awareness, and its presence suggests that you are within your optimal window. If at any time you lose orientation to the present time and experience a flashback that causes you to feel like you are actually back in that dangerous time and space without an anchor to the present, you have exited the window of tolerance that is your optimal healing zone. When this happens, it is more likely that you are reinforcing a trauma response rather than healing from it.

Siegel (1999) posits that if you have left your window of tolerance, you are experiencing either *hypoarousal* or *hyperarousal*. Both of these states are a survival response designed to help you survive a threat. Hypoarousal feels like under-stimulation of your nervous system and can include feeling emotionally numb, shut down, detached, or spacey. It is also known as the freeze response. If while doing this work you start to feel detached from your body, excessively tired and shut down, or like you should be experiencing emotions but can't, you might have exited your window of tolerance and could be experiencing hypoarousal.

By contrast, if you experience what feels like overstimulation of your nervous system, like crying combined with hyperventilation, rapid heart rate, shallow breathing, racing thoughts, and/or the impulse to flee, you might be experiencing hyperarousal. This state is referred to as "fight or flight," as your body prepares for action.

Both hypoarousal and hyperarousal are indicators from your nervous system that your sense of safety has been compromised. This can happen as a result of losing dual awareness. In other words, your body starts to think it is actually reexperiencing the trauma rather than remembering it. In an effort to protect you, it kicks you out of your healing zone and into survival mode. Even if you logically know you are safe, treat this as a cue from your body that it needs to feel more safe before proceeding, to avoid harm.

Our window of tolerance is not fixed; it can look different depending on the day and what is going on in our life. Perhaps at one time you are able to do a particular piece of inner work adequately and safely, staying in your healing zone. However, outside factors such as additional life stressors, sleep deprivation, certain medications, and/or hormone imbalances may create increased sensitivities and make you more vulnerable to being emotionally overwhelmed. Perhaps the most important part of this work is an ongoing assessment and honoring of your capacity to do it.

You will know you are within your window of tolerance when you have access to both your emotions and your logic. Being inside the healing window does not mean you will experience an absence of emotion. Remember that the goal is to experience the right amount of emotion for you in your healing work—it feels uncomfortable, yet tolerable and balanced by logic. Refer to this chart to help you determine whether you are in your window of tolerance or experiencing hyper- or hypoarousal.

Hyperarousal	
Fight-or-flight response	Shallow breathing
Pounding heart	Difficulty concentrating
Trembling	Increased blood pressure
Panicking	Sweating

Window of Tolerance or Healing Zone	
Dual awareness	Can feel emotions
Engaged	Feels safe
Rational	Open
Alert	Calm

Hypoarousal	
Freeze response	Can't process emotions
Feeling shut down	Disconnected
Detached	Zoned out
Numb	Spacey

This chapter is designed to teach you some anxiety-regulation strategies to help keep you in the healing zone by establishing and maintaining a felt sense of safety in your body. You can use these skills while engaging in this work; they can also be useful in your day-to-day life when you're working to regulate an anxiety response. These skills are not designed to be one-size-fits-all; what may be effective for one person might not work for another. In figuring out what works for you, it can be helpful to try a variety of different regulation strategies and keep a log or journal of your experiences, rating each for how effective they were for you, on a scale of 0 to 10.

The varying degree of effectiveness of these skills is highly dependent on your unique experiences, anxiety triggers, and preferences. When trying these skills or other anxiety-regulation practices, aim for breadth rather than depth. The more exercises you try, the more likely it is that you'll find the skills that are useful for you and can be added to your anxiety-management repertoire. It's helpful to try these skills while your anxiety is low and manageable, even if you think to yourself, *I don't have much anxiety right now; why would I need to practice these skills?* When our anxiety is high, it's likely that our fight-flight-freeze response is activated; when that's the case, it becomes incredibly difficult to problem solve and try a new skill. If, when your anxiety is high, you have already practiced these and discovered what works for you, you will require less innovation and troubleshooting in the moment and will feel more automatic, making it more likely these tools will be effective for you.

Self-Soothing

Self-soothing skills are exactly what they sound like: exercises designed to soothe your nervous system. Our five best-known senses (smell, hearing, taste, touch, and sight) play a large role in how our brains assess and respond to threats. For example, if you experience the felt sense of something crawling on your leg, and you are afraid of bugs, you are likely to immediately register some amount of danger and swat at your leg to remove the threat. If you have a bee phobia (or allergy) and hear a buzzing sound hovering around your ear, you will likely associate that sound with some amount of danger and run away (maybe for the hills). If you see or smell smoke coming from inside your home, your nervous system will do its job in recognizing that sight or smell as dangerous and will prompt you for action. You can see how our senses play an integral role in our sense of safety; they are designed to be the first line of defense against a threat by sounding the alarm. If our survival brains become activated by input through our five senses, it makes good sense that by soothing our senses we can in turn soothe our nervous systems.

What's soothing to me might be very different from what feels soothing to you based on your own unique experiences and past associations, which is why it's important to approach this with an open mind and confidence that you can recognize what's best for you.

Here are some examples of activities or objects that can feel soothing, broken down by the five senses.

Activities That Might Soothe Your Sense of Smell

- Baking bread

- Lighting a scented candle

- Going for a walk after it's rained

- Smelling fresh-cut flowers at a florist or grocery store

- Smelling freshly washed and dried linens

- Diffusing lavender or peppermint essential oils

- Smelling crisp mountain air

- Smelling coffee beans

- Smelling freshly popped popcorn

- Smelling sweet basil

- Smelling lemon balm

- Hanging an air freshener in your car

- Cooking with lemon zest, herbs, and spices

Sounds That Might Soothe Your Sense of Hearing

- Water sounds (ocean, rainfall, thunderstorms)

- Instrumental, ambient, or jazz music

- Humming sounds (engines, motors, fans, white noise)

- Laughter

- Hoofbeats

- Flutes, drums, or violin

- Chanting

- Crunching

- Shaking of a spray can

- A paintbrush stroking a canvas

- Gentle whispering

- Crash of pins from a strike in bowling

- Pages of a book being turned

Activities That Might Soothe Your Sense of Taste

- Eating a favorite childhood meal or snack

- Chewing peppermint gum

- Eating a popsicle on a hot day

- Eating dark chocolate

- Drinking hot tea with honey

- Drinking hot water with lemon

- Eating fresh fruits like oranges, mangoes, or strawberries

- Drinking hot coffee or warm milk with cinnamon

- Eating juicy fruits like watermelon, pineapple, and peaches

- Eating warm bread with butter

- Drinking cold lemonade

- Sipping hot soup

Activities That Might Soothe Your Sense of Touch

- Walking barefoot in the sand

- Getting a shoulder or foot massage

- Covering yourself with a fuzzy or weighted blanket

- Feeling the cool breeze on your face

- Petting your dog or cat

- Getting a tight squeeze hug from a loved one

- Stroking or massaging your hair and scalp

- Playing with Play-Doh or sand

- Wearing a soft sweater and noticing how it feels against your skin

- Popping bubble wrap

- Lying in blankets fresh from the hot dryer

- Walking on dried leaves or pinecones

- Holding grounding stones in your hand

- Lying on an acupressure mat

- Getting into a hot tub or bath with jets

Activities That Might Soothe Your Sense of Sight

- Looking at photos of baby animals

- Looking at photos of loved ones or people you admire

- Looking at nature (mountains, ocean, forest)

- Watching clouds go by

- Stargazing

- Bird watching

- Watching a lava lamp

- Looking at the colors of autumn leaves

- Watching the sunrise or sunset

- Watching video of a turning windmill

- Looking at art in a museum

- Watching someone paint

- Watching someone draw straight lines

- Watching someone concentrate

- Looking through color swatches

- Looking at Christmas lights

- Watching wood burning in a fireplace

If you can create these experiences in your current environment, that is great. If not, it can be just as effective to soothe your sense of sight or hearing by watching or listening to videos of these experiences on the internet. You will need to engage in these activities and practices mindfully to get the most out of them. For example, if you take a walk after it's rained but spend the entire walk talking on the phone, you may completely miss the soothing post-rain smell (there's a name for that smell: petrichor!) and will likely not benefit from the exercise as much as you might have if you were mindfully noticing your surroundings.

When you have had a chance to experiment with some of these sensory self-soothing techniques, reflect in your journal on what worked for you and what else you might try. This exercise offers some prompts.

REFLECTION: Self-Soothing—A Journal Exercise

1. Which of my five senses was easiest for me to soothe? Most challenging?

2. Which self-soothing techniques worked well for me?

3. Which self-soothing practices didn't work so well?

4. How did I know when something was soothing for me?

5. What might I try next time I want to self-soothe using my five senses?

Finding Your Calm Place

A potentially powerful anxiety-regulation strategy involves visualizing a place that you either have been or imagine being that feels exceptionally calming. The idea of an internal calm place is drawn from Francine Shapiro (2001), who called it your "safe place." Your calm place can be something as simple and familiar as your bed or as extravagant as a Greek isle. It can be a real place that you frequent or an imaginary, fairytale-like scene from your favorite Disney movie. The specific location matters less than the felt sense you get when you are there or imagine being there. The most important part of this exercise is that the place feels calming and soothing to your nervous system. Once you have a place in mind, you can begin the exercise. It's helpful to read through the whole exercise before you begin; you can also find an audio version to download in the online free tools at http://www.newharbinger.com/48756.

EXERCISE: Calm Place Visualization

Find a place in your home or office that is free of distractions. Sit or lie comfortably and start by turning your attention toward your breath. Take note of the sensations you notice as the air travels in through your nostrils and into your lungs, then is released through your nose or mouth. Take a couple of breaths here.

Now bring up the image of your calm place. Imagine yourself in this place, where you feel completely calm and completely safe. Begin to experience this place through your five senses, starting with sight. Experience this place through your eyes. What do you see? Take note of the colors this calm place has to offer. Now notice the shapes. Pay attention to any other sights this soothing place offers. Take a moment here. Breathe. If you notice stray thoughts entering, that's okay. Just acknowledge them and turn your attention back to your calm place.

Now turn your attention to your sense of hearing. Notice the sounds present in this calm place. Perhaps you hear wind or water. Maybe there are trees rustling. Maybe you notice a quiet hum, or perhaps it's completely silent. Take note of all of the different sounds you experience in this calm place, both near and far. Pause for a moment here.

Next, notice your sense of smell. What smells does this calm place have to offer? Perhaps you can smell crisp, clean air. Maybe you smell freshly baked bread coming from the oven. Maybe you're taking in the smell of wildflowers or salty ocean water. Allow yourself to fully experience this place through your nose. Notice.

Now turn your attention to your sense of taste. First, notice the moisture in your mouth. If you'd like, imagine sipping your favorite beverage or eating a delicious snack in this calm, soothing place. Savor the flavors as you imagine nourishing your body with this food or drink. If you find yourself distracted, simply notice the distraction and gently turn your attention back to your senses.

Finally, pay attention to your sense of touch. Notice the temperature on your skin. Do you feel the warmth of the sun, or perhaps a cool breeze? Can you notice how your clothes feel as they rest against your skin? Notice the surface that supports you. Maybe you are sitting in the grass, cool and damp, or beach sand that shifts and molds to your body. Perhaps you're lying on a cloud, or in your warm, comfortable bed. What textures are nearby that you can reach out and touch? Imagine touching them. Experience this calm place fully through the sensation of touch. Breathe.

Experience this calm place through all five of these senses. Remain in this place for as long as you'd like, taking in all it has to offer. If you'd like to revisit one of the senses in particular, return your focus there now. When you're ready to reorient yourself in the present moment, take a mental snapshot of yourself in this calm place. This image will serve as a reminder of this place, which you can return to at any time when you need a mental break. Now gradually begin to open your eyes and return your attention to your surroundings.

Once you've tried the calm place visualization one or more times, reflect in your journal on your experience. This will help you solidify your sense of how helpful this visualization is as a tool for you to self-soothe.

REFLECTION: Calm Place—A Journal Exercise

1. Where is your calm place? What was that experience like for you?

2. Which of the five senses felt most easily accessible to you? Which one brought the greatest sense of calm?

3. Did you notice any internal or external distractions? Were you able to acknowledge them and return your attention to the exercise?

4. How effective was this exercise in soothing your nervous system?

5. Would you return to this particular calm place, or would you choose another? What about this calm place did you like, and what didn't work for you?

My favorite thing about the calm place visualization is its versatility. It can be scheduled into your day as a twenty-minute mindfulness practice, or it can be done as a thirty-second exercise on the fly when you need a time-out from a stressful day. It can be done from a yoga mat rolled out on your living room floor, or in your car, or at the office. The important thing about the exercise is that it remains a calm place that feels soothing to your senses.

If for any reason your calm place becomes compromised and no longer feels calming, you'll want to pick a different place rather than force this place to feel soothing again. For example, you might begin to imagine last year's vacation destination, which starts off as very calming, but then your mind starts to wander and you begin to feel shame because of how you acted last time you were on vacation there. Now this calm place has a negative association, and you may need to pick an alternate place.

Returning to the Present

To be oriented to the present time is to experience the world through the eyes of your most current, present self rather than from a younger version. Many times, especially when we are experiencing anxiety or another emotion that doesn't fit the facts of the situation we're in, we are not totally oriented to the present. Anxiety often manifests as worry about the future, which might lead us to believe that when we are anxious, we are living in the future rather than in the present. While it is true that anxiety can cause future-oriented thinking, it is usually a symptom of some unresolved, distressing past experience. For example, if when I was twenty I was told by someone I trusted and thought was my friend that they didn't actually like me at all, this memory may be an unresolved little t trauma that affects my emotions in social situations now. Let's say that I'm now twenty-six, beginning to establish a close relationship with a new friend, and having difficulty trusting this friend because of my past experience. I am likely engaging in this current friendship from the eyes of my twenty-year-old self rather than my twenty-six-year-old self, which may cause me to be wary and guarded. In this scenario, I might be rationally aware that I'm twenty-six now and this is a completely different friend who has never caused me to distrust her, but my emotional experience of fear and anxiety may suggest that I am not completely oriented to the present time.

The work in chapters 4 through 6 involves taking a deeper dive and revisiting those past experiences to untether yourself from them. For the purposes of the work before the work, it's important to understand the difference between being time oriented and disoriented, and to get some practice orienting yourself to the present time.

To be oriented to the present time does not mean you will not experience emotions; rather, it means you will experience emotions that fit the facts of your current situation. For example, if you experience anxiety before giving an important presentation at work, this does not automatically mean that you are disoriented to the present time, even if you've had a past distressing experience with presentations. To be human is to experience emotions, and emotions are often helpful, necessary cues that can tell us important things about our values. In this case, it is possible that you would experience some anxiety before giving a presentation because the presentation is important to you and you want to do well. Perhaps the anxiety would be helpful in the week prior to the presentation because it would prompt you to do your research and prepare thoroughly. It might even be helpful to you on the day of the presentation if it prompted you to leave the house with enough time to find parking and review your notes beforehand. You can see how it's possible to experience anxiety and still be oriented to the present time.

When revisiting past distressing experiences, the goal is to have one foot in the present and one foot in the past. This concept—the dual awareness described earlier—was introduced by Francine Shapiro in 1995. With dual awareness, while we might experience the emotions associated with past distressing events while revisiting them, we never lose sight of the fact that we are reflecting on memories, and the danger is not currently happening. When we become overwhelmed or flooded with emotion that doesn't fit the facts of our current situation, it is likely that we have both feet in either the past or the future, rather than one foot here and one foot there. When we don't have *either* foot in the present, our nervous system will register a need for safety and activate a survival response, pushing us out of our healing zone. We can reestablish safety by using time orientation skills to pull ourselves back into the present moment, where there is no danger.

There's one essential component of practicing time orientation: it needs to be done when there is actually no present threat. If there is one, orienting yourself to the present will not be soothing and could cause more harm. For example, let's say you have a fear of dogs that stems from being bitten by a dog when you were ten years old. Now you're twenty-four, walking in a park. In the distance you see someone walking a dog on a leash—one that looks very much like the dog that bit you. You are hit with a strong wave of anxiety. In this situation, time orientation skills would help your nervous system get on board with what your logic already knows: that this leashed dog, walking fifty feet away, is very unlikely to harm you. These skills would allow you to focus on things in your present environment that are different from the experience you had when you were ten, and they provide evidence that you're not facing the same threat now, thereby soothing your nervous system.

Now let's say you are walking in a dark alley and all of a sudden you see a dog running toward you. The dog is alone, no owner in sight; it must be a stray. And it's acting aggressive: lips drawn back from its fangs, growling and snarling. In this case, it does not make any sense to practice time orientation skills, because the present situation is dangerous.

The more you tried to orient yourself to time—*what's actually happening, here and now*—the more danger you would feel. What's more helpful (and what is likely to happen automatically) is that your survival instincts kick in and you respond accordingly by either running away or defending yourself. If you feel anxiety the following day when walking through that same dark alley—however, this time there is no dog in sight—time orientation skills would prove useful again.

If you are experiencing anxiety that does not fit the facts or feels disproportionate to your current situation and there is no current danger or threat, time orientation skills will be useful. Time orientation skills are even more accessible than the calm place visualization, because you can practice them anywhere, and the people around you won't necessarily even know when you are practicing them. These skills involve turning your attention toward anything in your present environment, where there is no danger.

The benefits of time orientation are twofold. First, adopting a regular practice of orienting to the present time helps train you to approach life more mindfully. Decades of research have shown that regular mindfulness practice can improve both emotional and physical health via reducing anxiety and depression and improving emotion regulation. Time orientation exercises are also helpful because we humans are not good multitaskers; when we are given a mental task like listing things in our environment, we don't do very well at simultaneously ruminating about the past or worrying about the future. A common example of this phenomenon is when you're talking on the phone with someone, listening intently, and then someone nearby asks you a question and you suddenly realize you missed part of what the person on the phone said. We don't do well with paying attention to two things at once, despite what we'd like to believe, but this deficit serves us well when we want to shift our attention away from something triggering.

Here are two specific time orientation techniques that I encourage you to try:

- *Name ten things that you can see right here, right now.* These can be as general as a tree you can see nearby or as detailed and specific as the different shades of green on a patch of lawn nearby. Here's an example: in this current moment, while practicing time orientation, I noticed the numbers on the barcode on my bottle of water. The last four digits are the same numbers as the last four digits of my childhood home's phone number. This is something I never would have noticed had I not been intentionally practicing time orientation. The more detailed you can be in your observations, the better.

- *Mentally list details that serve as evidence that you are not your younger self.* Someone I once knew had childhood trauma that happened on the East Coast, where there is a very different climate than in Arizona, where she later resided. Whenever she experienced a trigger and needed to orient to the present time, she would go outside and look at the cacti and other features of the desert landscape around her. It helped her nervous system remember by providing evidence that she was in a completely different time and space—all the way across the country—from where the danger happened.

If you were a child or adolescent when the danger happened, notice the things in your life that point to your now being an adult. Perhaps you have bills lying on your kitchen table that you need to pay, or a grocery list posted on your refrigerator. These items can serve as anchors to the present time, providing evidence that you are older and no longer threatened in the same way. If the trauma happened before you could drive and you now have a car, turn your attention to your car: pull out your registration and driver's license and let these serve as a reminder that you have more resources now than you did then. If, since the trauma, you have a new supportive person in your life who provides safety and comfort, give them a call and allow them to support you, while noticing that this is a resource that didn't exist for you in the past. Anything that can serve as evidence of your different life circumstances in the current time that wasn't present at the time of the trauma can be a useful tool for time orientation.

REFLECTION: Time Orientation—A Journal Exercise

Give time orientation skills a try. What are ten details about your current environment you can notice now? They could be objects, colors, activities, sounds, smells, temperature. Write them in your journal.

Next, reflect in your journal on the following questions. These will help empower you to practice time orientation skills the next time a mismatch between your past or future and your present situation is causing you unnecessary distress.

- When would be a good time for me to practice time orientation skills?

- How will I know if my attention is in the past and I need to orient myself to the present?

- How will I know if I am worrying about a future scenario and need to pull myself back to the present?

- What are some people, places, or things that I can use to orient myself to the present?

- What is different about my life now from when things were more distressing?

Diaphragm Breathing

When it comes to regulating anxiety, there is no more powerful tool than your own breath. There are two main types of breathing: chest breathing and diaphragm breathing. Chest breathing is more shallow and occurs naturally when your body needs to get in a lot of oxygen quickly, such as after a sprint. When you are chest breathing, you'll be able to see and feel your chest rise and fall with each breath. Diaphragm breathing, also called belly breathing, involves breathing more deeply into your lungs; this causes your diaphragm—which is located below your lungs near the bottom of your ribcage—to flex downward, pushing out your abdomen. When you are breathing diaphragmatically, you should see your belly rising and falling with each breath, with little movement in your chest.

Our breathing and our survival response have a reciprocal relationship, each having influence over the other. For example, if you encounter a mountain lion on a hike, your fight-or-flight response is likely going to become activated, and your breathing will become more shallow and rapid to increase oxygen flow quickly and prepare you for action. This is an example of hyperarousal. Chest breathing is helpful in this situation, when there is a real threat of bodily harm, as it increases your chances of fending off danger and making it out alive. When we live with anxiety, we may register threats that don't actually exist or that exist on a much smaller scale than we are perceiving. This causes us to breathe in a way that prepares and encourages us to fight or flee when actually there is no danger. This can become a vicious cycle that perpetuates and reinforces anxiety over time. Perceived threat → anxiety → chest breathing → more anxiety caused by chest breathing → new perceived threats, and so on. Similarly to how you can communicate safety to your survival brain through self-soothing with your senses, by breathing deeply into the diaphragm you can help convey to yourself that the danger you perceived doesn't really exist. Breathing deeply activates the parasympathetic nervous system, which is in charge of regulating emotions and calming you down.

There are two ways I like to practice diaphragm breathing. The first is the hand method, a simple trick that helps gauge whether you're breathing into your chest or diaphragm. To practice this method, sit comfortably upright with your feet flat on the floor. Start by placing one hand on your upper chest and the other hand on your abdomen, just below your navel. As you breathe in through your nose, notice the movement of your hands. Try to breathe in deeply enough that the hand on your belly moves outward as your belly expands with each inhale, while the hand on your chest moves very little. Continue breathing deeply, trying to move the hand on your belly more than the one on your chest. When you achieve this, you'll know you are breathing into your diaphragm.

The second way to practice diaphragm breathing is called *box breathing* or *four-square breathing*. By either name, this technique has been used since the 1980s by the Navy SEALs and in other high-stress professions such as nursing and policing (Stinson, 2018). It is used to exit fight-or-flight mode and for general soothing, recentering, and concentration of the mind. To practice box breathing, find a comfortable position seated in a chair with your feet flat on the floor. Close your eyes and breathe in through your nose to the count of four, noticing the sensations of the breath entering your nostrils and lungs. Hold your breath in your lungs to the count of four, and then begin to slowly exhale to the count of four. After exhaling, pause for four seconds before starting your next inhale. Repeat this for several minutes. It can be helpful to picture a box while engaging in this exercise, like the one shown here.

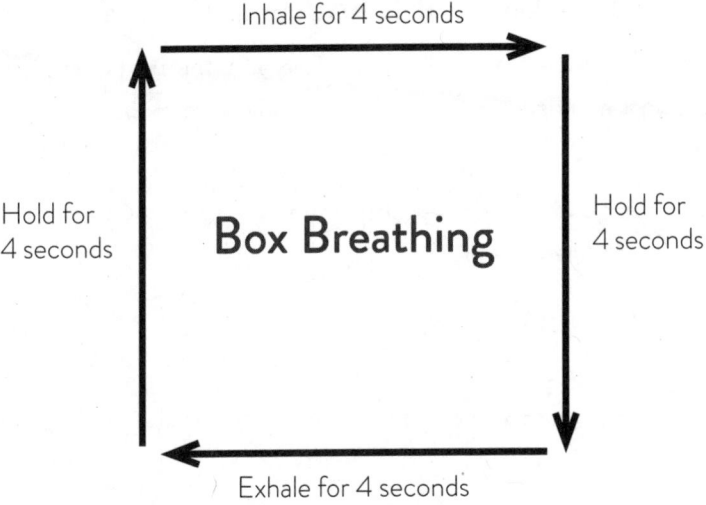

Inhale for 4 seconds

Hold for
4 seconds

Box Breathing

Hold for
4 seconds

Exhale for 4 seconds

REFLECTION: Diaphragm Breathing—A Journal Exercise

1. What were these breathing exercises like for me?

2. How can I tell when I am chest breathing versus diaphragm breathing?

3. Which breathing exercise was more effective for me: the hand method or box breathing?

4. When is a good time for me to practice diaphragm breathing?

5. How does breathing play a role in my experience with anxiety?

REFLECTION: Taking It All In—A Journal Exercise

Take some time to reflect on what you've learned in this chapter and how it's affected your experience with your anxiety, and record your answers in your journal.

1.   Which of the anxiety-regulation strategies in this chapter were most helpful? Least helpful?

2.   Are there other anxiety regulation strategies, not listed here, that have been helpful to me in the past? If so, what are they?

3.   How will I know when I am in need of increased safety in my body and mind?

4.   When do I experience anxiety most frequently? Which of these skills might be useful in those instances?

5.   As I move forward with the work, how will I know when I need to take a break and return to these skills?

6.   What more do I need to practice before moving on to the work?

My hope is that these practices will help you to feel more empowered in your ability to regulate your anxiety, in addition to equipping you to do the work of making peace with your anxiety by increasing the felt sense of safety in your body and mind. These tools have been proven effective at reducing anxiety in the moment; however, without getting to the source of why your brain is registering a threat that doesn't actually exist, the anxiety will always return. I suggest you think of these tools as helping with symptom reduction rather than addressing the root of the problem. When we use these tools as a long-term solution and replacement for doing the work, what may feel like a start at skillfully coping can morph into avoiding.

You should expect to revisit this chapter throughout the course of this work. Healing anxiety is messy and usually does not follow a linear path. As you are working through subsequent chapters, you may find that you have exited your healing window and are reliving past experiences. Or you may just want a break from the heaviness of the work. When this happens, return to this chapter and these practices. You may even find that you want to continue practicing these skills for months before moving on to later chapters. That is okay! Or you may feel ready to move forward with the work now. Move forward at your own pace, remembering always to tune in, assess your felt sense of safety, and honor it, even if you wish it were different.

Now that you have learned skills to help you temporarily take the edge off your anxiety, you are prepared to move on to the next step in the work: exploring avoidance, the primary behavior that keeps anxiety stuck. In the following chapter, you'll learn to distinguish the difference between helpful and problematic avoidance. Once you learn the difference, I'll help you let go of the latter, which will move you one step closer to healing your relationship with anxiety for good.

avoiding avoidance

All humans are hard-wired to avoid pain. It is natural for us to avoid painful conversations, experiences, and emotions, even if we know we will probably be better off long-term if we confront them. Avoidance is a defensive, protective strategy we're conditioned to use from a very young age, as it is a necessary part of survival. For example, when a toddler learns that touching a hot stove is very painful, he will likely avoid touching the stove again in the future. This is a necessary adaptation. Similarly, if a child learns that expressing her emotions is unsafe because when she cries her parents become increasingly agitated and tell her "Big girls don't cry," she will likely try to avoid crying in the future, in an effort to appease her caregivers and skillfully adapt to her environment. If she doesn't adapt in this way, she may be subjected to more disapproval and ridicule, which all children want to avoid. While stuffing emotions in this way is a behavior that can cause major problems later in life, in an environment in which emotional expression leads to compromised safety, avoidance of emotions may prove useful.

Another example of learned avoidance shows up when school-aged children discover what will help them fit in with a group. For example, if they find that if they wear a certain type of clothing or bring a certain type of lunch to school they will be teased by their classmates, any child will likely want to avoid wearing this type of clothing or bringing this kind of food in the future, to prevent the intensely painful emotions that teasing instigates. If the child is able to convince their parent to pack them a different kind of lunch or buy them a pair of the kind of shoes the other kids wear, it may be effective in reducing bullying. Of course, it is never a child's responsibility to make changes that reduce the likelihood that other humans will be mean to them; the responsibility to change falls on the person or people inflicting harm. However, this example gives insight into the ways in which avoidance of painful emotions is a deeply engrained, often automatic and effective attempt to protect our well-being.

By the time we're adults, we're usually pros at avoidance. We have had many years of experience avoiding what's painful or uncomfortable, and often avoidance behaviors are successful in helping us align with our goals. For example, you may have learned to avoid dating people who exhibit certain red flags early in a relationship, which helps you avoid later conflict or pain. Maybe you are lactose intolerant and have learned to avoid dairy ice cream, despite how much you love it, to prevent inevitable physical discomfort later. Perhaps you've learned to avoid shopping on Amazon when you've had one too many glasses of wine, which prevents you from feeling buyer's remorse the next day. All of these avoidance behaviors are useful because they prevent harm, sometimes by delaying short-term gratification in exchange for caring for ourself long-term.

Helpful Avoidance Versus Problematic Avoidance

Just as there are two types of anxiety, there are two types of avoidance: helpful, necessary avoidance, and avoidance that feels helpful in the short term but causes long-term problems. Throughout this book, I'll refer to these two types as *helpful avoidance* or *problematic avoidance*. Helpful avoidance can be obvious—like avoiding touching a hot stove— and easily accomplished with little inner conflict, or it can require delaying some short-term gratification for a long-term goal, like avoiding a potential relationship partner who excites us but exhibits clear red flags of emotional volatility. In the latter example, we can identify this as helpful avoidance because while it requires enduring the short-term discomfort of saying no to a date with this exciting person, it may help us align with our long-term values of finding a stable, dependable partner.

Problematic avoidance is avoidance that has the opposite effect of helpful avoidance: it prevents discomfort in the short term, but over time moves us further away from our goals rather than helping us become more aligned with them. For example, let's say you experience social anxiety, and one week ago you agreed to attend a friend's birthday party. The day of the party arrives, and as you are getting ready to go you begin to experience heightened anxiety. You may have an inner dialogue that goes something like *I could probably make up an excuse for why I'm not able to make it*, followed by *No, I should go. This friend came to my birthday party and it's important to me to maintain this friendship,'* followed by *But imagine how much better I'll feel if I just cancel.*

Sound familiar? And as this inner dialogue continues, it is likely that your anxiety continues to heighten. By the time you need to leave for the party, your anxiety might be so uncomfortable that you will do anything to reduce it, so you impulsively send your friend a text message to say you aren't feeling well and can't make it to the party.

It is very likely that this avoidance behavior is going to instantly reduce your discomfort. You might have a thought like *Thank goodness I don't have to feel that anxiety anymore. I'm so relieved.*

At this stage, it can be hard to identify this type of avoidance as problematic because it feels *so* right. After all, it may have been the only coping strategy out of several you've tried that was effective in reducing your anxiety. However, the next morning when you wake up, begin to scroll social media, and see photos posted from the party, with several people you would have loved to see all having fun together, you are likely to experience some unpleasant emotions. This is when you might start to identify your avoidance as problematic, because while it was effective in helping you avoid anxiety in the short term, it leaves you feeling worse the next day.

This type of avoidance can be problematic for two reasons. First, it involves short-term gratification, which produces an immediate but fleeting benefit that quickly wears off and is replaced with a painful emotion. The painful emotion is usually an indicator that you have not acted in accordance with your values. For example, if attending the party was in line with your values of being socially connected and a supportive friend, your avoidance of it might create feelings of missing out (FOMO), guilt, or shame.

The second reason this type of avoidance is problematic is the behavioral reinforcement it causes. Assuming there is no real threat associated with attending the party, when you are getting ready for it and experiencing heightening anxiety, your survival brain is registering a threat that doesn't actually exist. It's the anxious part of you that says things like *It's going to be awful. Just cancel. You'll feel so much better if you do.* This voice becomes louder and louder the more you try to counter it, because it thinks there is serious danger ahead if you do attend, and it is working hard to protect you from that danger. (In the following chapters, we'll explore together *why* your anxiety registers a threat that isn't really there, and how to help it recalibrate.)

As the tension between your logical brain and anxious voice increases, so do your heart palpitations, sweaty palms, chest breathing, rapid-fire thoughts, and other manifestations of anxiety you might experience. As soon as you send the text message saying you won't make it, the pressure is off, and your anxiety heaves a great sigh of relief: *Oh, thank goodness you listened to me. I'm trying to protect you! Don't you see how dangerous that would have been? I hope you realize you feel safe now because you listened to me. Best to let me take the lead in the future.* This narrative strengthens and reinforces the need to avoid in the future. Not only are you left feeling guilt about missing out on the party, but it will become just a tad bit harder to avoid avoidance the next time you're invited to a social gathering, because your brain has now made the connection that canceling plans = short-term relief from anxiety.

If you have social anxiety, you know that social encounters are usually not as bad as we build them up to be in our heads. When we do attend social events despite having anxiety, it usually reinforces the connection that following through with plans = not that bad, and we may even end up feeling glad we went.

Over time, problematic avoidance convinces us that the only way to reduce anxiety is to avoid hard things, even if it means abandoning our values. But learning how to avoid avoidance helps us build a life consistent with our values.

REFLECTION: On Avoidance—A Journal Exercise

Take some time to reflect on your experience of avoidance—both helpful and problematic—and any patterns that emerge. Record your answers to these questions in your journal.

1. What things did you learn to avoid as a child that were helpful?

2. What things did you learn to avoid as a child that were problematic?

3. As an adult, in what ways do you practice helpful avoidance?

4. As an adult, in what ways do you practice problematic avoidance?

5. In what ways does problematic avoidance threaten your values?

Self-Care Versus Avoidance

If you have been in therapy or done any reading about emotional health in the last several years, you have likely been exposed to the concept of self-care and the role it has in preserving mental health. Self-care is the practice of making decisions that prioritize our physical and emotional health. Self-care has become a hot topic in the last few years, both inside and outside of the therapy office. From the very first therapy session, therapists usually assess for the extent to which their clients are practicing care for themselves. After listening to the challenges their client is having that have brought them to therapy, a therapist will likely ask some version of "What are you doing in your day-to-day life to help you cope with these stressors?" Self-care practices are not limited to but can include the following:

- Taking care of basic needs (getting adequate sleep, eating well, taking medications as prescribed, drinking enough water, and so on)

- Practicing mindfulness or meditation

- Exercising or moving your body

- Spending time with friends or loved ones

- Journaling

- Engaging in enjoyable hobbies or activities

- Going on vacation

- Carving out "you" time for whatever makes you feel good

- Treating yourself to something that you don't normally indulge in, like an overpriced coffee

Self-care isn't limited to just bubble baths and fancy coffee drinks. It often includes practices that don't necessarily feel good while you're doing them, but are conducive to caring for yourself long-term, like:

- Scheduling and attending doctor and dentist appointments

- Setting boundaries with others

- Saying no to activities that deplete you

- Tackling responsibilities rather than procrastinating

- Prioritizing sleep over a night out

Self-care is very important, because adequate self-care practices can be an important starting strategy for managing anxiety. For example, let's say you are in therapy to address work-related anxiety. During the course of therapy your therapist learns that you often arrive early and stay late into the evenings at work in order to meet project deadlines, and to make this possible, you are skipping breakfast and missing your evening yoga class. Your therapist is likely going to see a need for improved self-care and might work with you on setting boundaries around your work hours; for example, having you make a commitment to eating breakfast every day and attending your yoga class at least a few times per week. It is likely that with improved self-care practices, your work-related anxiety will start to feel more manageable.

Similarly, if you are in therapy to address poor self-image, and in the course of therapy your therapist learns that you feel particularly bad about yourself after you spend time with a certain friend who often makes negative comments about your weight or appearance and who does not respect the boundaries you set, your therapist may well encourage you to reevaluate how much time you spend with this friend or whether you want to continue this friendship at all. It could be that your self-image begins to improve once you no longer spend as much time with this so-called friend. Bolstering self-care can serve as the first problem-solving approach in your larger effort to reduce anxiety.

While self-care is undoubtedly a necessary ingredient in the recipe for emotional health, the term has begun to be used to describe behaviors that appear on the surface to be self-care, but upon further exploration are actually avoidance in disguise. This can be problematic because we might think we're doing something helpful for ourselves when in reality we are reinforcing and perpetuating the anxiety cycle.

For example, let's say that you feel very overwhelmed with all of your responsibilities. You decide that it would be helpful to engage in a self-care practice, so you turn on your favorite show on Netflix. This may be a helpful, necessary exercise in carving out time to do something enjoyable for yourself and reduce the feeling of being overwhelmed. However, let's say one episode turns into a six-hour binge watch because each time you remember your to-do list it feels too overwhelming, so rather than thinking about it, you continue to watch more episodes. This practice may have started as necessary self-care but turned into avoidance once it started to serve the function of helping you avoid being overwhelmed rather than adding enjoyment to your life.

Let's say you are trying to distract yourself from the feeling of anxiety, and in an effort to do so, you go impulsively spend $300 at Target. This is likely an avoidance behavior rather than a self-care behavior because it's helping you run away from anxiety. However, if you recently completed an important work project and want to celebrate your accomplishment by treating yourself to an uninterrupted Target shopping trip, even if you spend $300 this behavior likely does not serve the same purpose of helping you avoid discomfort; it may be true self-care.

If you are prone to social anxiety, you may be tempted to label your isolation from others as taking care of yourself when in reality it may be that, given your unique circumstances, taking care of yourself actually requires you to do what's harder: persuading yourself to spend time with a friend. On the flip side, if you are introverted and require regular quiet alone time, perhaps choosing to skip out on plans with a friend and enjoy some solitude at home *is* actually an act of self-care. If you engage in compulsive exercise and call it taking care of your body, but the behavior is serving the function of helping you temper body-related obsessions, it is likely that engaging in compulsive exercise is a form of avoidance rather than true self-care. However, setting boundaries at work so you can leave on time to get to your workout class as a means to care for your body may be true self-care.

It can be challenging to distinguish between self-care and avoidance behaviors because the exact same behavior can be a self-care practice for one person and an avoidance strategy for another person. Additionally, the exact same behavior can be an act of self-care for you at one time but an act of avoidance at another time. It is important to ask yourself what function the behavior serves in order to determine if it is a true self-care practice or avoidance in disguise. To get a better idea, you may ask yourself the questions in the following exercise.

REFLECTION: Are Your Self-Care Practices Helping or Harming? A Journal Exercise

Take some time to reflect on your self-care habits, and record your answers to these questions in your journal.

- What are my go-to self-care practices? In other words, what practices do I most rely on to care for my physical and emotional health?

- Does my self-care practice feel like it's soothing my emotions— or helping me detach from them?

- After I engage in this self-care practice, do I feel energized and refreshed or more anxious?

- Do I engage in self-care impulsively to avoid discomfort, or do I plan my self-care activity ahead of time?

- Does my self-care practice feel like coping or escaping?

If a behavior that helps you detach or distract from painful emotions later causes you to feel more discomfort, or you do it impulsively, or it feels like an escape, it could be that it is actually avoidance rather than true self-care. By contrast, if the behavior is planned ahead of time, soothes your emotions, helps you cope with them, and/or leaves you feeling good afterward, that is a good indicator that it is true self-care. Behaviors that are likely to be avoidance in disguise include avoiding responsibilities for days, isolating from supportive people, practicing impulsive "feel-good" behaviors that leave you feeling worse off later, and subjecting yourself to continuous hurt in a relationship for fear of conflict.

We all engage in problematic avoidance from time to time, and it does not always have big consequences in our lives. For example, maybe I push off all my responsibilities on Saturday and binge Netflix instead, which means I have to cram all my weekend to-dos into Sunday afternoon. This is somewhat problematic, because I'm not going to feel great about it on Sunday, but at the same time, it likely won't cause dire problems in my life if I *can* tend to everything on Sunday. For this reason, I might not feel very motivated to dig deep into my behavior to explore the function of this pattern and try to change it. However, when avoidance takes over as the strategy we keep relying on for coping with anxiety and starts to reinforce and perpetuate the anxiety cycle, we need to acknowledge that we're avoiding and see what we can do instead that might be more effective.

REFLECTION: On Self-Care—A Journal Exercise

Reflect on this deeper dive into different kinds of self-care, and record your answers in your journal.

1. In what ways do I practice feel-good self-care?

2. In what ways do I practice the hard-but-good-for-me kinds of self-care?

3. In what ways do I practice avoidance masquerading as self-care?

4. Which of my self-care practices are likely to turn into avoidance behaviors?

5. What practices can I start to incorporate into my life to improve and expand my genuine self-care?

It Gets Harder Before It Gets Easier

Before you begin the work toward meeting and healing your anxiety, it's important to understand the role of exposure to anxiety-producing stimuli in this process. You can think of exposure as the opposite of avoidance. It is the practice of moving *toward* the thing that causes anxiety rather than away from it. Of course, practicing exposure often brings up painful emotions because it requires us to face what is making us anxious. However, the payoff is great. Each time we are exposed to our fears we become more desensitized to them and less anxious over time.

It is likely that during the course of this work you might question why you are being asked to lean into something that is painful, and especially why I encourage you to uncover old painful wounds that may have been the birthing place of your anxiety. It's only natural to ask this question, because often exposing yourself to the source of discomfort feels very counterproductive. Your anxiety voice will do everything in its power to convince you of this, because its main job is to identify and eliminate threats, preferably before they have even happened. In fact, I imagine it is possible that your anxiety voice is already screaming at you for reading this book and even thinking about doing this work. On the other hand, it could be that your logic knows you want to do this work—indeed, you *need* to do this work—so your anxiety is rather quiet at this time.

Regardless of how active your anxiety is now, there will surely be times throughout the course of this work when your anxiety raises its voice, persuading you to backpedal. This will be a convincing argument, because you've learned that the quickest way to avoid anxiety is to practice avoidance of the anxiety-producing stimuli. If the anxiety-producing stimuli is this work, it makes sense that your anxiety would do its best to persuade you to shove this book away in a bottom drawer, never to be revisited again.

As the many examples offered here have illustrated, avoiding this work will likely be effective in reducing anxiety in the short term; however, if you bought this book to get a better handle on your anxiety, then avoiding the work because it's uncomfortable will not be in accordance with your long-term values of creating and living a fulfilled, meaningful life. We must be willing to endure short-term discomfort for the long-term benefit of creating a values-driven life. Because of the likelihood that at some point you will question the productiveness of engaging in this work, the next exercise may be especially helpful now.

REFLECTION: What Is Your Why? A Journal Exercise

Reflect on the following questions and write your responses in your journal. You can revisit your answers at any time that your anxiety increases and you feel the urge to abandon the work.

- What arguments is my anxiety's voice likely to make while doing this work?

- In what ways will abandoning this work benefit me in the short term?

- In what ways will continuing with this work benefit me in the long term?

- What made me decide to purchase this book and engage in this work in the first place?

- How will I know when I need to take a break from this work because I need to do another, more immediately soothing kind of self-care?

- What are my values, and how does healing from anxiety fit in with them?

Note: There's a crucial distinction to be made between your anxiety's encouraging you to avoid this work because it is uncomfortable, and your body feeling unsafe while doing this work. In the former case, it may be appropriate to gently push through your anxiety to continue this work. In the latter, it's an indication that increased safety—and perhaps the oversight of a licensed therapist—is a necessary prerequisite to your continuing safely.

So how does exposure actually work? We discussed in chapter 1 that our survival brains are likely to draw a connection to a cause when we assess and respond to threats. For example, in scenario one, when my social anxiety gets the best of me and I cancel plans at the last minute, in the immediate rush of relief my anxiety voice will declare *I feel better because I skipped out on the party.*

The same concept applies when we practice exposure to the anxiety-producing stimuli. If, in scenario two, I face my anxiety head-on and attend the party, even if I have anxiety the entire time I'm at the party, I will likely feel that same relief when I am leaving the party *if attending was in line with my values.* In this instance, I might have the thought, *I feel really good because I was able to attend the party despite my anxiety, and I actually had a decent time.* The two outcomes here both result in my feeling good, and for both outcomes I draw causation. The first scenario left me thinking *I feel good because I avoided the party,* which is likely to be replaced with some unpleasant emotions over time; the second scenario leaves me thinking *I feel good because I attended the party.* The first scenario reinforces and strengthens the need to avoid parties in the future, whereas the second scenario reinforces and strengthens the need to push through my anxiety and attend parties in the future.

Our behavior choices are important because they always reinforce *something.* It becomes a matter of what we want to reinforce: anxiety and the limitations it imposes, or living freely.

When we pair an anxiety-producing stimulus with some degree of calmness, it begins to challenge our anxiety voice's argument that we need to avoid the anxiety-producing stimulus or else we will be in more danger. Let's revisit the chapter 1 scenario of healing from the traumatic dog bite in the park. When we revisit the place of the original trauma and practice the anxiety-regulation strategies outlined in chapter 2 to create the sensation of feeling calm, we begin to chip away at the narrative that the park is dangerous and start to increase the association between the park and feeling calm. It's like our anxiety voice says, *Wait a second. How is it that I can be in this park and feel relatively calm? Something is not adding up here.*

This contradictory experience is called *cognitive dissonance*. Cognitive dissonance happens whenever new information proves inconsistent with our previously held ideas about something. When you're doing this work, creating cognitive dissonance is an important indicator that your anxiety is starting to be challenged. The more times we expose ourselves to the original anxiety-producing stimulus and pair it with the sensation of feeling calm, the weaker the association between the stimulus and threat becomes, and our anxiety is replaced with neutral or pleasant emotions.

This behavioral association concept has been studied since the early 1900s. B. F. Skinner coined the term *operant conditioning* to describe the method of learning in which we are likely to either repeat or not repeat behaviors based on their positive or negative consequences. For example, a study was conducted in which lab rats pressed a lever when shown a green light and were rewarded with food. If they pressed the lever when the light was red, they were administered a mild electric shock. It did not take long for the rats to associate a red light with anxiety and press the lever only when the light was green. This is an adaptive response that helped keep them safe in this context. However, if the rats were moved to a different setting in which red lights caused the opposite result—a delivery of the food they were seeking—these rats would likely be in trouble because of the associations they had previously made.

Let's apply this concept to the scenario of being attacked by a dog in a park. Even if we had visited that park a hundred times before and it was always a pleasant or neutral environment, being attacked by a dog there just once is likely to be a strong enough consequence that we will begin to associate the park with fear in the future. Ideally, over time our logical brain would help us identify that the park is not actually dangerous; rather, that particular dog was. Then we would be able to return to the park with only mild anxiety, and the memory of the dog attack would not go on to cause problems in our lives.

If the traumatic memory of being attacked by a dog gets stuck and we do not integrate it properly as a single isolated incident, our brain may make other associations with the memory, and these will start to produce anxiety. Over time and with continued avoidance, we may become convinced that we need to avoid that park and dogs in general. This is how a past traumatic experience can start the cycle of avoidance and begin to cause more and more problems in our lives.

What Is Habituation, and How Does It Help?

So how do we prevent the cycle of avoidance from happening? Avoiding avoidance is the single most important thing we can do to stop anxiety in its tracks. In fact, exposure to the feared stimulus over time creates the opposite effect: *habituation*. Habituation refers to the decreasing of anxiety that happens when we are repeatedly exposed to the anxiety-producing stimulus. Each time we visit the park and are not attacked by a dog, the association between the park and being attacked becomes weaker. Over time, this means the park begins to cause us less and less anxiety, until going there becomes a neutral experience. If we can begin to pair the park with not only an absence of being attacked but also the presence of calm, pleasant emotions, we can begin to strengthen the association between the park and safety and enjoyment.

When anxiety does not fit the facts of the situation, there is a high likelihood that it developed as a result of some negative consequence you experienced at some point in your life, combined with repeated avoidance over time. The negative consequence can be real—like being made fun of—or only a perception, like assuming that people are silently judging you. When we continue to avoid the original anxiety-producing stimulus, we continue to reinforce the response of fear and anxiety. We cannot begin the process of habituation until we are willing to expose ourselves to the stimulus again.

For example, if my brain has paired social encounters with danger, the only way to extinguish this pairing is to attend social encounters while experiencing the absence of danger. If we avoid social encounters, we do not get this opportunity; instead, we reinforce the pairing of social encounters with danger, because we feel safer when we avoid them.

The same is true for my healing from anxiety while in professional meetings, which I mentioned in chapter 1. Although I did not avoid professional meetings, I did interpret ambiguous information during the meetings through the lens of I am stupid. For example, if I was not called on, or if, for an extended period after I had spoken, I sensed even the slightest bit of a chuckle from one of my superiors, I internalized that information as meaning that I was definitely stupid; as a result, strengthening the pairing in my mind between attending meetings and feeling threatened. Healing from this anxiety required me to expose myself to these kinds of encounters while feeling the absence of threat and instead a sense of safety. But because of the continuous pattern of pairing my meeting attendance with feeling stupid, my anxious voice had become so overpowering that it would not allow me to experience any amount of safety; instead, it would continuously alert me to the threat and implore me to avoid meetings altogether if I wanted to achieve safety. This cycle continued until my internship ended.

When Logic Isn't Enough

Getting caught in this cycle is usually an indicator that simply knowing these concepts isn't sufficient to break free of it. It's why logic-based solutions like "Just think calm thoughts" are unhelpful and invalidating. It's why I, a therapist with a master's degree in understanding these concepts, could not seem to wrangle my own anxiety.

Don't get me wrong: knowledge is power; it is important. Understanding from a scientific perspective how and why anxiety happens can help us comprehend the ways in which we are helping the problem and making it worse. It is an important starting place. But it is not enough. It is not the work. You can't logic your way out of an emotion—because emotions, by definition, are not logical. Healing from anxiety will require you to turn off your thinking brain and drop into your felt sense, your inner knowing, your intuition. This is not a skill that you have to cultivate; rather, it is an intrinsic strength that you can tap into. It has been there all along, pointing you in the opposite direction of your logic's roadmap. It is watching you struggle to climb the mountain of life while simultaneously being tethered to a boulder—the original little t trauma—where the consequence first happened.

In the next chapter, I will guide you through the process of pausing your ascent up the mountain of your life, tapping into your intuition, and turning around to tend to the boulders that are keeping you stuck. By doing so, you will untether yourself and begin to build a life in which all that energy you expend trying to dodge anxiety can instead be directed toward living in ways that are consistent with your values.

befriending anxiety

By now you are likely thinking of your anxiety in a new way. You are probably making logical sense of what happened to make you anxious, and you are starting to understand how anxiety developed out of a need to protect you from something. You might have come to accept that your efforts to avoid anxiety usually fall short, and that healing from it is going to require turning toward it. You may even be thinking about how your cycle of anxiety perpetuates itself, and the common goal that you and your anxiety share. This new way of conceptualizing your anxiety is an important prerequisite to doing this work, but it is not the work itself.

The next few chapters will guide you through the main work required to heal your relationship with anxiety. You will start to experience your anxiety as separate from you, as a force with whom you can have a conversation. Then you will be encouraged (and equipped) to turn your logical or thinking brain off, allowing you to get a felt sense and deeper understanding of your anxiety, so that ultimately you can work with it to discover what is keeping you stuck.

It is important to remember that you and your anxiety are separate; it has its own thoughts, opinions, and voice, separate from yours. If it were one with you, you would never be in conflict with it. When you can give it space to share its perspective, when you listen to it nonjudgmentally, you will be much more effective at figuring it out than when you try to decide for it. This is similar to a situation when you are worried that you upset your friend in your most recent conversation. You can do some serious mental gymnastics trying to figure out whether you said or did something hurtful, but what's most effective is to go straight to the source of the information and ask her, "Did I hurt you?" The same is true for anxiety. It has a voice. It knows its perspective and doesn't want you to fill in the gaps about its wishes and needs without including it in the conversation. In the exercises that follow in this chapter, you will practice listening for the answers rather than using your logical brain to try to figure them out. Remember, anxiety, by definition, is not logical.

When Anxiety Doesn't Cooperate

Just because anxiety has its own voice doesn't mean it's going to be enthusiastic about communicating with you right off the bat. Remember when we talked about having decades-long qualms about your anxiety? It's important to consider this when working to establish a healthy relationship with it. Imagine being estranged from a family member for twenty years or more and then sitting down one day for coffee. In that first conversation, you might hold back a little. Or a lot. You might be angry. You might want to scream. You might have so much to say that you don't know how to say any of it. That first conversation could produce a myriad of responses depending on the relationship you had with this family member. Then fast forward to your tenth conversation with this family member: it will probably look and feel a lot different from your first.

The same is true for the conversations you will have with your anxiety. Even if your anxiety has been screaming at you for some time, you may find that it becomes challenging to access as you work through these exercises. Or you may find that it has so much to say that it becomes overwhelming to take it all in. Either of these experiences is okay, as is anything in the middle of these two ends of the spectrum. The more you listen to your anxiety and work to understand it, the more trust you will build, further repairing your relationship with it. Whatever the outcome of these exercises, as long as you are holding space for your anxiety rather than trying to extinguish, numb, or outrun it, you are doing right by it.

Remember that painful emotions do not mean you are backsliding. In fact, many times the opposite is true.

The exercises in this chapter are meant to be not a quick fix, but rather an ongoing practice. If you find your anxiety is completely inaccessible one day, that is okay. Tomorrow you can show up and try again. If you find that your anxiety is so overwhelming that you're unable to take in all of the information it's throwing at you, let it know that you hear it and that what it has to say is important to you; however, it is going to need to respect your limits for how much you can digest in one sitting. Keep in mind that on one day your anxiety might show up with very strong feelings toward you—exhaustion, anger, indignation—and may not be pleasant to communicate with. The very next day you might find your anxiety is happy to be acknowledged and enthusiastic about communicating with you. (Remember the analogy of the dysregulated four-year-old having a meltdown? It applies here.)

Repairing any relationship takes time, and your relationship with anxiety is no exception. Think of this work as a marathon, not a sprint. Check in with yourself and honor your pace. It is recommended that you give yourself ample time between exercises to allow yourself space to digest and synthesize the information you are gathering from your anxiety. Remember to honor your feelings too. You may have strong feelings about your anxiety that require time to sit with and process. Whatever you experience is okay. Stay with each exercise for as long as you need to in order to be able to gather the information that you need to answer the reflection questions. If at any time during this work you become overwhelmed, simply take note, ease up on this work, and return to some of the self-regulation exercises you practiced in chapter 2.

Meet Your Anxiety

The purpose of the first exercise is for you to consciously meet with your anxiety for the first time. In many ways, of course, you already have a relationship, though not the kind that serves you well. This time, rather than pushing your anxiety away or resisting it, you'll approach it with curiosity and without judgment. You will explore who it is and what it's like, and start to consider why it does what it does and what it wants. (You can also find an audio version to download in the online free tools at http://www.newharbinger.com/48756)

EXERCISE: Consciously Connecting with Your Anxiety

Find a place in your home or office that is free of distractions, and take a comfortable seated position. Notice the surface that you are on; feel the weight of gravity grounding your body to the floor or chair. Pay attention to the way the structure that you're sitting or lying on supports you. Close your eyes and take a couple of full, easy, centering breaths.

Turn your attention inward, and just see what you notice. Perhaps you notice stray thoughts coming into your mind. You might be thinking *What is going to happen if I connect with my anxiety?* or *I'm not sure if this is going to work.* Maybe you're thinking about what to make for dinner tonight. Just notice. Take note of any physical sensations or emotions bubbling up to the surface. Perhaps you feel doubt, fear, anxiety. Maybe you feel somewhat blank. You might experience strong physical sensations like a headache or restless legs, or maybe your body feels calm and light. Just keep noticing without trying to do or change anything.

Now, see if you can connect with the part of you that feels anxious. You might find it easier to connect to a physical manifestation of anxiety, or perhaps an emotional one. Whatever ways your anxiety manifests right now, approach it with curiosity. Maybe you connect to it right away, or maybe it's aloof. Just notice this, not trying to change it.

See if you can identify where the anxiety is showing up in your body. This might come to you immediately, or maybe you can't seem to place it. It might feel like a small part of you in a specific location, or perhaps it feels like a surge of electricity coursing throughout your entire body.

Take note of whether your anxiety is moving in your body or staying in one position.

Notice its form—does it feel like a solid, liquid, or gas?

See if you can give your anxiety a color and a shape. Maybe it's many colors all jumbled together. Maybe it's scribble lines. Maybe it's a sharp object. Maybe it's a heavy weight. However it's showing up, see if you can acknowledge it as separate from you.

Continue to notice it without judgment. Maintain an intention of learning about it rather than fixing it. Sit with it for a few minutes. See if it can acknowledge your presence. Ask it to notice that, perhaps for the first time, you're not trying to smother it.

Once you've taken in all of the information you can about your anxiety, thank it for showing up today. Let it know that this is the start of a new relationship with it, and you're looking forward to getting to know it better. If it didn't show up today, acknowledge that and let it know that you'll revisit it again later.

With the experience fresh in your mind, take out your journal and answer these reflection questions.

1. How easy or difficult did it feel to connect with your anxiety?

2. Could you see your anxiety? Feel it? Both?

3. What did you notice about your anxiety? Did it have a color or shape?

4. Did your anxiety move during the exercise or stay in the same location?

5. How old did your anxiety feel?

6. How did you feel toward your anxiety?

7. How did this anxiety feel toward you? How did it feel about being explored?

8. How did you know that this anxiety was separate from you?

9. What else, if anything, did you notice about the experience of trying to meet your anxiety without judgment?

It's likely that something about this exercise surprised you. Just as we can't anticipate how we are going to feel after meeting an estranged family member of twenty-plus years for the first time, we can't know what reactions we might experience when going inside and connecting with anxiety in this way for the first time. I want you to remember something that's more important than the outcome of this exercise: that you have made the very real effort to stop running and start facing your anxiety, and that in itself is a huge step to be acknowledged!

Now let's unpack what came up for you during this exercise.

Building Trust

There is a lot of information that comes from how easy or challenging it was to connect with your anxiety. If it was challenging, that might tell you that your anxiety is somewhat distant and has a hard time trusting you. Imagine if you were invited to meet your estranged family member and you decided to no-show to the meeting. This ghosting behavior would probably be an indicator that you didn't feel emotionally ready to face this person or you didn't trust their intentions. The same is true for your anxiety; if it no-showed you, it's likely that it, or another part of you, feels apprehensive in some way about your connecting with your anxiety. Perhaps it doesn't trust your intentions. Perhaps it doesn't believe this exercise will work. Perhaps it fears that if you fully feel the emotion, you'll never be able to make it stop. If this is the case, it doesn't mean that your anxiety will never come around (after all, it's had no problem showing up before!); it just means that it's going to take some extra time to establish trust before it shows up for you in this context. The more you connect with it, the more trust will be established.

If you experienced the opposite and your anxiety was overwhelmingly present, it may be an indicator that it's been feeling silenced for a long time, and now it's working in overdrive to try and protect you. That is good information to have, and in the next exercise you will gain more insight into what it's working so hard to protect you from. You can also let it know that you understand it has a lot to say, but that you're going to need to work together on how much information it throws at you in one sitting. Remember, you share a common goal: It wants to be heard, and you want to hear it. So if you need it to scale back some in order to be able to hear it, it should be open to the compromise.

One strategy for lessening the overwhelming feelings you may experience when connecting to your anxiety is to imagine a barrier between you and your anxiety. Perhaps it's a brick wall with you on one side and your anxiety on the other side. You can imagine talking to it through a hole in the wall. Another strategy is to imagine talking to your anxiety on a screen, perhaps FaceTime, on which it appears in a small picture at a lower corner of your smartphone. Both of these exercises can help reduce the threat of being totally overtaken by anxiety.

In addition to noting the accessibility of your anxiety, it's important to take note of how old your anxiety feels, as well as how you feel toward each other. It's very common for your anxiety to feel younger than your actual age, because it usually presents as the age it was when it starting doing its job. For example, if your anxiety developed due to a little t trauma when you were eight years old, anxiety might feel eight years old too, because that's the memory it's responding to. Remember, anxiety that doesn't fit the facts of the situation is responding to a past threat as if it were a current threat. For example, when I had anxiety in my professional internship meetings, it was actually responding to the experience I had at age five of being laughed at during a family dinner. It makes good sense, then, that when I first met my anxiety, it felt like a five-year-old. If your anxiety does feel childlike, this can make it easier to develop compassion for it. You likely wouldn't tell a five-year-old to shut up and go away, and if your anxiety feels like it's five years old, you can treat it with the same patience and understanding you would have for any other five-year-old.

There are also benefits to your anxiety's feeling the same age or close in age to you. This means that while seemingly irrational, your anxiety has the logic and communication skills of an adult. An adult can be a little easier to reason, compromise, and settle disputes with than a child is, because an adult has the ability to think critically and see both sides of an argument. Having anxiety that feels similar in age to your own age may also indicate that your anxiety is responding to a little t trauma that happened more recently, which can sometimes make it easier to heal from because it doesn't have many years of being reinforced.

It's important to take note of how you felt toward your anxiety during this exercise and how it felt toward you. As you do this work, it's equally important to monitor how this shifts over time, as it likely will. The ultimate goal is to achieve mutual compassion for one another; however, be aware that often takes time to achieve. It makes sense for anxiety to lack trust in you or to feel any other emotion that an ignored person might feel. Similarly, it is common for you to feel fearful of your anxiety, particularly about its working too hard and causing more problems in your life. It also makes sense to feel annoyed or angry at your anxiety because of how it's impeded you in life. Over time, the goal is to be able to hash out your qualms with it and arrive at a place of compassion for the job it's doing, but it's important to honor the feelings that are showing up now because they are equally valid.

You Are Not Your Anxiety

The most important takeaway from this exercise is the ability to experience anxiety as separate from you, with a separate name and visual representation from yourself. Maybe you imagine it as an orange triangle, or maybe you think of the character Fear from the movie *Inside Out*. It doesn't matter so much what name and image you assign to it, but it's important to start thinking about it as a separate force. Before starting this work, you likely experienced anxiety as all-consuming. You might have had thoughts like *I'm anxious* or *I can't do that because of my anxiety* and labeled yourself as an anxious person. When we are fused with our anxiety, we become something we hate. *If I am anxious and I hate anxiety, then I hate myself.* This way of thinking about anxiety and oneself leads to secondary emotions such as shame, which can start to cause an entirely different set of problems. In reality, you existed before your anxiety. It is not you. It is a part of you that has a job to do, and you likely have many other parts of you that do different jobs.

If you need some convincing of this, think of all of the things about you that have nothing to do with anxiety. Perhaps you are an aunt who loves your nieces and nephews; maybe you like to cook; maybe you are a great writer, or a great friend. When you can experience your anxiety as separate from you, it opens up the opportunity for some really important dialogue. You can then work to understand it and befriend it, and you can work with it toward achieving your common goal. If there is one lasting skill that I hope you glean from these exercises, it is the ability to see your anxiety as separate from yourself.

Going Deeper

Once you have a felt sense of the who and what of your anxiety, the next step is to explore the when, where, and whys—when it shows up, where it shows up, and why it's showing up. The following exercise is designed to give you these insights into your own cycle of anxiety, in addition to the job it's doing for you. Remember to approach this exercise with the same open mind that you brought to the first one, and with the understanding that your anxiety may show up similarly, or perhaps completely differently from your first contact with it. Honor your limits, and take breaks as needed. Remember, this is a marathon, not a sprint. (You can also find an audio version of this exercise to download in the online free tools at http://www.newharbinger.com/48756.)

EXERCISE: Deepening Your Understanding of Your Anxiety

Find a place in your home or office that is free of distractions. In a comfortable seated position, close your eyes if it's comfortable for you, and take a couple of deep inhales, noticing the full course of each breath: the inhale, the pause at the top of the breath before the exhale, the exhale, and the pause before the next inhale.

Turn your attention inside, and see what you notice. Perhaps you notice various thoughts, emotions, and body sensations. Take note of what's there, acknowledging everything that's showing up. Try to maintain a perspective of curiosity rather than a judgmental one.

Now see if you can connect with the part of you that experiences anxiety. Let it know that you're here to check back in with it, rather than blocking it or trying to get it to go away. Once you are able to connect with it, see what you notice about it. How is it showing up today? Does it have the same color, shape, identity, or age as it did it in the previous exercise? Where is it in relation to you? Closer or farther away than previously? Is it moving or static? Does it have a larger presence than it did in the first exercise, or is it smaller and/or more quiet? Take in as much information as you can about it.

Next, let your anxiety know that you're here to learn more about it. Thank it for the information it has shared with you thus far, and then, when it feels right, ask your anxiety what goal it has for you. Tell it that you know it's doing an important job, and you want to understand more about that job it's doing for you. Don't respond just yet. Just listen.

Perhaps you can ask it what it's working to protect you from.

Ask it what it fears.

Ask it how it's helping you. Listen for the answer rather than trying to figure it out. See if you can listen with compassion.

Ask it when it feels most threatened.

Ask it when it feels like it needs to work the hardest.

See if you can acknowledge the importance of its job. Tell it that while you may not agree on how best to get that job done, you share a mutual goal.

Ask if there are ever times when it feels like it doesn't have to work so hard.

Ask what makes it feel soothed.

Let your anxiety know that without trying to change it, you'd like to see if it can acknowledge the problems that it's caused in your life.

Try to get a felt sense of what anxiety's goal is and the job it's doing. Try to understand when it works the hardest, and when it gets a break.

Acknowledge its effort. If it feels right, thank it.

Ask it if it has anything else it wants to share with you now.

Once you've taken in all of the information you can about your anxiety, thank it for showing up today. Let it know that you are working hard to try and understand it, and you're looking forward to continuing to learn about its role. If it didn't show up today, acknowledge that and let it know that you'll revisit it again later.

With the experience fresh in your mind, take out your journal and answer these reflection questions.

1. How challenging or easy was it to connect to your anxiety today? Did it feel more or less accessible than last time?

2. Could you see your anxiety? Feel it? Both?

3. What did you notice about your anxiety? Did it have a color or shape?

4. How did you feel toward your anxiety today? Did this differ from last time you explored it?

5. How did your anxiety feel toward you today? Was it more or less open to communicating with you?

6. Where did your anxiety show up today? Was it closer in proximity to you than last time? Further away? Did it move during your time together?

7. What did you learn about anxiety's goal for you?

8. When does your anxiety work the hardest?

9. When is your anxiety most calm and soothed? When does it get a break?

10. What is it working to protect you from? What are its fears?

11. In what ways is it trying to help you?

12. Were you able to acknowledge that you share a common goal with your anxiety? Could it acknowledge how it's caused problems in your life?

13. What else did you notice about your anxiety?

These exercises can and should be used as a tool for reflection anytime you experience anxiety that does not fit the facts of the situation you are in. When anxiety shows up, the initial impulse is usually to extinguish it as quickly as possible. If you can learn to turn toward your anxiety with curiosity sooner after you experience it, you will spend less time and energy fighting it.

As you continue to move through these exercises, it's important to take note of any shifts in how you experience your anxiety. Hopefully, as you continue this work your anxiety will feel more easily accessible, closer in proximity to you, more trusting and easier to talk to. Any shifts you notice, whether you perceive them as positive or negative, are usually indicative of progress. Returning to the example of your estranged family member, if you no-showed the first scheduled meeting but showed up to the second and got angry, that would show forward movement even if it felt more painful to yell and scream than it did to no-show. Movement in any direction is progress. Of course, if your anxiety initially shows up with a hostile presentation and over time becomes more calm and easy to talk to, this is an indication that it is likely experiencing increased trust and safety in its relationship with you. No matter what shifts might happen, it's important to notice them.

Your Anxiety Wants the Best for You

Perhaps the most important information you will gather from these encounters with your anxiety is a better understanding of the job it's doing. We know that anxiety usually develops from a wound, and it is working to protect you from reexperiencing that wound. While no two experiences of anxiety are the same, there are some common themes that emerge in the types of jobs anxiety usually takes on. Many times this understanding does not come easily, but rather requires many conversations and reflections. Anxiety might not even be totally clear on its job (especially if it's presenting as a five-year-old!), and if it isn't really sure, it's going to have a hard time communicating it to you clearly. Patience is really important here. With patience and continuing effort, you and your anxiety can work together to come to a mutual understanding. A helpful question you might ask yourself when working to uncover the threat that anxiety is protecting you from is *If this bad thing happens, what does it say about me as a person?*

Often anxiety is working to protect you from rejection of some sort. This was certainly the case for me when I kept experiencing anxiety related to looking or sounding dumb in my professional work environment. I didn't always know that I feared rejection, however; I just knew that I didn't want to sound dumb. In doing this work, I was able to collaborate with my anxiety on what exactly the threat was, and I realized I was sure that if I sounded dumb, I was going to be laughed at. It followed that if I am laughed at, that means I won't be respected. If I'm not respected, I am rejected. If I am rejected, I am unworthy. As soon as I uncovered this fear, it made perfect sense why my anxiety was working *so* hard. To my anxiety, my worth as a human was at stake.

Other times, anxiety might be working to protect you from failure. This kind of anxiety might show up when you are goal-setting, future planning, or taking forward steps that feel in line with your personal or professional growth. Other threats that anxiety often responds to are a sense of being out of control, being unsafe, feeling defective, or being responsible for something bad happening.

Once you understand the main threat that your anxiety is responding to, you will likely get a better grasp on when it is most likely to show up. For example, if you identify that your anxiety fears being out of control, you will start to notice that it works harder whenever your sense of control is threatened. Similarly, if your anxiety seems to strike unexpectedly, you may be able to better pinpoint the trigger for your anxiety by asking yourself, *In what ways am I feeling out of control right now?* This is important for many reasons:

- It affirms that your anxiety is separate from you.

- It acknowledges that your anxiety is working hard at its job.

- It allows you to acknowledge that you share a common goal of feeling in control of your life and adopting some compassion toward it.

- It will eventually give you the opportunity to ask your anxiety to ease up some and trust that you can take it from here.

When these steps become part of your response to anxiety, major transformation happens.

What Do You Need from Anxiety?

The last step in this piece of the work is to acknowledge how your anxiety has hindered your life. This relationship is a two-way street, and while you are working very hard to understand and develop compassion for your anxiety, it's equally important that your anxiety considers your needs and perspective as well. While you can acknowledge that it's doing a really important job, you can also ask it to acknowledge that the way it's been doing that job has been less than helpful. Facilitating this conversation can feel threatening to your anxiety, just as it might feel threatening to you if a friend came to you to tell you how your presence has been causing problems in their life. Defensiveness is bound to come up, and that's okay. Remember that any shifts in experience are likely indicative of forward movement.

It's important to let your anxiety know that you're not trying to get it to go away; in fact, quite the opposite. However, you would like it to see that when it works as hard as it does, there are consequences. Maybe you shy away from participating in social gatherings for fear of anything negative that might happen. Perhaps when things seem to be going "too well" in a new intimate relationship, your anxiety about being emotionally vulnerable causes you to sabotage the relationship so you can't end up getting hurt. Or maybe you hold yourself back from achieving your goals because it's more comfortable to stay put. Once your anxiety can acknowledge that there might be a better way to respond to these perceived threats—a way that cause less negative impact in your life—and you can work with it to find this balance, the gates to healing swing open.

Preparing to Work with Stuck Memories

Now that you have consciously connected with your anxiety, developed curiosity and compassion for it, and have a better understanding of the job it is doing, you can prepare to work with it to uncover stuck memories.

We'll spend the next pages—and some hours of your time—practicing some of the skills that will help you uncover and unstick stuck memories. You will increase your skill at getting quiet and turning your attention from external stimuli to your inner world. When you live with anxiety, learning to do this can be tricky. You have probably gotten very good at tuning out your inner experience, since it is so uncomfortable. You might notice that you are often caught up in what is going on in the world around you, investing emotional energy in other people's problems more easily than you can sit with your own emotional experiences. It may seem counterintuitive to actually turn your attention within, where the anxiety lives.

Another obstacle that some people face when learning to go inside and work with their stuck memories is feeling blocked from doing so. In this context, I'm not talking about being blocked by external forces like a busy schedule or chaotic household. I'm referring to feeling blocked from the inside, like you want to go there but there is a protective force inside that won't allow you to.

This can be an indicator that there is another part of you that feels threatened by doing this work. Just as anxiety may be trying to protect you from embarrassment, shame, or some other emotion, there can be a part of you that develops to protect you from anxiety. Or it could mean that a part of you believes it needs to protect you from accessing this memory because it will be too overwhelming to process. Remember that we are hardwired to avoid pain. Leaning into painful past memories in this way is counterintuitive, so patience is key. Trust that your body and brain are working hard to keep you safe. With a little reassurance from you, combined with being shown that this work actually is not dangerous after all, over time a beautiful working relationship between you and your anxiety can and will unfold.

If you experience this blocked sensation when you try to go inside, you will need to spend some time with the part of you that feels resistant to exploring these memories. Ask it how it's trying to help you, what it fears, and what it would need from you in order to feel safe to explore your inner world in this way. If you learned early on in your life that emotions are not safe to experience, and as a result you have spent the rest of your life pushing them away, breaking through this barrier will take several conversations with your anxiety. You might ask your anxiety the following questions to facilitate this unblocking:

- What do you need in order to feel safe accessing this memory?

- If we do explore these past memories and it becomes too overwhelming, how will we know that we need to back out?

- What exercises from chapter 2 can we practice to help reorient to the present and feel safe again?

- What is the benefit of doing this work (our why)?

Again, patience is key. You might make an agreement with the part of you that is blocking you from these memories to explore your inner world in very small doses, perhaps thirty seconds at a time, so that it remains a safe experience. Or you might imagine looking at the memory as if it was on a TV screen rather than in real life, so the sensory experience is less vivid. Or you could imagine a wall between you and the memory, so that it is accessible yet there is a barrier between you and the memory, keeping you safe from it.

If after exploring this for several sittings you still feel blocked, it may mean that the memory is not in fact a little t trauma but rather a *big t trauma* that needs the support of a licensed therapist to help you process it. If you attempt to charge ahead into these memories before it feels safe for all parts to do so, it is likely you will continue to feel more and more blocked. The goal is not for it to feel totally comfortable to go inside and explore your anxiety (after all, the point is to experience and lean into some discomfort), but it does need to feel accessible. You will know it is accessible if you can revisit it while remaining in your healing window of tolerance; that is, the memory comes to mind, you can experience some sensory information that it contains (images, sounds, emotions), and you can do so without experiencing hypo- or hyperarousal. Refer back to the image of the window of tolerance in chapter 2 to use as a guide.

Once you are able to turn your attention inward, you must then be able to notice and experience your anxiety as a force separate from you that can guide you through your past experiences. If you can notice your anxiety and experience it as an energy separate from your adult, logical self, you can allow it to successfully show you what it needs to without becoming completely immersed in the experience.

Remember the concept of dual awareness? When I work with my clients, I ask them to achieve this by imagining having one foot in the present (in the therapy room with me) while having one foot in the past, exploring past trauma memories. This way, they always have an anchor to safety—right here, right now, with me, where there is no danger.

Throughout the trauma work, I will often ask them to pause, take a break, and notice their present surroundings where it is safe. This helps them remain in their healing zone.

It may be helpful for you, too, to find some kind of safety anchor in the present while diving into past memories. That can be anything that feels calming in your environment: a pet, an essential oil, a picture of you and a loved one. When going back into past experiences, imagine having one foot in the past experience while also remaining in the present where it is safe. Your safety anchor can be a helpful reminder that you are revisiting a memory, not reliving it.

The last prerequisite to working with your anxiety in this way is establishing trust between you and your anxiety. You have to trust that anxiety is working hard to protect you from something and to have some compassion for the job it's doing, even though it inconveniences you. Your anxiety has to trust that you are a safe adult who can help it not have to work so hard, rather than trying to extinguish it (as you probably have been trying to do for some time!).

If you feel angry, contentious, or resentful of your anxiety, it is likely that you could benefit from establishing more trust prior to exploring stuck memories. Your anxiety is going to be your tour guide into these memories, and the more you can trust it to guide you, the more collaborative and successful an experience you will have. Once you can adopt a curious and compassionate stance toward your anxiety and can trust that it has valuable information for you to see, you are likely ready to move forward.

At this point, you are likely starting to see your anxiety as a force separate from you with whom you can have a conversation. If you have not yet been able to have a dialogue with your anxiety, it's important to stick with the exercises in this chapter before moving on.

This chapter has taught you skills and practices for exploring your inner experience without becoming blocked; to see your anxiety as separate from you; and to develop a mutually trusting relationship with your anxiety. These skills prepare you to allow your anxiety to guide you into your past experiences to show you where it is stuck. The newfound trust you have established in your relationship with your anxiety will be the force that allows it to guide you through your past experiences safely and to help you uncover and untether from the boulders keeping you stuck, so that your past experiences no longer have to dictate your current emotions. Setting forth on that guiding relationship is what the following chapter is all about.

welcoming anxiety as your guide

In the last chapter, you learned to experience your anxiety as a separate entity with its own motives—and one with which you can have a conscious relationship. In this chapter you'll learn to go inside, trusting your anxiety enough to allow it to show you the boulders or little t traumas that are keeping your anxiety active and you feeling stuck. If you haven't yet been able to have a dialogue with your anxiety, you should spend some more time on the practices in chapter 4, establishing a more curious, conscious relationship with your anxiety. Here, you'll begin to see how that work can transform your life.

The work you do in this chapter will equip you with all of the tools needed to heal your relationship with your anxiety. You will, perhaps for the first time, let go of trying to suppress anxiety symptoms and will instead uncover the source of your anxiety. Now that you have been able to connect with your anxiety and adopt curiosity and compassion toward it, you can allow your anxiety to guide you into your past experiences and show you where you are tethered.

In this chapter you will ask your anxiety to share with you its most fundamental fear, and from there you will participate in a float back exercise that will help you identify where this fear originated. Next, with your anxiety as your guide, you will create a timeline of little t trauma events that are the boulders keeping you stuck. This will become your roadmap for untethering from these boulders. You will then create an adaptive timeline of events that will highlight past experiences that support what your logic knows to be true (that is, *I am good enough*). This timeline will provide evidence to the contrary of your anxiety's fears, and serve as a logical anchor as you begin the untethering.

Must You Go Back There?

If you are wondering if it's really necessary to go back to past little t trauma experiences in order to heal from anxiety, you're not alone. When I ask a new client, "What prompted you to seek therapy at this time in your life?" I usually do not hear "I want to revisit the way my mother treated me when I was a kid" or "I'd like to dive into my past emotionally abusive relationship with my ex-boyfriend." Most people talk about symptoms they are currently experiencing that they want relief from. My clients Sara and Meg (names and some details changed) are good examples of this.

Sara had lived almost her whole life with high anxiety about exposure to blood. On a couple of occasions she had found herself unable to do things that were very important to her because of her anxiety. Sara was an ally of the LGBTQ+ community, and after the 2016 Pulse nightclub shooting she wanted to be able to donate blood to help the survivors who were in desperate need. Despite her strong desire to help in this way, her anxiety made it impossible. Not long after this, Sara witnessed a motor vehicle accident and felt a strong urge to pull over and render aid. But she couldn't bear the thought of seeing people injured and bleeding.

Sara came to therapy wanting to address her blood phobia because, as just described, it had started to interfere with her ability to live according to her values. She did not come to therapy saying, "I want to address my traumatic childhood experiences with blood." It wasn't until we started doing the work that Sara acknowledged that we needed to address her first traumatic experience with blood at age eleven, when her dad was badly injured and she feared the worst.

Similarly, Meg came to therapy to address her social anxiety, as it had recently prevented her from doing what she had long dreamed of: rushing for a sorority. She had such a strong fear of rejection that she couldn't bear the thought of participating in rush week and not matching with any sororities. So instead, she did not participate at all. When this left her feeling depressed and isolated after seeing all of her friends match, she sought therapy.

In Meg's first therapy session, she said she wanted to address her feelings of depression and anxiety. We explored where her anxiety and depression stemmed from and discovered an underlying fear of rejection, which Meg had not yet been consciously aware of. After doing this work together for some time, we discovered that in the sixth grade Meg had experienced an unresolved little t trauma, in which a group of girls announced that they no longer wanted to be friends with Meg. This rejection had devastated her. I was not surprised that Meg had not come to therapy saying she would like to address this experience of bullying that happened to her in sixth grade. She had come because she wanted to stop feeling so depressed and anxious *right now*. For her to do that, we needed to look at what purpose anxiety was serving for her. As it turned out, it was working hard to prevent her from ever again feeling the way she had in sixth grade. Once we discovered this, she was able to heal that wound and change her relationship with anxiety.

Again, you are probably not reading this book because you cannot wait to dive into the painful things that have happened in your past. It is more likely that you are reading this book because you want to get a handle on your anxiety in the present. But to get you there, we must explore what past trauma the anxiety is protecting you from.

How Trauma Memories Get Stuck

Francine Shapiro developed the adaptive information processing (AIP) model to describe why and how past trauma memories get stuck and cause problems later in life. According to Solomon and Shapiro (2008), our brains assimilate new experiences into already existing memory networks. You can think of a memory network as a web of experiences that are connected in your brain by related images, thoughts, emotions, or body sensations. And you can think of your trauma timeline as one particular memory network, and your adaptive timeline as a different memory network. Each memory network contains various experiences that are grouped together in your brain based on the common way they made you feel about yourself, others, or the world.

These memory networks are the basis for our perceptions, attitudes, and behaviors. When this process is working supportively, the new information we take in connects and integrates with our existing memory network, allowing us to make sense of it with no problems. For example, when I have a random and delightful encounter with a nice dog at the park, the sensory information will connect to previous pleasant experiences I have had with dogs and integrate smoothly into that memory network (*dogs are great*) and without inner conflict. But if I have a traumatic experience with a dog at a park, this experience and the new idea that comes with it—*dogs can be dangerous*—creates inner conflict because it does not fit with what I previously knew to be true about dogs.

Shapiro's AIP model explains that an experience that is particularly distressing or traumatic may create its own memory network when it is unable to connect with other memory networks that hold helpful, true information. This can happen when we have an experience that is overwhelming to our nervous system because it is in direct conflict with a belief we previously held about ourself, others, or the world. When this happens, we can't make sense of the new information, given the way we understand the world.

For example, let's say I'm studying for an important exam, and I hold a memory network full of past experiences of doing very well on exams. I may believe that I'm a smart and capable person. If I study as hard as I always have in the past but end up failing the exam, I will need to find a way to make sense of this. Ideally, I will make sense of this in a way that allows me to maintain the idea that I am smart and capable. That is, this memory will integrate into my existing memory network seamlessly. Perhaps I will come to the conclusion that I failed the exam not because I am not smart, but because I didn't get any sleep the night before, which compromised my powers of concentration and recall on exam day. Once integrated, this memory becomes an exception to the rule and is not likely to cause ongoing problems in my life.

When we can't make sense of memories in a way that integrates them into our existing memory network, the memories can get stuck in their own network and become boulders that we get tethered to. If I cannot find another way to make sense of failing the exam, this will challenge my belief that I am smart and capable. If this experience cannot integrate, and I make sense of it by thinking I am not as smart and capable as I once thought, it will form its own memory network and carry with it the belief that I'm actually incompetent. This creates a feeling of disconnection between what my logic knows to be true and what actually feels true. I may have the experience of logically *knowing* I am smart and capable, but *feeling* like I'm actually an imposter. There is an inner conflict when we have separate memory networks holding conflicting ideas, creating a stuck feeling.

This stuckness is what occurred for me as a result of the way my dinner table memory of being laughed at was integrated into my memory network. Prior to this experience at age five, I had likely had several experiences that had taught me I was capable and smart. For example, when I took my first steps, learned the alphabet, or created anything artistic, I was applauded and told some version of "Wow! Great job!" This started to develop the memory network of adaptive information that said that I was adequate.

Later in life, I had experiences that suggested that I was smart and capable, like when I got a 4.0 GPA in college, when I landed a really competitive internship, and that time when my graduate school classmate referred to me as "the smartest girl I know." I would have told you that logically I knew I probably wasn't stupid, but in those internship meetings when I was called on to speak and trembled with fear, it certainly did not feel true. And knowing logically that I was smart had almost no impact on the anxiety I felt associated with sounding dumb.

According to the AIP model, this disconnect between what I logically knew to be true and what felt true happened because the experience I'd had at the dinner table at five was existing in a different, isolated memory network that carried with it the belief that I am stupid. The memory networks were not integrated; they existed separately and were not communicating with one another. When this disconnect happens, we can assume the memory that is stuck in its own memory network is either a little t or a big t trauma.

Not Every Distressing Experience Is Traumatic

You might be wondering, *Does every upsetting experience cause trauma, then?* The answer is no. We take in tons of sensory information all day long, a lot of which conflicts with our preexisting beliefs. Not all distressing events will be stored in their own memory networks. We can have an experience that conflicts with existing information in our memory network and still integrate the memory without consequence. When our brains do this successfully, even a very scary memory will not be stored as a trauma memory.

For example, if I'm bitten by a dog but hold a preexisting belief that dogs are wonderful, trustworthy creatures, this attack may cause inner conflict, but I can still successfully integrate the memory into an existing network without its getting stuck. I might make sense of this experience by adopting the belief that, generally speaking, dogs are safe and wonderful; however, there are times when a particular dog feels threatened that may cause it to act out aggressively. I may think that I was bitten because I carelessly reached down to pet the dog without allowing it time to sniff my hand and give me permission. This allows the memory to integrate into my current memory network without getting stuck and causing problems later.

Distressing memories will integrate into an existing memory network based on the meaning we assign to them. This is why you could have one experience in your past that would be universally labeled as traumatic, like a near-death experience, but not require specific therapeutic intervention or cause any problems later in your life. Meanwhile, something like being rejected in sixth grade, which others might see as a normal, everyday childhood experience, can cause crippling social anxiety into adulthood.

Because of the significance of the thoughts we have about our experiences, two people can experience the exact same traumatic event together, and one might integrate it successfully while the other goes on to develop posttraumatic stress from it. For example, several years ago, when I was driving in my car with my friend as a passenger, we got into a car accident. I was distracted while driving, and the accident was my fault. Both my friend and I experienced the same sensory event—hearing the screeching of the tires and the crunching of the metal on my car. We both felt the same impact of the collision and had similar injuries from it. While both of us experienced a lot of fear and stress from the incident, my friend was able to make sense of it and integrate it into her memory without its causing later problems. She had the thought that car accidents happen often; she will learn from this event, and in the future when she is the driver she will take extra precautions to ensure she is very alert, which may prevent accidents and keep her safe. On the other hand, I walked away from the accident thinking that my negligence had put someone else's life at risk, which meant I was a bad person. This memory got stored in its own memory network because it could not coexist among my other memories that suggested the opposite. The same distressing event was stored traumatically for me, but was only temporarily distressing for my friend, based on our different beliefs about the event.

According to the AIP theory, when an experience is stored in its own dysfunctional memory network, the memory becomes frozen in time and can be retriggered when we experience sensory information similar to the original event. This information can include images, thoughts, emotions, or body sensations. When we experience an emotional reaction that feels disproportionate to the facts of our current situation, it is likely a result of an unresolved past event becoming reactivated.

How Can You Know if You Need to Revisit a Memory?

A good indicator that you are experiencing a disconnect between memory networks is when you know something to be true about yourself, other people, or the world, yet in certain situations the opposite *feels* true. In my work as a therapist, my clients often remark that what they *know* to be true is not connecting to what *feels* true, and they are puzzled by how this can be. Shapiro's AIP theory suggests that this points to an experience or experiences that are frozen and cannot integrate into a memory network. In this case, the frozen experience is causing the feeling, while your existing memory network is what your logic knows to be true. When this disconnect exists, we have to revisit the experience that is frozen and help it get unfrozen. There are many therapeutic modalities that offer different approaches and interventions for how best to accomplish this. For our purposes here, I hope to teach you to rely on the part of you that is trying to alert you to danger (your anxiety) to be your guide into your past experiences. It can show you where you are stuck and give you a route to healing.

The following exercise will invite you to connect to your anxiety and allow it to guide you into your past experiences to start gaining an understanding of the boulders keeping you stuck. (You can also find an audio version of this exercise to download in the online free tools at http://www.newharbinger.com/48756.)

EXERCISE: Exploring Fear

Find a place in your home or office that is free of distractions. In a comfortable seated position, take a couple of deep breaths into your diaphragm as you close your eyes and turn your attention inward. Start by noticing the sensation of your breath entering your nostrils, moving into your lungs, and then exiting from your nostrils or mouth. Stay here, noticing your breathing, for as long as it feels right.

Next, see if you can connect with the part of you that feels anxious. Perhaps its presence is obvious and you notice it immediately. Maybe you feel calm right now and the anxious part of you is more distant and difficult to connect to. Don't force anything to happen; just be still and notice what's going on inside. Let any stray thoughts pass by like clouds in the sky. If you have trouble connecting to your anxiety, bring up a recent experience in which you felt anxious. Do your best to feel into that experience. As you revisit this experience, notice if the part of you that holds anxiety becomes more noticeable. Again, don't force anything to happen. If it is still not showing up, perhaps it is not the right time or place; you can try again another time.

Once you do connect with your anxiety, notice where it is located in your body. Take note of its size and shape. If it had a color, what would it be? Perhaps it takes the form of an inanimate object, or perhaps it feels like a childlike part of you. However it is showing up, acknowledge its separateness from you. See if you can notice where it is in proximity to you. Perhaps it is a younger version of you sitting or standing right next to you, or maybe it's farther away. Notice the energy between the two of you. How do you feel toward it? Perhaps there is tension or reluctance or distrust. Perhaps there's a compassionate, loving energy.

As you sit with this part of you, see if you can engage a little more curiously or compassionately. See if you can let go of any judgment, so you can see your anxiety more clearly.

Once you feel mutual compassion and curiosity, ask your anxiety to show you its biggest fear. Turn your thinking brain off and just listen. This part of you has the answers that you seek, but you cannot access them by figuring them out; you must listen for them. Approach your anxiety as you would approach your most beloved friend who is sharing with you their most vulnerable truth. Be curious.

Allow anxiety to show you what it fears. Maybe it will show you a visual scenario that feels very familiar to you. Perhaps it will blurt out its fear using words. However it communicates with you, stay with it and stay curious.

Give your anxiety as much time and space as it needs. It may take some time to sort through all of the fears it wants to show you. Be patient. Continue to breathe. Once you have a sense of what your anxiety fears, sit with it for a minute. Can you notice how important this is to your anxiety? Can you see how hard it has been working to prevent this from happening? Even if this doesn't make logical sense just yet, acknowledge the fear. It is very real to your anxiety. Practice validating your anxiety as you would validate a scared child.

Once you have a sense of the fear, ask anxiety to go a little deeper with you. Ask anxiety, *And if this feared scenario happens, what will that* mean *about me as a person?* Listen. Breathe. Perhaps it means you are unsafe. Maybe it means you're unworthy. Maybe it's that you aren't in control. Listen without judgment. You are not trying to rationalize right now. You are listening to understand.

Once you have a clear picture of what your anxiety fears, thank your anxiety for showing up today and providing you with this important information. Ask your anxiety if it has anything else it wants to share with you right now.

When you are ready, open your eyes and return your attention to your surroundings.

With the experience fresh in your mind, take out your journal and answer the following reflection questions:

1. How accessible was your anxiety today? Did it feel louder or more distant than in past exercises? If it was more distant, what do you need to adjust the next time you approach this exercise to make it safer for your anxiety to communicate with you?

2. What information did you gather about what your anxiety fears?

3. Can you see how you and your anxiety share a common goal? (Avoiding rejection, feeling safe, and the like.) What is that common goal?

4. Was there anything that surprised you about this exercise?

Exploring Fundamental Fears

When exploring the fears of your anxiety, it's important to get to the most fundamental fear. The fundamental fear is exposed when we peel back the superficial layers of our fears and uncover a negative core belief about ourselves, others, or the world. The fundamental fear also helps make sense of the intensity and urgency our anxiety adopts. For example, if we revisit the example of my anxiety during professional meetings, my initial fear was of sounding stupid in my internship meetings. Once I went deeper, I found that if I sounded stupid, it meant that I would be laughed at, which meant that I would be rejected, which meant I am defective in some way. At the core, I didn't fear sounding stupid; I feared not being good enough. Sounding stupid was just a means to my biggest fear. A symptom of the fear rather than the fear itself. Once I understood this fundamental fear, the intensity of my anxiety started to make more sense. My anxiety was responding to the idea that I was not good enough, not just that I could be laughed at. Once I uncovered the fundamental fear, I could then explore other times I felt not good enough, which reinforced this fear. The point is, if we don't know what the fundamental fear is, we won't have an accurate picture of what our anxiety is actually responding to and working to protect us from.

You can uncover your fundamental fear by asking *If this happens, what does it say about me as a person?* To ensure that you get to the root, you may continue to ask your anxiety, *What happens then?* For example, if it is showing you a situation in which you put effort into your school work and then fail the class, ask it, *What happens if I fail the class?* Perhaps it answers, *You will disappoint everyone.* Then you might ask, *And if I disappoint everyone, what happens then?* It may then say, *You're a disappointment.* To take it a step further and really get to the root, you might ask, *And if I'm a disappointment, what does that say about me as a person?* The answer: *You're inadequate.* Failing the class, then, is not the root fear. Failing the class is how your anxiety is manifesting, just as a weed manifests above the ground where we can see it. Underneath the soil is the fear of being inadequate or defective—which is one of the four categories of *negative cognitions* defined by Francine Shapiro:

- Defectiveness; that is, the belief *I am inadequate, I am not good enough,* or *I am not lovable.*

- Responsibility; that is, the belief *I did something wrong* or *It's my fault.*

- Safety; that is, the belief *I can't trust anyone, I am in danger,* or *I am not safe.*

- Control/choice; that is, the belief *I am not in control* or *I am powerless.*

Fundamental fears take the form of these negative cognitions. And negative cognitions are always "I" statements. For example, *I'm not good enough* versus *He doesn't love me.* If you don't yet have an "I" statement, it likely means you need to continue to go deeper and explore what that *means* about you if that belief were true. You can use the questions *What does that say about me as a person?* and *What happens then?* interchangeably, based on which seems to fit better for your situation. Either one should help you uncover the negative cognition associated with your fear.

Let's say you experience heightened anxiety in your intimate relationship. You go inside and ask anxiety what it fears, and it responds,

He's going to leave you! You then ask, *And if he leaves me, what happens then?* Your anxiety responds, *You'll be all alone!* You ask, *And if I'm all alone, what does that say about me as a person?* Your anxiety may respond, *You're unlovable.*

In this case, the root fear that your anxiety is trying to protect you from is being unlovable. This manifests when your intimate partner has not responded to your text in several hours and your mind starts going to worst-case scenarios. You might feel compelled to run from the relationship, because if you get out first, you can't be broken up with and therefore you've dodged the feeling of being unlovable. Anxiety is often working to protect you from these kinds of bigger, scarier feelings. If you try to solve anxiety by challenging your thoughts about what may be happening when your partner is MIA, you are only working with what's above the surface, rather than the actual fear: of being unlovable.

To move on to the next phase of this work, where anxiety will show you where it is frozen in time, you must have accurate information about what is keeping it frozen in the first place. You have to understand the fundamental fear, not just the symptoms. This requires an open mind and a willingness to get uncomfortable. After all, you may be exposing your most vulnerable, painful fears from which you have been trying to escape for years. If, after learning more about these fundamental fears, you feel the need to revisit the Exploring Fear exercise earlier in this chapter, please do so.

On one hand, uncovering your fundamental fears is a stepping stone to reaching the ultimate goal: becoming unstuck from your past experiences and relieving yourself of the anxiety associated with them. On the other hand, understanding what is really driving your symptoms can be a huge point of awareness and healing in itself. For example, let's say you were having a text message conversation with your intimate partner. It's early in your relationship, and you shared a detail about your personal life that felt vulnerable. After you send this text, your partner stops responding, and the more time passes without a response, the greater your anxiety becomes. You may start wondering, *Was that too much?* Prior to engaging in the exercise in this chapter, you may have very little awareness about what is actually causing your anxiety; you just know that you feel very uncomfortable and might feel compelled to send your partner rapid-fire texts like "Sorry if that was too personal LOL." The more time passes without a response, the more you might feel inclined to make other desperate attempts to soothe your anxiety. Once you do this work and have more awareness of what is typically underneath your relationship anxiety, you may be able to go inside, explore what is actually happening, and remember that you fear being unlovable. Then you will more likely be able to engage in some mental dialogue that imparts logic and suggests that there are a thousand reasons why your partner may not be responding that do not indicate you are unlovable.

Anxiety has been trying to alert you to past little t traumas where these fundamental fears originated, and it is simultaneously working hard to protect you from feeling the emotions associated with them. Once you uncover these fundamental fears, it can feel nerve-racking to your anxiety, because now you are in touch with what it was working hard to prevent you from feeling. At this stage, anxiety will sometimes up the ante in its efforts to protect you. You might notice that your anxiety feels heightened as you move through these exercises. If it becomes overwhelming, you can always take a break and return to the self-soothing exercises in chapter 2. If it feels safe to continue, you can acknowledge that this is a normal part of the process, and that sometimes it feels worse before it gets better. You can be reassured that this work may feel threatening *and* that doing it does not actually pose any danger. After all, you are *revisiting* memories, not reexperiencing them. By uncovering these boulders keeping you stuck, you will help your anxiety become unstuck, and, as a result, it will not have to work so hard.

Where Does Your Fundamental Fear Come From?

Once you have uncovered the fundamental fear underneath your anxiety, you will then work to understand where this fundamental fear originated. The method I like to use in my therapy practice for uncovering past unresolved wounds was developed by Francine Shapiro; it is called the *float back technique* (Shapiro, 2012). The float back technique will allow you to uncover earlier little t traumatic experiences that are the boulders keeping you stuck and responding to past events as if they are current threats. These boulders are the experiences in your past from which you learned these negative beliefs about yourself. They are what anxiety is working so hard to protect you from. These experiences are existing in their own memory networks, unable to integrate with your adaptive memory networks, and causing your present symptoms. When you're doing this exercise, it's important to have a pen and paper nearby so that as anxiety shows you the boulders keeping it stuck, you can make a note of them and return to them individually to do the work that is required to become untethered.

Now that your anxiety has showed you its most fundamental fear, you need it to show you where this fear originated and became reinforced over time. You can think of this fundamental fear as being its own memory network, and you are going to ask anxiety to show you all of the memories that exist within that network—in other words, all of the times you felt defective or unlovable or unsafe. As you might imagine, this can be an uncomfortable exercise. Set yourself up for success here—bite off only as much as you think you can chew. You are not expected to come out of this exercise with a crystal-clear picture of every life event that has contributed to your anxiety over time. Take things slowly, and do not overexert yourself in this exercise. Perhaps anxiety will show you one boulder, and you will need time and space before you feel ready for it to show you another. It may be useful to return to some of the soothing exercises in chapter 2 when you need a break from this exercise. It's important to maintain trust between you and your anxiety, and if you push yourself too hard, it can cause a tear in the relationship, only reinforcing the perceived need to avoid this work in the future.

Come up with some ground rules for this exercise. Let your anxiety know that you are willing to allow it to lead you into some uncomfortable memories, and you trust it to show you what you need to see. If this exercise becomes too overwhelming, you will let it know that you need to back off and out for now and will revisit the exercise at a later time. Ask it to have patience with you as you approach this new, unfamiliar territory. Hold true to your word, backing out of the exercise if and when it becomes overwhelming. This is not a race. (You can also find an audio version of this exercise to download in the online free tools at http://www.newharbinger.com/48756.)

EXERCISE: Float Back

Find a place in your home or office that is free of distractions. In a comfortable seated position, close your eyes if you'd like, and notice your breath. Stay with your breath for as long as feels necessary. Then turn your attention inward and see if you can connect with your anxiety. As always, do not force it. If your anxiety is hiding today, just notice what it feels like to experience the absence of anxiety. Once you can connect with it, notice where and how it is showing up today. If you are having difficulty connecting to it, think of a recent experience in which you felt anxious. See if you can connect to that feeling again.

Once you have made the connection, take note of how you feel toward your anxiety. Can you be compassionate and curious toward it? Imagine sending these emotions toward it. Let it know that you're going to allow it to guide you into your past experiences to show you where it is stuck.

Share with your anxiety how you feel about engaging in this exercise, and let it know that you'd like to cover some ground rules. Tell your anxiety that this is very important work, and it's equally important to do this work carefully and with attention to your nervous system. Let it know that you're going to strive to remain time oriented in the present, bearing witness to these past experiences rather than becoming fused with your anxiety. If at any time you lose orientation to the present and you begin to relive these memories, that's an indicator to you that you might need to back out and reground yourself. Share with your anxiety how you will alert it to the need to back out, if it comes up.

Ask your anxiety if, for its part, there are any ground rules it wants to set with you. Listen. Breathe. Let your anxiety know that, once you begin, you're going to be writing down what it shows you, so that you can be sure you make note of the boulders accurately and thoroughly. When you are ready to do the untethering work, you will give each boulder the attention it deserves.

Now, ask anxiety to show you its fundamental fear. Maybe it has a few, but focus on the most pressing one for now—the one that seems to be driving your current symptoms of anxiety. Perhaps it's feeling unlovable, feeling not good enough, or feeling unsafe. Try to think of a recent experience that prompted that feeling, and embody that feeling now, even though it is uncomfortable.

Once you can tap into the emotions and body sensations associated with your fundamental fear, allow your mind to float back to an earlier time when you experienced a similar feeling. Turn your thinking brain off. You are not trying to think of an earlier memory; you are trying to *feel* for it. If your fundamental fear is of being unlovable, embody the feeling of unlovable and allow your mind and body to float back to an earlier time you felt unlovable. When a memory pops into your mind, open your eyes and write down the following:

1. Your age at the time of the experience (say, twenty-one)

2. A brief description of the experience (David ghosted me)

3. How upsetting this experience feels to you now on a scale from 0 through 10, if 0 is not at all or neutral and 10 is the most upsetting you can imagine (let's say your feeling rates a 6)

Close your eyes again and return to the exercise. Thank your anxiety for showing you this boulder, and let your anxiety know that you have it recorded and will return to it at a later time.

Next, bring back up the emotions and body sensations associated with this negative belief, and allow your mind to float back to an even earlier time you felt this way. Record the same three pieces of information about this earlier experience. Then close your eyes and float back even further. Write down each experience that comes to mind until you get to the very earliest time you can remember feeling your fundamental fear, which is usually in childhood. Keep in mind that you are reflecting on memories rather than experiencing this threat in the present. You are in a different time and space now, with the resources of an adult. You have more information and choices than you did when you were a child. You have the ability to keep yourself safe from danger, which was not true when you were a child. See if you can experience compassion for your younger self, who didn't know then what you know now.

You may complete this exercise in fifteen minutes, or it could take you multiple sittings. Once you cannot float back any further in time, you likely have a complete list of the boulders that have been keeping you stuck and are finished with this exercise.

Congratulations! This is a huge step in recovering from your anxiety.

Now use your journal to reflect on the following questions:

1. What was this exercise like for you?

2. Were there any surprises? Were there any memories that, until now, you hadn't remembered or realized were impacting you today?

3. How accessible were these memories to you? Did they come to you quickly and easily, or do you have a sense that you still do not have all of the information you need?

4. What is the earliest memory you have in which you felt this fundamental fear?

5. Which of these memories feels most distressing to you? Was this surprising to you?

It is very common to have past wounds come to the surface that you would not have originally connected to your current anxiety. You might find yourself having thoughts like *What does that have to do with this?* or *I thought I was over that!* Resist the urge to use logic to discredit what your inner guide, anxiety, shows you. Remember, you are moving away from trying to solve anxiety with logic, and moving toward trusting your anxiety as an intuitive guide that will show you what it needs to heal.

Many of my clients have remarked at the end of therapy that creating this list of past painful experiences is the toughest part of the entire therapeutic process. From here on out, you will turn your attention and energy to only one boulder at a time. You will not move on from that boulder until it feels resolved enough to do so. For most clients, looking at one past painful experience in depth feels more manageable than the effort to take an inventory of all the times they felt unlovable or unsafe or defective. The point is, the exercise you just completed is no easy feat. If you were able to access the information, you should feel good about yourself, as you are one step closer to healing from your anxiety. If it doesn't feel complete yet, that is okay. Stay with the exercise until you feel confident that you have at least one boulder that you can work with. If more memories pop up later, you can add them to the list at that time.

A note on generational trauma and implicit memories: Research on generational trauma suggests that we can be psychologically impacted by trauma that happened to our caregivers in generations before us. If, while completing these exercises, you have a hard time pinpointing a single traumatic event in your past, and you have a sense that the trauma occurred before you existed, it could be an indicator of generational trauma. In this case, it might be helpful to imagine and write down the trauma your parent, grandparent, or ancestor endured that was passed down and its effects internalized by you.

Similarly, we can be impacted by trauma that happens in our first few years of life even if we don't have explicit or concrete memories of it. For example, if your mother had postpartum depression and was withdrawn and unresponsive to your needs during your first few weeks of life, you probably were psychologically impacted by this, but your memory of it will be implicit —more of a felt sense of unsafety than vivid, tangible memories of not being cared for.

If it feels appropriate to do so, you can include both generational and/or early implicit memories of childhood trauma on your trauma timeline—which you will create in the following exercise—even without being able to recall specific details of the memory.

EXERCISE: Create a Trauma Timeline as a Roadmap

When you are ready to move on from the float back exercise, organize your list of boulders into a *trauma timeline*. You can think of your trauma timeline as a visual depiction of the memory network that holds the painful emotions or experiences.

1. Using the list you created in the last exercise, rearrange it in chrono-logical order, starting with the earliest memory you can remember and ending with the most recent.

2. Title this timeline with the fundamental fear (for example, "Unlovable Timeline").

3. On this new timeline, record your age at the time of each event, a brief description of the event, and how upsetting the event feels to you now, using a 10-point scale.

If you have only a couple of boulders in this memory network, this may be a quick and easy exercise. If you have several, it may require several sheets of paper and a substantial amount of time. Remember: this is not a race. Once it's completed, you may have a trauma timeline that looks something like the one shown here.

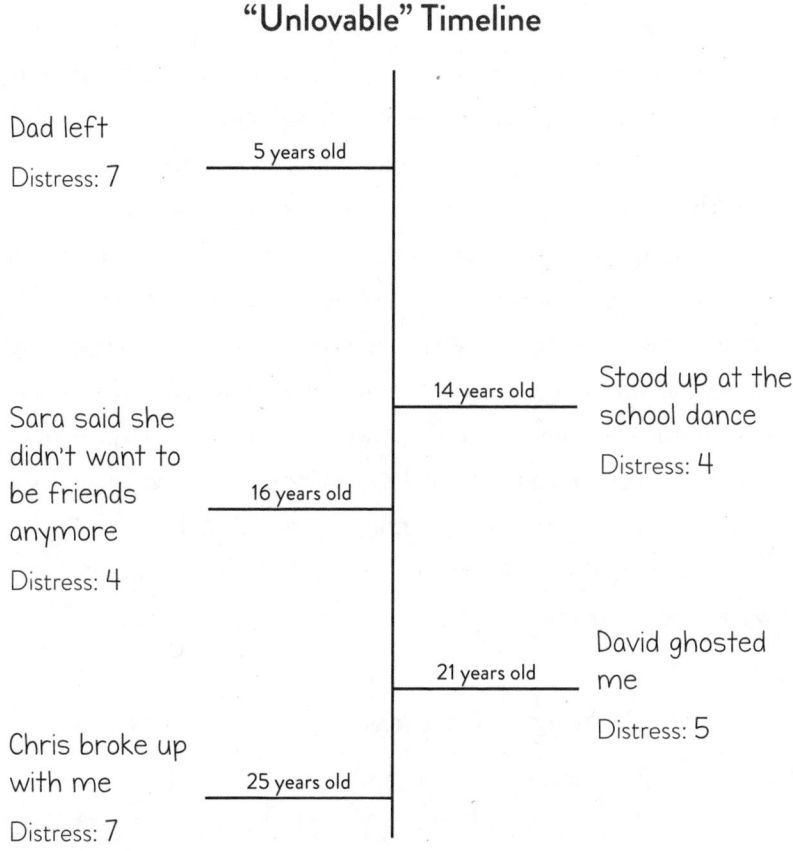

"Unlovable" Timeline

Dad left
Distress: 7

5 years old

14 years old — Stood up at the school dance
Distress: 4

Sara said she didn't want to be friends anymore
Distress: 4

16 years old

David ghosted me
Distress: 5

21 years old

Chris broke up with me
Distress: 7

25 years old

Creating your trauma timeline is important because it shows you first, the point from which your anxiety likely originated, and second, the events that have added to this memory network and perpetuated this negative belief over time. My client Sara was able to identify her earliest traumatic memory with blood at age eleven, and she had many other experiences with blood over the course of her lifetime that reinforced the fear and still caused her distress to think about. While we did not end up having to address each memory individually, it was important for her to know about them so that we could ensure, at the end of therapy, that they were no longer a source of distress for her that could continue to impact her current emotional state.

Knowledge is power when it comes to anxiety recovery, and the float back exercise provides a clear picture of the events that likely led to the symptoms we currently experience. Shapiro (2012) posits that, generally speaking, we have about ten to twenty unprocessed memories in our history that contribute to the majority of the suffering we experience in the present. You may have more or fewer depending on your age and history, but this gives you a sense of how long this exercise can take.

Equally as important as creating an accurate trauma timeline is creating a timeline of important events that are in the adaptive memory network—the experiences that shape what your logic knows to be true. These experiences often reinforce the opposite of your fundamental fear. For example, if you created a timeline of events stored in your "unlovable" memory network, you'll want to create a timeline of events in the "lovable" memory network.

EXERCISE: Creating an Adaptive Timeline as an Anchor

There are two good ways to assemble this timeline.

First, simply get out a piece of paper (or a journal page) and write down past events that created or reinforced the opposite feeling of your fundamental fear as they come to mind. For this timeline, record your age, a brief description of the event, and how lovable you felt on a scale of 0 through 10. If you have trouble accessing these memories, try closing your eyes, tapping into the sensation of feeling the *opposite* of your fundamental fear (feeling lovable, for example), and allowing your mind to float back to times in which you felt lovable, then recording them on paper.

For many people, creating the adaptive timeline can feel more challenging than creating the trauma timeline. If this is your experience, do not be discouraged. Do your best to find at least one adaptive memory, regardless of how fleeting or insignificant it seems. It can be something as small as a teacher who encouraged you or a childhood friend's parent who welcomed you to eat dinner with their family.

Once completed, your adaptive timeline may look something like the one shown here.

"Lovable" Timeline

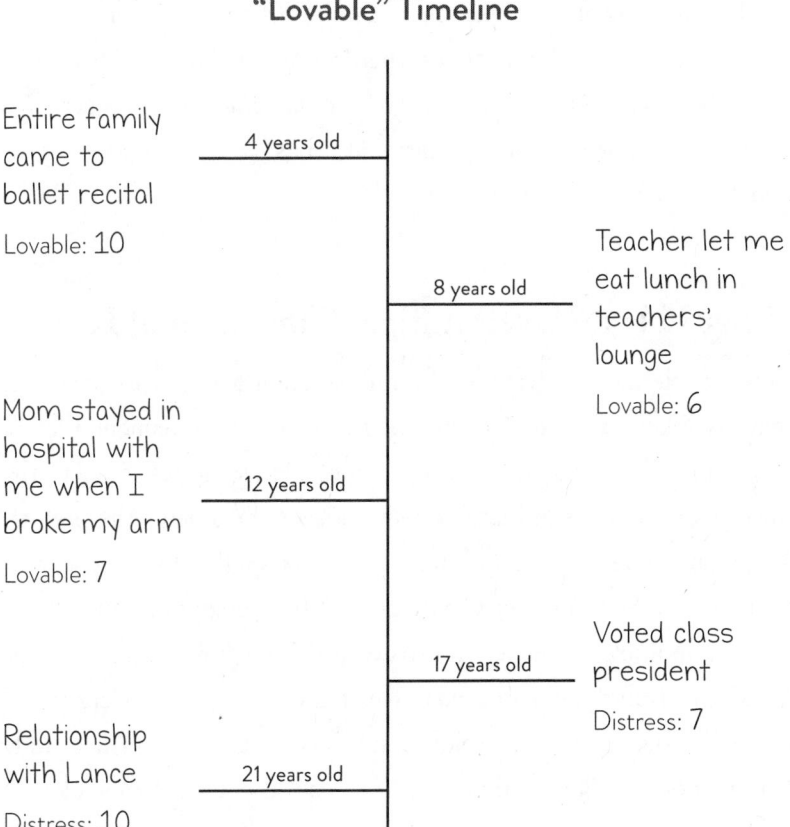

Entire family came to ballet recital

4 years old

Lovable: 10

8 years old

Teacher let me eat lunch in teachers' lounge

Lovable: 6

Mom stayed in hospital with me when I broke my arm

12 years old

Lovable: 7

17 years old

Voted class president

Distress: 7

Relationship with Lance

21 years old

Distress: 10

The second approach is to make a timeline of events that support what your logic knows to be true (*I am lovable*) and a separate timeline of events that have perpetuated what feels true when your anxiety is high (*I am unlovable*). This adaptive timeline of events can serve as an important anchor while you're doing this work and when you're experiencing anxiety in your day-to-day life. If you have a high-anxiety day in which you are feeling particularly unlovable, it may be useful to pull out your adaptive timeline and review the past experiences that have indicated otherwise. To take it a step further, you can close your eyes and embody the feelings that come to mind when you really put yourself back into these pleasant experiences, and allow that feeling to course throughout your body and expand.

Because anxiety can feel all-consuming when you experience it, it can be useful to remember times when you felt differently. This can be soothing because although you may be experiencing a lot of anxiety now, the adaptive timeline is a reminder that it has not always been this way and it will not always be so.

What If You Have Multiple Fundamental Fears?

Most people have more than one fundamental fear. For example, you may get relationship anxiety that boils down to a fundamental fear of being unlovable, and you may also experience some test anxiety that uncovers a fundamental fear of being not good enough. Although the sensations these fears produce might feel very similar, they are separate fundamental fears and likely exist in separate memory networks. If you uncover multiple fundamental fears, you will need to create two time-lines, one trauma and one adaptive, for each fear you identify. For example, you may create a Not Good Enough trauma timeline and a Good Enough adaptive timeline. You may also create an Unlovable Trauma Timeline and a Lovable Adaptive Timeline. You can revisit the Exploring Fear and Float Back exercises to uncover the fundamental fears and the associated past experiences stored in that memory network. You will work on one fundamental fear at a time as you enter the next phase of the work; in that phase, you will revisit these past boulders one by one and work to become unstuck from them.

Congratulations on making it this far; you are doing great. This is not easy work. If this does not come as easily or as quickly as you had hoped, be gentle with yourself. Diving into our past experiences may feel counterintuitive. And it takes time and patience—two things that our anxiety does not always have to spare. You may need to return to these exercises time and time again before feeling like you have documented a clear timeline of boulders to move forward with.

You will know you are ready to begin the untethering work in the following chapter when you:

- Can experience your anxiety as separate from you

- Can feel curiosity and compassion toward your anxiety

- Have identified a fundamental fear(s)

- Have an idea of where this fear originated and the experiences that have reinforced it over time

healing wounds together

Some would argue that once you have gotten to this point in the work, the hardest part is behind you. In creating a trauma timeline, you have gotten past the uncomfortable truth that your past experiences may hold the key to unlocking and releasing your anxiety. You likely have accepted that you probably do need to go back there. You have demonstrated willingness to dive into those past experiences, even though doing so brings up uncomfortable emotions and might feel counterproductive. All of this is something to be celebrated.

It is not uncommon for people to resist diving into their past experiences. I often work with clients who ask, "What can I do about my anxiety?" When I propose the idea of leaning into anxiety, getting to know it better, and exploring where it is stuck in the past, I sometimes get a perplexed look followed by a reiteration, "Okay, but what do I actually *do* about it?" Generally speaking, people do not want to look backward. It's not in our nature. We are conditioned to look ahead, to set goals and accomplish them. But you have tried that. You've attempted to outrun and extinguish your anxiety. You have told it that it doesn't make any sense. You've tried working harder, pushing through, doing more. And you have decided to open your mind to the possibility of approaching it another way. At this point in the work, if you've been doing the exercises you have likely already made leaps and bounds of progress, and for that I commend you.

Having created a timeline of events that have contributed to and reinforced your anxiety over time, you are ready to begin the untethering work. When you get to this stage, it is like having your own personal blueprint for healing from your anxiety.

If you haven't already, thank your anxiety for showing up and cooperating in showing you where it is stuck in trauma time. Because of your anxiety's willingness to communicate with you, you have an opportunity to do what you need to do to get you both unstuck. You can't do it without anxiety as your guide, and your anxiety definitely cannot work less hard without your willingness to explore where it came from. The next step in this work, the untethering, is mutually beneficial in that it will allow you to live a happier, healthier life with some freedom from anxiety, while allowing anxiety the freedom to kick back and relax a little rather than constantly alerting you to danger.

Note that the untethering work is almost always easier to navigate when you are working with a skilled therapist. Should you get stuck in this chapter or anywhere else while navigating this work, it may be an indicator that you could use a therapist's support. Keep in mind that we all have times when we aren't able to guide ourselves out of a particular painful experience and require the support of others, and this work is no exception. I often hear new clients say "I knew I needed help because my normal means of coping haven't been working for this particular issue."

You might find that you are able to make good progress in untethering from some of your boulders, but there are one or two that you cannot get unstuck on your own. Perhaps seeing a therapist for a couple of sessions could cause a shift that you need in order to return to this work on your own. It could also be that you experience a clinical mental health condition that this self-help work is not suited for, such as complex posttraumatic stress disorder (CPTSD), OCD, or a dissociative disorder. Regardless of what is preventing you from making progress in this work, a licensed therapist from whom you seek individual, personalized care will support you in reprocessing trauma memories in a way this book cannot.

That said, Francine Shapiro acknowledges in her self-help book *Getting Past Your Past* (2012) that the processing of past trauma memories "doesn't only have to take place in a therapist's office." She says, "Many things can happen in our everyday lives that cause our emotions to change and insights to occur." These can include new experiences that enter and reinforce your adaptive memory network, profound life experiences that shape you and cause you to view the world in a new way, or simply a series of small shifts in perception that come naturally with the passage of time.

Knowledge Is Power

Many people make progress in their emotional health simply by gaining an understanding of what is contributing to their pain, which you have done in the last chapter. For example, when you experience anxiety, it may be enough for you to be able to say to it *Ah, you again. I know why you're here. You're alerting me to that time in seventh grade when I was mocked after school. I can see how you think this situation might pose that same danger, but I've evaluated the risk, and I think we're in the clear.*

Perhaps you have already gained more insight into your anxiety and have experienced shifts that will be more than enough to change your relationship with it moving forward. I have had clients get to this stage in therapy, when they have a greater understanding of why their symptoms came to be and how they're impacting them today, and decide that they feel well equipped enough with this key information alone to discontinue the therapeutic process without ever doing the untethering work. Increased awareness, by itself, can be what allows you to move forward in your life with less anxiety and greater spontaneity and ease, as you so deserve. My hope is that you have already started to notice some minor shifts in how you experience and relate to anxiety that will prove useful in your life, regardless of how far you get in the following untethering work.

Most people, however, feel empowered by the increased awareness and education, but still need help addressing the source of anxiety so that they can eradicate the symptoms. I've heard countless times in my therapy practice "I know where this comes from and why it's happening. But I still can't stop it." In these cases, anxiety is no longer a puzzle to be solved. In fact, its origins may be crystal clear. If you sense that you have good insight into your anxiety but still need to go deeper into this work to fully heal it, this chapter will be helpful to you. I will guide you through the next step in the work and will offer an opportunity for you to revisit these past wounds safely so that you can become unstuck from them. In doing so, you will reassure your anxiety that it can live with you in the present, doing its job in alerting you to danger only when danger actually exists.

The untethering work in this chapter will include the following steps in this order:

1. First, I will teach you how to access a calm, centered internal state which will prepare you to do the untethering work successfully. If you cannot access this state easily, we will come up with a representation of what this state would be like for you.

2. You will connect with your anxiety and work to establish mutual compassion.

3. You will then allow your anxiety to guide you into your stuck memories, one at a time. You will bear witness to the memories in which anxiety is stuck, then explore what you needed but didn't get at the time of the event. You will then uncover ways in which you can help meet those needs now.

4. Finally, you will bring your anxiety with you into the present, where the danger is no longer happening.

Untethering

The first step in the untethering work is to get in touch with the most centered, calm version of yourself. Internal family systems (IFS) therapy calls this state *self-energy* and purports that everyone has it already within; it does not need to be created or cultivated. According to IFS, you know you are in self-energy when you experience eight Cs: curiosity, calmness, confidence, compassion, courage, creativity, connectedness, and clarity (Anderson, 2020). When you feel disconnected from self, it is because other parts of self (such as anxiety) are working hard inside and may be at the forefront, blocking you from experiencing the eight Cs. This can cause you to feel distant or detached from your calm and confident self-energy, but is not an indicator that self-energy does not exist. It's important to note that not everyone feels the eight Cs wholeheartedly even when in self-energy, and that is not a requirement for you either. The better question is, can you tap into curiosity, calmness, confidence, and the rest? You do not have to experience all of these all of the time.

It may be that this calm, centered version of yourself is just ordinary you minus anxiety. Perhaps you know self-energy very well because you experience this version of yourself often when your anxiety is well managed. If you experience anxiety related to a specific experience, such as public speaking, it may be that you are relatively cool, calm, and collected most of the time until it is time to talk in front of a group, in which case your anxiety hijacks your self-energy. Or perhaps you experience more generalized anxiety that feels constant, and the possibility of being centered and free of anxiety feels so foreign to you that it's causing you anxiety just to think about it! Regardless of how accessible self-energy feels to you now, there are different exercises that will help you get in touch with this version of you in a way that is necessary for untethering. I will guide you through these exercises now.

Now, let's come up with an image and felt sense of your highest-functioning, centered self. There are many ways to do this, and I've provided the following four exercises as options for this step in the work. I recommend that you read through all of them and then decide which feels like it will work best for you. You can certainly try all four of them and learn by doing which works best. The more resources you have, the better, so don't be afraid to spend too much time here. If none of these feels accessible, it may be that you need to revisit these exercises at a later time. Remember: this is not a race. (You can also find an audio version of these exercises to download in the online free tools at http://www.newharbinger.com/48756.)

EXERCISES: Find Your Most Centered Self

Option #1

Find a place in your home or office that is free of distractions. In a comfortable seated position, close your eyes, and turn your attention inward. Notice any thoughts, feelings, and body sensations you may be having. If you notice any unpleasant thoughts, just allow them to pass by as quickly as they came in. If you experience any anxiety or other uncomfortable emotions, simply acknowledge them and let them know that you are aware of their presence. Then ask these unpleasant emotions one by one if, for the purposes of this exercise, they would be willing to ease up and give you some space so that you can connect with your self-energy. Ask permission rather than demand this from them. You're not asking these emotions to go away, but rather to simply become unfused from you so that you can observe them from a place of curiosity.

Notice what it feels like for them to ease up for you. If these emotions aren't willing or able to give you space right now, perhaps it is not the right time or place for you to engage in this exercise. Once these uncomfortable emotions have stepped aside, turn your attention back to your breath, allowing it to continue to flow naturally.

Notice the experience of feeling calm, curious, and centered. This is self-energy. It is a deep inner knowing that has always been there and will always be there. Notice where it is showing up in your body. Perhaps it is located in your heart or solar plexus, or maybe it rests somewhere in your mind or elsewhere in your body. Or it could be a sensation that permeates your entire body. You might experience it as eternal, conscious, and intelligent. Maybe it is playful, sensitive, and creative. This part of you is calm and connected. Breathe into it, allowing it to expand. Just notice.

Now notice what image is associated with this part of you. Perhaps it looks like you in a certain time and space, or maybe it's an energy flowing through you like water. It could be a bright white light radiating from within or a solid, unwavering force like a mountain. Keep noticing this centered part of you.

Now turn your attention to how it feels to be connected to this part of you. Perhaps there is a warmth or a tingling sensation coursing throughout your body. Breathe. Notice any sounds associated with this part of you. Perhaps you notice a soft buzzing, or maybe there is stillness and silence. Spend a few more moments connecting with this part of you. Then take a mental snapshot of this version of you, which exists so freely, calmly, and confidently, so that you can return to this part of you at a later time.

Finally, thank this inner wisdom for showing up today, and let it know that you'll be connecting with it again very soon.

Many people find it hard to access the sensation of calm early in this work. If this first exercise was not accessible for you, I invite you to give this next one a try.

Option #2

As preparation, revisit one of the adaptive timelines that you created in chapter 5, particularly one that outlines experiences in which you felt safe,

okay, and/or enough. Choose the event on the timeline that feels most powerful to you now.

> Find a place in your home or office that is free of distractions. In a
> comfortable seated position, turn your attention to your breath.
> Close your eyes and bring to mind that positive experience. Don't
> just think about this experience; try to feel into it again. Put yourself
> back there and notice how it felt to be lovable, worthy, enough.
> Really get a felt sense of it. Let the feelings you had at that time
> course through you now. You are just as lovable, worthy, and *enough*
> now as you were then.

> If your brain starts to make any negative associations, just notice
> them, like railroad cars on a passing train. Let them go, and turn your
> attention back to the pleasant feelings associated with this memory.
> Notice where you feel these sensations in your body. Perhaps they
> bring a warmth or a vibration. Maybe they feel like stillness.

> Create a snapshot of the version of you that felt these feelings.
> Perhaps it's an image of a younger you, or an image that represents
> the feelings this memory brings you now, like an anchor or a bright
> light. Notice as many details about this snapshot as you can, so that
> you can return here at a later time.

When working on option #2, it's important that the image you come up
with does not become compromised by a negative association. This is the
same concept we discussed in the Calm Place Visualization exercise in chapter
2. For example, if you begin thinking of a memory in which you felt completely lovable, and then your thoughts wander to how this was an exception
and you are actually not truly lovable, try to bring your attention back to the
feeling of being lovable. If this is not possible and the memory is now associated with a painful emotion instead, it may not be a useful resource for you in
this work. If this happens, do not spend more time on it; simply move on to
another pleasant memory on your adaptive timeline or to a different exercise
altogether.

The next exercise is another version of the second option. Rather than revisiting an earlier version of yourself, however, this exercise invites you to tap into your future older, wiser self.

Option #3

Get comfortable, close your eyes, and turn your attention inward. Notice any thoughts, feelings, and sensations you may be having. If you notice any unpleasant thoughts, just acknowledge them and allow them to pass by. If you experience any anxiety or other uncomfortable emotions, simply acknowledge them and let them know that you are aware of their presence. Then imagine asking them, one by one, to give you a little space for the purposes of this exercise.

Next, create an image in your mind of an older, wiser version of yourself. It could be you five years from now or fifty years from now. Imagine this older version of you as having been through many important experiences that have allowed that self to develop great knowledge and wisdom. Imagine your older self as being mostly freed from anxiety and fear, and being content with yourself and the world around you. Find awe in the inner beauty, awareness, and insight that this self possesses. Breathe.

Now imagine this older, wiser version of you coming into the present moment with you. Perhaps you sit in adjacent chairs while sipping cups of tea together. Maybe you hold hands or hug. Imagine this older version of you telling you what you need to hear right now. Notice how it feels to have that self close. Breathe. Allow these pleasant emotions to course through you, and allow yourself to be comforted and soothed by this supportive resource that is your older, wiser self. Take as much time as you need here.

Now create a mental snapshot of yourself experiencing the pleasant emotions you feel when you are with this resource. Try to encapsulate the images and associated feelings and body sensations in this snapshot. Keep it close so that you can return here when you are ready to continue the work.

If these three exercise options were not accessible for you today, it could be that now is not the right time and space for the untethering work, and it may be more appropriate to return to it at a later time. It could also mean that your anxiety and perhaps other emotions have been working so hard and for so long that it's tough to imagine yourself without them, even in a different time and space. When this is the case, it can be useful to find external resources that can help you tap into the sensations of calm rather than relying on inner resources. If this feels true for you, I'll invite you to try the following alternate technique for getting in touch with your most centered self.

Option #4 (Alternate)

Get comfortable, close your eyes, and turn your attention inward. Notice any thoughts, feelings, or sensations you may be having. Act as a mindful observer of your inner experience rather than clinging to or pushing away anything. Breathe.

Now bring to mind the image of someone or something you have had or imagine having in your life that offers unconditional protection and love. It could be something imaginary, like your favorite Disney character or superhero. It could be someone special in your life who provided this love, care, and protection to you in the past—like a teacher or a childhood friend's parent—or in the present, like a current intimate partner or friend. This resource could be someone who is no longer alive, like a deceased family member or pet. It could be a higher power, like God or a spirit guide. It matters less who or what this resource is and more the felt sense that you have when you imagine them being with you. Perhaps this resource comes to you immediately, or maybe you need more time. Take as much time as you need. The goal is to experience an increased sense of safety and calmness when they are with you.

Once you have this resource in mind, imagine them coming into the present with you now. Bring them nearby and notice the sensations you experience when they are close. Breathe. Allow the pleasant emotions to course through you, and allow yourself to be comforted and soothed by this supportive resource. Perhaps you want to inter-act with them in some way, or maybe it is enough to simply feel their presence.

Create a mental snapshot of yourself experiencing the pleasant emotions you feel when you are with this resource. Try to encapsu-late the images and associated feelings and body sensations in this snapshot. Keep it close so that you can return here when you con-tinue the work.

Ideally, your own "self-energy" will become the resource that you need in order to help your anxiety heal from the wounds it is stuck in. This is the goal because if and when you are done with this work, and you're in a situation where you encounter anxiety that does not fit the facts of the situation, it is usually most simple to tap into your centered self to help manage it. Your centered self will always be with you, to assist you in working through whatever challenges you are facing at any given time. This makes it an invaluable resource.

If, for example, you use your spouse as an external resource for the unte-thering work you are doing now, and a year from now you are going through a hard time with your spouse and are having anxiety as a result, it is likely that your spouse will not be the best resource to help you revisit this work when needed. However, when it's not yet possible to access your own centered self, option #4 can be a useful tool to identify a strong resource that can help you become untethered from the boulders that are your past traumatic experi-ences. Identifying an external resource will not require you to be able to tap into self-energy if that feels inaccessible. However, as much as you can, it's important to turn your attention to the way you feel in the presence of this resource, rather than the resource itself. This way, the resource shifts from an outside person to an inside feeling and can be more universally applicable.

After completing one or more of these exercises, take out your journal and reflect on the following questions.

1.   What was it like to experience self-energy? How did you know when you were tapped in to your most centered self?

2. What emotions did you experience when you were connected to your self-energy?

3. What body sensations are associated with your centered self?

4. Write about or draw a picture of the mental image you came up with.

5. How do you think this state of being might help you untether yourself from past boulders keeping you stuck?

Now that you have an image and felt sense of your most centered self, it's time to connect this version of you to the part of you that is anxious. To do this, I will guide you through an exercise adapted from the dissociative table technique created by George Fraser. The technique is designed to provide a forum for various parts of self to communicate and work together in healing trauma (Martin, 2012). Both your most centered self and your anxious self will revisit these wounds together. You can think of it as two forces with a common goal, teaming up to do what needs to be done to achieve that goal. This untethering takes teamwork and communication, which you will facilitate in the following exercise. (You can also find an audio version of this exercise to download in the online free tools at http://www.newharbinger.com/48756.)

EXERCISE: Introducing Your Most Centered Self to Anxiety

Find a place in your home or office that is free of distractions. In a comfortable seated position, turn your attention to your breath. Close your eyes and feel yourself melting into the surface you're resting on. Notice how the furniture or floor beneath you is holding you up, supporting you. Breathe.

Now imagine a meeting place where you will bring together your anxiety and your most centered self or resource. It is a space with exactly enough seats or room for you. Make sure this meeting place feels comforting and calm. Maybe it is a boardroom; maybe it's a treehouse. Once you have a meeting place in mind, ask the anxious part of you, who will be in charge of leading you back to the boulder you are tethered to, to enter the meeting place with you and take a seat wherever it would like. When it does, thank your anxiety for showing up today.

Next, bring your most centered self or external resource to the meeting place. This part will take the role of assisting anxiety in the untethering. Allow these two parts of you to come together and see if they can experience mutual compassion for one another. Acknowledge the common goal of becoming untethered from these boulders. Maybe it's a goal of feeling lovable, or good enough, or safe. Acknowledge the goal of this work: anxiety will not have to work quite as hard, and you will experience some relief. Ask your anxiety to notice the resource you brought in, and the fact that it has a new team member—one that it didn't have in the past—to support it now. Ensure that these two parts have a supportive relationship before you proceed. If there is any contention, they will need to spend more time together, with you as the mediator, until they have resolved any issues so they can move forward as a team. Once they can experience mutual curiosity and compassion, it is safe to continue.

Now that you have introduced your most centered self to your anxiety, take out your journal and reflect on the following questions.

1. How accessible was your anxiety today? Your centered self?

2. What was it like for you to create a meeting place for the parts of yourself?

3. What was the felt sense of the relationship between these parts of self?

4. Did you feel blocked from this exercise at any point? If so, what can you do to move forward (for example, try again later, eliminate distractions, explore the part of me that's fearful)?

5. Do you have a sense that these two parts share a common goal?

6. Do you have a sense that these two parts are capable of working together on a team, or is more relationship building needed?

The introduction of your most centered self to your anxiety can feel complicated. When we go inside, it is common for multiple different emotions to come up, even conflicting ones. Perhaps there was a part of you that felt angry. Or maybe there's a part of you that feels indifferent and isn't sure that it wants to go further in this work. Or perhaps the blocked sensation we discussed in chapter 5 is happening because this work feels threatening. As we discussed in earlier chapters, you shouldn't expect this work to feel seamless; in fact, it is often messy. However, it should feel accessible. To make this determination, you might go inside and ask yourself, *Is there any part inside that does not want us to revisit these boulders?* If any part of you screams in opposition, it is a good indicator that this part of you needs to feel a little more safe before moving forward. If you get an agreement, even a begrudging one, it is safe to move forward.

If you have a part of self that you sense is interfering in some way, you will need to spend some time with that part before you go charging ahead in the work. You'll want to explore what the part's job is, what it is fearful of, and what it needs from you in order to feel okay with continuing. Come up with an agreement with the part about how you will proceed in a way that is safe for all. Once you sense that all parts of self are on board to revisit your past boulders, it is time to continue the work.

How Can You Know Where to Start?

Your most centered self and your anxiety have to come up with a game plan for which boulders should be addressed first. The good news is that you have already written down a map of your boulders: your trauma timeline. I will share with you a couple of theories on the order in which to best approach these boulders, so you can make an informed decision on where to start. There is no right or wrong answer here, so don't let making this decision hold you up.

The first theory suggests that if you tackle the earliest chronological memory on your timeline first, healing from that memory may have a cascading effect on later memories. In other words, if you connect the earliest trauma memory to an adaptive memory network, it may by default connect other, later trauma memories to that same adaptive network. This would mean that you could revisit one trauma memory, become untethered from it, and then realize that a subsequent memory spontaneously no longer causes you any distress, because it had been grouped in your brain with the original memory.

Another theory holds that you will get the most relief the fastest if you start with the memory on your timeline that causes you the most distress or anxiety now. It's likely that the "worst" memory on your time-line is currently the biggest contributor to your anxiety. Therefore, revis-iting that memory first may offer the greatest and fastest relief. Francine Shapiro, in describing a roadmap for addressing past trauma in EMDR therapy, refers to these two potential starting places as "first or worst."

I recently worked with a client who had anxiety every time she felt sick or dizzy. On her trauma timeline was an incident three years earlier in which she had passed out in her bathroom after experiencing a bout of dizziness. She reported that since that incident, any slight indication that she could pass out again—dizziness, nausea, or lightheadedness— caused her anxiety to spike. The incident in which she passed out in her bathroom was listed on her trauma timeline as a distress level of 10 out of 10. Since this event three years before, she had experienced other related incidents that were less distressing, such as the time she got sick with the flu. Together we decided to first address the time she got the flu, as she wanted to have some practice with the untethering process prior to revisiting one of the scariest things that has happened to her. Once we completed the untethering of this memory, she felt confident to move on to the scarier ones.

When considering which boulder to address first, it's important to start with one that feels manageable. If there is a memory on your time-line that causes a distress level of 10 out of 10, and you feel a strong impulse to avoid it, honor that for now. Similarly, if you have a memory on your timeline that causes some detachment or emotional flooding when you think about it (a sign that you have exited your window of tolerance), that is probably not the best place to start either. In fact, that may be a memory that warrants the support of a professional therapist to reprocess. Conversely, if all of the memories on your trauma timeline cause a relatively low amount of distress, it may be that you can start with the one that causes the most distress, because it is likely still a manageable amount of distress that feels tolerable to revisit.

Take a look at your trauma timeline and the boulders listed, as well as their corresponding distress levels. Is there a boulder with a distress level of 4 to 6 that may be a good starting place? Make sure that both your most centered self and the part of you that is anxious agree on the starting place. You can do this by going inside and connecting with your most centered self or external resource and the anxious part of you. Let them know which memory you'd like to start with, and see if there are any objections. If there are, see if there are any ideas about where is a better starting place. Once you have a mutually agreed upon starting place, you can begin the next exercise. (You can also find an audio version of this exercise to download in the online free tools at http://www.newharbinger.com/48756.)

EXERCISE: Healing Wounds

Find a place in your home or office that is free of distractions. In a comfortable seated position, turn your attention to your breath. Close your eyes and feel yourself melting into the surface you're resting on. Notice how the furniture or floor beneath you is holding you up, supporting you. Breathe.

Now bring up the image of your meeting place. This place is calm and comfortable, with exactly enough space for all. First, imagine yourself in this meeting place. When you feel ready, imagine inviting your anxiety into the same meeting place. Imagine your most centered self or external resource in the meeting place with you. Ensure that you have permission to move forward by asking all parts if it's okay to proceed. If any part inside you objects to moving forward, explore what this part of you might need to feel it's safe to continue. Maybe it doesn't want to participate but is willing to watch from an adjacent room. Perhaps it wants to be able to speak up when it is time to back out. Maybe it needs to be with an external resource to provide protection as you revisit past wounds together. Do not force things; rather, ensure that you have permission from all parts of self to move forward.

Next, in your mind's eye, imagine anxiety leading you and this resource back to the boulder. Perhaps anxiety is in the front, with you and the resource following behind. Or maybe you are the leader, with anxiety giving you directions from behind. Maybe your most centered self or resource is leading, perhaps holding anxiety's hand or carrying it on its back, ensuring that it is safe. Maybe you ride in on a plane or a magic carpet. Go with whatever your imagination conjures up.

Let your mind float back to this earlier traumatic experience. Maintain the awareness that you are in a different time and space now than you were when this memory happened. You are revisiting the memory rather than reliving it.

When you get to the boulder, allow your anxiety to show you what it needs to. Be a supportive observer, a silent witness. Give your anxiety as much time as it needs to show you what is important about this experience. Breathe. If you notice any emotions coming to the surface, make space for them. Allow them to flow over you like ocean waves. If this becomes too overwhelming, try putting a partition between you and the memory. Perhaps you revisit the memory from behind a brick wall with one brick missing, allowing you to see through. Maybe you get on your magic carpet and hover above the memory, looking down on it.

Let your anxiety know that you and your resource are watching and listening and are here to bear witness to this experience. Take as much time here as you need to ensure that your anxiety has shown you everything it needs and wants to. Let anxiety know that it didn't have you at the time of the memory, but you are with it now. Listen. Stay present with it.

Now, ask your anxiety what it needed at the time of this experience but didn't get. Don't try to figure out the answer; instead, listen for it. Breathe. Maybe it needed a supportive adult to tell it everything was going to be okay.

Maybe it needed someone to keep it safe. Maybe it needed a hug. Allow anxiety to tell you what it needed. Breathe. Listen.

Now imagine providing to your anxiety what it needed then but didn't get. Take your time here. Breathe. Tell the younger you what they needed to hear. If needed, allow your external resource to step in and help. If this is a scary memory, allow the resource to provide protection. If it's a sad memory, allow the resource to console you. Use your wildest imagination as you revisit this boulder, letting happen whatever feels like it needs to happen. Let any emotions well up and flow over and out of you. Tell your anxiety that at the time of this memory, it was all alone, but now it has you, its biggest resource. Let it know that you're here with it and it won't ever have to be alone again. Breathe.

Spend as much time here as necessary. Do not rush this process. Anxiety might have a lot to show you, and it may need a lot from you now. Stay with this exercise until you feel some relief and closure. If it becomes too overwhelming, simply honor that and back out for now.

Then, when you're ready, ask your anxiety if it would like to be able to leave this memory in the past. If it says no, see what needs further addressing. Ask what else it needs to show you now. If it says yes, imagine doing anything more that feels necessary while in this memory.

Now imagine bringing anxiety out of this memory and into the present with you, where this danger no longer exists. Where does anxiety want to go? Perhaps it wants to go with you to a comforting place. You may return to your safe meeting place or somewhere different. Check in with your anxiety and see how it is feeling. Tell it that it won't ever have to go back there again.

Check in with the other parts of yourself, see if any of them were able to witness what just occurred, and survey their thoughts and feelings. Thank your anxiety for leading you back to this boulder, and thank your higher self and/or external resource for showing up and providing for your younger self what it has always needed. Rest now.

Now take out your journal and reflect on the following questions.

1.   What was that experience like for you?

2.   What did anxiety need to show you? What did it need from you now that it never got then?

3. Were you able to give anxiety what it needed? If so, how?

4. Was there any part of this exercise that felt inaccessible or blocked? If so, what is your sense of that?

5. What is important to you to remember from this exercise?

When It Doesn't Go as Planned

Don't be discouraged if you didn't get the results you were hoping for from this exercise. Sometimes it can take a few days for this new information and experience to fully integrate and for you to start to feel better. Many clients, immediately after completing this phase of the work, say they feel generally lighter and sometimes a little confused or disoriented. Then when I see them a week later, it is not uncommon for them to experience greater clarity and for this memory to feel much less distressing. It can take some time for your brain to integrate new information and connect old memories to adaptive memory networks.

Other times, there can be factors that get in the way of successful untethering. The first factor is when the memory you are revisiting becomes too overwhelming. This can cause you to exit your window of tolerance and enter hyperarousal (emotional flooding; fight or flight) or hypoarousal (emotional shutdown; freeze). When you exit your optimal healing zone and enter hyper- or hypoarousal, you are no longer reprocessing past trauma but are instead reliving it. This signals to your body that danger is imminent, causing your body to enter survival mode and elicit the fight, flight, or freeze response. When you are in survival mode, you cannot do this work safely or effectively.

If you think you exited your window of tolerance while working through this exercise, it is an indication that you need increased safety before proceeding. The exercises in chapter 2 will help activate your parasympathetic nervous system and bring you back to a more regulated, restful state. Remember that your window of tolerance can look different from day to day. If you are hungry, angry, lonely, or tired, or if you have more stressors than usual in your life, you may experience greater emotional vulnerability. This can reduce your capacity to revisit past trauma memories safely. It is important that you get the timing right. It may be that on one day this exercise is way too overwhelming, but the next day, after a full night's sleep, the work feels totally accessible. Listen to your body and make sure it's a good time to do this work.

If you have ensured that you are well rested and well fed and have your stressors relatively well managed but you are still finding this work to be too overwhelming, you can try a couple of strategies, called *emotional distancing* techniques. These are useful for keeping your nervous system more regulated, enabling you to do this work. These skills are designed to create some distance between you and the emotions associated with past traumatic events so that you can approach them safely. I briefly mentioned these emotional distancing techniques in the previous exercises; now let's delve into the details.

The first technique is to imagine some kind of barrier between you and the trauma memory. In the preceding exercise, I gave the example of imagining a brick wall between you and the memory, with you bearing witness to the memory through a hole in the wall the size of one brick. Many people report that imagining a barrier like this can help the memory feel more accessible, while remaining safe enough that the brain does not trigger a survival response. As you reexperience the memory with your highest self and/or external resource, it may become increasingly safe to imagine more bricks coming out of the wall. Perhaps eventually the wall will disintegrate completely, giving you full access to the memory. Other possible barriers between you and the memory can be a glass wall or a wall with a window in it for you to see through, or a canyon or a body of water.

Another emotional distancing technique is to imagine displaying the memory on a small TV or smartphone screen. Then you can watch the memory happen on the screen rather than experiencing it yourself through all your senses. The key here is that you have the power to change the channel or turn off the phone anytime the memory becomes too activating. You can imagine watching the trauma memory on the screen, while your higher self or external resource is with your younger self in the memory. Then, when it feels safe enough, you might imagine actually entering the memory yourself.

The final emotional distancing technique involves imagining the memory in black and white or otherwise muted in some way. Sometimes the colors of the experience can make it feel too vivid and can be overwhelming to your senses. Imagining the experience in black and white can tone down the associated emotions. A client I worked with reported that imagining the memory in black and white helped her remember that the memory is in the past, keeping her oriented to the present.

Another factor that can get in the way of successful untethering can arise when you have another part of you that is in a protective role and doesn't want you to access this memory. Rather than the memory feeling too vivid, this intervening part usually causes the memory to feel blocked. When this happens, it is important to turn your attention to the part of you that feels threatened by approaching this work and trying to gather more information about it. This would ideally happen in the meeting place prior to revisiting the memory. You might ask yourself *Are there any parts inside me that feel resistant to approaching this boulder?* If there is a part of you that screams *Yes!*, you will need to spend some time with that part and make sure you have its permission before proceeding. Otherwise, you can expect that it will do its best to keep you from accessing it. While this might be frustrating, it's important to remember that these parts of you are doing their very best to keep you safe. They just don't understand that revisiting a memory is actually not dangerous, just as a small child might not understand that their caregiver's leaving the room for a few minutes is not dangerous. Spending some time with this part and getting to understand its fears and what it needs from you in order to proceed safely will save you time (and emotional labor) down the line.

Perhaps this part would agree to proceed on the basis that you use one of the emotional distancing techniques just described. While doing this work, watch for some indicators that you may have a part like this: feeling sleepy, zoned out, or generally detached or disconnected from the process, or feeling panic or the need to run away.

If you are feeling like this exercise was helpful but the memory doesn't quite feel fully resolved, you may need to revisit the exercise and do something different. Peter Levine developed a therapeutic modality for releasing trauma responses that he named Somatic Experiencing, in which he posits that trauma gets stored in our bodies due to thwarted survival energy that is locked up in the body and needs to be released (Levine, 2020). Levine studied the stress response in the nervous systems of animals, who are under constant threat but do not develop PTSD. He came to understand that after animals enter the "freeze" survival response, if they survive the threat, they tremble and shake to discharge the energy that prepared them to fight or flee. He theorizes that in humans, when that energy is not released, it stays stored in the body, causing us to think we are still under threat. Somatic Experiencing is a comprehensive therapeutic modality that is performed by a trained professional; however, the concepts may resonate with you and provide some insight into what can be done to facilitate the releasing of trauma memories that feel stuck.

Many times when a client is revisiting trauma memories, they will get cues from their body about movements or actions they need to take, even if they can't logically understand why. In my own personal experience with releasing a trauma memory in therapy, I told my therapist I felt compelled to enter the fetal position. I have to admit, it was sort of awkward to say that and even more so to get into that position on the floor of his office. However, I had a sense that my body needed to get into that position to complete the movement it had needed to do at the time of the memory but didn't because it froze instead. Once I allowed myself to get into that position, the reprocessing happened.

Similarly, I once had a client who, while engaging in this work, felt the strong urge to scream at her mother. I could almost feel the pent-up energy in her body and could see that she needed to complete this movement. She too wanted to scream, but her adult self was holding back because she did not want to disturb the sessions in adjacent therapy offices. Because I could see this was an important part of this work for her, we went outside, and I invited her to scream there. I screamed with her. She did it several times, and I could see the emotional energy being released from her body each time.

As you approach this work, you too may feel compelled to complete the movement somehow. Maybe you feel like you physically want to shake it off; perhaps you need to scream, or cradle yourself, or punch a pillow. Other practices that can be useful for releasing energy stored in the body include exercise or movement, massage, reiki, and yoga. It's important to listen to your body and trust that it knows what it needs to do, and then create a space where it is free to discharge this energy in whatever way feels best. Our bodies are powerful and hold important information about our emotions and what is required to heal. Often our "doing" minds take over and neglect what our bodies are asking of us, simply because what they are asking doesn't make logical sense. As you navigate this work, I invite you to continually push your logical mind to the side and tap into the inner wisdom of your body's felt sense. It has the answers you seek.

Remember, this work is messy. You are probably feeling a mixture of emotions at this point—maybe lighter in some ways, perhaps more confused or perplexed, maybe relieved, maybe angry. One emotion that is very common to experience in this stage of healing is grief. Even if the processing you've done feels productive and helpful, the relief can be accompanied by grief about how the trauma has impacted you up to this point. I recall that at this stage in my own process, I had to grieve over how harsh I was to myself for years while sitting in professional meetings.

Grief about what anxiety has taken from you is necessary and adaptive, and it deserves to be acknowledged, just as any other emotion does. See if you can make space for whatever emotions you are feeling right now. If it feels helpful, take out your journal and try free-writing all of the thoughts and emotions you are experiencing; this can help you gain some clarity.

The work you have done thus far deserves to be celebrated. Diving into past experiences takes tremendous effort and courage, and it may seem easier to just keep on avoiding your anxiety. You have chosen the harder but necessary path, and that is something to be proud of.

Spend as much time as you need to on the untethering work in this chapter. Depending on your history of trauma, you may feel ready to move on from untethering now, or you may need to go through the steps outlined in this chapter with several more trauma memories. Feel free to take breaks! You are not a constant self-improvement project, and you deserve time and space for rest and leisure in addition to the healing work you are doing. If you need to take a break from revisiting past trauma before returning to another boulder, that is perfectly okay. It may be that the work you have done thus far has gifted you a new lens through which to see the world, and you might want to give yourself a few days or weeks to adjust to it before you move on to another memory.

When you're ready, take a look back at your trauma timeline and rerate the distress level associated with each memory. From that vantage point you can decide which memory, if any, to tackle next. Repeat the steps in this chapter until you feel little to no distress associated with each memory on your timeline. In general, if a past trauma memory causes a distress level of no more than 1 or 2, it may be okay to move on from it. Some memories will always hold some level of distress, because the fact that they happened is inherently sad or upsetting. They don't have to reach a distress level of 0 to be fully processed.

Once you feel satisfied with the distress level associated with the memories on your trauma timeline, it is time to start the future-oriented work. The following chapter will help you develop a working relationship with your anxiety moving forward so you can continue to reap the benefits of the processing work you have done thus far, and your anxiety will remain well managed enough to allow you the space and freedom to live your life to the fullest.

a working relationship with your anxiety

It is likely that revisiting past little t traumas brought up some big emotions for you. In fact, you may have experienced emotions that have been trapped inside for years. Perhaps your emotions felt rather straightforward, or maybe they were surprising, confusing, or conflicting. The path to healing from past trauma is not always predictable or linear, and neither are the emotions experienced along the way. Whether you tapped into deep sadness, fiery rage or fear, you can trust that the emotions you experienced were necessary. Though these painful emotions may not feel like progress in your healing, rest assured they come naturally with the work of learning and growing.

What Does Healing Actually Look Like?

After working through the exercises in chapter 6, your relationship to your trauma memories should have shifted in some way. Doing this work does not mean that you should forget the trauma or the way it impacted you, nor does it mean that you should feel grateful that it happened or experience any other pleasant emotions when you think about it. You may always wish it hadn't happened, and that is okay. It is more realistic that the outcome of healing from a trauma memory means it becomes less vivid and distressing. You may start to think about it in a new way.

It may become something that happened to you rather than something that defines you. You will realize that you are bigger than that past incident or situation.

One of my former clients used a tree metaphor to describe what healing felt like to her. She said that when she initially came to therapy, it felt like her life was a tree and her trauma was the main trunk. Every branch of her life was connected to and impacted by her trauma: her social relationships, work, and family. (Note that this was a big T trauma rather than a little t, and likely would have been beyond the scope of self-help work.) At the end of therapy she said her trauma became a smaller branch at the top of the tree. While it still had its place in her memory, it became an isolated experience that no longer touched every part of her life. She was now the trunk, and the branches were her experiences. Although this was a big T trauma, you should experience a similar shift in that your little t trauma no longer impacts you the way it did before.

Once there is a shift in the way you relate to your trauma, there is a good chance that the way you experience emotions will shift too. When a trauma memory integrates, it becomes stored in its correct time and place: the past. This means that your anxiety will stop responding to this traumatic memory as if it presents current danger. It will be able to assess current threats more accurately.

For example, let's say you revisited a past memory of being left out of a social group. Before this memory was resolved, you may have experienced anxiety when an ambiguous social situation triggered this past experience—say, not yet receiving an invitation to a friend's upcoming event. Once you have revisited and healed the wound of being left out when you were younger, you probably won't experience the same degree of anxiety when you are waiting to receive an invitation. You might have more adaptive thoughts, like *There is still a lot of time before the event. I may still receive an invitation.* Or *If I'm not invited, it won't be the end of the world. I don't really like gatherings anyway.*

Healing from past little t trauma memories does not mean you will experience a complete eradication of anxiety. To be human is to experience a wide range of emotions, anxiety included. It is inevitable and necessary. But once anxiety is no longer stuck in trauma time, it becomes useful. It will remind you of what is important to you and will prompt you to act in a way that is in line with your values. It will also alert you to danger that actually does exist, which, again, is an important survival mechanism.

You don't want anxiety to go away completely. To determine whether your anxiety warrants your attention and intervention, you can ask yourself the simple question *Does my anxiety fit the facts of the situation I am in?* For example, if you are anxious about whether you will get fired from your job after sleeping through a scheduled shift, that anxiety fits the facts, because your job is important to you and you need to pay your bills. You can problem solve it by reaching out to your boss, apologizing, and reiterating the job's importance to you. If you are anxious because your partner said he would be home in thirty minutes, but two hours have gone by without his arriving home, the anxiety fits the facts of the situation and would prompt you to make calls to make sure he is okay. Experiencing anxiety usually feels very uncomfortable, but that does not mean it is wrong and should be eliminated from your life.

This chapter will help you build a working relationship with your anxiety so that you can reap its benefits moving forward. Through this relationship, you will experience anxiety as no longer something to be feared or extinguished. While it may always be an uncomfortable experience, anxiety will become a key messenger in your life—a helpful signal that you learn to respect, honor, and trust.

Step One: Establishing a Communication Plan

The first step in building a working relationship with your anxiety is to establish a communication plan for future interactions with it. Having great communication with your anxiety is as important as having great communication with any other person in your life. It will help you avoid feeling like your anxiety is in control of your life and will help anxiety know that you care about it and realize the importance of what it has to say. When anxiety can trust that you will hear and understand it, and you can trust that anxiety will loosen its grip so that you can enjoy your life, living with anxiety becomes not so bad after all.

The nice thing about anxiety is that it usually follows predictable steps when it is trying to communicate with you. It's common for anxiety to come on gradually, as if it is trying to subtly nudge you to see something. Because it is not always logical, you may not automatically be able to put the pieces together and understand what it is trying to say. This is something that you will learn to do with practice.

Regardless of how quickly it escalates, anxiety always begins with a nudge. You might be objecting: *No way! What about panic attacks? They spring on me full-blown!* It can definitely feel this way. However, when I work with my clients to break down what led up to their panic attack, there is some subtle evidence that anxiety was building over a short time before the explosion happened. For example, a client I worked with recently told me that she drove to a birthday party to pick up her son. While waiting in the car for him to come outside, she started to feel panic coming on. She originally reported that it came out of nowhere; there were no apparent triggers. Because this anxiety did not fit the facts, we decided to do a little more digging. After examining the panic attack further, she said that she and her husband had gotten into an argument a few hours before, and the encounter was still weighing on her. Immediately following the argument, she had started having doubts about whether she was a good spouse and whether her marriage would last. She began to wonder if she wasn't a burden to everyone in her life. At this point, her anxiety sent the nudge—it pointed her to the threat of losing everyone she cared for. As would be the case for most of us, she didn't have awareness of what was happening in the moment, so she ignored her anxiety's nudges and later got into the car to start driving (another situation that caused her anxiety). As she continued to push her anxiety away, it became louder and louder until it evolved into panic.

Your anxiety probably manifests in your body in similar ways each time. Maybe it feels like butterflies in your stomach, a weight on your chest, a lump in your throat, a shaky voice, or jitters throughout your entire body. These body sensations may be the first sign that your anxiety is trying to communicate with you. No matter when, where, or how your anxiety manifests, having an intimate understanding of it will make you more responsive to it and ultimately contribute to a proactive, effective working relationship.

When you don't acknowledge or understand your anxiety's nudges, it will usually keep trying to get your attention. If you either fail to recognize or actively ignore these attempts, it will almost always just keep getting louder until you have to acknowledge it. At that point, it can feel like you have lost control and anxiety has taken over the driver's seat of your life. In some instances it may feel like anxiety goes from 0 to 100 within minutes. Other times it will become louder over a period of months or even years.

The goal in communicating effectively with anxiety is to be tuned in to it enough that you can acknowledge its subtle nudges. If you can make anxiety feel seen when it is small, it has no reason to make itself bigger to get your attention.

There may be periods in your life in which anxiety is relatively quiet and in the background. When this happens, you can trust that its needs are generally being met, and you may not need to be having ongoing, intentional conversations with it. Even if your anxiety is well managed, it helps to stay tuned in to it by having a good understanding of when, where, and how it typically shows up. When you do, you can almost predict the onset of anxiety and proactively intervene when it is in its early, more manageable stages.

For example, let's say you RSVP'd yes to a bridal shower scheduled in a couple of weeks. You know that your anxiety tends to show up in social situations in which you are required to mingle. You are pretty confident that you won't know many people at the shower and you will feel pressure to engage in small talk with strangers for some period of time. Your relationship with the bride is important to you, so you want to do your best to contribute to her having a good time.

The night before the event, your anxiety sets in. It is uncomfortable, so to drown it out, you feel the urge to have a few glasses of wine and binge a show on Netflix. As the night progresses, so does your anxiety, and you start having thoughts like *Tomorrow is going to be awful* and *I could just say that something has come up and I have to cancel.* These are examples of early nudges from anxiety that you should notice and tend to.

When you notice a nudge from anxiety, you have two choices: (1) Continue your efforts to extinguish your anxiety by numbing and avoiding and hope that works, or (2) acknowledge that your anxiety wants your attention and the only way to get it to chill is to spend some time with it. In the bridal shower example, your friendship with the bride is important to you, and you'd like to be there for her and take part with as little anxiety as possible, so the second option is the better choice. It might work like this:

1. You pause your show, put the wine down, and turn your attention inward. You say, *Okay, anxiety, what is it that you want?*

   Your anxiety tells you that it fears you are going to be super awkward and embarrass yourself.

2. You acknowledge that you too would like to avoid embarrassment at the shower. You thank your anxiety for alerting you to this. Now to come up with a plan with your anxiety for decreasing the likelihood that this will happen.

3. The plan: You make sure to take care of your basic needs first. You make a plan to get adequate sleep tonight, be sure to eat a good meal and avoid caffeine the next morning, and take a yoga class before you go to the shower. You then reach out to a mutual friend who confirms that she plans to attend the shower too. You make sure to get there early, sit near your mutual friend, and limit your mimosa intake to a maximum of two. You prepare a few conversation starters to use when the conversation gets awkward or stale, like "Have you seen the venue where Steph is getting married? It's so gorgeous!"

4. You feel good about this plan. Your anxiety breathes a sigh of relief. You feel slight relief from your anxiety.

Managing anxiety effectively requires awareness of when it is likely to show up and a willingness to respond to its nudges. The more information you have about when you can expect your anxiety to show up, the better you can predict and respond to it. When you know that you tend to get anxiety in social situations because you fear embarrassment, you can almost predict that it will show up the night before a social event. Because you have this knowledge, you can catch it early, when it is nudging you, and be proactive about how you're going to address it.

In addition to getting to know when your anxiety shows up, you should also have awareness of where and how it manifests. Maybe you know that you tend to get anxiety when you are in a crowded grocery store or a professional meeting. Perhaps your anxiety starts to nudge you when you go to a specific area of town or when you board an airplane.

Maybe it creeps in when you're at your family's house or at the doctor's office. When you have plans to go to a specific location where your anxiety is known to rise, you can check in with it beforehand and come up with a game plan together for navigating being in this place together.

REFLECTION: Getting to Know Your Anxiety— A Journal Exercise

Spend some time reflecting in your journal on the when, where, and hows of your anxiety. Get to know your anxiety's nudges versus its more urgent ways of communicating.

1. When is your anxiety most likely to show up? What is it trying to protect you from in these situations?

2. Where is your anxiety most likely to show up (meetings, airplanes, doctors' offices, and so on)? Do you know why this is? In other words, are these places connected to past little t traumas?

3. How does your anxiety usually manifest in your body? Do you typically become aware of body sensations first, or do these come later once your anxiety has progressed?

4. What are the first signs of a nudge from anxiety? What happens if you ignore these nudges?

5. What can you do when you experience the first signs of anxiety?

Step Two: Understanding Anxiety's Needs

The second step in building a healthy working relationship with your anxiety is to get clear on what your anxiety needs from you and to share with anxiety what you need from it. Just like in any relationship, this one is more likely to be successful if both partners have clear expectations of what they need in the relationship and have communicated those needs directly. Your relationship with anxiety is no different. It will take introspection, communication, and perhaps some negotiation to keep both parties happy and the relationship functioning well.

In chapter 5 you explored what anxiety needs from you while approaching past stuck memories. Now you are asked to gather more information about what your anxiety needs from you moving forward. Assume that experiencing anxiety in the future in inevitable. There will be future situations and places you encounter that will trigger your anxiety to alert you to something. It is likely that your anxiety will need you to be open to its concerns and to trust that what it has to say is important. It could be that your anxiety needs you to do your best to avoid situations or people who seem to pose a real threat to your well-being.

As in previous exercises, it is best to go inside and listen for information and answers from your anxiety rather than trying to figure out the answers with your logical mind. Approach the following exercise with a curious, open mind. (You can also find an audio version of this exercise to download in the online free tools at http://www.newharbinger.com /48756.)

EXERCISE: What Does Anxiety Need from You?

Find a place in your home or office that is free of distractions. In a comfortable seated position, close your eyes and turn your attention inward. Spend a few moments noticing, with an open mind, what is going on inside. Pay attention to your breath.

Now connect with the part of you that experiences anxiety. This part of you may show up right away, or perhaps it feels more distant and hard to reach. Don't try to force or make anything happen; just continue breathing with a curious, open perspective.

Once you are able to connect to the anxious part of you, find a place where you and your anxiety can have a conversation. Let it know that you're here to get to know what it needs from you from this point onward. Tell it that it is your goal to develop the best working relationship possible. If it feels right, share with it that you know it has an important role in keeping you safe, and you want to nourish your relationship with it as best as you can. Share with it what you've gathered about when, where, and how it shows up. Tell it that you're working hard to understand it.

Next, ask your anxiety if it wants to share any information with you about what it needs from you. Get quiet. Listen. It may give you an answer right away, or it may take more time to get this feedback. If you need clarity, ask your anxiety to tell you more. Tell it you would like as clear of information as possible, with all the detail it is willing to share.

Notice how you feel in response to what your anxiety has to say. Let go of any judgments or strong emotional reactions. Just observe. Listen. Now is not the time for arguing or negotiation; that can come later. Right now you are just gathering information. If necessary, take notes, as it's important to remember what your anxiety is telling you it needs moving forward.

Once you have a clear understanding of what it is saying, ask if there is anything else it needs. Let it continue to show you what it wants, while you remain curious and open. Once there is nothing more it needs to say, thank it for showing up today, and let it know you will take all that it has told you into consideration.

With this experience fresh in your mind, take out your journal and answer the following reflection questions.

1. How accessible was your anxiety today? How difficult or easy was it to communicate with it?

2. What did your anxiety communicate with you about what it needs from you?

3. What are your reactions to what your anxiety had to say? Do you notice any feelings of resistance or pushback coming up for you?

4. Are there any asks from your anxiety that you think you'll need to negotiate, or do they all seem fair and agreeable?

It could be that your anxiety made fairly simple requests, like *Listen to me* or *Don't push me away*. Or it could be that your anxiety had an overwhelming request that you're not sure if you can agree to, like *End that troubled relationship*. Ultimately, you are the one in control of your life. While it will benefit you to work with your anxiety on its requests, remember that anxiety often does not have all of the information that you do. It may take some time to process anxiety's requests and get clear on what you're willing to agree to versus what you aren't.

It is possible that you will need to negotiate some of anxiety's requests. For example, if anxiety made a request like *Don't go to any more social gatherings* and this is a request you are unwilling to fulfill, you will want to politely let your anxiety know that you hear its request and aren't able or willing to do this. However, you can do your best to come up with a plan with your anxiety to help it feel as safe and soothed as possible when these situations arise.

You may go inside and tell your anxiety something like, *I hear that you want me to stop going to social gatherings altogether. I know that these are uncomfortable and feel dangerous to you; however, they aren't actually dangerous, and there are times when attending a gathering is really important. When this happens, I will make sure to check in with you beforehand and come up with a game plan for making this as tolerable as possible for both of us.* Just like in any relationship, expression of needs from either party may require negotiation and meeting in the middle.

Step Three: Communicating Your Needs

Now that you have taken the time to hear what your anxiety needs from you, it is your turn to share with your anxiety what you need from it. Keep in mind that complete eradication of anxiety is not possible. Therefore, it is not in either of your best interests to ask it to go away completely. Think about what needs to happen so that you can experience anxiety while still living a values-driven life. Perhaps you need it to be willing to comply when you ask it to ease up somewhat on the feelings it triggers in you. Maybe you would like it to give you more clear nudges when it is trying to get your attention, as opposed to subtle ones that are followed by coming on suddenly and hard. You might want it to let you take the reins when navigating your intimate relationship so that anxiety does not sabotage it.

Spend some time reflecting on how you can cohabitate with anxiety effectively. If you imagine yourself a year from now living a life consistent with your values, with anxiety fairly well managed, what does that look like for you? How is that scenario different from the way you experience anxiety now?

Answer the following reflection questions in your journal.

- What do you need from anxiety as you navigate life moving forward?

- How you do envision living a fulfilled, meaningful life while still having some anxiety?

Once you have an idea of what you need from anxiety, you will need to communicate your needs with it. It is not enough to just think about what you need; for this to stick, you need to tell your anxiety and get its acknowledgment and feedback. In the following exercise, share with anxiety what you need from it. (You can also find an audio version of this exercise to download in the online free tools at http://www.newhar binger.com/48756.)

EXERCISE: Share Your Needs with Anxiety

Find a place in your home or office that is free of distractions. In a comfort-able seated position or reclining, close your eyes and turn your attention inward. Without judgment, start by noticing what is going on inside. Pay attention to your breath.

Now see if you can connect with the part of you that experiences anxiety. This part of you may show up right away, or perhaps it feels more distant and hard to reach. Don't try to force or make anything happen; just continue breathing with a curious, open perspective.

Once you are able to connect to the anxious part of you, invite your anxiety to a meeting place where you can have a conversation. Let it know that you appreciated it sharing its needs with you, and now you are going to do the same. Tell it that your goal is to establish great communication with it. When you have its attention, gently let anxiety know what you need from it. Ask it to just listen for now until you are finished. If any negotiation is necessary, that can happen later. Try to communicate with your anxiety in a compassionate, warm voice. Be specific and clear.

When you are finished communicating what you need from your anxiety, let it know that you are open to feedback. Ask it directly if it is willing to agree to your requests. Notice the energy in the room between you and your anxiety. Is it open and safe? If not, what needs to happen to make it more so? Take breathers as necessary. Take turns respectfully sharing your thoughts until it feels like you have come to an agreement. This may take more than one conversation.

With the experience fresh in your mind, reflect in your journal on the following questions :

1. What requests did you make to your anxiety?

2. What was your anxiety's response? Did it agree to your requests?

3. Are there any needs that will require future discussion or negotiation?

4. Are there any additional needs you want to communicate to anxiety but haven't yet?

Step Four: Negotiation

Just as in any relationship, good communication with your anxiety requires an ongoing effort from both parties. It is not typical that you can have one conversation in which you assert a need of yours and it is then met perfectly forever after. Even if you clearly communicated your needs and the other party acknowledged and agreed to them, it is likely you'll need to revisit the conversation at some point in the future. Additionally, it may take multiple conversations until you feel like your need was truly acknowledged and agreed to.

For example, if you asked your anxiety to loosen its grip in your relationship, it could be that your anxiety was skeptical, as it fears what might happen if you let your guard down. Negotiating this could require lots of dialogue over the course of several conversations. Remember that anxiety has been reinforced over and over again through time and will need some practice to loosen its grip. Perhaps you have gone inside and told anxiety that you would like it to stop sabotaging relationships at the first sight of conflict. Maybe you helped it understand that conflict in relationships can actually mean your (human) partner wants to preserve the relationship, not abandon you. In your initial conversation, anxiety seems to grasp this concept and agrees to ease up the next time you disagree with your partner. A few months go by, and things are great, and then out of nowhere your partner sends you a text saying that something has been bothering him and he'd like to talk to you about it later. Your anxiety spikes. It continues to escalate throughout the day, despite your conversation with it months ago. When this happens, you will need to have another conversation with it.

If you sense that your need(s) requires some negotiation with your anxiety, consider the following questions to ask anxiety to propel the discussion forward:

- What do you need in order to trust that it is safe for you to ease up?

- What can I do to help you not have to work so hard?

- If you agree to ease up, what signal will you give to me if you need to get my attention?

- How can I help you trust that I hear your concerns and will take them seriously?

- Are you willing to do an experiment in which you ease up for a short period of time and see how I do?

After you and your anxiety come to an agreement on how to move forward together, you will want to have follow-up conversations in which you may renegotiate your needs. For example, let's say you ask your anxiety to ease up in your relationship so that you don't inadvertently sabotage it. Anxiety agrees, and it begins to trust that you can navigate relationships without its constant input. Then your partner unexpectedly breaks up with you. It is possible that your anxiety will want to swoop in and take back control, believing that you were hurt solely because it had become less vigilant. Your anxiety does not have all of the information that you have, and it may become more rigid in its perspective on what it needs from you in relationships and vice versa. If this happens, you'll need to renegotiate.

In this example, you would want to go inside and allow anxiety to share its thoughts and feelings about what happened. Then you would share yours. You might help anxiety understand that despite the relationship's ending, it was one of the most fulfilling ones you've had because you were willing to be vulnerable. You might think of all of the growth you had in this relationship, and how it will make you better equipped for the next relationship. You might ask your anxiety to continue trusting you, despite the relationship's ending. You might help it understand that the end of a relationship isn't actually always the worst thing. You also might help it to see that the ending of the relationship wouldn't necessarily be less painful if you had been hypervigilant throughout its duration.

Revisiting Trauma

There may be times when it feels like you get stuck when trying to come to an agreement with your anxiety. This may be one indicator that there is a past little t trauma that must be addressed before any future working relationship can be established. If, for example, your anxiety will not budge in your request that it ease up in your relationship, it could be an indicator that a little t trauma in your past remains as a boulder to which you are tethered, keeping you stuck. In that case, you may need to revisit chapters 5 and 6 to help you become unstuck from that event and then revisit your communication plan with anxiety from here on out.

It could also be that you need to revisit a past memory that you had already addressed and thought was processed. This does not mean that your initial work was ineffective or that you have lost any progress. It simply means that you need to revisit a topic with your anxiety, much as you might revisit the same conversation with your intimate partner despite thinking it had previously been resolved. This work is not linear; indeed, it can feel like two steps forward, one step back. (This is normal—and we'll explore this truth further in the next chapter.) You will know you need to revisit a past memory when it feels like your anxiety is stuck in trauma time, does not fit the facts of the current situation, and/or is showing up frequently and not responding well to logic and reasoning.

You may be thinking, *This sounds like a lot of work!*—and if you are, you are correct. But it is also a lot of work to live with anxiety in the driver's seat of your life. All healthy relationships take effort, and if you want a healthy relationship with your anxiety, the effort required is no different. You likely have certain people in your life whom you value enough that you are willing to put in the work to keep the relationship healthy and functioning well. My hope is that you see the value in putting in the work to keep your relationship with your anxiety healthy and well-balanced. After all, your relationship with anxiety may be the one relationship in your life that has the power to influence all the others.

In the next chapter, we'll delve into how to manage future anxiety setbacks (which are inevitable) without becoming discouraged; we'll also consider how to deal with anxiety about not having anxiety. We'll explore the job that you'd like anxiety to do now that it will no longer be alerting you to danger that doesn't actually exist. Now that you will be less consumed by anxiety, what do you actually want to do with your time? What kind of person do you want to be? To start discovering these possibilities, together we'll explore your values.

beyond the boulders

At this point, you have been offered a new way to think about anxiety, opportunities to repair your relationship with anxiety, avenues for uncovering and processing the root of your anxiety, and strategies for building a working relationship with your anxiety for the future. While it was necessary to present these steps in a linear, orderly way for the flow of this book, healing from anxiety is not typically linear, and it is never one-and-done.

When you sprain your ankle, you are almost guaranteed complete healing in a few weeks if you follow the instructions of your doctor. Once your ankle has healed, you will be able to put the injury behind you and will not need to continue to tend to it. Anxiety does not work this way, because it is not an injury; it does not need to be fixed or remedied. It is an adaptive emotion that, when working correctly, helps you avoid danger and live meaningfully. You'll need to continue understanding and collaborating with your anxiety if it is to continue helping you live a fulfilled life consistent with your values.

Anxiety Relapses

I hope that by this point in the work you are feeling like you have made some progress in understanding and working with your anxiety. Perhaps your anxiety has become more distant, like a quiet observer rather than a force to be reckoned with. With the work you have been doing, it may even seem as if anxiety has completely gone away for now, and you feel more clear headed and calm. Regardless of the progress you have made thus far, it is highly likely that you will experience times in the future in which anxiety still gets the best of you.

For example, you might have done some good work on social anxiety and experienced improvement in your ability to engage in groups with more spontaneity and ease. You may feel like social anxiety is a thing of the past. Then all of a sudden one day you are getting ready to go to a small gathering at a friend's house and you experience a panic attack, seemingly out of nowhere. If you've felt like you were past this by now, this can be highly discouraging. The thought that you have regressed and lost your progress can be seriously depressing.

When this happens, it is useful to pay attention to primary versus secondary emotions. Primary emotions are emotions that come first. Secondary emotions are emotions that we have *about* primary emotions. Secondary emotions tend to complicate things and prolong our pain. For example, if you have a panic attack before a gathering at a friend's house, fear may be the primary emotion. It sets in, peaks, and then is over, usually within a few minutes. Following the wave of fear and panic, you experience frustration because you start thinking that maybe you didn't make the progress you thought you had made. You might also be discouraged because you think nothing is ever going to work for you and you will have to live with panic attacks forever. Then hopelessness and depression set in, and you cancel your plans to attend the gathering.

In this example, fear was the primary emotion, which then elicited a panic response. It lasted just a few minutes. Then came the secondary emotions about the panic—frustration, discouragement, hopelessness, and depression. In this case the secondary emotions—the emotions about your primary emotion—cause more distress and suffering than the primary emotion you initially experienced.

When you have what feels like an anxiety relapse, acknowledging and releasing your secondary emotions can keep you on the path toward healing. To do this, you might repeat thoughts like *The healing journey is not linear* or *This was a minor setback* or *Two steps forward, one step back* or *This does not erase my progress*. Once you have worked through and released your secondary emotions, you clear up space in your mind to gather more information about what led up to the primary emotion. Then you can go inside, initiate a conversation with your anxiety, and explore the factors that contributed to its sounding the alarm. Gaining this new information and insight becomes the next step forward on your healing journey.

Once you understand the probability that you will succumb to anxiety at some point in the future, you'll feel less taken by surprise when it happens, and you'll be better able to keep secondary emotions at bay. Anxiety relapses can happen for a multitude of reasons that have nothing to do with the progress you have already made. An unexpected big wave of anxiety is usually the result of an accumulation of lots of smaller factors. When you get curious and explore what led up to the anxiety relapse, you may find the basis for it: perhaps you are running on very little sleep, or dealing with the stress of a new job or a move, or taking a new medication that is affecting your brain chemistry. Or perhaps a new little t trauma has been activated.

When you have an anxiety relapse, it can be useful to journal about the thoughts, feelings, and body sensations you had leading up to the anxiety spike, during the spike, and afterward. When you start to examine the internal and external factors present before the spike, you will get good information about what contributed to your anxiety. Take the example of my client who had a panic attack while in the parking lot. When she first described the event to me, she said she panicked "out of nowhere." After exploring it further, we identified several potential triggers: a fight with her husband, having not eaten lunch that day, and a recent change to her medications. Once she had this context, she was able to adopt some self-compassion and see that her anxiety had not come out of nowhere after all.

Regardless of what led up to the setback, it's important to do the reflecting work early so that you can get back on track quickly. Don't allow an anxiety setback to convince you that this work is futile and you should give up now. Take the time you need to process what happened, let your secondary emotions subside, and get curious and open about what your anxiety needs to share with you. Then take this information and get back out there in the world. Go to the next gathering.

Anxiety About Not Having Anxiety

In addition to anxiety spikes or setbacks, you may have times when your anxiety feels very well managed. You could even experience times when it feels nonexistent. When this happens, I imagine your primary emotion is relief or contentment. After all, you have invested a lot of time and energy into making it this far. But then, if you are like many people prone to anxiety, something curious may happen: you may start to experience being *anxious about not being anxious*. You feel like you must not get too comfortable, because something terrible could be around the corner. You are concerned about being caught off guard, and you don't yet trust that things could just be okay. Feeling calm feels good, but ominous—it's like you're waiting for the other shoe to drop.

This is an indicator that your anxiety is trying to alert you to the danger associated with thinking things are okay or feeling calm. While this might make your head spin, because it feels so ridiculous, it actually is no different from any other function of anxiety. It could be that there is a little t trauma associated with being caught off guard that needs to be addressed. Was there an earlier time when you felt calm and then something bad happened? Was there a time when you thought things were okay and then you were blindsided? Where, when, and how did you learn that feeling calm is not safe? You may find it helpful to go back there and work through it, as you already did with other little t traumas.

The other possibility when experiencing anxiety about not having anxiety is that your anxiety is not used to being idle, and it isn't sure what else to do. In other words, your anxiety needs another job to occupy it. All parts of ourselves have an important job description; they have gotten quite good at their jobs and probably take pride in them. Doing this work creates changes to anxiety's job description. You are essentially removing items from its job description when you show it that it doesn't need to alert you to looming events like social gatherings and public speaking, or concerns like the expected *not* happening; say, when your partner still hasn't texted you back and it's been a good half hour! (Well, a good fifteen minutes.)

Think about how you would feel in the unlikely event that your boss told you they'd eliminated 80 percent of your job description. You might initially feel relieved, thinking *Finally this job will feel manageable!* Then it's likely you'd start to twiddle your thumbs and wonder what you're supposed to do with all that extra time. Over time, you might feel bored and seek out other things to do. This is what your anxiety is experiencing when you cut back its workload. Anxiety is high achieving—it wants a job to do!

It can be useful to explore with your anxiety what it would like to do instead of alert you to danger all of the time. Then you can renegotiate its job description in a way that honors your preference for it to relax on the tasks it used to do, while replacing those things with other tasks that it finds meaningful. The following exercise guides you through this process.

EXERCISE: Exploring Anxiety's New Job

Find a place in your home or office that is free of distractions. In a comfortable seated position or reclining, close your eyes and turn your attention inward. Spend a few moments with openness and curiosity about what is going on inside. Pay attention to your breath.

Now connect with the part of you that experiences anxiety. This part of you may show up right away, or perhaps it feels more distant right now. Don't try to force or make anything happen; just continue breathing with a curious, open perspective.

Once you are able to connect to the anxious part of you, find a place inside where you and your anxiety can have a conversation. Let it know that you're here to get to know what it needs from you now. Tell your anxiety that you can see the effort it is making to ease up some. Ask your anxiety: *Now that you no longer need to work as hard at alerting me to danger, what would you like to do instead?*

Before you start making suggestions, let anxiety tell you what it would like to do. If it is stumped, offer some alternative jobs you can think of. Perhaps it wants to work on some other important task. Maybe it wants to play or create. Maybe it is fine with just resting for now. Come to a mutual agreement. Shake on it if you'd like. Reassure your anxiety that this new role comes with more fulfillment, fun, and payoff for everyone. It is a promotion. Invite anxiety to assume its new role, and agree to check in with it in a week or two to see how it feels about its new job. Reassure your anxiety that you can always make modifications to its job description as needed.

A client I worked with had anxiety about people leaving her. This interfered with her ability to make and maintain healthy friendships, because she worried that people would just leave. She traced this fear back to a big T trauma of her dad leaving her family when she was little. We revisited this memory together, and in the course of therapy, she relieved her four-year-old inner child of the responsibility for her dad's leaving. She exclaimed, "It was not my job to make sure he stayed around."

Once her inner child no longer needed to alert her to threats of abandonment in her current friendships, she wondered what to do instead. Rather than make suggestions to my client or her inner child directly, I invited my client to go inside and ask her inner child what she would like to do. To her surprise, her inner child responded quickly and confidently that she wanted to have fun playing with dolls instead. We agreed on the new job, and since then, her anxiety about being abandoned in friendships has been nearly extinguished.

Waning Motivation for This Work

You may find that your motivation to do this work waxes and wanes over time. This is a natural, expected part of the process of healing. When you get this far in the book and the work, you'll likely still feel at least somewhat motivated to work on your anxiety. But once you finish the book and more and more time passes in which you are not actively engaging in this work, you may find your motivation to stay in touch with your anxiety drops off. You can't be expected to maintain 100-percent motivation for all things self-improvement all of the time. That sounds a lot like missing out on the fun stuff life has to offer.

While declining motivation is to be expected, it is also something to be mindful of, because it can mean you slip back into old habits of trying to work against your anxiety. I hope that the methods you have learned here will give you a new way of looking at your anxiety that you will keep with you forever, so that running away from your anxiety will not be your default response. It's human nature to avoid things that cause us discomfort, so your natural impulse, without a concerted effort to do otherwise, will be to avoid or extinguish anxiety. You'll need some motivation to maintain a working relationship with your anxiety.

A big part of maintaining this motivation is to assess and reassess your values—the things you care about at the most fundamental level. Values are different from goals. Goals are achievements that can be checked off on a to-do list, like graduating from college, getting a job, or saving money for a trip. Values are how you want to live your life and be remembered. You can't ever "achieve" them; they require ongoing effort. Values are a way of being rather than doing.

When helping my clients explore their values, I like to ask these two questions:

- If you were to die tomorrow and the people you love most were gathered at your funeral, reminiscing about the kind of person you were, what would you want them to say about you?

- If you knew you had twenty-four hours left to live, what would you do with that time? Where would you go? With whom would you spend it? What would you say?

When asked about her values, one of my clients recently reported that she wanted to be remembered as helpful and funny. She quickly made the connection that unmanaged anxiety was a hindrance to being both of those things. Her anxiety often caused her to be a recluse—canceling plans with friends and shutting out the world around her. The reflection on her values was an important reminder to her of her *why* for doing this work. It is not to live with less discomfort; rather, it is to live more fully.

Spend some time considering how you might answer these questions, then reflect in your journal.

- How do you want to be remembered when you are no longer here?

- What would you do with just twenty-four hours left to live on this earth?

- What did you learn from your reflections about what you value most?

If you are unsure about your answers, consider the following list of possible values and how those might be reflected in those remembrances of you, and in your wishes for that final day:

Kindness

Generosity

Honesty

Adventure

Fun

Creativity

Service to Others

Humor

Loyalty

Strength

Friendship

Courage

Helpfulness

Spirituality

Compassion

Your values are your why for doing the work you're doing in this book. Once you have identified your most fundamental values, you might start to see how anxiety gets in the way of carrying them out. Untreated anxiety likely pulls you further away from your values. It can convince you that you should avoid taking risks or being spontaneous or adventurous. It can also get in the way of being a reliable friend, a helpful neighbor, or a compassionate partner.

When you participate in life despite your anxiety, you are more easily able to live a life consistent with your values. When you are in tune with your values, you may experience a newfound motivation to do the work to keep your anxiety well managed. Engaging in the inner reflection conversations with your anxiety, as you've been doing here, is not just about having conversations with anxiety. You're not revisiting the origins of your anxiety just to see where it came from. And as you practice the exposures necessary to confront rather than avoid anxiety, you're not just challenging yourself for no good reason. You're working to live a life that is meaningful to you—to act right now in accordance with how you want to be remembered when you are gone. It's the difference between existing and living fully.

One of my former clients had anxiety about leaving the house. Her anxiety started as much more specific, but had progressed and generalized over time. Once she was informed she would have to return to work in person after the COVID-19 pandemic, she knew she needed to seek therapy. Together we created a list of exposures, which included leaving the house to go for a five-minute walk, then driving to her local Target store, followed by driving to a shopping mall in the nearest town over and spending a couple of hours there. Some anxiety setbacks made her question whether the therapeutic work was worth the effort. She felt waning motivation to keep doing the exposure homework I assigned her between sessions.

As a way to tap into more motivation, I asked her how she would like to spend her last twenty-four hours on this earth. I wanted to know what she valued. With tears in her eyes, she told me this beautiful story.

She used to host annual crawfish boils in her neighborhood. She would invite all of her friends and family, and people would even fly in from out of town to attend. People brought their kids from all over; they would come together and play in the neighborhood. There was laughter,

games, and good food. Everyone would stay up late into the night, celebrating nothing but life itself. But because of my client's anxiety, she
hadn't been able to host or attend a crawfish boil in years. People had
been asking her when she would host again. She usually responded by
saying she wasn't sure. She wasn't comfortable telling people that she
didn't know when her anxiety would ease up enough to allow her to.

Hearing this story showed me that she valued family, friendship,
connection, fun, and laughter. Once we uncovered these values, the
homework I assigned her served a completely different purpose. When I
asked her to leave her house to go shopping outside of town despite the
anxiety it would cause, it wasn't for the sake of being able to purchase
goods that weren't available in her town. In fact, that was hardly a moti-
vator. Doing this work, getting anxiety under control, would bring her
closer, step by step, to being able to host another crawfish boil. That
became her why.

Considering your values will help you discover your why for doing
this work. It is usually deeper than wanting to not feel so anxious. You
already know that you can tolerate anxiety. You have been coexisting
with it for some time now. If you just wanted tools for managing anxiety,
you could have stopped reading this book after chapter 2. This work isn't
about wrangling anxiety.

Think about all the reasons that made you buy this book. You are
not doing this work to eradicate symptoms. You are doing it for the doors
that will open in your life when your anxiety loosens its grip. This work
is about being able to say yes to attending social gatherings and having a
blast at them. It is about showing up authentically and unapologetically
in new relationships without hiding parts of yourself. It is about taking
spontaneous trips. It is about dancing the night away. It is about taking
risks and maybe making some bad decisions. It is about courage. It is
about your inner child being proud of the life you are living. It is about
hosting that crawfish boil.

The work it takes to repair your relationship with anxiety is no easy feat. You have made it this far, and you should be proud of the effort you have put in to better yourself and improve your relationships. It is much easier to maintain the status quo than it is to face your anxiety—and the memories that caused and reinforced it over time—head on. It takes serious courage to be willing to walk into your past experiences and poke around at what hurts. Just as your brain and body would not like you to rip off a bandage and start poking at a wound on your arm, it is counter-intuitive to explore the wounds that led to your anxiety in this way. To do so means you are courageous and committed to living a life with purpose and meaning. Regardless of the outcome of this work for you, your effort is something to be celebrated.

If, as you near the end of this book, you have the thought, *Darn it! I've finished the book and I still have anxiety!*—please know that you are not alone. Never in my therapy practice have I had a client come to their last therapy session and say, "That's it! I am healed. I no longer have any anxiety, and I'm ready to end therapy!" More commonly, termination from therapy happens after a series of conversations about what realistic growth looks like, how the person might start to incorporate newfound tools learned in therapy into their day-to-day life as they move forward without therapy, and the option to return to therapy in the future when extra support is needed. The same is true for you with this work. The bad news: You probably won't ever arrive at the destination of Healed—because it doesn't exist. The good news: Nobody arrives there, so you don't have to either. This work is an unfolding journey that can and should be returned to as needed. It is a process rather than a milestone.

Committing to self-improvement is commendable. At the same time, you are not a constant self-improvement project. Perfectionism has no place in this work (or anywhere)—it can only lead to feelings of inad-equacy. To be human is to experience emotions, including the uncom-fortable, messy ones. Even with crippling anxiety, you are worthy of love, acceptance, and belonging.

Perhaps you are experiencing newfound ease, calm, and confidence as a result of doing this work. Perhaps it has also stirred up some conflicting or confusing feelings within you. You might feel like you still have a lot to learn about your anxiety. Regardless of how much progress you feel you have made, or how much more you think you still need to make, remember to have grace with yourself. You can be simultaneously working to better yourself and knowing that you are already enough. You are inherently whole.

I hope that this book has brought you closer to yourself. I hope it has shown you that you are to be trusted. With *you* by your side, you can climb the mountain of life without restriction. You are simultaneously free—and home.

References

Anderson, F., PhD. 2020, April 22. "Treating Complex Trauma with Internal Family Systems." Lecture presented via PESI, Inc. in Phoenix, AZ.

Martin, K. M. 2012. "How to Use Fraser's Dissociative Table Technique to Access and Work with Emotional Parts of the Personality." *Journal of EMDR Practice and Research* 6(4): 179–186. https://connect.springerpub.com/content/sgremdr/6/4/179.

Levine, P. A., PhD. n.d. Somatic Experiencing (SE). Retrieved November 8, 2020, from https://www.somaticexperiencing.com/somatic-experiencing.

Shapiro, F. 1995. *Eye Movement Desensitization and Reprocessing: Basic Principles, Protocols, and Procedures.* New York, NY: Guilford Press.

Shapiro, F. 2001. *Eye Movement Desensitization and Reprocessing: Basic Principles, Protocols, and Procedures.* 2nd ed. New York, NY: Guilford Press.

Shapiro, F. 2012. *Getting Past Your Past: Take Control of Your Life with Self-Help Techniques from EMDR Therapy.* Emmaus, PA: Rodale.

Siegel, D. J. 1999. *The Developing Mind: How Relationships and the Brain Interact to Shape Who We Are.* New York, NY: Guilford Press.

Solomon, R. M., and F. Shapiro. 2008. "EMDR and the Adaptive Information Processing Model: Potential Mechanisms of Change." *Journal of EMDR Practice and Research* 2(4): 315–325.

Stinson, A. n.d. "Adult-Onset Asthma: Causes, Symptoms, Treatments, and Management." *Medical News Today.* https://www.medicalnewstoday.com/articles/325302.

Jaime Castillo, LCSW, is founder of Find Your Shine Therapy, and a licensed clinical social worker specializing in the treatment of trauma and anxiety disorders. She is a certified eye movement desensitization and reprocessing (EMDR) therapist and EMDRIA-approved consultant, and has additional training in internal family systems (IFS) and exposure therapy. She specializes in working with adults experiencing post-traumatic stress disorder (PTSD), obsessive-compulsive disorder (OCD), phobias, and generalized anxiety disorder (GAD). Jaime has been featured for her trauma expertise in *The Arizona Republic*, *The Verge*, and *Phoenix Voyage Magazine* where she was named a Top Inspiring Phoenix Professional. She was a speaker at the 2020 Global Resiliency Summit alongside world-renowned mental health professionals, and appeared as a guest trauma and shame expert on *The Things We Couldn't Say* podcast.

Real change *is* possible

For more than forty-five years, New Harbinger has published proven-effective self-help books and pioneering workbooks to help readers of all ages and backgrounds improve mental health and well-being, and achieve lasting personal growth. In addition, our spirituality books offer profound guidance for deepening awareness and cultivating healing, self-discovery, and fulfillment.

Founded by psychologist Matthew McKay and Patrick Fanning, New Harbinger is proud to be an independent, employee-owned company. Our books reflect our core values of integrity, innovation, commitment, sustainability, compassion, and trust. Written by leaders in the field and recommended by therapists worldwide, New Harbinger books are practical, accessible, and provide real tools for real change.

 **newharbinger**publications

MORE BOOKS from
NEW HARBINGER PUBLICATIONS

THE NEGATIVE THOUGHTS WORKBOOK

CBT Skills to Overcome the Repetitive Worry, Shame, and Rumination That Drive Anxiety and Depression

978-1684035052 / US $21.95

LIVING UNTETHERED

Beyond the Human Predicament

978-1-648480935 / US $18.95

Copublished with **sounds true**

THE MIND-BODY STRESS RESET

Somatic Practices to Reduce Overwhelm and Increase Well-Being

978-1684034277 / US $17.95

ADULT CHILDREN OF EMOTIONALLY IMMATURE PARENTS

How to Heal from Distant, Rejecting, or Self-Involved Parents

978-1626251700 / US $18.95

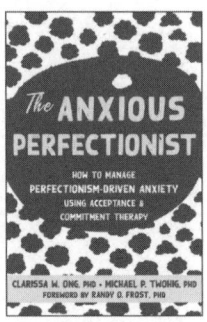

THE ANXIOUS PERFECTIONIST

How to Manage Perfectionism-Driven Anxiety Using Acceptance and Commitment Therapy

978-1684038459 / US $16.95

CRAVINGS AND ADDICTIONS

Free Yourself from the Struggle of Addictive Behavior with Acceptance and Commitment Therapy

978-1684038336 / US $17.95

newharbingerpublications

1-800-748-6273 / newharbinger.com

(VISA, MC, AMEX / prices subject to change without notice)

Follow Us 📷 📘 🐦 📺 📌 in

My Bloody Life

My Bloody Life
The Making of a Latin King

Reymundo Sanchez

CHICAGO
REVIEW
PRESS

Library of Congress Cataloging-in-Publication Data
Sanchez, Reymundo
    My bloody life : the making of a Latin King / Reymundo Sanchez.— 1st ed.
      p. cm.
    ISBN 1-55652-401-3
      1. Sanchez, Remundo 2. Puerto Ricans—Illinois—Chicago—Biography. 3.
    Violence—Illinois—Chicago. 4. Chicago (Ill.)—Social conditions—20th
      century. I. Title.

    F548.9.P85 S26 2000
    977.3'11004687295'0092—dc21
    [B]
                                                                    99-054261

Cover art and design: Frances Jetter
Interior design: Rattray Design

First edition
Published by Chicago Review Press, Incorporated
814 North Franklin Street
Chicago, Illinois 60610
ISBN 978-1-55652-427-1
Printed in the United States of America
26 25 24 23 22

For those who have tragically lost their lives due to
gang violence and for those who continue to live that lifestyle

My Bloody Life is by no means a justification for gang involvement or gang crime. It is not an attempt to glorify any one gang or its members' actions. Nor is it intended in any way as the confession of one person's crimes. *My Bloody Life* is the story of a lifestyle and the destruction it creates.

Oh my friend let me apologize,
For not obstructing your path of wrong,
For not having my eyes open,
While I led you on a crazy route.
For letting you follow my misfortunes,
For sharing with you the drink of the devil,
For inhaling with you the smoke of hell,
For encouraging you to hurt, maim, and kill,
For making you laugh when you should have cried.

Oh my friend, oh how sorry I am,
For not shielding you,
For not being the one,
For letting you be unaware,
For watching you die in my arms.

Oh my friend will you ever forgive me,
for surviving, for living,
For being the one in whose arms you died.

Contents

Preface

ALTHOUGH THIS BOOK is based on the truth, the names of those involved and places where events occurred have been changed. The order of events has also been changed. However, all of these events did take place in the city of Chicago and the names of the gangs are real. I still have relatives who live in these gang-infested neighborhoods, so I've made these changes to protect them.

My real name and age are not important. I've written about every-day occurrences in the neighborhood I grew up in, a place where parents swap tragic tales about what Latino youths do to each other. Anybody who has been in or around a gang can tell a similar story, some even more tragic than mine. I choose to remain just another ex-gang member, one who opened his eyes in time to survive.

The point of this book is not merely to tell stories of gang life but to also provide some explanations for why kids join gangs and to point out that most kids are driven to gangs by adults, not by their peers or the dreaded "white man" who is blamed for every problem. I hope this book can save the life of at least one kid.

This book is also my attempt to make the brothers and sisters in gangs realize that the gang leaders are living the good life at their expense. Unfortunately, the people who need to hear this message the most will probably never read this book.

LATINO GANG MEMBERS kill other Latinos as part of their daily routine, but instead of changing themselves they blame police harassment and discrimination for all their social ills. In the meantime the Latin Kings and other street gangs continue to grow. They victimize Latino families by giving kids a false sense of belonging—something their parents fail to do. Police do nothing to create a feeling of trust within gang-infested communities, and so they remain part of the problem. There are police officers who genuinely care, but they number too few.

The gang problem has become a billion-dollar revolving-door industry for justice systems across the United States. The police, lawmakers, and attorneys profit—no one stands to gain from a decline in gang crime except for those who live where gangs flourish.

People in these communities must wake up before it's too late.

My Bloody Life

1

La Familia

Puerto Rico, 1963. I was born in the back of a 1957 Chevy on the way to the hospital. I may have been born where I was conceived. Considering that my mother went into labor while sitting in the outhouse, being born in a car was not so bad. My father passed away when I was very young. I was almost five years old when he died. I don't have too many memories of him other than what my mother has told me and the personal memory of seeing him on his deathbed. I wish he could have been there to guide me through life, to give the advice that only one's father can give.

My mother was a young girl when she married my father. She was sixteen, he was seventy-four. He was a widower with six children, all older than my mother, and he had several grandchildren her age. His children resented my mother for being so young and marrying such an old man. To this day one of them still does not really accept my sisters and me as siblings.

I don't know much about my father. I never bothered to ask, but those who claim they knew him say he was a good man. I'll take their word for it I guess, but even Richard Nixon was considered a good man after he died. As you can expect from an old geezer marrying a teenager, my father died while my sisters and I were still very young. To me, the fact that a seventy-four-year-old man fathered three kids with a teenage girl is incredible. After my father passed away, my mother, still a young woman, remarried quickly. I don't remember my mother's courtship or ever meeting the man before she married him. Perhaps I was too young to remember or maybe she never stopped to think that what we thought of him was important. I do remember being beaten, almost tortured, by my aunt and cousins when my mother went away on her honeymoon. I guess I wasn't that young; after all, I do remember the pain.

We lived in a little hilltop village in central Puerto Rico. It was a village of farmers. Everybody lived off the land. My father's family was from the city. I don't remember ever meeting any of them. The village where we lived was very tranquil. There was a great deal of undeveloped land. We played baseball in an open, grassy field where we would sometimes lose the ball in the tall grass. We played hide-and-seek in the woods, climbed trees for oranges and grapefruits, and picked guavas for snacks. Our family harvested coffee, rice, and various other fruits and vegetables. It was an easy-going life until my father died and my mother remarried and went on her secret honeymoon.

I was five years old at the time. My mother left us with her sister, who had seven kids of her own. My cousins' ages ranged from three to eighteen. For some reason that I'll never comprehend, my aunt allowed her kids to brutally beat us. At any given moment we could be kicked, punched, or made into a bloody mess for no reason at all. My cousins were not punished; in fact, I remember laughter from the adults.

Alberto was our oldest cousin. At that time he was the biggest jerk in the world. Alberto would make my sisters and me run up and down a rocky hill, knowing we would fall and hurt ourselves. He would initiate the abuse by sending his little brothers to punch us, kick us, whatever. He was a very sick individual.

Our house was about one hundred yards up the hill from my aunt's house. It was unoccupied and unlocked while my mother was gone. One morning Alberto led me up to our house with the promise of giving me a slingshot and showing me how to use it. I was excited. Once we got to the house he pulled a slingshot from his back pocket and told me that mine was inside on the kitchen table. I hurried inside, happy and excited, but found nothing. When I turned to go back outside, Alberto was there behind me. Alberto picked me up, carried me into my mother's bedroom, and threw me on the bed face down. I tried to turn around and get up but he held me down by the back of my neck. Alberto pushed my face into the mattress, almost suffocating me. I felt him grab the elastic waist of my shorts and pull them down. With one strong pull Alberto had my shorts down to my ankles. I struggled. He put his other hand on the back of my head and pushed down hard. I was nearly motionless. Alberto released my head and began fumbling with my buttocks while he continued to hold me down by the neck. I felt pain as Alberto shoved his penis into my anus and I started to struggle again. Alberto laid over me and held me down. Within seconds the ordeal was over. Alberto got up and released me. As he fixed his pants, he threatened to kill me if I told anybody. I lay there in shock, catching my breath as Alberto repeatedly made threats against my life. I couldn't move, couldn't talk, couldn't even think. Alberto's voice got further away; I realized he had left the room, but then he came back. I felt something cold and wet brush against my inner thighs, up to my testicles, and between my buttocks. Alberto lifted me by the legs and tossed me toward the foot of the bed. My body turned as my legs flew through the air. He was cleaning a spot on the bed with a wet rag. I then realized that the cold wetness I had felt was Alberto cleaning me up. Slowly, with no emotion or thought, I pulled my shorts back up and stood there like a zombie. Alberto left the room, came back without the rag, and walked directly up to me. He grabbed me by the neck and lifted me so that I was face to face with him. Alberto said, "*Si dices algo, te mataré como un perro*" ("If you say anything, I will kill you like a dog"). He threw me on the bed and left. I sat numbly on the foot of my mother's bed for I don't know how long. I don't remember when I left the house, with whom, or how long after the rape took place.

I don't remember feeling shame or anger. I don't remember crying or feeling pain or discomfort after the incident. In fact, although I remember that episode as if it was yesterday, I can remember little else about life in Puerto Rico from that day forward.

2

Chicago

OUR NEW FATHER'S name was Emilio. He was a short man with a light complexion and light brown hair. I never got to know much about him. I heard he had children from a previous marriage. Other than that, Emilio was a total mystery. My mother must have been pregnant months before she and Emilio were married. Shortly after we moved out of the village she gave birth to a baby girl. I now had three sisters. Soon after the birth of their daughter, Emilio moved the family to the United States.

The first couple of years in the States were great. We lived in Chicago, the Windy City, the city of broad shoulders, and all that other bullshit. I was going on seven years old when we first came to Chicago. I was very curious about everything that surrounded me. How fascinating were the things in this great city, so different, so new. I remember sitting on the back porch of our very first apartment in Chicago and getting excited about the silver and green train going by on the elevated tracks located about a half-block away. I dreamed of some day riding that big green machine that decorated the skyline.

People were everywhere in Chicago. They socialized at all times of the day. This city was alive. In Puerto Rico the nearest neighbors were a quarter-mile away and they were usually relatives. The houses were made of wood and the toilet was a simple outhouse. In Chicago strangers lived next to, above, and below each other. Oh, and the miracle of indoor plumbing. What a difference there was in lifestyle and scenery. I fell in love with Chicago. I had trouble learning English, but other than that I was in heaven.

At school I was placed in a preschool setting because of my language barrier. It wasn't so bad. At almost seven years old I was the biggest kid in class and I got to go home at noon. (I discovered that I had to attend school only in the morning after spending half the afternoon searching for the "go home" room on my first day. If it hadn't been for a Spanish-speaking teacher that I ran into that day I might still be wandering the hallways.)

We lived on the South Side of the city around Twenty-sixth Street. It was a predominantly Mexican neighborhood. For the most part they weren't very friendly to Puerto Ricans. Their favorite chant was "*Arriba Mexico, abajo Puerto Rico*" ("up with Mexico, down with Puerto Rico"). I think their dislike of Puerto Ricans stemmed from the fact that while we were citizens of the United States at birth, they had to literally sneak into this country. But that seemed to be predominantly an adult attitude; the kids didn't seem to care. I made friends with kids who spoke Spanish as fluently as they did English. That helped my sisters and me learn English faster.

At home, Emilio's attitude toward us changed as his daughter got older. In short, he became an asshole. He would do things like padlock the refrigerator so that only his daughter could drink milk. He would hang a box of crackers from a rope high up on the ceiling so that we couldn't have any. All of his anger was taken out on us. Whether it was money problems, the baby crying, or an itch he couldn't scratch, we were beaten for it. Why my mother let him do those things I'll never know, but I'm sure it had a lot to do with avoiding my stepfather's anger. By the time I was eight the only thing my two sisters and I had to look forward to was going to school. We were pretty much confined to our bedroom in order to avoid Emilio's wrath. We went outside only when Emilio wasn't around, which was usually when we were in school.

Then Emilio lost his job. I didn't know what he did for a living to begin with . . . but during this period he was always at home. With him there all the time, the ranting and raving was constant. Then suddenly and for no apparent reason, Emilio started leaving the house early and would not come back until late at night.

With Emilio not around, our childhood became a joy again. The city, the snow, our new friends—my sisters and I loved every minute of it. Meanwhile Emilio got himself in some sort of trouble trying to scam the Social Security Administration. The rumor was that the FBI had picked him up for questioning. And just like that, Emilio disappeared. No goodbyes, no "I'll be back"; he just left and never returned. My mother, a very attractive woman and somewhat ignorant for a woman of her experience, was alone with four kids and on welfare. My mother's mother didn't let her go to school so she could learn to be something other than somebody's housewife. Now here she was in the land of opportunity, illiterate and with no skills, counting on others to do for us. She didn't stay single for long, though. I guess she used the only survival skill she knew—she found another man.

His name was Pedro. He was from the North Side of the city, where most of Chicago's Puerto Ricans lived. Pedro was five feet, five inches tall, weighed three hundred fifty pounds, and was fat, toothless, stinky, and loud—a truly trifling individual. He was a widower with a grown son named Hector. Pedro had this habit of cleaning his snot on his T-shirt, sometimes even blowing his nose into it, then walking around like that. The man rarely bathed and even when he did he smelled horrible.

Pedro was a very successful illegal lottery dealer. He bought a brand-new car almost every year and carried a large amount of cash on him at all times. My mother looked like a frail toothpick next to Pedro. I don't think it was any secret that the only thing my mother saw in Pedro was his money. It's how she chose to provide for her children; it's the only way she knew how. When he would come over my mother would send us outside. After a couple of months of that we all moved to the North Side.

Pedro's son Hector was a younger, taller version of his father. He was twenty-three years old, six feet, three inches tall, and weighed four hundred pounds. He was a sports fanatic and had a particular taste for big flashy cars. An orange Cadillac Coupe de Ville with a white top or a powder blue Lincoln Mark IV—these were the kinds of cars Hector drove. He had the personality of a kid. Hector enjoyed playing practical jokes on people and had a knack for making people laugh. Like his father, Hector also dabbled in the illegal lottery. Unlike his father, Hector was also a drug dealer. Although he himself didn't drink, smoke, or use drugs of any kind, he was always surrounded by junkies. Hector sold heroin. His girlfriend

Missy, a junkie, was a tiny woman whose teeth had rotted away because of her craving for sweets. Missy's sister Jeannie was also a junkie. In fact just about everyone who hung around Hector was a junkie, including his previous girlfriend, the mother of his child, his sister-in-law, and her boyfriend. Hector enjoyed their company. They worshipped him. They did anything he wanted at his command.

It wasn't until we moved that I realized how big and racially diverse Chicago was. So many worlds collided with each other on the way north from the Mexican area of Eighteenth Street and Western Avenue toward the Puerto Rican area at Western and Potomac Street. We went past an African American neighborhood, then through Polish and Italian areas. I saw railroad tracks, parks, and kids enjoying themselves in the spray of water coming from a fire hydrant. The buildings changed in style, each telling their own unique architectural story. It seemed like the city embraced its dwellers the way a mother demonstrates love for her child. My love for Chicago grew stronger by the day.

3

Humboldt Park

I MADE FRIENDS very quickly on the North Side. We all seemed to have something in common other than being of the same race. I was eight and a half when we moved to the North Side. The area we moved to seemed predominantly white but there were also plenty of Puerto Ricans. We lived in the Humboldt Park area. Humboldt Park was the most beautiful park I had ever seen. There was a beach for swimming, a lake for fishing, and many baseball diamonds. To me it was like a world within a world. Our home was a second-floor, three-bedroom apartment above a grocery store. There were wooden porches in the back with stairs that led down into a walkway that went into an alley. Next door to us was a three-story building with a bar on the street level.

I was enrolled at Von Humboldt School, which was located about six or seven blocks from where I lived. By now I had become somewhat proficient in English, but there was still a lot I did not understand. I was still very ignorant in the ways of American youth. I was going on nine years old. At Von Humboldt I was put in the fifth grade with kids my own age. Having spent the last two years with kids much smaller than myself, I wasn't prepared for such a drastic change. I went from being the biggest kid in class to being one of the smallest. I didn't like it at all. On the very first day of school the school bully confronted me. His name was Ricardo, but everyone called him Ricky. He was a big, ugly, black-skinned Puerto Rican. Ricky wasn't muscular, but he was big. He had a big afro and could easily have been mistaken for an African American until he spoke. Ricky proclaimed himself the toughest guy in school and pointed out a certain girl as his girlfriend. He warned me to stay away from her. Her response to Ricky's claim was, "I'm not your girlfriend. You better stop saying that." The next person I met was a guy named Jorge. He was short with big feet and curly hair and was an easy person to get along with. Jorge introduced me to his buddies Noel and Julio. Noel looked more like a white boy than he did a Puerto Rican. He had dirty blond hair, blue eyes, and rosy skin. Then there was Julio. He looked more like a stereotypical Puerto Rican. He was brown skinned with pushed-back black hair and a very deep Latin accent. Jorge and Noel were born and raised in Chicago. Their families had been some of the first Puerto Ricans to inhabit the Humboldt Park area. They told me a lot of horror stories about white violence toward Puerto Ricans. As new additions to the neighborhood, Julio and I could only take their word for it.

The stories the guys told about the white people in the area were never pleasant. Jorge showed me scars he claimed were caused by a group of white boys who jumped him because he was Puerto Rican. They assured me it wasn't as bad as it once was but warned me to avoid any groups of white boys. I don't know why, but deep down I didn't believe a word the guys told me. All the white people I had encountered since coming to Chicago were friendly and nice. I told the guys about some white boys I had passed on the way to school. They seemed friendly enough. They kept pointing at the sky with their middle fingers. I thought they were showing me how beautiful it was. They also yelled words that I understood to be friendly gestures. I had never heard these words before. They yelled "punk," "spic," "pussy," "son of a bitch," and I think they even offered me a pork chop. Julio, Jorge, and Noel laughed uncontrollably as I told them about these white boys. After the laughter they explained to me what I was being called and what the middle finger pointed at the sky meant. I felt like an idiot. All day long I kept thinking about what the white boys were saying to me. Now I was scared. I had never experienced such hatred. I became wary and cautious of the company I kept.

One morning there was a group of about four white boys teasing and pushing around some Puerto Rican kid I didn't know. Noel, Jorge, and Julio wanted to confront the white boys but hesitated because of the presence of a police officer. The officer was standing near his patrol car about four or five feet from the white boys by the edge of the sidewalk. He looked at the boys with this half smile, half smirk on his face, but did nothing. It seemed like he was enjoying what was going on. The Puerto Rican kid, apparently pushed to the limit, suddenly lunged at the white boy nearest him and tackled him to the ground. He then began swinging his fists wildly at the white boy's face. The white boy covered his face with his arms as his friends backed off, yelling, "Leave him alone, leave him alone!" The police officer walked up to the two boys and grabbed the Puerto Rican kid by the hair. He lifted the kid up and pulled him toward the patrol car. The officer opened the back door of the car and tossed the kid in as he kicked him in the rear end. "See how tough you are in jail, you fuckin' spic," the officer said as he slammed the car door. He then turned around and yelled, "Get in school, all of you." I hurried inside and went to my classroom. There were only a few kids there. About ten minutes later Noel, Jorge, and Julio walked into the classroom along with the rest of the class. "I told you. The white boys get away with everything," Noel said as he walked past me toward his desk. "They'll probably put him in juvi [Juvenile Detention]," Jorge said. From that point forward I was always leery of white people. Whether they locked the kid up in juvenile detention or not, I don't know. I never saw him again—not in school, around the neighborhood, or anywhere. Maybe his parents had been scared right back to Puerto Rico. That episode certainly put the fear of whites in me. I immediately recognized that when a Puerto Rican complained about abuse from a white person they were classified as weak, cowardly, not able to conform to American ways. However, when a Puerto Rican became the aggressor, he was classified as an animal, not fit to live within American society.

At school I hung out with Puerto Ricans, mainly the guys, and avoided whites. This became easier as time went on. It seemed like they were moving out to get away from the Puerto Ricans. Jorge, Noel, Julio, and I became inseparable. We soon started meeting each other on the corner of Rockwell and Potomac Streets. There was a candy store located there that we routinely shoplifted from. The store was called

Gloria's. The most popular item in the store came in a little folded brown paper envelope that cost five dollars, called a "nickel bag." I always wondered what kind of candy could be so expensive. Anyway, it was because of the popularity of the nickel bag that we were able to steal candy so easily. The boys and I played around on that corner until it was time to go to school. The best thing that came from hanging out with Julio, Jorge, and Noel was how quickly I learned English. They spoke in a mix of Spanish and English that made it easy for me to follow and understand what they were saying. They took the time to explain what I didn't catch on to. After, they had a good laugh—at my expense, that is. In no time at all I was using the most popular words in the English language in complete, proper sentences. "Fuck you, you stupid mother fucking asshole," was my first English sentence.

On the North Side of Von Humboldt School was a chain-link fence with a hole in it. We called it "the escape hole." Kids our size could jump right through it but a grown-up, like, say, a truant officer, would have a hard time. By the time they did get through we would be gone. On the other side of that fence was an alley that led to Washtenaw Street. When we came out of the alley there was a game room right across the street. The place was called Carmen's; it was the school hangout. It had two pool tables, an air hockey table, a foosball machine, and various kinds of pinball machines. The most popular item there was also the "nickel bag." At Gloria's the bags were sold over the counter, but at Carmen's they were sold by a couple of teenage guys. One sold them inside and the other worked outside on the street.

Back in school I was in heaven. Being able to read, write, and understand the English language better made school even more fascinating. I was a model student, always on time, my homework neatly completed, and always attentive and eager to learn. My three *amigos* and I were all pretty good students. We were all on the honor roll, which didn't do anything for the cool dude reputation we so very much wanted to have. To make up for it we used to cut school once in a while and spend the day running around Humboldt Park and hanging out at Carmen's. On several occasions Noel took us to his house. We spent the day looking through his father's *Playboy* magazines. It was the first time I had seen an adult female body in the nude. I was kind of embarrassed at first, but I was also definitely excited. Noel seemed a bit more experienced in sexual matters than the rest of us. He spoke openly and proudly about what he would do to a woman's breast if he got the chance. Noel would show us a centerfold and say something like, "I would eat her for so long, I'd have to go to a dentist for a haircut."

After school we would rush home to watch our favorite cartoon, *Speed Racer*, get a bite to eat, and then meet at the school playground for a couple of games of baseball. While we were having a good time with our ball game, the neighborhood teenagers would group up by the mobile classrooms. They would play loud music, drink Old Style beer and Richards wine, and, to my surprise, make the contents of the infamous nickel bags into cigarettes. I finally found out what the nickel bag was used for.

The best-looking girls always hung out with that group. The girls also drank and smoked the expensive cigarettes. They were always tongue kissing the guys and would let themselves be touched and grabbed in places that I had thought were sacred to the opposite sex. They would do these things right out in the open with no shame. My friends and I were so envious. Most of the guys playing baseball with us had their minds made up—they wanted to be part of this cool group when they got older. Noel's older brother was already part of that group. Noel pointed him out as the "one with the blue baggy pants with black All Stars that's grabbing a girl's ass." His name was Oscar. It was obvious that he and Noel were not the offspring of the same father. Oscar looked more like Julio, only his skin was just a little lighter. Noel's brother was known as Chico. His name was spray painted or written in marker all over the place. Wherever his name appeared, so did the letters *L D*. They stood for Latin Disciples. That was what they called themselves.

That afternoon after we finished playing baseball, I bombarded Noel with questions about his brother and the Latin Disciples. Noel told me that people in that group were considered the coolest guys in the neighborhood. They protected and helped each other in times of need. They were all known by nicknames—everybody who joined them was given one. He also told us about how sometimes he would see the Disciples chasing white boys and blacks out of the neighborhood, and sometimes even all the way out of Humboldt Park. I asked him why. Julio answered, "Because we're Ricans, that's why!"

That summer went by quickly and left a lot of unanswered questions in my mind. We played a lot of baseball, tried to hang out with the Latin Disciples, and talked a lot about girls. My stepbrother Hector would come by once in a while and talk sports with me. Sometimes we played catch together and once he played "fast pitching" with us.

Fast pitching was what we called a game of baseball played against a wall. The wall acted as the catcher. A box representing the strike zone would be drawn on a wall that had open space in front of it. An imaginary playing field was created, depending on the space available. All pitches that landed inside the box were strikes and any outside the box were balls. Any number of players could play, but the usual number was one to three players per team. No base running took place. Boundaries were agreed upon to determine base hits, doubles, triples, and home runs. All balls hit in the air that weren't caught were ruled using these boundaries. Of course, if they were caught it was an out. Any ground balls hit past the pitcher were base hits but if caught beforehand it was an out. The playing surface didn't matter as long as there was a wall and space to hit.

It was a thrill seeing Hector's fat ass trying to catch a grounder or chase down a pop fly. When he ran we all made believe there was an earthquake. Hector didn't seem to mind—he laughed along with us. Surprisingly, Hector was a pretty good athlete for a man his size. He had a hell of a curveball and had a good swing when at bat. When he hit the ball solidly in the air, man, it went a long way. I was so happy playing baseball and going to school.

During the winter the Latin Disciples were rarely seen hanging out. Most of the time we would run into them hanging out at Carmen's or when they would go by Gloria's to buy nickel bags. Other than that, it was rare to see them hanging out like they did during the summer. Noel said they had some kind of clubhouse where they congregated to stay out of the cold.

Winter was pretty boring except for the snowball fights we used to have at school, the few snowmen we built, and, of course, Christmas. Mostly I stayed at home watching television because my mom didn't want me to get sick.

I got to know my stepfather Pedro about as much as I would ever know him, which wasn't much. He spoke in a loud voice that made it seem like he was always screaming. Because of the illegal lottery business, the police would raid our apartment every so often. As a kid, I wondered why they did that. I really didn't pay much attention to it. I thought they were just making sure that our house was safe. (I got this idea from the annual "Officer Friendly" visit at school. While he passed out coloring books and crayons he described his job and how the police were there to help us. He always painted the world as being so sweet and honest.) Pedro was pretty good to us. He would buy us anything we wanted and would always supply us with candy money. Toward the end of the summer my mother became pregnant with her first child by Pedro. The family was so joyous, especially Pedro. In the beginning of June my mom gave birth to the newest addition to the family—a boy. They named him Pedro Jr. Suddenly, like Emilio before him, Pedro Sr. started to change drastically.

4

The Beatings Begin

SUMMER WAS HERE, school was out, and I had become part of the "in" crowd. I was no longer the new kid in school. I studied everything and everyone around me. Still, I shied away from personal attention. I was embarrassed to talk in front of girls or in class and I had a serious case of stage fright. I learned how to draw and developed a knack for writing poetry. These things got me unwanted attention from the teacher, so I mostly kept them to myself. I loved school because I felt special there. My first full year at Von Humboldt School went by too quickly. I didn't learn enough, didn't hang out enough; it was over before I could enjoy it fully.

Jorge, Noel, Julio, and I started making plans to join a Little League team at Humboldt Park. We always tried out for teams, but we wouldn't play if we didn't all get on the same team. A firefighter that lived in the neighborhood told us if we got a team together, he would coach us. Finally, a team we could all play on together!

Pedro, my stepfather, had other ideas about what my sisters and I were going to do all summer. Pedro demanded that we stay home or in the vicinity of home while he was out with my mom showing off his newborn. All of a sudden I was not allowed to go to Humboldt Park or to hang around with Jorge, Noel, and Julio. I complained about wanting to play on the Little League team with my friends. Pedro's response was to talk to one of his lottery connections who had a son on a Little League team and, just like that, I was on a team that played in Lincoln Park. I hated being on that team but stayed on it because of my love for the game. All that summer I wondered what Jorge, Noel, and Julio were up to. I was not allowed to use the telephone or leave the neighborhood, so I had to wait to see them in school. I was dying to tell the guys about the dorky baseball team I played on. We were going to be seventh graders in the fall, which meant we would go to Von Humboldt Branch, which was a separate building located on California Avenue and LeMoyne Street. Von Humboldt Branch was for seventh and eighth graders only. Our minds were constantly on girls. We were planning to join the Latin Disciples so that we could get to know the nice, touchable girls who hung out with them. I didn't want to drink or smoke. I just wanted to be cool and get girls.

Life at home was becoming pure hell. Pedro had lost whatever affection he had for my sisters and me. He became very abusive. I guess he thought that since he now had a child of his own he didn't have to care for the hand-me-down children anymore. My mom also changed. She became very protective of my sisters. Pedro could not get away with doing anything to them, but it was a different story when it came to me. It seemed like my mom didn't care that Pedro was kicking my ass just because I let out a loud cheer when Billy Williams or Ron Santo of the Cubs hit a home run onto Waveland Avenue. She would just scream, "Shut up, stop crying, and turn off the television." I felt alone; my sisters had my mother, Junior had his father, but I had nobody. I found myself counting the days until school started again so that I could be with my friends. I knew that once school started I wouldn't be alone anymore. I thought I would have all the friends I needed once I joined the Disciples. There would never be a lack of attention for me. Everything was going to be so great once school started. I was wrong.

The city was building a new high school for the Puerto Rican community. That was the reason why the houses were being demolished at the southeast corner of Western Avenue and Potomac Street when we first moved into the neighborhood. They were being cleared to make room for what would be the new school's playing field. The school was to be named after a Puerto Rican hero, Roberto Clemente. The new school was built on the corner of Western and Division Street and the baseball/football field stretched for one block down Western to Potomac.

We lived on Western, a quarter-block from Potomac. We could see the school from where we lived, and it was beautiful. The old neighborhood high school was Tuley High, which was located on Claremont Street between Hirsch and Potomac Streets, one block north of the new school. While Clemente was being prepared for the first school term, Tuley was gearing up to become a grammar school. High school students enrolled at Tuley and the incoming freshman class were the first students at Clemente. About two weeks before the start of the school year my mom received a letter from the Board of Education informing her that I would no longer be attending Von Humboldt School. I would be transferred to the new Tuley Educational Complex simply because I lived closer to it. Kids from a school named Shuley would also be attending Tuley. Shuley was closed down and demolished to make room for the Clemente parking area. My dreams of going to Von Humboldt Branch and reuniting with my friends Jorge, Noel, and Julio after a bad summer just flew out the window.

Not going back to Von Humboldt felt like when we left Puerto Rico to come to Chicago. I would have to make new friends and find out where the hangouts were. Or I could try to sneak over to Von Humboldt every day after school and hang out with the boys. I decided to make new friends. I was afraid of the beating I would get from Pedro if he found out that I was hanging around with my old friends behind his back. I had to face the fact that my buddies would soon become just a memory. Even though they lived just six or seven blocks away, it was like they lived in another country because of Pedro's newfound attitude.

The first day of school that summer was different than I expected. Instead of being in a group where everyone wanted to hear what I had to say, I was an outsider being talked about. Because of this, school became boring and not worth going to. I went from being on the honor roll at Von Humboldt to being an average student at Tuley. I became a class clown, hoping for attention.

There was a group of boys that lived across the street from where I lived. I got the nerve to talk to them because they were always outside playing catch. Our mutual interest in baseball brought us together. Finally, I had some new friends. My new friends were five brothers. The oldest was Heraldo; he was in high school. He was the type of guy who didn't like trouble and always had some good advice for kids younger than he was. The next one was Rodolfo. He was about a year or two older than me and was very popular in the neighborhood. His nickname was Papo. He was short in stature, but very muscular and cocky. He had a reputation for being a bully. The third brother was Ernesto. He was the same age as I was. Ernesto was pretty laid back and easily influenced by others. Everyone thought that he was gay, but he was far from it. The other two were twins, Antonio and Jaime. These guys were always together and kept to themselves most of the time. Papo, Ernesto, and I were all in the same classroom because Papo had flunked a grade.

The brothers knew me as the guy who was always getting his ass whipped by his parents. They had seen my mother slap me around out on the street in front of our house on several occasions. They had seen her and Pedro beating me through the window. I was embarrassed when they told me this. The guys made light of it, then never mentioned the incidents again.

As time went by, Papo and I became good friends. He said he got along with me so well because I wasn't afraid to hit him back. (Actually, in the incident he was referring to, I hit him back because I thought he was playing around with me. Had I known that he was testing me, I probably would have failed.) Papo was part of the "in" crowd, just like Noel's brother Chico, and he invited me to join his group. I said I had to think about it. I had not seen Papo's group hanging out. I wanted to make sure the girls that hung out with them were as attractive and friendly as the ones that hung out by Von Humboldt. I told Papo about the Latin Disciples. He knew more about the Disciples than I did. He told me their colors were black and blue and their leader was a guy called Cadillac Joe. I didn't know whether what he said was true or not; I just knew they had some hot chicks hanging out with them. I asked Papo the name of his group. He didn't tell me. All he said was I would find out soon enough.

My new friends made it much easier to avoid Pedro. Because they lived right across the street I could hang out with them almost all day and then seclude myself in my bedroom at night. I played a kind of tactical game to avoid Pedro. I would rush into the house to eat, watch television, or whatever once I saw him leave the house. When I heard him coming I'd hurry out the back door. Nevertheless I couldn't avoid him all the time. Sometimes I would get hypnotized watching a Cubs game and I wouldn't notice Pedro come in. He would either try to hit me or he would go around ranting and raving, yelling obscenities about me for no reason. (I really never tried to find out why Pedro acted this way toward me. I don't think I would get anything near a sensible answer anyway. I do sometimes wonder if he even has a remote idea of the damage he did to my life. I wonder if he even cares.)

Winter was back in the air and there was snow all over the place. As a kid, I grew to love Chicago winters; it turned the city into a wonderland. The only bad thing was that I had to stay in the house most of the time, which meant too many confrontations with Pedro. One Friday I came home from school and asked my mother if I could go out and play football. I explained that even though there was snow on the ground it was still pretty warm out. She agreed but said I had to do my homework first. The only homework I had was math. I picked up a pencil, sat at the dining room table, and tried to finish my homework as fast as I could.

About five or ten minutes into my homework I heard Pedro come in. He walked over to me, looked over my shoulder, and started screaming in rage about the numbers I was writing. You see, the asshole was uneducated and illiterate; to him, all numbers were illegal lottery numbers. Before I could react, I felt a sharp pain across my back and then again, and again, and again. I fell to the floor screaming and crying in pain. I begged my mother to stop him from beating me. My dear mother responded by kicking me and whipping me with an extension cord. She picked me up by the hair and told me she was going to kill me. I believed her, I truly believed her. Somehow I got away from her, ran into my bedroom, and hid under the bed.

I could feel the pain in my back as I laid there crying, begging God for mercy. About a half an hour later my sister came into the room and told me to come out from under the bed. Pedro and my mom had gone out. I came out and took off my shirt. It hurt like hell. The shirt had stuck to the blood that was dripping out of two or three different places on my back. The asshole had taken off his leather belt and hit me with so much force that the skin in the places where he struck me was either black and blue or gone altogether. On my legs were the red, black, and blue stripes reflecting the help my loving mother gave me with the extension cord.

I stayed in my room for the rest of the night, crying, and wondering what I had done to deserve such punishment. I was afraid to fall asleep. I figured my mother and Pedro would probably continue their abuse once they returned. Every time I heard the front door open I got under the bed. Most of the time it was my sisters. They were running around playing, laughing, as if nothing had happened. I envied them. I hated them. I wished them dead. I knew it wasn't their fault but I just couldn't understand why I was the only one being treated abusively. I heard my mother's voice and immediately put my shirt back on and got back under the bed. She was laughing with Pedro Jr. I heard her in the kitchen talking to my oldest sister, something about Puerto Rico. I heard Pedro come in talking loud as hell, asking where I was. I got as close to the wall as possible, bracing myself for another beating. Pedro was cursing and saying he would kill me if he ever caught me writing numbers again. My mother didn't reply. I heard her tell my sisters to go to bed. Pedro continued ranting and raving for at least another hour. Then all was silent. I was sure everybody had gone to bed, but I was still too scared to come out from hiding. I knew that at any given moment, and for no reason, Pedro could charge into my room and commence beating me. I slept under the bed. It was uncomfortable, but at least I felt safe.

Saturday I crawled out from under the bed feeling discomfort and pain. My shirt had again stuck to the wounds on my back. I didn't realize this and just pulled the shirt off normally. The pain intensified tenfold. To make matters worse, I awoke to some very bad news—my mom was pregnant again and she and Pedro had decided to pack up and move back to Puerto Rico. I kept thinking to myself how impossible it would be to avoid getting my ass beat by Pedro once we were on the Island. My older sister and I expressed an interest in finishing school in Chicago and talked about how hard it would be for us to adjust. To my surprise, even my sister's pleas went unheard.

The beating I had received the night before was still fresh in my mind. I kept waiting for my mom to tell me she was sorry and take a look at the wounds, then do the things mothers do that make kids feel better and heal more quickly. It never happened.

Pedro was not home when my mom broke the news to us about moving. The first thing he told me when he came home was that I was lucky he hadn't killed me. He told me I had better watch myself because we were going to Puerto Rico to live in "his" house and I wouldn't have anywhere to run or hide. My mother heard him say these things to me but dismissed them by saying that Pedro didn't mean what he said. Just the thought of being trapped in Puerto Rico with that asshole brought tears to my eyes and made me fear for my life. I spent all day Sunday crying and wondering how I would survive. I had this idea that if Pedro actually tried to kill me and failed, my mother would probably finish me off. I spent half the night twisting and turning in my bed, wondering what I had done to deserve what was happening to me. The weekend was over and it was time to go back to school. What a relief. I had a reason to leave the house!

The hatred I felt for my mother was undeniable. I didn't talk back to her or attack her, but it wasn't out of respect. It was because of fear. Fear that she would unmercifully beat me into submission, that she would torture me for the pleasure of hearing me scream. In my mother I saw all that was evil in the world. She was Satan, she was Hitler, and she was a venomous snake disguised as a harmless flower. My mother was that warm, safe, inviting place that turned into an inferno once an entry was made. The way she would act after beating me, as if nothing had happened, burned me up inside. Somewhere in her warped mind she must have thought she was teaching me some kind of lesson. Oh, how I hated her, how I wanted her to die. This was my first thought of committing a violent act, and it was against my mother.

Papo was waiting for me outside of his house so we could walk to school together. I tried to avoid him but he caught up to me and asked me why I didn't come out all weekend. I kept silent. I was lost in thoughts of the embarrassment I would feel if anybody saw my back. Papo was unusually quiet. He usually kept messing with me until I broke down and started messing with him back. We were the class clowns but that day it was obvious to the whole class that something was wrong. Papo and I just sat there while everybody else, including the teacher, waited for one of us to start acting up.

The teacher called us outside the classroom and asked us if there was some kind of disagreement between us. We told him there was nothing wrong. He kept asking questions. Finally, I told him that my family was moving to Puerto Rico and I didn't want to go. He expressed his sorrow but assured me that Puerto Rico was a beautiful place to live. I thought to myself, "Yeah, right, if you only knew."

After school I was trying to hurry home and lock myself in my room away from all the violence that was constantly awaiting me. But Papo pushed me into a hallway as we walked through a gangway and locked the door behind us. He told me that he was on his way up the stairs of my house on Friday night when he heard me screaming and begging my mother for mercy. He said my mother was a bitch. When he said that I took a swing at him in defense of my mom. Papo grabbed me in a bear hug so that I wouldn't hit him; this accidentally peeled a scab from the wounds on my back. I winced from the pain. He let me go and I showed him my back. I couldn't believe his reaction. Tears actually came out of the corners of his eyes. I told him that what I had told the teacher about leaving Chicago was true. He just put his head down and said, "Come on, let's go home."

Even with the hatred I felt for my mother I felt the need to come to her defense when Papo called her a bitch. That's just the way it is. Honor thy mother no matter how much pain and suffering she inflicts on you. That's why no one gets blamed but the kids—a mother's name is sacred.

At home everybody was smiling and happy. My mom had company and she was bragging about moving to the Island. She called me over as she told her friends that I was such a good boy, how my grades were always good, and about how obedient I was. She acted as if she was sure I had forgotten the pain, as if I didn't have belt marks on my back.

5

The Spanish Lords

THE NEXT DAY Papo and I met at the usual place. I begged him not to tell anyone about my back. I told him that I was going to cut school that day. It was gym day and all the guys would see my back in the locker room. I didn't want to have to answer questions about my wounds. I didn't want to be faced with the need to protect my mother's honor again. After a little deliberation, he decided to cut school and keep me company. It was the first time I had cut school since I started going to Tuley. I had thought about it before but realized how close to home the school was, and always decided against it. Papo took me to the clubhouse of the group he belonged to. I still didn't know too much about these groups. The only knowledge I had was that they were always the most popular guys and the most attractive girls always hung out with them. That's all I had to know.

The name of the group Papo belonged to was the Spanish Lords. Their clubhouse was located right across the street from the school. It was in the basement of the house of one of their members. Papo told me that the guy's father had also been a member of the Lords when he was younger, so he let them have the basement as a hangout. I asked what the difference was between his group and the group from Von Humboldt, but before he could answer we were at the clubhouse door. Papo advised me not to ask any questions about the group in the clubhouse and promised to answer my question later. He knocked on the door and replied, "Lord Papo," when a voice on the other side asked who it was. The door swung open. He stepped inside and told me to wait outside for a minute. I didn't see who had opened the door. Papo was being very secretive, as if he was hiding something. I became nervous, wondering what Papo was doing and why he was taking so long. A couple of minutes later the door opened and Papo asked me to come in.

Inside the basement we walked over to another door and entered through it. The room was dark; the only light was from several purple florescent lights. The walls were decorated with various glow-in-the-dark posters. A song by Daryl Hall and John Oates broke the silence. "She's a rich girl and she's going too far but you know it don't matter anyway," the song said. The room was filled with smoke and the distinctive smell of marijuana was in the air. After my eyes adjusted to the lighting and focused, I could see two sofas and several chairs. There was a big console television at the end of the room with a stereo system on top of it. A couple of the chairs were occupied, two by guys and one by a girl. They were just sitting there drinking, smoking, and looking at me like "Who the hell are you?" On one of the sofas there was a couple making out. They were really getting into it. Papo had to pull me over where he was to stop me from staring at them. I went with him into another room where there were two older guys, about twenty or twenty-one years old. They had a big plastic bag of what looked like dried leaves. They were busy stuffing it into little brown paper envelopes. So that's where the nickel bags came from. All this time I had thought some company manufactured them.

Papo introduced me to these two guys. They were called Rican and Lil Chino. Lil Chino was Puerto Rican but resembled someone of Asian descent. He had a light complexion, brown eyes, and long brown hair that he tied into a ponytail. Lil Chino had a slim build and had many tattoos on his arms. The most noticeable of his tattoos was one on the left side of his chest. He had a tombstone with the name *Loco* and the letters *R.I.P.* written inside of it. I told him my name. He glanced at me and said, "What's up," then went back about his business. Rican was bronze skinned and had a big afro. He looked more African American than Puerto Rican. Rican was into weight lifting and was really huge, but seemed friendly. He told me that he was looking forward to having me become one of the brothers. Rican instructed Papo to introduce me to the others.

We went back into the smoke-filled room. Papo went over to a corner and turned on the lights. Simultaneously, everyone began complaining about the light being turned on. When Papo told them that Rican had told him to introduce me, they suddenly all came to attention. They were all older than my eleven years.

The two that were making out were busy getting their private parts back into their clothes. Papo introduced the guy as Snake. He had a Cubs cap on and had no eyebrows. Snake had an ugly scar on his neck, as if he had been badly burned at some time in his life. The girl was still trying to clip on her bra. Nevertheless she stopped what she was doing, got up half-naked, and said her name was Nancy. She said everyone called her Sexpot. She was a heavyset white girl with gigantic breasts and a badly done, homemade tattoo on her upper left arm that said *S L's*. Sexpot was in no way a beauty queen, but she had the reputation of being easy to get into bed. The other girl in the room walked over to Sexpot and said, "You're such a fuckin' whore," then walked out.

The other two guys there started laughing and introduced themselves. One was called Joker. He was about eighteen and was a high school dropout. In fact, everyone in that room except for Papo and I were dropouts. Joker was high on marijuana and kept giggling and teasing Sexpot. The other guy was called Pothead. He smoked pot for breakfast, lunch, dinner, and in between meals. Pothead was tall and muscular. He stuttered a little and had this "tough guy" attitude about him. It seemed like he didn't like me too much. He told me that if I ever backstabbed one of the Spanish Lord brothers he would kill me himself. Papo quickly stepped in between us and told Pothead to cool out and give me a chance to prove myself. Joker offered me a cigarette. I took one and studied it. It was a Kool. I had no idea what to do with it. Sexpot started laughing and said, "Well, lookit here, Papo done brought me a virgin to teach. Come here, honey, let me teach you how to smoke." Before she could go any further I put the cigarette up to my mouth and proclaimed that I wasn't a virgin. I lit the cigarette and taught myself how to smoke by watching Pothead. Papo turned off the light, sat down next to me, and told me to kick back and relax.

About an hour passed. Lil Chino came out of the other room and asked us if we wanted anything from the store. "Yeah, man, some brewskies," replied Snake. Shortly after, Rican stepped out of the room and turned on the lights. He asked me how I was feeling. I told him I was fine and asked him for a cigarette. At this point I would have done anything to pass the time. Rican told me that the only kind of cigarettes he had were the funny looking ones. I wondered why everybody in the room started laughing, but told him to give me one anyway. As Rican handed me the joint, Papo took it from him and said that he would light it up. Everyone was surprised and asked why he had suddenly decided to start smoking pot. He said that since it was going to be my first time he wanted to join me. Papo lit the joint up, inhaled the smoke, and handed it to me. I watched his face turn tomato red as he tried to hold the smoke in his lungs. He gasped out and started coughing. Everybody laughed, including him. Now it was my turn. I put the funny-looking cigarette in my mouth, inhaled, and held the smoke in my lungs just like Papo had done. I started getting dizzy and began coughing and gasping for air. The room was going around in circles and everything was blurry. I could hear laughter and then I heard chanting, "Hit it again, hit it again, hit it again." I knew they meant for me to take another puff from the joint but everything was blurry. I couldn't see the joint. I thought to myself, "What the hell, I don't have to see it." I brought my hand up to my lips and went through the motions only to find that I didn't have anything in my hand. The chants were for Papo, not for me. I had dropped the joint without realizing it and Papo had picked it up. Everybody was hysterical about that. Rican embraced me and told me that I was "all right, man." At this time Lil Chino came back and started passing out beer to all of us. After several hours of drinking and smoking, it was finally time to leave the Lords' clubhouse.

I had entered the world of drugs and alcohol without even realizing it. There was no peer pressure—it was more the desire to be like everyone else, to belong.

The school day was over. It was time for Papo and me to blend in with the rest of the students going home. We had smoked two joints and drank a couple of beers apiece. We were pretty high and acting silly. Papo told me he was going back to the clubhouse and that he would see me later or tomorrow. I walked home hoping that Pedro and my mom wouldn't notice that I was high. I got home and went directly into my room. My mom didn't find that suspicious—I had made it a habit ever since I started getting beat up by Pedro. I lay there thinking how much fun I had had and how accepted I felt when I was with the Lords. The beer I drank and the marijuana I smoked relaxed me and made me feel like I had no worries in the world. I felt like I had finally woken up from the nightmare my life had become. Everything was better.

I couldn't stop thinking about having seen Sexpot's breast. Although I found her very unattractive I couldn't stop fantasizing about her. I thought about how I would go up to her the next time I saw her and make out with her. I thought about how fat and ugly Sexpot was and how attractive the girl was who cursed her out. I wondered who she was. Too bad she left before I could meet her.

My mind was racing at a thousand miles per minute, leaving me behind. My thoughts made me panic, smile, then panic again. It was an awesome experience. I was falling asleep when my sister knocked on my door and told me to come and eat. I told her I would eat later. She advised me to unlock the door before Pedro noticed that I had it locked and started trouble. I thought about it and knew she was right. I got up and unlocked the door, then went to sleep.

I woke in the middle of the night hungry as hell. I had a bad case of the munchies. I got up, went in the bathroom and washed my mouth, then went into the kitchen. I didn't turn on the light in order not to wake anyone. I was nervous about going into the kitchen because my mother and Pedro's bedroom was next to it. The hunger, however, overpowered the fear I had of Pedro. In the darkness I could see what looked like a dinner plate sitting on the table covered by another plate. I figured my mother must have left it there for me. I reached for the plate to take it back to my room. Before I touched it someone grabbed me by the hair and threw me to the floor. I felt a crippling pain in my stomach where I had just been kicked. I heard Pedro screaming and then the light went on. I heard my mother scream, *"Pedro, que haces?"* ("Pedro, what are you doing?") I lay there in pain saying to myself, "Man, what's with this guy? What have I done to him?" A sudden rage came over me. I didn't feel the pain anymore.

I walked over to the table, grabbed the plate of food, and hit Pedro in the face with it. By this time everybody was awake. After Pedro got over the shock that I was fighting back, he ran into his bedroom and came out with a gun. He pointed it at me and pulled back the hammer. My mom and sisters jumped in front of me. Pedro put down the gun and went into his bedroom. I was surprised that my mom had come to my defense. Had she changed? Was she going to hold me and tell me everything was going to be all right? No. She slapped my face three times. As she hit me she yelled obscenities. She paused, then swung at me again. This time she left an ugly scratch on my neck. Once again I ran into my room and hid under the bed, only this time she came after me with a broom and continued to hit me. A few minutes later everything was dark and quiet, as if nothing had happened.

My mind was fucked up. I lay under that bed weeping and begging for mercy but my cries went unheard. I thought about suicide, murder, or running away from home. I didn't know what to do or how to act to keep myself from being the victim of my mother's and Pedro's need for violence. I was afraid of everything around me. I withdrew into my own little world where everything was somehow connected to terror and violence.

I woke up the next morning and realized that I had slept under the bed again. I was scared to come out of my room, but I also knew that if I was late for school I would be whipped again. I didn't know whether to try and sneak out or to get back under the bed for protection. I heard my sisters talking and opened the door to see why they hadn't left for school yet. My older sister told me that my mother and Pedro were not home. They had gone to our schools to let them know that we would no longer be attending because we were moving back to Puerto Rico. I was petrified. My body literally trembled.

I immediately started thinking of ways to stay in Chicago. I could become a Lord and sleep at their clubhouse or I could sleep on the streets—anything would be better than going to the hell that Pedro was preparing for me in Puerto Rico. When they returned we found out that their plans had changed again. Pedro and Hector had won a big sum of money through the illegal lottery. They had decided to buy an abandoned building located two houses away from where we presently lived and have it remodeled. That was to be our new home.

My mom kept me home from school until the scratches on my neck weren't visible. By the time the scratches were even close to being healed, it was time for Christmas vacation. I didn't go back to school until January. When I did finally go back I felt free. I actually felt as if I had been locked up somewhere and had been set free.

At school my grades continued to drop and I became more unruly. I threatened a teacher because she insisted I write a paper on what I did during Christmas vacation. I told her I was going to get the Spanish Lords after her. I disrupted classes with my clownish behavior and started a food fight in the cafeteria. My mother was called to the school on several occasions, but she never went. She didn't care. All she did was beat me when I got home. She didn't even know why she was beating me. All she knew was that she got a call from school, so therefore I must have been bad. The more violence I experienced at home the more I acted up at school. Still, I could master any subject when I exerted myself. However, I purposely worked only just enough to pass. Getting attention was much more important to me than making good grades.

The violent behavior shown toward me at home directly translated into negative behavior at school. No longer did I love school because of what I could learn or for its challenges. School became nothing more than my escape from my home life. My aggressive acts toward authority figures were my way of getting back at my mother. Only, my mother couldn't have cared less. She blamed my poor school performance on my stupidity; she didn't think it had anything to do with her. Her answer to the problem was, of course, to knock the stupidity out of me.

It was a cold winter so I wasn't allowed to go outside until the weather got better. During that time I spent a lot of time in my room talking to myself. My fear of getting whipped just for being there made me turn to imaginary friends. I played imaginary games and visited imaginary places. I began talking to myself at school also. Only the embarrassment of realizing that other kids were looking at me stopped this from becoming a habit. I did continue to have imaginary conversations with myself, but in silence. This earned me many trips to the principal's office for not paying attention. As the number of trips to the principal increased, so did the beatings at home. According to my mother and Pedro, I was an idiot who would never amount to anything. Well, that was actually the nicest thing they said. I learned to ignore them and everybody around me.

I explored masturbation for the first time. Sex had been on my mind for a while but I had never actually done anything. I didn't even know what to do. I finally experienced an orgasm and found it to be a great feeling. Only the shame I felt about what I was doing kept me from masturbating on a regular basis. From that moment on my desire to experience sex became an obsession. Sex involved touching, kissing, passion. It involved love. I began to think that I could find all the feelings I was missing in my life in sex.

Even though I kept to myself, Pedro still found reasons to start fights with me. But since I had hit him back he wouldn't just start beating me. He would threaten me with his gun instead. Pedro's gun was the first real gun I had seen up close. It was silver and shiny. It wasn't big but it was loud. (I knew that from hearing it fired on New Year's Eve.) As far as I was concerned, Pedro's gun was a threat to my life. I had to get rid of it before it could get rid of me. I told Papo about my plan to steal Pedro's gun. He told me that if I did he could get someone to buy it off me. I began looking for the opportunity to make my move. I noticed that Pedro would get up early to go see how the remodeling of the new house was coming along. My mom would go with him. One morning when they left I went into their room and found the gun in the closet inside a coat pocket.

I took the gun and gave it to Papo. I suggested that we cut class that day and sell the gun. Papo suggested that we should hide the gun and go to school just in case Pedro came looking for me or called the police. Sure enough, the police showed up at school and questioned me. I told them that I didn't know anything about a gun, only that Pedro threatened me with it. The police officers didn't pressure me too much; they just said they would be watching me. For the rest of the day all I could think about was the beating waiting for me at home. Papo advised me to leave the gun where it was until the heat was off. I went home that day and came in through the back door. Pedro was waiting for me in the living room. I heard him talking about the beating he was going to give me. By the time he had noticed I was in the house, I had grabbed hold of a baseball bat.

The coward froze in his steps. He had beaten me when I couldn't fight back and pulled a gun on me, but now that I was fighting back and he didn't have his gun, he was shitting in his pants. Still, I wasn't safe yet. Pedro stood away from me but my mom took over. I had always thought that if Pedro stopped hitting me for no reason my mother would too. Again I was wrong. I guess she became addicted to beating me. It seemed that every time she got upset about something she would take it out on me. Once again I had to hide under the bed.

About two weeks after I took the gun, Papo and I sold it to a gang called the Insane Unknowns. We wanted to sell it to the Spanish Lords but they didn't want to take a chance with it because I hung around with them. The Spanish Lords and the Insane Unknowns were united. They partied together and backed each other up on the street. Any gang that had problems with the Lords usually had problems with the Unknowns as well—it was as if they were one gang with different names. I was glad to finally get rid of the gun. I had been a nervous wreck during the time the gun was hidden. On the other hand, so was Pedro. He had it in his mind that I was just waiting for an opportunity to kill him.

We sold the gun for one hundred dollars and used the money to buy marijuana, beer, and wine. The Spanish Lords consumed the majority of it. I didn't care; I was just happy to know that I was welcomed somewhere. I also knew better than to show up at home totally wasted. I did, however, take about ten joints from this stash with me. At night I would open my bedroom window and smoke a joint. I enjoyed the way I felt when I smoked marijuana. When I was high I could think about doing evil things and feel good about it. I would imagine killing Pedro and my mother over and over again, and be forgiven. My imagination would roam in worlds that didn't even exist. My fantasies and imaginary friends became lifelike. Marijuana became my way out of the horrible reality that was my life.

6

Murder in the 'Hood

SOON SUMMER WAS in the air, school was out, and the family was getting ready to move into the new house. I spent that summer like all my other summers—playing baseball. Only now instead of having a soda or water after the game I was smoking a joint and drinking beer. My mother didn't know or maybe she did and didn't care. Papo's brothers were in a group called the Western Boys. They were not a gang; they were a team that participated in all kinds of sports together. They would challenge guys from other neighborhoods to games of baseball, football, basketball, and more. Papo and I started hanging out more with the Western Boys than with the Spanish Lords; however, Papo was still one of their members.

The time came to move into Pedro's house. (I didn't call it our house because Pedro constantly reminded me that it was "his" house.) The apartment we vacated was quickly occupied. I recognized the boy in the family who moved into our old apartment. He was from Von Humboldt. His name was Victor. We had played baseball together many times. I invited him to join the Western Boys. He was a welcome edition to our team. He could hit the ball and it would fly for a mile. He was also the only one who volunteered to play catcher when we played league ball. We gave Victor the nickname Flaco because he was tall and thin. We became very close and so did our sisters and mothers. We slept at each other's houses on a daily basis and knew each other's family problems. My problem was, of course, Pedro. Flaco's problem was his sister Millie. Millie was seven years older than he was. She was tall and very attractive. Millie's problem was that she had a very active sex life. She went beyond being promiscuous—she was a nymphomaniac. Millie was also bisexual. Millie's lifestyle infuriated Flaco to the point of having fistfights with her. What bothered him the most was that she was so open about her ways. As her brother, Flaco was ashamed and always felt like he had to protect his family's dignity. It didn't help that his mother always came to Millie's defense. Flaco knew about Pedro's habit of abusing me. He told me that he would rather be in my place than to have a bitch for a sister. Our problems did one thing—they kept us talking and made us good friends.

I felt that my problems were the only ones that truly mattered. Flaco's problem wasn't a problem at all. That was my attitude. I was learning to think about myself and myself only. All the problems of the world were unimportant compared to mine. Feeling sorry for myself also became an excuse for accepting failure. Like my mother, I blamed everything and anything. Nobody felt the pain I felt. Nobody else suffered but me. That way of thinking became imbedded in my mind and became my way of life for a long time.

On Artesian Street, which is located one block west of Western Avenue, another gang was being formed. They called themselves the Spanish Cobras. Their graffiti began appearing all over the place. My old friend Julio from Von Humboldt School was one of their members. I tried to talk to him on several occasions but he ignored me. Bad blood was brewing between the Lords and the Cobras, and I didn't even know it. I was still ignorant about gang life. I still thought of gangs as a sure way to get girls and party, but nothing more.

School was about two weeks away and the Spanish Lords and the Spanish Cobras were having some kind of dispute. Papo explained that the Cobras were hanging out in the Lords' 'hood and had begun disrespecting them. That weekend while we were playing baseball we watched the Spanish Lords group up and walk toward Artesian. They carried cans of paint and paint rollers. They painted over the name *Spanish Cobras* everywhere they saw it. That night I could hear gunshots coming from the direction of Artesian and Hirsch Streets, about a block away. I heard police sirens, ambulances, and fire trucks zoom by the house, traveling up Western. The next day there was talk about what had happened the night before all over the neighborhood. Even the older people were talking about the incident between the Lords and the Cobras. Apparently the Lords had demanded that members of the Cobras become Lords or move out the neighborhood, or else they would go to war. The Cobras chose war. A shoot-out broke out between the Lords and the Cobras. The Cobras stayed in a building on the northwest corner of Artesian and Hirsch. The Lords shot the building up from outside while the Cobras returned fire from inside. Ultimately, the Lords threw cocktail firebombs through the windows of the building and shot at people as they came running out to escape the fire. Only the arrival of the police and fire departments kept the incident from becoming a massacre. The Cobras disappeared after that night; they would not be heard of again until the following summer. However, bad blood remained between the youths that lived west of Western and those who lived east of it. It was the first sign I witnessed of divisions within the Puerto Rican community.

This incident with the Spanish Lords and the Spanish Cobras was my first experience with gang violence. I didn't understand it and therefore classified it as a confrontation between enemies and not a part of everyday gang activity. I still had the desire to join a gang because of the females. However, my experiences with the Spanish Lords gave me a strong feeling of belonging, respect, and love. These were feelings I didn't receive or expect anymore at home. I began to see that gang membership had its advantages. I was prepared to accept whatever gang life had to offer.

On Artesian there was a sports team called La Familia; we all knew each other. Since we lived so close to one another and played against each other so often, they were our archrivals; but it was all in fun. That year on Halloween we kept the tradition of having an egg fight with La Familia. There were some Lords helping us out and La Familia members were getting help from the Disciples. The Lords and Disciples were not fighting each other. They were not allies in any way, but they did have a peace treaty between them. After we got through bombing each other with eggs, we all gathered at the Clemente School field and decided to go bomb the Gaylords and the Vicelords. The Gaylords were a white gang whose motto was "The only good Puerto Rican is a dead Puerto Rican." All the Latino gangs fought the Gaylords. They were known to have killed their share of Puerto Ricans in their time and wouldn't think twice about killing another. The Vicelords were a black gang; the Latino gangs all fought them too. I didn't know much about the Vicelords—only that they were bigger on the South Side of the city and that the ones on the North Side were supposedly a bunch of cowards. At least a hundred of us gathered at the Clemente School field. We broke up into two groups—one headed toward the Gaylords, the other toward the Vicelords. I went with the group that was going toward the Gaylords. Flaco, Papo, and I walked together. We had no idea where we were going; we just followed the older guys ahead of us. The Gaylords hung out on Campbell and Moffat Streets about six blocks from North Avenue. The bombing party was over quickly; only the first ones to arrive at Moffatt and Campbell actually got to throw eggs at the Gaylords. By the time the rest of us got there, the Gaylords were gone. We had to hurry out of their 'hood before they came out shooting. Those of us who didn't get to bomb the Gaylords threw our eggs at windows of homes in their 'hood. Who cared if the homes that were vandalized didn't house any members of the Gaylords? These homes were in the Gaylords' 'hood—that was all that mattered.

When we got back from our egg-bombing game everybody split to their respective 'hoods. Papo, Flaco, and I began getting some money together to get a bag of weed. We were walking toward Tuley down Potomac Street when we heard about seven gunshots and a lot of screaming. The Spanish Lords had shot one of the guys from La Familia. They mistook him for a Cobra. The guy was not in a gang. He was a friend of our family. The Lords had started to identify any young Latino that lived west of Western as a Spanish Cobra. That included all the members of La Familia. Even with that knowledge I couldn't understand why the Lords would do this. They all knew him. They knew that he and his friends were not gang members. Papo knew the guy who had been shot and felt really bad about the whole incident. He told me that he was planning to quit the Lords. Most of the guys in La Familia accused the Western Boys of knowing what was going to happen that night. After that incident, everything in the neighborhood changed. The sports competitions between the Western Boys and La Familia ceased. The members of La Familia were rarely seen on Western anymore, and then only on their way to or from visiting someone.

There was tension between the Spanish Lords and the Latin Disciples. The Lords usually hung out by Tuley School, but they were making themselves more visible on Western and Potomac. That was the last year that the Halloween egg fight took place. Puerto Rican youths were dividing into rival factions.

I was in eighth grade and ready to graduate. Three of the Western Boys and Papo were in my graduating class. We were looking forward to attending Clemente High School. Most of all we were ready to party on graduation night. On graduation eve Papo, Flaco, and I went party hopping. We must have gone to about six or seven different parties. I got so drunk that I somehow got separated from the guys without realizing it. I wobbled back to the neighborhood and was told by the Lords that my mom had come around looking for me. I wobbled home. Pedro was at the horse track with his friends that night, so I didn't have to worry about him taking advantage of my drunkenness. That night my mom beat the shit out of me, or so my sister told me. I don't remember a thing. Supposedly my mother slapped me about twenty times and broke a broomstick over my back. All along I just looked at her and said, "*Matame, matame, es lo que quieres, matame*" ("Kill me, kill me, that's what you want, kill me"). I only wish I had some memory of that night. It would have been the only memory I'd have of not running under the bed when my mother beat me. On the other hand, there were rumors that I made a fool out of myself at several parties. I'm glad I have no memory of them.

With eighth grade graduation out of the way and high school in the near future, I was ready for the summer. The summer started out with a bang. Every year in June, Puerto Ricans celebrated their independence from Spain with a parade. The parade began in downtown Chicago and ended in Humboldt Park. However, that year tragedy struck the celebration. Somehow a couple of Puerto Rican men got into a confrontation with the police. Some say that a police officer was seen in Humboldt Park burning a Puerto Rican flag. Others say the problem stemmed from two Puerto Ricans who were members of a revolutionary group called the Armed Forces of National Liberation (commonly referred to as the FALN). The FALN wanted Puerto Rico to be an independent country, not a commonwealth of the United States. The real reason the confrontation started remains unclear, but it ended with police officers shooting and killing the two Puerto Ricans. As the news of the incident spread, the independence celebrators became hostile. The result was a riot that lasted a week. Puerto Ricans began fighting with police on California and Division Avenues, a corner of Humboldt Park. They overturned and burned police cars. They destroyed and looted businesses all down Division. Only the mobilization of the Illinois National Guard put an end to the rioting. From then on there was this fear of the police in the community coupled with a desire to create confrontations with them. The police were the enemy. I just hoped the damn incident didn't delay school from starting so I could get out of the house and away from Pedro.

That riot was the first incident of Puerto Rican self-destruction I witnessed, although I didn't recognize it as such at the time. I was very ignorant and indifferent about the whole situation. I watched on television as people went on a path of destruction in the name of all Puerto Ricans. Maybe I was too young to acknowledge or receive whatever message the riot was supposed to be sending. What did destroying our own neighborhood prove? I just didn't get it.

PEDRO AND MY mom put the idea of moving back to Puerto Rico into action once again. My mom had two kids with him now, a boy and a girl. All four of them went to Puerto Rico for a week so my mom could check out the house Pedro had built over there.

While they were gone, Pedro's son Hector looked after us. He occupied the third-floor apartment above us with his girlfriend Missy. All of his junkie friends were at his place all the time. He had total control over these people, and he knew it. Hector would order a pizza and have a couple of junkies steal the other food from the car while the delivery person came up to the apartment. He once called the police and reported a robbery in a rear third-floor apartment of the building across the street from us. He then had a junkie slash their tires while they were gone. The junkies did just about anything to keep Hector happy.

During the time my mom and Pedro were in Puerto Rico, it seemed like we lived alone. Only the fear of my mother's friends telling on us kept us from staying out all night. I found a way to stay out by climbing out the window at night. Between the building where we lived and the one next to it there was a two- or three-foot gap on the side where my bedroom was. I would put one foot on one building and one on the other, then ease my way down. The grip of the rubber on my gym shoes kept me from slipping and my hands kept me balanced. I got back up the same way. It was quite an acrobatic feat to get in and out, but I mastered it. Once I escaped I'd go by Tuley and hang out with the Lords.

I'd get information about what was going on in the gang community by listening to the Lords. There was conversation about the Spanish Cobras being back. They were now hanging out on Division and Maplewood Avenue, close to the Latin Disciples. The Cobras had not forgotten their little disagreement with the Lords and they wanted revenge. They began vandalizing up and down Western and at Clemente. They had added the word *insane* to their name; they were now called the Insane Spanish Cobras. They wrote *Spanish Lord killers* next to their name. They were definitely making their presence and their hostility toward the Spanish Lords known. The Spanish Lords began vandalizing in retaliation, writing anti-Cobra graffiti, and began mobilizing against them. Papo told me that the Lords had gone into Cobra territory on several occasions and shot at their members. He didn't say whether anybody had been killed or wounded; he just bragged about how the Lords were handling the Cobras. Little did he know that the worst was yet to come.

On a hot Saturday night, I sneaked out at about 10:30 P.M. and met Papo, who had also sneaked out. We tried to get Flaco to do the same but he could only get out through his third-floor bedroom window, so he stayed behind. Papo and I met up with one of the Lords who I had never met before. He introduced himself as Afro. He was tall and stocky with a giant afro. He had just gotten out of juvenile detention. Afro was Rican's little brother. He was the same age as Papo but much bigger. He already had a mustache and beard—facial hair we only dreamed of having. There was a liquor store on the corner of Western and Hirsch. Afro knew the owner and could buy liquor there even though he was underage. We walked to the back porch of a house located on the east side of Western. Snake, Sexpot, Afro's girlfriend Lisa, and her sister Jenny waited for us there. Lisa and Jenny didn't live around the neighborhood. They had snuck out of their house so that Lisa could see Afro. Lisa and Jenny's uncle owned the building where we met. It was being remodeled so it was empty and they had keys to get in.

We pitched in money to get some Old Style beer and Richards wine so we could go up on the roof and get high. Snake had already announced that he had an ounce of weed. We gathered about sixteen dollars and gave it to Afro. Afro walked out the back door that led to the alley and headed for the liquor store. A few seconds later we heard someone shout "Lord love" and then there were gunshots. We freaked out. Snake told us that Afro was probably shooting off the pistol he was carrying. "That brother is crazy," Snake said. "He just got out and is already acting a fool." Snake went out into the alley and let out a scream of horror. "Oh, no! Shit, no! Afro! No! No! No!" We ran out into the alley and saw a body lying at the end of it. It was Afro. He was shot three or four times in the head and face from point-blank range. Snake kneeled next to him and cradled his head, crying, "Don't die, my brother! Please don't die." He reached into the front of Afro's pants and pulled out a gun. He gave it to Papo and told him to get rid of it. I was in shock. I couldn't believe what was happening. Lisa and Jenny were crying and screaming hysterically and now so was Snake. Tears were rolling down my face but it was caused more by fear than anything else.

Papo pulled me with him as he took off with the gun. He told me to go home before the police came. We ran down the alley and into a gangway. I noticed the anger on Papo's face. He kept looking up to the sky and saying, "Don't worry, my brother, revenge is a bitch." When we got out on Western I noticed some of Pedro's friends standing in front of the bar next door to where I lived. I told Papo that there was no way I could go home at that moment. Papo went home; I turned around and hoped I could get back into Lisa and Jenny's uncle's place without being noticed. When I went in I found Lisa and Jenny there.

They told me that Rican had come by and told them to get lost so that the police wouldn't find out they were there. I sat there quietly for about five or ten minutes until I saw the flashing lights of police cars. I went up on the roof to take a look at what was happening.

The police had taken their sweet time, but now it seemed like every cop in the city had arrived on the scene. They were asking questions and looking around the surrounding area. A couple of detectives had Rican against a car and kept asking him who did it. Rican kept saying he didn't know, but the cops persisted. Rican screamed, "That's my little brother, let me be with him," but to no avail. The detectives handcuffed him, put him in their car, and drove away.

Afro was pronounced dead on the spot. The ambulance never got there; it wasn't needed. They covered the body, picked him up, and threw him in the back of a paddy wagon like a sack of potatoes. I didn't understand why the police treated Afro's body with such disrespect. And why did they take Rican away instead of letting him be with his dead brother? The reasons for the hate and fear that Puerto Rican youth had for the police were becoming more apparent to me.

Jenny came up on the roof to join me. Lisa was too hysterical to come up. She just sat on the stairs crying and asking us to please leave her alone. Jenny and I watched police cars go up and down the streets in every direction as we talked about Afro's death. Jenny told me she would be attending Clemente High School that year. I expressed the hope of seeing her there. The cops cooled off their search and I decided to try to get home before the sun came up. I climbed up into my room and got into bed. After all that had happened that night, the only thing I could think of was seeing Jenny again. Afro's death did not once cross my mind as I lay there. Was I turning into an insensitive animal? Or was it that since I didn't know Afro I didn't care? Anyway, I thought, let him rest in peace.

THE SUMMER WENT by mighty quick. The Spanish Lords did not do much about avenging Afro's death. But we knew that sooner or later it would happen. School was on again. I was looking forward to going to Clemente and meeting Jenny there. High school was all I thought it would be—there were gorgeous girls all over the place. There were a lot of guys from the neighborhood who had been there for a couple of years, so I felt right at home. It seemed like the don't-hang-with-the-freshmen rule didn't apply to me. In my homeroom class there was a member of the Unknowns named Speedy; he was supposed to be a sophomore but he didn't pass, so they had him in a freshman homeroom. Papo was also in school; so was Flaco, only he was hanging around with his friends from Von Humboldt who were in Clemente now. Flaco also stopped coming by my house. He told me that he didn't want to be mistaken for a Lord. I didn't understand what he meant by that, but didn't pursue any other explanation, either. We rarely saw him any more; we didn't miss him. I saw my old friend Jorge at Clemente but he ignored me as if he had never known me. To hell with him, I thought, I had new friends now anyway. But I did wonder why he acted like that and if Julio and Noel were there also. Speedy showed Papo and I the ropes and made sure that we were invited to all the parties.

Jenny and I began seeing a lot of each other. She was an intelligent girl with a beautiful personality and she also had some kind of body on her. Jenny looked much more mature than I did, and she had a lot of older guys asking her out on dates. I worried about that but made it a point not to let my feelings show. Speedy kept telling me to forget about Jenny, saying that she was a freshman and he could set me up with some sophomores and juniors who would do anything once they got high. I was interested in Speedy's offer but had no intention of forgetting about Jenny.

Jenny lived on Lyndale Street, which was north of the school and a pretty long walk. That gave us the opportunity to talk and get to know each other a whole lot better. It also gave us plenty of time to stop somewhere and express our feelings for each other. Jenny was pretty filled out for her age. She was the first girl I kissed whose breast I felt pressed up against me. Actually, she was the first girl I kissed. On the way to her house we had to walk through the Gaylords' 'hood. It was broad daylight and there were a lot of kids walking that way so it was fairly safe. On my way back I would take the bus to make sure I didn't run into any trouble. Jenny's older brother belonged to a gang called the Latin Kings, which was the biggest Latino gang in the city. They called him Lil Man. He had a reputation as a tough guy, and he acted that way. Lil Man was about my height but he was older and more muscular. He walked with a jump in his step that was known as pimping. Lil Man had a tattoo on his left arm of a crown with a ribbon on the top on which was written *Almighty*, and one on the bottom that read *Nation*. The letter *L* was on the right side of the crown and a *K* was on the left, written in old English-style lettering. It was honestly the best-looking tattoo I had ever seen. The first time Lil Man saw me with Jenny he was more worried about what gang I belonged to than about what I was doing with his sister. I told him that I wasn't in a gang but he refused to believe me. Jenny told him that I lived by the Lords but that I wasn't a member. He seemed satisfied then but he warned me that if I ever hurt his sister he would kill me. For some reason I didn't doubt him at all.

This was how all Latino youths seemed to classify each other—gang member first, human being second. Ironically, Latinos complain that police treat all youths as gang members first and human beings second.

7

My Teacher Maria

ONE NIGHT I went to the Unknowns' 'hood on Leavitt and Schiller Streets, just a couple of blocks from the Lords' 'hood. I was going to take Speedy up on his invitation to set me up with older high school girls. The Unknowns were a pretty big gang. There were always at least ten or fifteen guys on each corner. They had a mural on a wall that took up the whole side of a building. The mural consisted of two reapers holding shotguns standing on opposite sides of a shield that had the letters *U K* written in the center. The word *Insane* was written in a ribbon above the shield.

I found Speedy smoking a joint in front of the building where the mural was painted. I asked him about the wild girls he was talking about. He told me that if I had money for some weed we could get laid that very afternoon. We picked up Papo to see if he had any cash. Papo was as broke as we were. We went walking, trying to find someone who did have money to join us. We walked by Tuley and ran into Rican and Snake. Rican had become very friendly with me and stopped to talk to me. He asked me about the night his brother got killed. I told him that I didn't see what happened, that I just heard the gunshots. Tears flowed out of his eyes as I spoke to him. He swore that the Cobras would not get away with killing his brother. I didn't doubt him for a minute.

I knew that Rican sold bags of weed so I asked him for one. He gave me two and told me that whenever I wanted some all I had to do was ask. I thanked him and left with Papo and Speedy. As we walked, the guys explained that Rican's very friendly treatment was his way of recruiting me for the Lords. It didn't matter to me as long as I was getting free weed. Besides, I intended to join the Lords.

Speedy took us to a house located across the street from Wicker Park. Wicker Park is located on Damen Avenue between Division and North Avenues. He said that four women lived in the third-floor apartment. Three of them were teenagers and the other was one of their mothers. Speedy said they were so easy that their apartment was known as the fuck house.

The mother and daughter were named Maria and Lucy, respectively. Maria was one wild woman. She was about thirty-five years old but dressed, acted, and looked like she was in her early twenties. Her son had been killed in a car accident and her husband, a Latin King, was in jail serving forty years for murder. Lucy was seventeen years old, with short, kinky hair and brown eyes. She was a little flat-chested, but she made up for it with the rest of her body. Speedy called her Miss Ass for obvious reasons. The other two girls were runaways. Their names were Yolanda and Myra. Yolanda was a chubby, sixteen-year-old girl with shoulder-length dirty blonde hair and brown eyes. Yolanda wore tons of makeup and skimpy, revealing clothing. Every other word that girl said was a curse word. Myra was also sixteen, with short black hair and brown eyes. She was a very beautiful girl with a body you would kill for, but according to Speedy you didn't have to. All you had to do was get her high and she was yours. Myra went out of her way to be sexy. She exaggerated her walk and spoke with a low, almost moaning type of voice. I found Myra's ways very attractive and couldn't help staring at her. She was the one I wanted to be with but I didn't know how to approach her. I decided to sit and wait for things to happen; then I would make my move.

We rolled up the weed and split the joints evenly among Papo, Speedy, and myself so that we wouldn't have to bother each other once we got the girls alone. Papo and Myra quickly got into a conversation and went into another room after he whispered something in her ear. Lucy excused herself, saying she was going to the bar on the corner to see if her mother Maria was still there. Speedy sat next to Yolanda and they started whispering and giggling. I thought that they were talking about me because every time something was said Yolanda would look my way and giggle. After a few minutes of giggling they got up and proceeded to a room in the back of the apartment. Speedy came back and told me not to waste any time when Lucy came back. "After one joint, you will never forget why they call her juicy Lucy," Speedy told me.

It was bad enough that I was already nervous; now I was scared. I had never had sex before. I was a virgin and I just knew that after tonight I would be the joke of the neighborhood. These girls were very sexually experienced. It wasn't likely that Lucy would keep my virginity a secret. But I decided the hell with it. As long as I got laid for the first time in my life, everything would be cool.

It seemed as if Lucy had gotten lost on her way to the corner. She was taking a long time to return. There I was, sitting in the dark, anticipating my first sexual experience, fantasizing about what would happen when I heard her voice. My heart nearly jumped out my mouth and my body began to tremble. As I listened closely, I realized that her voice was coming from outside. I looked out the window and saw Lucy inside of a car kissing and letting herself be touched by a man who was twice her age. He started the car and they drove away.

I was very disappointed. I listened through the door of the room where Papo and Myra were and heard giggling, laughter, and moaning. I felt depressed and envious. I sat in the darkest corner I could find and lit up a joint, hoping I could get the image of Lucy and me having sex out of my mind. The reason Speedy and Papo got lucky and I didn't had to be because they were in a gang. I began to regret coming with them but at the same time I couldn't wait to return another day, regardless of the outcome. I sat and entered my imaginary world, fantasizing about things and rubbing my crotch. As I prepared to light up my second joint I heard the door open and shut.

The first thing that came to my mind was "All right, juicy Lucy is back." Then I became nervous. After some debating I found the courage to go into the kitchen and make my move on Lucy. I found her mother Maria there instead. Maria was bending over, looking in the refrigerator. She had a really short, tight skirt on. I couldn't help but stand there and stare. She was muttering something about not having any beer. She turned around and saw me staring at her and said, "Who the fuck are you? I never seen you here before. Did you get a kick out of looking at my ass?" I didn't answer. I panicked. She walked over to where I was and took the joint from my hand. She walked to the table, pulled a lighter out of her purse, and lit the joint up. Maria opened the back door that led into a closed-in porch and said, "Come on if you wanna smoke." I stood there motionless. "Don't be scared, I don't bite," Maria said as she motioned me over to where she was.

Maria took me into a porch area that had been converted into a room. There was a small table, two chairs, and an old couch there. I was so scared my body trembled and I couldn't talk. Maria told me to sit down and relax while she laughed at my nervousness. Maria puffed on the joint, then asked me if I wanted a "shotgun." (A shotgun is when you put the lit part of the joint into your mouth and blow out so that a lot of smoke comes out the other end where someone else inhales it.) I thought why the hell is she offering me a shotgun. I didn't know what she was talking about, so I didn't answer. Maria put the joint in her mouth and kneeled in front of me, inches from my face. She blew so much smoke in my mouth that it made me choke. My eyes became blurry with tears. I could hear Maria laughing, telling me to hold the smoke in.

After the effects wore off, Maria asked me to give her a shotgun so that I could learn what to do with all the smoke. Maria sat down on the couch and I stood in front of her. I carefully put the lit part of the joint in my mouth, closed my lips around it, bent over close to Maria's face, and blew. She inhaled the smoke like a vacuum. Then she stuck out her tongue and licked my bottom lip. I jumped back, fell, and burned my tongue on the joint. I sat there gagging while Maria laughed at me hysterically. When she stopped laughing she said, "What's wrong? Just learning, huh?" "*De donde eres, nunca te a via visto*" ("Where are you from, I've never seen you before"). I got up off the floor and sat on the chair directly across from her. I stared at her, scared, wanting to get up and run but too nervous to do so. Maria sensed my nervousness and began teasing me. "Good-looking guy like you with hazel eyes, are you Puerto Rican or gringo?"

Her skirt was hoisted almost up to her waist and I could see her panties. I couldn't stop myself from trying to see more. She was very aware of what I was thinking and kept opening her legs slightly and then crossing them. I re-lit the joint and tried to act cool but she saw right through it. "You must be gringo," Maria said, "*a Boricua ya me habia comido*" ("a Puerto Rican would have already eaten me").

Maria got up, locked the door, sat next to me, and began asking me questions I had no answer for. I just nodded to everything. She asked me if I found her attractive. Did I think she was sexy? The truth was that Maria was better looking than her daughter Lucy but she had a strong odor of alcohol and cigarettes that was making me sick. I nodded my approval of her looks as I felt her hand rubbing my leg. She rested her hand on my groin and began squeezing. Then she stopped. I was so nervous I couldn't move. She looked at me and said, "You're a virgin. I love virgins. I'm going to teach you everything you need to know about pleasing a woman." Maria stood up and undressed herself slowly while explaining how I should go about undressing a woman. I forgot all about how bad she smelled. I stared at her naked body with no clue as to what I should do.

Maria made all the moves for both of us. Never once did she open her eyes and look at me until we were finished. That night I became a man, or so I thought. Maria taught me all about sex. She showed me the pleasures of oral sex. Maria held my head down on her as she instructed my every move. "Women will fall in love with you if you do it to them right," Maria explained. I asked her if she was in love with me. She giggled and said, "No, but with more practice anything could happen. Don't be so shy, or you'll miss out on a lot of things," she advised. When it was all over she kissed me deeply, then began getting dressed.

I was only thirteen. I was too young to understand that what Maria did was wrong. At the time I thought sex with an older woman was the stuff of dreams. Now I know that's bullshit. Yes, I learned about sexual feelings that night, but nothing else—no emotions or thoughts were shared. It was sex and nothing more.

In every neighborhood I ever hung out in, there was a home like Maria's—adult women having sex with young men, or, in my case, boys.

There were always homes where runaway kids could be found, places where they were welcomed, where there were no rules. Every neighborhood had fuck houses where kids could hide from the truth.

Papo, Speedy, Myra, and Yolanda were in the living room smoking weed. Myra yelled, "How was he, Lucy?" Maria answered, "He was great. And you better stay away from him, he's mine," as she left the house giggling. Everybody looked at me like I was crazy. Nobody said a word. They just stared at me with a look of disbelief on their faces. It was getting pretty late so we left.

On the way back to the 'hood all we talked about was Maria. I felt like some kind of stud, especially after the things I had learned from Maria. The guys wanted me to tell them what happened. Maria had told me that women love men who didn't kiss and tell so I told them that we just got high. Back in the 'hood Papo told all the guys about Maria and me. "Ol' boy fucked Maria," Papo said. I was just hoping that Jenny didn't find out. In fact, I couldn't wait to try the techniques Maria had taught me on Jenny. I had always had sexual thoughts about Jenny. These suddenly became graphic. I would picture her in my mind as my sex student. I imagined what her naked body would look like and how she would react to my sexual advances. After that episode with Maria, graphic thoughts of sex occupied my mind on an almost constant basis. Every attractive woman that passed before my eyes, whether in real life, on television, or in a magazine, became a subject of my graphic sexual fantasies. If I found a woman attractive I fantasized about her.

Maria was thirty-five; I was thirteen. She led; I followed. Yet in the eyes of the guys in the 'hood I was a stud. Maria prepared me for sexual encounters with females but she did nothing to prepare me for the emotional beauty sex involves. In the long run, Maria's lesson hurt my subsequent relationships with women more than it helped.

I went home, climbed up between the two buildings, and went into my room through the window. Once in my room I listened quietly for activity in the house. I didn't hear Pedro or my mother. I came out of my room to find my sisters watching television. My mom and Pedro were out. My older sister told me that my mom and Pedro were talking about moving to Puerto Rico again. Pedro had already bought the plane tickets for the trip. He was going to the Island first to prepare what was to be our home. We would follow shortly.

As soon as my sister told me the news, I began making plans to make sure that I would miss that plane. A couple of days later my mom went to our schools and got our transfer records. Now I knew that she was serious. I went over a thousand plans in my mind for how I could stay here in the United States. All of them were interrupted by sexual thoughts of Jenny. It was obvious that I would be going to Puerto Rico whether I liked it or not. I made up my mind to have sex with Jenny before I left—nothing else was important.

The day before we were to leave I walked Jenny home for what I thought would be the last time. I told her about my inevitable move to Puerto Rico. She expressed disappointment and said she didn't want me to go. We made our usual detour so that we could be alone. This was the first time I had been alone with Jenny since that night with Maria. Jenny's reaction to my sexual advances shocked me. She responded to my blowing in her ears and kissing her face and neck with loud moans and heavy breathing. That studly feeling came over me again—the things Maria taught me actually worked! I was surprised that I was able to touch her breast and groin area without her getting mad as she usually did. I opened her blouse but couldn't find the clip on the back of her bra. Jenny took my hands and showed me where the clip was in the front. I became somewhat nervous, but not enough to make me stop what I had started. I tried to pull down her pants but she put a stop to that. I got upset and bit her nipple.

At that point the only thing on my mind was sex. Jenny's feelings were not important to me. Jenny noticed my anger and apologized. She didn't have any reason to but she did anyway. I went on trying to get her to have sex with me but she kept saying no. She reminded me that I would be leaving Chicago. She said if I wasn't leaving she might go all the way. I told Jenny that I was not going to Puerto Rico, while still wrestling with her pants. She didn't believe me but promised that if I didn't go she would give herself to me. From that moment I didn't care what happened, I was not going to Puerto Rico. We fixed our clothes and continued our walk toward Jenny's house. We held hands but did not say a word to each other. I don't know what was going through her mind, but all I was thinking about was where I would stay if I didn't go to Puerto Rico. At Jenny's we didn't talk like we usually did before saying good-bye. We kissed and then she went inside her house and I went to the bus stop. Not a word was said.

I went back to the neighborhood and ran into Rican. He invited me to smoke weed at the Lords' clubhouse. He asked me if the rumor going around about Maria and me was true. When I told him it was, he busted out laughing. He said that Maria had robbed the cradle and referred to her as a child molester. I assured him that it was all right as long as I was the child she was molesting. "You're a kid," Rican said, "Maria is an old woman. She shouldn't be doing things like that with you." "Yeah, she's a fine old woman," was my response. I told him what happened that night in detail. He just sat there with a freaky look on his face and shaking his head in disbelief. "What a bitch," Rican said as he handed me a joint.

Rican sat there silently for a moment, then asked if I wanted to become a Lord. I said I didn't know. He reminded me that the Lords considered me one of the boys. I told Rican about my family getting ready to move to Puerto Rico and that I didn't want to go. He was surprised by the news and began to tell me stories about Puerto Rico. He then expressed his disappointment that I wouldn't be joining the Spanish Lords. I told Rican that I felt like I was walking into a cage where Pedro could beat my ass any time he wanted to. Rican said he understood; he also had an abusive father. He told me that if I decided to stay I could sleep in the Lords' clubhouse if I wanted to.

Rican's words coupled with my desire for Jenny made me decide to stay. I just had to figure out how to get away from my mom. We were to leave for the airport at 6:00 A.M. the following morning. I went home that night and unpacked the things that I wanted to keep, basically some clothes and my school transfers. I went to sleep and woke up at about 5:00 A.M. My mom was already up and looking forward to the trip. She went in the bathroom and turned on the shower. I took the opportunity to leave the house. I grabbed my clothes and headed out the door as quickly and as quietly as I could. But I found I just couldn't do it. I was too scared—the thought of being on my own at thirteen with no home and no food terrified me. I would just have to put up with Pedro. Puerto Rico, here I come!

8

No Paradise

PUERTO RICO WAS just like I remembered it: green with a bright blue sky and so beautiful. We lived on a hilltop village outside the city of Caguas. There were very few people in the village and most of them were related to Pedro. Still, I was somewhat mesmerized by the sugarcane fields, mango trees, and banana plants that bordered the road up to the house. The house was a modern structure made of cement with inside plumbing. I had expected to be living in a wooden shack with an outhouse for a toilet. Thank God for modern changes.

From the moment we stepped in the house Pedro began to assert his authority over my sisters and me. He threatened to kill me if I got out of line, while my mother ignored his words as all talk. Pedro had bought a machete that he carried at all times and he often threatened me with it. I cut a baseball-bat-sized piece of guava tree for protection and carried it with me at all times. Not one day went by without a confrontation between Pedro and me.

Pedro had told as many people as possible that I was a criminal and a drug user. That made it hard for me to make friends. The few people who did talk to me usually asked if Pedro's accusations were true. I became a loner. I would walk on the land behind the house and lose myself in my own little world. I spent my days climbing orange and mango trees talking to myself and wishing I were dead. In my conversations with myself I conjured up a group of friends and romantic interludes. I had many imaginary torrid sexual affairs, which I made real by masturbating. It was only in my own, nonexistent world that I found any kind of happiness.

My sisters, on the other hand, got along just fine. They made friends who would pick them up and take them places. They always ignored me. I began to think that maybe something was wrong with me that had nothing to do with Pedro. Nevertheless, I began to adore sitting high up alone in the trees, eating fruit and fantasizing about Jenny, Maria, and Chicago.

After six months of loneliness and hell my mother decided to send me back to Chicago to live with Pedro's son Hector. She grew tired of breaking up fights between Pedro and me, and said I was the cause of all her troubles. She said she didn't know what else to do with me so she sent me away. I should have been hurt that she felt that way but instead I was elated. I only wished she had gotten tired of me much sooner.

My mother's decision to rid herself of me did not surprise me. I was just surprised that she didn't beat me all the way to the airport like she said she was going to. I never bothered to ask her why she treated me with so much hatred. I'm sure she must have had some logical explanation for her actions; after all, she was my mother. "*Un hijo de la gran puta*" ("a son of a bitch") was what she called me. I wonder if she ever stopped to think about those words. Maybe she was right.

9

No Home

I ARRIVED IN Chicago near the end of February. A couple of Hector's junkies picked me up at the airport. It was cold and I only had on a sweater. The junkies stopped by a K-mart on the way home and one of them went in and stole a coat for me. For the remainder of the drive they discussed how much dope they could get from Hector for stealing the coat.

Living with Hector was like living alone. Actually, it was worse. There were junkies in and out of his house at all times of the day and night. Every three to four months there was a drug bust. I watched people shooting up heroin and even helped some of them do it. I became an expert in preparing and shooting heroin into junkies' veins. I would volunteer to do it for them in return for marijuana or money.

There was a nineteen-year-old girl who shot up between her toes. It was easier if I did it for her. Her name was Gina. Gina was a very attractive girl—she didn't look at all like a junkie. She was always clean and nicely dressed. Gina smelled good, unlike the rest of the junkies, who smelled like cigarettes and liquor. Gina was a prostitute. Judging by the cars that dropped her off at Hector's I would say she was a high-priced prostitute. She would often perform oral sex on me in return for the favor of shooting her up. All this went on in my bedroom at Hector's house. Hector thought it was cool that I used the junkies to make money and used Gina for sex. It was all part of being a man, being hip. Only the help of God and my fear of needles kept me from becoming a junkie.

I was out in the streets at all times of the night. Sometimes I wouldn't come home for two or three days, and no questions were ever asked. I became a regular at the Lords' clubhouse and at Maria's house. I rarely slept any more and when I did it was either at Maria's or at the clubhouse. I wanted to have sex with Maria again but she refused. In fact, I was so occupied trying to lay Maria again that I had forgotten all about Jenny.

Time and time again Rican invited me to become a Lord, but I was always too high to answer. I became a pothead. I smoked pot just about every hour of the day and night. Rican was being pretty cool with me. I knew Rican was only treating me in this manner so that I would join the Lords.

One day he took me to his house where his girlfriend fed me and told me I could take a shower if I wanted to. Rican's girlfriend was Marilyn, a very pretty, petite girl. She had two kids with Rican. Marilyn looked out of place as the girlfriend of a gang leader. She just seemed too pure and intelligent for that. Marilyn went into the back room, brought out a plastic bag full of clothes, and told me to go through them and take what I wanted. The clothes had belonged to Afro. I refused to take any but Rican assured me that it was all right. I would be disrespecting him if I didn't accept them, he said.

I showered, changed clothes, and sat down for dinner with Rican and Marilyn. All through dinner I studied Marilyn and the way she walked and moved with such finesse and sophistication. Marilyn spoke so clearly and was very articulate—like a teacher. She didn't use slang or curse words in her speech like Rican did. Marilyn expressed herself with pride. I couldn't help but wonder what circumstances had led her to end up with Rican.

After dinner Rican and I went into the living room to smoke weed. Marilyn took the kids in the back bedroom and locked the door. Rican talked about the advantages of being a Lord. He showed me a Lord sweater and promised to buy me one if I became a Lord. His recruiting tactics were good; however, I listened to very little of what he said. Mostly I sat there fantasizing about having sex with Marilyn while still nodding in agreement with everything he said. Marilyn came out of the room to tell Rican to stop smoking so the kids could watch television. I found myself staring at her with desire but snapped out of my dreams before I was caught by Rican. I knew I couldn't have Marilyn, but I was excited by my fantasies. In an instant Jenny's last words echoed in my mind. "If you don't leave Chicago, I'll give myself to you." I immediately excused myself and headed toward Jenny's house.

10

Jenny

I SNEAKED ON the bus at Western Avenue and Hirsch Street and sat way in the back. I thought about Jenny in purely sexual terms. I wasn't worried about what I would say to her or how she was going to react when she saw me. I only thought about what I was going to do to her once I got her naked. My intentions were only to get sex.

When I got to Jenny's house her brother Lil Man and her sister Lisa were outside smoking a joint. Lisa was surprised to see me back from Puerto Rico so soon. She welcomed me with a hug and a kiss. Lil Man yelled for Jenny to come down, that her boyfriend "the Lord" had arrived. I corrected him by telling him that I wasn't a Lord. At that point some friends of his who also belonged to the Latin Kings arrived in a van. They said something about the Gaylords needing to be taught a lesson. Lil Man opened the side door of the van and pulled me inside with him. Before I had a chance to jump out, the van was speeding up Western, headed towards the Gaylords' 'hood.

The guys in the van asked Lil Man about me. He told them that I was his sister's boyfriend and that he wanted to find out what I was about. He looked at me and said that he didn't want his sister going out with a punk. The guys told Lil Man that a carload of Gaylords had gone into Humboldt Park, beat up an older man, and tore the top half of his wife's clothes off. They did it simply because the couple was Puerto Rican. I got angry just hearing about this. In my mind I thanked God that my mother and sisters were in Puerto Rico.

The Gaylords hung out on the corner of Moffat and Campbell Streets. They also had a faction on Palmer Boulevard. We were headed into that area. I had never been there before and had no idea where it was located. When we got there, the Gaylords were all over the place. The Kings had decided to get anyone they could; they didn't care who got hit as long as they were white. I looked out of a small window on the backside of the van and saw a wooden fence that was painted black. It had a Nazi cross with a swastika in the middle, an American flag on one side, and a Confederate flag on the other. Above the cross was a ribbon with the word *Palmer* written inside it. Below the cross was another ribbon with *Gaylords* written inside it. But what really caught my attention was the big bold writing, in red paint, that said *THE ONLY GOOD PUERTO RICAN IS A DEAD PUERTO RICAN.* I wondered what the Puerto Ricans had done to the Gaylords that warranted such hatred. I was angry and my adrenaline rose to the point that I was telling the driver to stop the van so we could get a Gaylord. I thought that the Kings were going to jump out of the van, grab a couple of the Gaylords, and beat the shit out of them. I grabbed a baseball bat that was laying on the floor of the van. I wanted to make sure that I hurt one of the assholes who thought that I was only good dead. Lil Man turned to me and told me that the bat was not going to be enough. He reached under a blanket, pulled out a shotgun, and told me to stay out of sight and to be ready for anything.

I couldn't believe what was about to happen—these guys were actually going to kill someone. Lil Man instructed the driver to pull up by the crowd that was on the corner and told the other guy to be ready to pull the side door open. I just sat there thinking, "What the hell am I doing here?" and then all of a sudden the van stopped and someone inside flung open the door. Lil Man's shotgun went off three times, boom, boom, boom. Screams could be heard as we quickly drove away. My ears were ringing and my heart was beating a thousand beats a minute. I was paranoid. We drove about four or five blocks and dumped the van in an alley; it was stolen so it didn't matter. Lil Man told me to wipe off everything I had touched. We walked out of the alley and got into a waiting car. These guys had no remorse whatsoever. They were laughing and joking about how the people who got shot "fell like bitches" and about how the "mother fuckers" had better not mess with the Kings' nation. I sat there petrified and grinned every time they looked at me but I really didn't find it amusing.

I confess that I wanted to hurt a white person just as much as the others did. However, killing was not something I had a desire to do. It was my first up-close lesson in street justice—Latinos hunting whites and vice versa. Innocent people, like those who were attacked in the park by the Gaylords, were usually the victims. Racial hatred just seemed natural, as if it was somebody's right to kill others as long as the victims were of another race.

Lil Man and I got dropped off at his house. Jenny and Lisa were outside waiting for us. Lil Man went through the gangway on the side of his house. Jenny grabbed me by the hand and followed him. Lisa followed us. They led me through a door that led to the basement of the building they lived in. Lil Man called to us from inside to hurry up and lock the door. The basement was well lit with a lot of chairs and a table. There was a crown spray painted on the wall in black and gold—the colors of the Latin Kings.

Lil Man continued bragging about the shooting as he lit up a joint. He sent Lisa upstairs to get a bottle of wine that was in the refrigerator. Jenny asked me about the incident. I told her that I didn't want to talk about it. Lil Man told her that I wanted to jump out and hit a Gaylord with a baseball bat. Jenny looked at me, smiled, then kissed me. It seemed as if she was proud that I was involved in a crime. After that kiss all I could think about was having sex with Jenny. The violence that had had me so upset was completely gone from my mind.

Lisa returned with the wine and handed it to me. I opened the bottle, took a big swallow, and then gave it to Lil Man. He in turn gave me the joint. After the wine was gone Lil Man decided to leave. I was going to leave myself but Jenny whispered in my ear to stay with her. Jenny and Lisa walked to the door whispering to each other. Lisa left and Jenny returned and kissed me.

We began kissing passionately while undressing each other. Soon we were both naked and all the things Maria had told me about pleasing a woman were running through my mind. It was a matter of what to do first. Jenny must have thought that I was scared or something because she told me not to worry, that Lisa was watching out for us. I wasn't scared—I was anxious. I was so anxious that I picked her up, laid her on top of the table, and got to the business of having sex. Jenny was a virgin; Maria had not prepared me for that. I was really having a hard time and was unable to penetrate her so I tried to perform oral sex on her. Jenny grabbed me by the hair and pulled me up toward her face saying, "Don't do that." Again I eagerly tried to penetrate her but couldn't. Fortunately Jenny was patient and eager to lose her virginity. I began thinking about the things Maria had told me. "Take your time, look at what you're doing so you can enjoy yourself," Maria had said. Finally I controlled myself enough to realize what I was doing wrong and was able to penetrate Jenny. It was over almost as quick as it started. I wanted to do it again but Jenny said no and that there would be other times. Then she began to get dressed.

After we had sex, Jenny asked me what I would do if she became pregnant. I was startled by the question. I had never really given that possibility any thought. Jenny looked at the expression on my face and started laughing. She told me that she had told Lisa about wanting to have sex with me long before I tried to talk her into it. Lisa got her some birth control pills and taught her how to use them. Jenny invited me up to her house to wash up before I left. She told me not to worry, that her parents had probably gone out anyway. After I cleaned up Jenny led me into her bedroom. Immediately I laid Jenny on her bed and started pulling off her clothes. Jenny wrestled herself away from me and demanded I stop. She took me to the window and told me that if I could get up there I could have sex with her anytime I wanted to. The anger that was building up inside of me because of her rejection turned into a smile. I knew climbing up to Jenny's bedroom window would be no problem at all. I kissed her and told her that I would see her later on that night, then walked to the bus stop. It was almost 10:00 P.M., but that didn't matter. I had no curfew.

My first sexual experience aside from Maria was not all that I had expected. Maria prepared me for everything except being too young to have sex to begin with. What happened between Jenny and me when I was fourteen was more of a wrestling match than it was making love. The episode left me confused and somewhat embarrassed. Why did Jenny freak out when I went down on her when Maria had said that oral sex was something women loved?

11

Lords of Nothing

I WAS STANDING at the bus stop when Maria and Lucy pulled up in front of me and told me to get in the car. Maria asked what I was doing so far away from the neighborhood so late. I told her I was visiting my girlfriend and that what she had taught me worked. She laughed and mentioned that if I wanted to learn some more to let her know. I guess Myra and Yolanda had not told Lucy about what happened between her mother and me. She just sat there looking at us and wondering what the hell we were talking about.

Maria asked me where I lived so she could drop me off. I told her that my mom was in Puerto Rico and that I was staying with my stepbrother Hector. Maria told me that if I ever needed something from her, not to hesitate to ask.

I asked Maria to drop me off by Tuley so I could hang out and maybe get high. Rican, Papo, and all the rest of the Lords were out there. They began to chant "child molester" when they saw me get out of Maria's car. Maria ignored them and drove away. Sexpot began teasing me about having sex with an old lady instead of her. I responded by telling her that the old lady was four times better looking than she was. Everybody laughed except for Snake. Snake was in love with Sexpot because she was the only girl that ever let him have sex with her. I didn't know that all the other girls ignored him because of his looks. I thought that because he was a Lord he had his choice of whichever girl hung around with them, but that was not the case. Snake told me, "You better watch what you say, you fuckin' punk, before I whip your ass." "Keep your lady in check, nobody is desperate enough to fuck her except your ugly ass," I responded. Snake made a move toward me. I prepared to fight him. Pothead grabbed me from behind and held me in a headlock. Rican stepped between us and told us to chill out. Snake persisted. He said, "That punk ain't no Lord. Why you protecting him?" Rican told him that I was from the 'hood and we shouldn't be fighting each other. Still, Snake persisted. I stood next to Papo and smoked a joint while Snake argued with Rican. I got into a conversation with Papo and forgot all about Snake. Snake charged me and threw me to the ground. He tried to hit me, but Rican and Papo pulled him off before he had the chance. I got up and went after Snake. Rican grabbed and pushed me away. I lost my balance and fell. Rican stood over me and screamed, "Take your little ass home before you get killed. You're not a Lord and don't forget it!" I got up and walked away mad as hell. I couldn't believe the Lords, especially Rican, would treat me that way. I thought they would be fair and let me fight Snake. Instead they ganged up against me. I got to Hector's, got some weed from a junkie, and locked myself in my room. I was too pissed to go by Jenny's house. I didn't even think about her. I smoked a couple of joints and then went to sleep.

I woke up at about noon the next day. Hector's girlfriend Missy told me that one of my friends had just come by looking for me. I looked out the window and saw Papo across the street by his house. Papo saw me and motioned for me to come down. I cleaned up and went outside. Papo, his brothers, and I went to Clemente field to play football. We played a couple of games, then split up. Papo and I went by Tuley and his brothers went back home. It was pretty cold out so we went to the Lords' clubhouse. I didn't feel right about going to the clubhouse but Papo told me Rican wanted to talk to me. "Man, I don't want to be a Lord, not after last night," I told Papo. Papo explained that after I left Snake kept insisting on fighting me one on one. Rican and Lil Chino decided to let us fight. Papo was to take me to the clubhouse so the fight could take place. I began to wonder if they had decided to kill me. Would Papo still have led me there if that were the case? I became nervous. I was scared of what would happen if I beat Snake. Would the Lords let me be or would they avenge Snake's loss? Well, I could either go fight

Snake or I could lock myself in at Hector's and never come out. I decided to take my chances with the Lords. If things got out of hand, I thought I could just tell Rican that I wanted to become a Lord.

It seemed like all the Lords and Lordettes had slept in the clubhouse. They were all there except for Rican. Snake began talking shit as soon as he saw me. Lil Chino told him to cool out until Rican got there. Lil Chino and Papo were the only ones who were being friendly toward me. All the other Lords were hostile and kept trying to instigate a confrontation. I stood quietly smoking weed and drinking wine with Lil Chino and Papo.

By the time Rican got there I was pretty high. I was also upset about all the bullshit and nasty things the Lords were saying about me. When Rican walked in, Pothead said, "It's party time." Snake walked up to me, got in my face, and said, "Let's take it outside, punk." He walked outside and all the Lords followed. I took off my coat and went out. The Lords had formed a circle in the alley behind the clubhouse. Snake stood in the middle waiting for me. As soon as I walked into the circle he punched me twice in the face. I had blood dripping out of my nose. I felt the same rage I had experienced when Pedro beat me. My mind went blank; all I could think about was killing Snake for hitting me. Nobody had hit me since my mother sent me back to the city. I wasn't about to let anybody else start abusing me. The next thing I knew I felt somebody grab me and pull me back; then I heard Papo telling me to be cool. I told him to let me go, that I was going to kill that ugly bastard. I thought the Lords were ganging up on me and began to struggle. I was held until I calmed down. When I was released I realized that there were four guys holding me: Lil Chino, Papo, Pothead, and Crazy One. Snake was on the floor holding his midsection and bleeding from his nose and mouth. He was mumbling something about going to get a gun to shoot me. Rican told him that he got beat fair and square so he better just forget about it and leave me alone. Rican helped him up and told us to shake hands. Snake didn't shake my hand; he walked off angry. Sexpot ran after him. Everybody else went into the clubhouse.

I knew I had done it, but I didn't even remember hitting Snake. The rage I went into was fiercer than it had ever been with Pedro. I was not aware of what I had done or how I had done it. It was as if my body was programmed to attack if I was hit. I didn't know how to fight. I didn't even know what fighting felt like. Snake had a swollen eye with a cut above it. He had a broken nose and both his lips were busted but I didn't remember ever hitting him. (I wonder if my mother remembers hitting me.)

Crazy One put his arm around me and invited me to smoke a joint. He said I was as crazy as he was. Crazy One got his nickname because he had overdosed on Valium when he was about thirteen and ever since then he was in and out of mental hospitals. He was a twenty-year-old white boy who, along with his brothers, had helped out many Puerto Rican families when they first moved into the neighborhood. His brothers were also members of the Lords; one of them was doing life in jail for killing some Vicelords. Crazy One's family was one of the few white families who remained in the Humboldt Park area. He lit up a joint and we began walking down Claremont Street to Clemente field. Rican and Lil Chino joined us shortly. Lil Chino told me not to worry about Snake and advised me to kick his ass again if he messed with me. Rican disagreed. He told me that if Snake approached me I should ignore him and let Rican know about it. Rican said if I were to kick Snake's ass without letting him know what was happening, the Lords would have to take care of me. I asked Rican why it had to be that way. He said, "Snake is a Lord; you're not," then walked ahead of me.

We walked through Clemente field and then headed down Western Avenue. We were headed to a restaurant that was located on Western Avenue and Haddon Street right across the street from the high school. The place was a school hangout, but since it was the weekend it was empty. We got there and ordered some food, then started playing with the pinball machines. After a couple of minutes Lil Chino stepped outside and said something about some Chi-West coming down the street. The guys stopped what they were doing and went outside. I got curious and followed. The Chi-West was a gang of white boys just like the Gaylords; their feelings about Puerto Ricans were basically the same. There were about six of them walking right toward us. Crazy One took off his red and black Lord sweater and handed it to me. I stood by the door as the guys walked toward the Chi-West.

Crazy One pulled out a switchblade from his back pocket and opened it. The Chi-West yelled their gang name and began to scatter around the street. They began yelling racially derogatory remarks at us. "Dirty spics, pork chops, go back to the island and take the roaches you brought with you," they said. The Lords went after them. The Chi-West guys ran in every direction and the Lords followed. Seconds later they were all out of sight. I didn't know whether to go after them or go back to the 'hood for help. I had to keep my tough guy image so I decided to join them. I stepped out of the restaurant and went looking for the Lords. I hadn't walked past two houses when I felt someone grab me from behind.

I turned around and was pushed to the ground. I looked up and there standing in front of me were two white guys, both in their early twenties. Both were Chi-West. They snatched Crazy One's sweater, punched and kicked me, then ran off. I lay there on the ground in pain, swearing that I would get those assholes back. The Lords came back and picked me up off the concrete. Crazy One immediately asked for his sweater. I told him the Chi-West took it from me. He went ballistic. He grabbed me by the throat and told me that I better get his sweater back or he was going to kill me. Rican saw the fear in my face and stepped between us. He told me not to worry, that we would get that sweater back.

When we got back to the 'hood everybody already knew what had happened. Crazy One had walked ahead of us screaming and mumbling about the whole incident. I told Papo what happened. He told me that I was in big trouble. Lil Chino told us to come to the clubhouse later that night. We both assumed that I was going to be beat up, or *violated,* as they called it. I couldn't figure out why loosing a sweater was such a big deal. Papo explained that since Crazy One told me to hold the sweater he would probably get a violation also. I wasn't a Lord; by putting me in charge of "the colors" he had violated a rule. (Gang colors are precious to their members. Gang members are willing to maim, kill, and die for colors that have a special meaning only to them. It would be one thing if they kept this practice among themselves but all too often an innocent bystander gets involved in this stupid game. At any given time someone could get shot, beat up, or killed because of the color of the clothes they're wearing.)

That night we reported to the clubhouse at about 8:00 P.M. When we got there all the Lords that were my age were told to step outside. I was instructed to close the door behind them. As I expected, the meeting was about the sweater. The Lords asked me what I was going to do about getting the Lords' colors back. I told them I didn't know. They said they did. Lil Chino explained that they were going to wait until it got warmer outside. That way there would be a better chance of catching the Chi-West hanging out. The Chi-West were probably expecting quick retaliation but the Lords were going to let them forget before making their move. Rican pointed at me and said, "You're going to get that sweater back." He pointed at Papo and said, "You're going to help him since you brought him around."

"Fuck them honky punks. We'll get our colors back right now if you want," Papo said. I didn't say a word. I was afraid to even look anybody in the eye. "It's cool," Lil Chino said. "We'll wait and see." All the other Lords were let back inside the clubhouse. We all began getting high. Shortly afterward, I was told I had to leave. I would not be allowed back in the clubhouse until I got the Lord sweater back from the Chi-West. I thought Papo would come with me but he only walked me to the door. I was on my own.

12

Chi-West

FOR THE REST of the winter I spent most of my time playing football with Papo's brothers. The Lords confronted me every chance they got, not letting me forget about the sweater. Because of that I stopped going by Tuley or to Maria's apartment. I did, however, go every day to pick up Jenny after school and walk her home. I had not been in school since leaving for Puerto Rico. I don't think Hector even considered enrolling me.

At Jenny's I began to get to know a lot of Latin Kings through Lil Man. I would get high with them. Sometimes I'd hide out in Jenny's bedroom until everybody went to sleep and then we'd have sex. When I didn't get the chance to hide out, I would come back and climb up to her window. Jenny was always ready and willing. In fact she would get upset if I didn't show up to have sex with her. Jenny became more open-minded about sex. She finally let me perform oral sex on her and learned to love it. She also became more aware of what to do for my pleasure. Jenny and I became kind of obsessed with sex. We rarely talked about anything other than what we would try the next time we got together. Jenny would take her father's pornographic magazines so I could see them. Most of the time she would point out a picture of a position she wanted to try. Over time Jenny seemed to become more experienced with sex than I was. She would often tell me to slow down or not to be so rough. She even went as far as showing me how I should perform oral sex on her so that it wouldn't hurt. (I hadn't even known that I was hurting her.) We learned a lot of things together that Maria didn't teach me.

Jenny was great. Being with her kept my mind off the situation at home and the Spanish Lords. I still, however, fantasized about other women, older women for the most part. Whenever I had sex with Jenny I would fantasize that I was with an older woman, usually ones I had seen on television such as Marilyn Monroe, Jaclyn Smith, Farrah Fawcett, Raquel Welch, and others. I had sex with all of them through Jenny. When I saw them on television I would smile as if I had really been with them.

That winter Joker from the Spanish Lords decided to leave Chicago for Puerto Rico. He had beaten an attempted murder rap and didn't have the desire to hang around anymore. In the days before his trip Joker was excited. "It will be a new start," he said. Several going-away parties were given in his honor. Guys were talking about taking the same route as Joker. The brother was being smart. He predicted a destructive future if he stayed on the path he was following and decided to get out before it was too late.

The day before Joker was to leave for Puerto Rico he went to get a haircut at a barbershop on North Avenue and Campbell Street. As he sat in the barber's chair a guy wearing a ski mask walked in and shot him. Joker died right there in the barber's chair. He made it to Puerto Rico, but in a coffin. Rumor was that the son of the barbershop owner was a Spanish Cobra. The barber himself supposedly had some kind of gang affiliation. As far as I know nobody got arrested for Joker's murder. For the Spanish Lords it was an act deserving revenge. Those who had thought about following Joker's lead found a reason not to.

WARM WEATHER WAS now in the air. The trees were sprouting leaves, the Cubs were in spring training—all signs that winter was finally over. It was an exceptionally warm spring that year. By the middle of April it seemed like summer. The Lords decided it was time to take action against the Chi-West. They came by Hector's several times looking for me, but I was always at Jenny's house. The Lords began saying that I was hiding from them. Papo saw me at Clemente waiting for Jenny and approached me in a hostile manner. "Trying to hide, punk? Go by Tuley today or you're dead," he said. His attitude took me by complete surprise. I kept forgetting he was a Lord and I wasn't.

I told Jenny about my predicament with the Lords and she understood why I couldn't walk her home that day. Jenny was actually excited about the idea that I was going to take part in a hit. "You're my man. You can get that sweater, I know you can," Jenny said as she kissed me. I promised that I would come see her that night. Jenny got on the bus. I walked to Tuley and sat on the front stairs of the Lords' clubhouse waiting for the Lords.

It didn't take long for them to arrive. Pothead sat next to me but didn't say a word. Papo arrived and said, "Make sure he doesn't go anywhere," then walked toward the back. I was surrounded by the Spanish Lords. Most of them were talking *about* me, but none were talking *to* me. "Yo, come on back," somebody yelled from the back of the building. I was sandwiched by Lords; they wanted to make sure I couldn't get away from them. We walked through a gangway to the back of the building and into the clubhouse.

Inside the clubhouse everybody sat along the sides of the room. I was left standing in the middle in front of a table occupied by Lil Chino, Rican, Crazy One, and another guy I had never seen before. Papo was told to join me. Rican began preaching about what the colors meant to them and what the consequences were for losing them. He said that the consequences are twice as bad for those that lose the colors and are not Lords. In the meantime Crazy One kept mumbling, "I want my sweater, punk. I want my sweater back."

Rican introduced the guy I didn't know as Mouse. He explained that Mouse would be joining us on our mission. Rican handed each of us a gun. Our mission was to either get the sweater back or to kill one of the Chi-West. Failure to do one or the other would result in a violation for Papo and an all-out beating for me. Papo quickly agreed with them. I got nervous as hell and remained quiet. I watched as Papo put the gun inside the waist of his pants and I did the same. Mouse headed toward the door; Papo followed. I hesitated but then followed them too. "If you don't bring my sweater back you're dead," Crazy One yelled as I walked away. As I walked out, Papo came back in. "We're going to wait until it gets dark. Mouse will be back for us," Papo announced.

We sat there killing time. Papo was laughing and joking around with the Lords and getting high. I was sitting on the floor in a corner being ignored. It seemed like an eternity before Mouse walked in and said, "Let's go, brothers, let's go." Papo received handshakes and hugs as he departed; I received evil looks and threats.

(There is a very fine line between being welcomed by and being in danger with a gang. Even those closest to you can become hostile in an instant. Being an actual member has its advantages, but these can disappear at any moment. Papo was a member of the Spanish Lords, yet he was being forced to put his life in danger for a sweater just as I was.)

We left the clubhouse with Mouse and went out to the alley where there was a car waiting for us. It was a green Ford LTD with a black vinyl top. There was a girl inside. I made her out to be the girl that was in the clubhouse the very first time I went there, the one that cursed Sexpot out. Her name was Maribel but they called her Morena. Morena was a Latin Queen, which was the female faction of the Latin Kings. She was also carrying a gun. Mouse asked for our guns and walked off to hide them so we could get high. He came back, got in the car, and pulled out a plastic bag half-full of marijuana. Mouse and Morena rolled several joints, lit them up, and passed them to us. While we smoked, Mouse told us that he had cruised by the Chi-West's 'hood on his way over. They were hanging out at a schoolyard. He said we were waiting for them to get drunk; that way they would be easier to surprise. Morena sat quietly, moving only to pass or receive a joint. About an hour passed and not a word was spoken.

Finally, Morena said, "Let's go, man." Mouse retrieved the guns, handed them back to us, and we were on our way. I looked at Papo as I tried to stick the gun in my pocket. I watched as he put his gun inside the waist of his pants. I did the same but it was too uncomfortable so I held it in my hand instead. I was scared. I kept looking Papo's way to see if he was as scared as I was. Papo didn't look at me once during the ride to the Chi-West's 'hood. He was playing this macho role, saying how he couldn't wait to kill a Chi-West.

The only one who looked my way was Morena. I quickly turned my face away from her so she wouldn't notice my fear. I looked out the window, watching the buildings go by and thinking about what was about to happen. I thought about the gun I was carrying. I convinced myself that I would use it. I couldn't, however, bring myself to even imagine how it would feel to pull the trigger or shoot another human being. How could I? I had never done it before. For a moment I felt as if I was alone. I could not hear or see the others in the car with me. Papo brought me back to reality by bumping me in the arm with his elbow. "We're almost there, man, we're almost there," he said. We were on Augusta Avenue. Mouse told us to get ready; we were almost at our destination.

The Chi-West hung out by a school on Augusta Avenue. We arrived there and walked quietly through the playground toward the mobile classrooms where we heard loud rock music. The Chi-West were partying between two mobile classrooms, out of sight from the main street. We split up into two groups to cut off the only two exits available to the Chi-West. Papo and I headed toward the back while Mouse and Morena covered the front. When we jumped out, the Chi-West freaked out. The guy who took the Lord sweater from me was there with the sweater on. To show his disrespect for the Lords he had taken off the emblem and sewed it back on upside down. There were also three other guys and three girls. Mouse instructed me to get what we came for. I pointed the gun at the guy with the sweater and demanded he give it to me. Papo kept saying, "Shoot him, shoot him." The girls with the Chi-West began crying and telling the guy to give me the sweater. He had other ideas. He walked toward me and said, "Kill me, punk." The fear I felt was evident to everyone present.

My body shook as if the ground was trembling. I broke into a cold sweat and just stared at this guy as he said things like "You fucking coward, shoot" and "All you fucking Ricans are cowards." All I could think about was why wasn't he just giving me the sweater. But no, he kept asking me to kill him and I couldn't. Mouse took the gun from my hand and shot the guy in the leg twice. Morena also opened fire. She was shooting anything that moved. Papo also joined in the shooting party. Mouse took the sweater from the guy, stood over him, and prepared to shoot him again. There was a girl on the ground next to him clutching a wound on her arm. The guy noticed that Mouse was about to shoot him again and tried to cover himself with the girl's body. Mouse pulled the trigger. I watched in shock as the bullet entered one side of the girl's face and came out the other. Mouse again pulled the trigger and again he hit the girl, this time in the chest. Blood splattered all over the place when the second bullet struck her. I froze. I kept seeing the bullet strike the girl and the blood splatter over and over in my mind. I heard police sirens but I couldn't move to run. I felt someone grab me and pull me. I thought it was the cops but then realized that it was Morena. She had run but came back for me.

We jumped over the fence surrounding the school and ran down an alley. We could hear and see the police cars zoom by with sirens blaring and lights flashing. We knew we were not going to make it out of that neighborhood without running into the cops so we started looking for a safe place to hide. We ran through a gangway and found an open door. We went inside and locked the door behind us. From inside that hallway we could hear police officers walking in the alley; one of them even tried the door and moved on when he found it locked. We heard him tell his partner that he couldn't wait to get his hands on some spics. We sat quietly with no movement for about an hour. Morena was going to open the door to see if it was clear to leave but we heard voices coming from the alley. We decided to wait it out right there. I was trembling and tears were running down my cheeks. Morena comforted me, assuring me that everything would be OK.

Morena and I talked in whispers for the rest of the night. I told her about my problems with my mother, Pedro, and Hector. Morena told me about her ex-boyfriend. He was a Latin King. He had been shot and killed by the Vicelords. She met him after her mom kicked her out. Morena told me she was an only child. Apparently her mother's boyfriend didn't like her. He tried to sexually abuse her. When she prevented him, he told her mother that she had come on to him. Morena's mother believed him and threw her out. She began living with her boyfriend only because she had nowhere else to go. Eventually she learned to love him. One day they were walking hand in hand down Damen Avenue by Wicker Park when two shots were heard. He grabbed her and then fell to the ground. He was shot twice in the back and bled to death right there on the street. Morena shed tears as she told me this story. She explained that that was why she didn't care about killing people. She told me that the incident opened her eyes to reality; she advised me to open my own eyes before it was too late. Morena told me that to survive street life I had to be ruthless. "You have to learn to hurt people before they have a chance to hurt you," Morena said. She advised me not to trust anybody and not to do anything I didn't want to do. "Be a leader, not a follower," she said. "Always be a leader."

To be a leader and not a follower meant I had to be cold-blooded, violent, and uncaring. It wasn't right to feel empathy for the suffering of others. I wasn't supposed to react to the sight of blood dripping out of a human body. I was supposed to ignore and even laugh at the screams for mercy and the terror. Death was supposed to be a normal thing that would make me a leader—a leader, not a follower. I would hear this phrase many times in my life. Only later did I understand that it never fit the occasion.

13

Coward

WE NOTICED THE daylight creeping in under the door. It was time to try and make it back to the 'hood. The plan was to act like we were boyfriend and girlfriend walking hand in hand, as innocent as could be. Hopefully we wouldn't run into any white people. The plan worked. Back in the 'hood we split up. I went to Maria's and kept knocking on the door until somebody answered. Maria opened the door screaming, mad at me for waking her up. "*¡Que carajo quires tan fuckin' temprano!*" ("What the hell do you want so fuckin' early!") I stared at her with watery eyes, not knowing what to say. She noticed that something was wrong and asked me about it. I promised to tell her but first I had to get off the street. Once inside I told her what had happened the night before. She cradled me in her arms and told me I could stay there as long as I wanted. I was relieved in more ways than one. I had somewhere to hide and I wanted to have sex with Maria to get the shooting out of my mind. Going to Hector's didn't even cross my mind. I kept myself locked in Maria's bedroom all day. Nobody knew I was there except for Maria's daughter Lucy. Lucy knew that I was hiding out because of the shooting but did not know the complete details. She thought I had participated fully and was therefore impressed. She acted seductively toward me. I could have told her the truth but didn't. It wasn't to my advantage.

That evening Maria came into the room and asked me how I felt. I assured her that I was OK and tried to kiss her, but she pushed me back. She told me that her boyfriend was on his way upstairs and that

I would have to come out of her room. I was very disappointed but I accepted it.

For the next few days all I did was pace from the living room to the kitchen and back again, thinking about the attack on the Chi-West. I couldn't sleep. Over and over again I imagined the bullets piercing that girl's face and chest and the blood splattering. Smoking marijuana put me at ease but when I came down from that high I became paranoid.

Myra and Lucy were constantly making sexual advances toward me. I couldn't believe how sex crazy these girls were. Their whole world revolved around getting high and having sex. Some days they would have multiple partners and would then sit around comparing them with each other. My first four days there I either slept with Myra or Lucy. I never slept alone. After the fourth day that started to change.

Myra never complained about me touching her, regardless of where she was or what she was doing. All of a sudden she began to snap at me whenever I got near her. She said she liked brave guys, not cowards. Lucy made remarks about me thinking I was big and bad but that I was really a big pussy whose life was saved by a girl.

On the fifth day I left their apartment feeling angry and embarrassed; but mostly I was afraid. I had to try to make it to Hector's before I ran into the Lords. Papo, Pothead, and Crazy One were hanging out by Tuley as I passed by. I thought they were going to try to jump me so I began looking for ways to run. But they just looked me up and down and didn't say a word. I stopped in front of them and said, "Hey, what's up?" Pothead said to get the fuck away from them. They didn't want any cowards hanging around with them. I got angry and started cursing at them. Papo grabbed me in a full nelson and said, "Pull up before you get jumped, punk." He told me that I was on my own; the Lords didn't want me around anymore. I walked up Claremont Street feeling lonely as hell. I kept hearing people calling me names like *pendejo* ("punk" or "idiot"), coward, pussy, and *maricon* ("faggot") just to name a few. I don't know why, but I just didn't want to go to Hector's place.

I walked up Western Avenue toward Hirsch Street and ran into Morena. I thought she was going to add a couple more names to the ones

I had already been called, but instead she walked up to me and surprised me with a kiss on the cheek. Morena asked me where I'd been. I told her I was at Maria's hiding out. She laughed and invited me to smoke some weed. We walked back down Hirsch and headed toward the Unknowns' 'hood a couple of blocks away. As we walked, we lit up some joints and talked about the past. I told her about how I was being treated in the 'hood. She told me that she didn't have anything against me for reacting the way I did. She said she understood. Morena went on to tell me that Mouse had been caught by the police with the gun he used that night. Snake was with him and he was locked up, too. She also told me that Papo was the one that suggested that I be thrown out of the 'hood. I was kind of shocked that my "best friend" Papo would act that way toward me. I guess he was angry and disappointed because I didn't meet his expectations as a gang member.

In the Unknowns' 'hood I saw Speedy with Jenny's brother Lil Man. I expected to get the same shabby treatment from them that I had gotten from the Lords but that wasn't the case. It seemed like the only ones who were talking shit were the Lords. Lil Man asked me where I'd been. He said his sister was worried about me. Lil Man, Morena, and I got in a car with a Latin King from Beach and Spaulding Streets called Tito. The Beach and Spaulding area was home to what was supposedly the biggest faction of Latin Kings in the city. I had heard about that area before but had never been there. I had thought it was in the suburbs somewhere. Lil Man instructed Tito to drop me off by his house so that his sister could see me. I didn't want to go there. I wanted to hang out with the Kings, but I said nothing. Reluctantly I stayed at Jenny's place, knowing that at least I could get sex if nothing else.

Jenny had already heard about what had happened with the Lords. She was being careful about what she said concerning the subject. It was obvious she didn't want to hurt my feelings, but she seemed bothered by something.

Jenny was alone. Her parents had taken Lisa to be fitted for a dress she was to wear at a wedding she was going to stand up in. We talked for a little while about where I'd been for the last four or five days and then we started kissing. She invited me to her room. I laid her on the bed and got on top of her. She pushed me off. "Why didn't you shoot that white boy?" Jenny asked. I stood there quietly, staring at her and at a loss for words. "You can't be my boyfriend and be a punk," Jenny said. "My boyfriend has to be brave." I stuttered, searching for words to protect my manhood. "It's OK. I know next time you won't back down, right?" Jenny told me as she began kissing my neck and face. All was forgotten and we began making love. Then suddenly we heard someone calling her name. We stopped to listen. When her name was called out again we realized that it was her father calling from outside. We got up and began getting dressed. Before I could get my pants on her father was knocking on her bedroom door. Jenny pretended she was awakened by her father's knocking and told him to wait a minute. I picked up all my belongings and crawled under the bed. I heard Jenny's father questioning her about why she was asleep at that time of day. Then he told her to start cooking so that her mother could relax for the day. The light in the room was turned off, the door was shut, and then there was silence.

Even with my mother and Pedro gone I still ended up under a bed. Jenny's words—"You can't be my boyfriend and be a punk"—were prophetic. Being violent was required not only by the gangs but also by girls. Why a girl would desire a guy who could kill in cold blood is beyond my understanding.

Seconds, minutes, and then hours went by and I was still under the bed. Jenny came in the room several times, but she was with her mother and never stayed for very long. Every time the door opened, my heart skipped a beat.

Then I heard the door opening again. This time I saw only one pair of feet walk in. It was Lisa. Lisa bent down, handed me some food, and told me to stay quiet and be patient; her parents would be going to bed soon. I got out from under the bed and looked out the window to see if the coast was clear to jump out. Lil Man and some of his friends were standing in front of the house so jumping was out of the question. I sat there and ate the food Lisa had brought me. I had just finished eating when I heard footsteps near the door; quickly I crawled back under the bed.

Jenny, Lisa, and their mother walked in and sat on the bed. They began talking about the upcoming wedding that Lisa was going to be in. I was being squashed between the floor and the bed while trying desperately not to be discovered. Lisa decided to get her dress and try it on. Jenny suggested that they do it in her mother's room but Lisa refused, saying that it wasn't going to take long. Lisa stepped out and came back with her dress. I saw her pants drop and wanted to get a better look but stayed still, fearing that if I made any significant move Jenny's mom would notice. Finally, after about forty-five minutes of physical and mental cruelty, Lisa and Jenny led their mother out of the room. They returned shortly and began jumping on the bed, laughing quietly. Lisa called me out and told me that her parents had gone to bed and as soon as Lil Man and his friends left I could jump out the window and go home. Jenny went to take a shower; Lisa and I stood looking out the window waiting for the guys to leave. They were drinking, smoking weed, and flashing gang signs at the cars that drove by. Several times they went as far as chasing a car and throwing bottles at it. Jenny came back into the room. Lisa said good night and left. Jenny locked the door behind her, walked over to me, and kissed me. She let her robe drop to reveal her naked body. We started kissing passionately and soon we were making love to each other again.

The next thing I knew it was daylight. I could hear Jenny's parents up and about. I panicked. I looked out the window and saw that the coast was clear. I got dressed, gave Jenny a kiss on her forehead, and prepared to leave. "Come back tonight," I heard Jenny say as I climbed out the window. I stood at the bus stop thinking about Jenny and her sexual hunger. I laughed to myself thinking about what would have happened if her parents caught us. The bus came and I snuck in through the back door. I looked out the bus window, watching the buildings go by, lost in thoughts of the previous night. I knew that I was headed toward the Lords' 'hood but I didn't know where I was going once I got there. I hated going to Hector's; everybody there looked like zombies and he was their master. But it didn't matter. I had to go to Hector's house. I was scared of what the Lords would do to me if I stayed out on the street.

14

Can't Be Normal Even If I Tried

I GOT OFF the bus on Western Avenue and Potomac Street, walked to Hector's, and then went upstairs. Junkies were sitting on the steps waiting for Hector to open the "drugstore." They were happy to see me but only because they knew that I would wake Hector up to let me in. I knocked and kicked on the door for about five minutes. Finally I heard a woman's voice say, "Motherfucker, come back later, shit." "It's me," I said, "Let me in." "Are you alone?" the voice asked. "No, there's a line out here," I responded. I was instructed to tell everyone to go downstairs. I didn't have to say a word. The junkies on top of the steps heard this and started down. All the rest followed. "They're gone. Let me in," I said, then waited as the door opened.

When the door opened, Gina was on the other side. She unlocked the two locks on the heavy-duty gate that protected the door and let me in. "Hector wants you," Gina said as she closed the gate and door. I walked to Hector's room and asked what he wanted from outside the door. "How many are out there?" Hector asked. "About ten," I answered. "Here, tell them that's all until tonight," Missy said as she stuck her arm out to hand me a butter canister containing bags of heroin. "How many are here?" I asked. "Twenty dimes," she answered. "Hold the money," she said, and then closed the bedroom door.

I opened the front door and exchanged drugs for money with the junkies. I sold twenty bags of heroin at twenty dollars apiece in two minutes. "Don't come back until tonight, there's no more," I told the junkies as I handed them their fix. I sold twenty bags but still had two left; apparently Hector or Missy had miscounted the bags. "How many did you sell?" Hector yelled. "Twenty," I responded. Gina put her hand over my mouth and said, "I'll buy those from you," before I could tell Hector there were two left. I walked into my room with her, lay down on the bed, and watched Gina prepare her fix. She pulled a half-ounce of weed from her purse and tossed it to me. "Light up," she said. I pulled two already rolled joints from inside the plastic bag and told her I was going to keep the rest for myself. Gina "cooked" the two bags of heroin in a soup spoon with a cigarette lighter. She put a small piece of cotton in the spoon and then filtered the liquid through the cotton into a syringe. "Do me a favor," Gina said. "Take off your clothes," I responded. "You're a nasty kid," Gina said as she handed me the syringe; then she pulled off her sundress.

All Gina had on underneath her dress were G-string panties. She sat on the bed and put her leg on my lap. I handed her a joint and told her to light up. I parted her second and third toe, inserted the needle, and then tried to draw blood into the syringe. I had to insert the needle twice before I found her vein and drew blood. I let the blood and heroin mix together inside the syringe and then slowly inserted the mixture in her vein. Gina closed her eyes and moaned as I emptied the syringe into her bloodstream. When the syringe was empty I pulled it out and put it on the windowsill. "Thank you," she said. "Take off your pants and I'll take care of you." I stripped naked, then lay there smoking a joint and watching Gina perform oral sex on me. Gina would do something that Jenny and Maria never did—she swallowed my semen. I thought she was a sick bitch for doing that but I loved the feeling.

It never occurred to me that there was anything wrong with a four-teen-year-old kid injecting heroin into a junkie, not to mention getting his penis sucked by a prostitute on a consistent basis. Yet it all seemed so normal; that was what my life was all about. Not once did I or any-one around me worry about the repercussions of our actions. My childhood had been stolen from me and I didn't realize it. I thought it was my duty as a "man" to involve myself sexually with every and any woman who offered me sexual favors. In reality I was only a boy, a little boy.

I slept until 3:00 P.M. that day. I looked out the window and saw Papo's brothers playing baseball at Clemente field. I worried about a confrontation with the Spanish Lords but went out and played with the brothers anyway. After the game, Papo's older brother, Heraldo, invited me to their house. He told me that he had heard about the incident with the Chi-West. Heraldo assured me that I had done the right thing by not wanting to shoot anyone. He advised me to stay away from his brother because he was a troublemaker.

The things he said made sense but somehow I still felt like I had done something wrong and would now have to prove myself as a "tough guy." I knew the hostility between the Lords and me would continue unless I proved to them that I wasn't a punk. Jenny telling me that she didn't want a punk for a boyfriend also kept ringing in my head. I had to find a way to erase the memory of that night we confronted the Chi-West. The only way I knew how to do that was to approach Rican and ask for another chance. Getting to talk to Rican proved to be a task in itself. Every time I tried to talk to him, he would either tell me to get the fuck away from him or tell someone else to say the same thing.

School was to begin in a couple of weeks and I wanted to get enrolled. I had to figure out how get myself enrolled at Clemente. I went and asked Maria to pretend she was my mom. She said she'd do it as long as I had the school transfers. I ran home to look for them. I knew I had them but I had forgotten where I put them. Hector was sitting at the kitchen table with a white guy I had never seen before. They were counting money. He called me over and introduced me as his little brother. The white guy had a gun holstered to his side. He didn't look like a junkie or anybody who would hang out with Hector. His name was Schwartz, Detective Schwartz. Detective Schwartz said he was a good friend of Hector's and that I should mention his name if I ever got stopped by the cops. I didn't say a word. I just kept thinking about Hector having a cop for a friend. It didn't make sense. I guess I was still a little ignorant to the whole drug scene. They were counting a lot of money and talking about something that was to happen at Hector's on Thursday of the following week. I went into my room and found my school transfers. I asked Hector for ten dollars and went back outside after he gave me the money.

I didn't know what to do about school clothes. My current wardrobe consisted of three pairs of pants and five T-shirts. I thought about the clothes Marilyn (Rican's girlfriend) had offered me and somehow found the courage to go claim them. I got to Rican's house and hesitated to knock at first but decided to risk it. Marilyn opened the door and asked me to come in. I asked her if could take the clothes she had offered me previously. She pointed toward the back room and told me to help myself. I took a close look at Marilyn and noticed she had a black eye. She was trying hard to hide it by letting her hair fall over her face. I asked her about it but all she said was to hurry up and get out before Rican came back home. She said Rican had told her not to let me come inside anymore. I picked up the bags of clothes and left as quickly as I could. I went to Maria's house instead of Hector's. I couldn't get Marilyn out of my mind. If Rican could be so brutal to the mother of his children, imagine what he would do to me.

I got to Maria's house and asked her if I could keep my things there. She said it was OK. Then she asked me for a joint. I told her I didn't have any pot, so she gave me money to go buy some. I went by the Unknowns' hangout and found Speedy. He was selling nickel bags. After a little joking around with Speedy I bought a bag and headed back to Maria's apartment.

Maria was sitting in the living room drinking a beer when I got back. She told me to roll a joint and light it up. As I rolled the joint I noticed Maria seemed depressed. I had never seen her that way before; she was usually gracious regardless of what was happening. We smoked about four joints without saying a word to each other. I wanted to come on to her sexually but realized it wasn't the right time for it. I looked out the window and saw that night had already fallen. I wondered out loud where Lucy, Myra, and Yolanda were. They were usually in the house or out front with guys by nightfall. I thought maybe the girls' absence might have something to do with Maria's depression. Without answering, Maria got up, went in her bedroom, and locked the door behind her. I decided that it was time to go pay Jenny a visit.

I walked to Western and North Avenue and sneaked on the bus headed toward Jenny's house. I figured that Lil Man would be outside with his friends getting high but there was nobody there. I went through the gangway and climbed up to Jenny's window. I peeked in, saw that she was alone, and went in. Jenny was, as always, happy to see me. In no time at all we were naked and having sex. I talked Jenny into performing oral sex on me. Actually I forced her to do it. I threatened to make a lot of noise if she didn't comply with my wishes. Jenny kept saying she didn't want to and begged me to not make her do it. But I was determined. I told her to pretend it was a lollypop but not to bite. After relentless debating, Jenny began to do as I instructed. Her lack of desire made the feeling kind of awkward. I closed my eyes and imagined that it was Gina there instead of Jenny. I felt an orgasm coming and put my hands on Jenny's head. She tried to pull away but I grabbed on tight to her hair to make sure she swallowed my semen. I had forgotten that it wasn't Gina I was dealing with. Jenny began gagging and pulled away as hard as she could. "Get the fuck out of here, you asshole," she whispered angrily. "Get me something to clean myself with," I demanded. "You sick bastard! Why did you make me do that?" Jenny said. "Because I love it," I answered as I cleaned my groin area with her bed sheets. "You like when I do it to you, don't you?" I asked. "Well, I want the same." "You do it because you want to. I never asked for it," Jenny replied as I got dressed. I got up real close to her face and said angrily, "But you love it, don't you, you love it," then pushed her to the bed. "I'm going out to smoke a joint but I'll be back and you better be ready," I told Jenny as I made my way out the window. Jenny closed the window and locked it when I got out. "Fuckin' bitch," I said to myself and then went to the back of the house to smoke a joint.

When I got done smoking I was determined to get back into Jenny's room and have sex with her. I climbed up and found the window still locked. Jenny saw me and closed the curtain. "I'll break the window, you bitch, you better let me in," I demanded. When I didn't get a response, I hit the window hard enough to break it, but it didn't break. That was enough to scare Jenny into letting me in. She opened the window and said, "Come in already, just be quiet." Jenny lay down and turned her back to me. She was still naked. I took off my clothes and lay down next to her. I was determined to have sex with her. She refused all my advances. I kept getting angrier. "Bitch, I'll kill you if you push me away one more time," I told her. She turned around and began kissing me. She cried and said, "I hate you," as I kissed my way down her body. "Don't do that, I hate you," she said. I ignored her completely. All I was worried about was my pleasure. As long as she stayed on the bed she could cry all she wanted. When I was finished, she told me I had to leave. I refused until she threatened to tell her brother about what had happened that night. I got dressed, kissed her on the forehead, and left. I hopped the bus back to the 'hood. It was about 3:30 in the morning. Nobody answered the door at Hector's. Nobody answered the door at Maria's, either. I sat in the hallway stairs that led to Maria's house and fell asleep.

My experiences with adults influenced my everyday actions. My brutality with Jenny took place without regret, as if she was my property to do with whatever I wanted. My wish was her command, or else. No thought was given to what our relationship would be like from that day on. There was no tomorrow, or at least no advantage in thinking about it. It was as if nothing happened.

"Wake up, you can't be sleeping in our hallway," someone said as they shook me awake. It was Lucy; she was just coming in. It was already about noon. I had slept in that hallway for quite a while. I went to Hector's, showered, asked for money, slept for another five hours, and then headed back to the streets. I stopped at the store and got some Twinkies and a pint of milk, which I devoured on my way back to Maria's. I had to go there and change my clothes. I also wanted to give her my school transfers and discuss what we would do to get me enrolled at Clemente. I was going up the stairs to Maria's when I heard someone screaming. It was Maria and Lucy arguing. The door was closed but unlocked, so I let myself in. I found Speedy and Papo there along with Lucy, Maria, Myra, and Yolanda. I asked Speedy what was going on. He told me the argument was about Maria's boyfriend. Maria was obviously drunk. She kept calling her daughter a cheap bitch and told her that she should sell herself instead of being a free neighborhood sperm bank. Lucy replied by saying, "I came out just like you and you're only known for your blow jobs." Maria charged Lucy and punched her in the face. Lucy fell to the floor. Maria sat on her, grabbed her by the hair, and continued beating her while calling her every bad name in the book. Things had definitely gotten out of hand between them.

Speedy, Papo, and I separated them. As soon as Lucy got off the floor Maria punched her again. She fell, crawled over to Speedy, and held on to him. Maria went into the kitchen and came back with a beer in her hand. She stood in the middle of the floor and said, "I want to tell you little bitches something; this is my house! I let you whores get all the dick you want here so when I decide I want some dick I don't want to hear shit from any of you! Do you fuckin' understand that? This is my house! I'm the boss here!" Everybody just looked at her. Lucy was still crying, hanging on to Speedy, and talking shit to Maria. "You bitch, you even fuck little boys," Lucy said. After that remark Maria really lost it. "Who the hell do you think you are to tell me who I can and cannot fuck? Huh, bitch?" Maria said as she reached for Lucy's hair. "If I want to fuck little boys it's my business!" Maria slammed the can of beer in her hand against the wall and started ripping her own clothes off. She was grabbing her own body and saying, "I'm horny, I'm fuckin' horny, I want some prick." She stood in front of Papo, spread her legs, and yelled at him to fuck her. Papo was in shock; he didn't even blink. Maria moved away from him and said, "You little faggot, you don't know what you just missed." She then came over to where I was sitting, kneeled in front of me, and began wrestling with my pants. "This is the little boy I fucked, and I'll fuck him again," Maria said. She was just about to get my pants undone when I panicked, jumped up and over her, and ran out the door. Everybody looked at me like I was doing something wrong. I was doing the only thing I could do.

15

First Kill

THE NEXT DAY that episode at Maria's was the talk of the neighborhood. The rumor was that, after I left, Papo and Speedy had their way with Maria. I wondered if that part of the rumor was true, but it didn't matter; what mattered was what was being said about me. First I was a coward for not shooting at the Chi-West and now I was a faggot for not having sex with Maria. I wanted to go talk to her and see how she was, but I couldn't find the courage to do so. I got the feeling that our relationship would never be the same.

I couldn't hang out with the Lords and now I was scared to go by Maria's. I would either have to stay at Hector's all the time or find somewhere else to hang out. With that in mind I headed toward Maplewood Park to hang out with Lil Man and the Latin Kings. At Maplewood Park it seemed like they had some kind of party going on. They were drinking, smoking, and had music turned up really loud. Morena was there. She greeted me with a kiss on the cheek and took me around to meet everybody. She introduced me as a future King. We walked over to a van and went inside. Morena told me to sit down and relax. She began rolling joints. Some guy sitting on the front passenger seat came into the back, handed me a bottle of Richards wine, and introduced himself. His name was Leo. He was a Latin King. Leo was a little taller than me and was very skinny, with brown eyes and curly hair. He had an ugly scar above his right eye. Leo was about nineteen years old. He was rather puny for his age. His arms were covered with tattoos, mostly homemade ones of girls' names. Leo sat next to me and began telling gang war stories. He rarely looked at me. Instead, he stared at the joints Morena was rolling, anticipating lighting one up. When Morena gave him a joint and a book of matches, Leo sighed in relief. He didn't say a word afterward; he just enjoyed the marijuana.

Morena left the van and came back shortly with another girl. She was introduced as Pebbles. Pebbles was petite, with short black hair and blue eyes. She had a beautiful smile and a sculptured body to go with her porcelain complexion. Pebbles sat next to me and began talking to me. I lit up a joint and gave it to her. She took a hit, held the smoke, and moved in on me as if to kiss me, but at the last second blew the smoke in my face and laughed. I was embarrassed but laughed along with her so she wouldn't notice. After a few bags of weed had been smoked and about three bottles of wine downed, I was acting super silly. Leo had left the van and another King called Hercules joined us. Hercules was a big, muscular guy. Hercules had dirty blond hair and blue eyes and was about six feet three inches tall. Hercules didn't drink or smoke and also didn't talk much. In fact, whenever he said something, it was whispered into Morena's ear. I was acting like a clown. Pebbles, Hercules, and Morena just kept cheering me on. It was like I was the life of their party. Hercules came up with the idea of going for a drive to find some Vicelords. The girls quickly agreed and so did I. As we were pulling out, someone asked Hercules where we were going. Hercules shouted back, "To find out what the newcomer is all about." I sat there laughing like a fool, not realizing that the newcomer he was referring to was me.

The Vicelords hung out on Hoyne and Evergreen Streets not far from the Unknowns' 'hood. That's where we headed. Pebbles and I sat in the rear of the van, Hercules drove, and Morena sat in the front passenger seat. Leo called Pebbles up to the front. I heard him say, "Give this to that brother so he can take care of business." Pebbles came back to where I was and handed me a sawed-off shotgun. I was scared out of my mind. I was about to be tested again. Damn, I wished I was in Puerto Rico!

The van stopped a few seconds later. Hercules came to the back and asked for the shotgun. I was relieved, thinking that I wouldn't have to use it on anybody, but he had only forgotten to load it. Hercules loaded the shotgun and demonstrated how to use it. "See, my brother, you pull the trigger, then pump it, pull the trigger again, then pump it again until it's empty," Hercules instructed me. Shotgun shells flew out of the top of the gun every time he pumped it. (He never actually pulled the trigger.) Hercules reloaded it, gave it to me, and again we were on our way. Pebbles lit up a joint and sat next to me. She gave me the joint and started kissing my neck and whispering about what she would do to me if I shot a Vicelord for her. I stared at the shotgun, not knowing what to do. Pebbles took it out of my hands, put it under a blanket, then kissed me. I was tongue kissing her and feeling up her body when Morena came back and told us that we had arrived at our destination. She advised me to get ready, then went back into the front.

Pebbles looked out the window and pointed out the Vicelords for me. She grabbed my groin, squeezed gently, kissed me, and told me that the sooner I got it over with the quicker I could have her. I made up my mind right then and there to go ahead with the whole thing. "What the hell, it was only some niggers. Who would care anyway?" I rationalized. I told Hercules to go around once again. I lit up a joint, drank half a bottle of wine as if it were water, and grabbed the shotgun. Morena looked back and whispered for me to get ready. I pumped the shotgun and moved to the side door of the van. Pebbles was looking out the window and instructing me as to what corner the Vicelords were standing on. Suddenly the van stopped and Hercules yelled "Now!" I jumped out, ran toward the northeast corner, and opened fire. I did just as Hercules had instructed: pump and shoot, pump and shoot. People were screaming and running all over the place. I ran up on the curb and saw a couple of people pleading for mercy as they bled to death. Some guy came running out from the back of a car. I reacted by turning toward him and pulling the trigger. The shots hit him in the back and head; he fell forward and lay there motionless. I ran back inside the van and slammed the door. We flew out of there and back to Maplewood Park. Inside the van I felt an adrenaline rush as if I had just done something good. Pebbles hugged and kissed me as she told me how proud she was of what I had just done. At Maplewood Park Hercules drove the van directly into a garage and then took the shotgun to get rid of it. I lay on the floor of the van and smoked a joint with Pebbles.

For some reason the incident did not affect me the way the one with the Chi-West had. I felt relaxed and proud of myself. Maybe it was the weed and wine or maybe it was being with Pebbles. I really didn't know what the difference was and I didn't care. What was important was that I had proved myself.

Pebbles never kept her promise to make love to me. She never had any intentions of doing so. It was all Morena's way of getting me really pumped. It worked. I found myself bragging half the night like an idiot about what I did.

"IT'S ONLY NIGGERS," I reassured myself before committing the crime. "Only niggers." I wonder how many times the Gaylords rationalized in the same manner before killing a Puerto Rican. I'm sure the Gaylords said, "It's only a spic," after slaughtering a Puerto Rican. It's that racial blindness we all live with. Pebbles offered sex for spilt blood and the anticipation of her passion became the basis of my courage. It was the first time I saw blood spill because of my actions. It was a coming out, evidence that I could be, and was, as cold-blooded as anybody else. It was also the beginning of my tenure as a gangbanger. There was no turning back.

I WOKE UP with a giant headache. I turned to see Pebbles lying next to me and everything started coming back to me. I woke Pebbles up and just watched her as she stretched. I tried to kiss her but she pushed me away. She said that if her boyfriend ever found out we were together he would kill me.

Pebbles took me to her sister's apartment where we washed up and had breakfast. I talked to Pebbles and found out that her real name was Josephine. She was eighteen and had just graduated from Orr High School. She told me that she used to be a cheerleader. She definitely had the body for it. I didn't understand why she was gangbanging. We walked to Maplewood Park and played on the swings like two little kids. In fact we were two little kids trying so hard to be grown up.

Some Kings showed up on bikes and began selling weed. I asked one of them to lend me his bike so I could go home. He asked if I was the little brother who went on that mission with Hercules the night before. I told him I was. The guy got off the bike, shook my hand, gave me the bike and a nickel bag of weed, and said that I was welcome there any time. I got on the bike and started to leave. *"Amor de Rey"* ("King love"), yelled the guy as I rode away.

16

The Acceptable Difference

I RODE THE bike to Hector's apartment and went upstairs. The junkies were already out looking for their fix. Hector opened the door only for certain junkies; most of them just slipped their money under the door and got their drugs the same way. I knocked and told him to open the door. He asked how many people were out there with me. "Three," I told him. He told me to come back later. I didn't want to. I was afraid the police would be looking for me, but I didn't have any choice.

I got on the bike and rode to Maria's as fast as I could. The shooting had taken place just four blocks from Maria's apartment. When I got there I walked in as always—as if it was my home. This time Lucy confronted me about walking in without knocking. She even went as far as saying I wasn't welcome there anymore. I asked for Maria with the excuse of enrolling in school. She said, "I don't know where that bitch is at," and disappeared into the kitchen. Myra filled me in on what Maria had done that night after I ran out. Reportedly Maria's drunken state coupled with her anger led her to have sex with both Papo and Speedy. At least that's what Papo and Speedy were saying. Maria had kicked the girls out of the house and did not let them back in until the next day. Myra mentioned that Lucy didn't care because her mother was known as the neighborhood bitch anyway. I think Lucy was hiding her feelings; it hurt her to know her mother wasn't respected. (I think Lucy was the way she was because of the pain she carried around inside her.)

I went into Maria's room, laid down on her bed, and fell asleep. I slept till sundown. I was awakened by Myra. She told me that some guy was outside looking for his bike. When I went downstairs I saw Lucy in the hallway getting kissed and touched by some guy as if the incident of the other night had never happened. She stopped only to tell me her mother wanted to talk to me. Morena and the King brother who lent me the bike were outside waiting for me. They put the bike in the trunk of a car and invited me to come with them and get high. I turned them down, explaining I had to wait for Maria because she was going to enroll me in school the next morning. I headed toward Western Avenue. I was going to sneak on the bus and go by Jenny's house.

As I walked down Hirsch Street I heard someone calling me. It was Crazy One and Papo. The first thing that came to mind was that Crazy One was going to start with me about the Chi-West incident. Instead they walked up to me, shook my hand, and congratulated me on what I had done to the Vicelords. The same guys who had kicked me out of the 'hood were now patting my back because they thought I had shot someone. I began to realize that only violent acts were rewarded in the world of gangs. To be accepted you had to be violent. I made a mental decision to do anything and everything to keep my newfound popularity intact. We walked by Tuley smoking weed, then headed down Potomac Street toward Western.

When we got to the corner Papo spotted some guy spray painting a wall by the alley on Potomac in between Western and Artesian Street. He ran over there to take a closer look. Like a dummy, I followed. It was a Spanish Cobra. He saw us and shouted, "Cobra love, Lord killer," and took off running. The Spanish Cobras were growing into a pretty big gang after their move to Division Avenue and Maplewood Street, mainly because of their alliance with the Latin Disciples.

The guy with the spray paint must have thought we were punks or maybe he had a death wish. After a few minutes he reappeared in the alley behind the fire department building, yelling "Cobra" and writing the letters *ISC* (Insane Spanish Cobras) all over the walls. I thought it was funny that Papo was irritated by this guy taunting him.

Papo chased the guy down the alley; I followed. As we got closer, the guy threw the can of paint at Papo but hit me on the side of my head instead. I became angry and gave chase as aggressively as Papo. In no time at all we had him cornered. Papo and I proceeded to beat the Spanish Cobra without mercy. I repeatedly kicked and stomped his groin and stomach as Papo slammed his head against a brick wall.

We would have beaten him to death if someone who lived where the beating was taking place had not come out, shouting to leave him alone. We ran up the alley and headed toward Potomac. Before we could make it out we found ourselves surrounded by members of the Spanish Cobras. Some were about our age but most of them were older. One of those in the group was our old friend Flaco. Flaco had outgrown us. He had hair on his face and had developed a very muscular physique. He still considered me his friend, but he didn't feel the same way about Papo. Flaco was the leader of that group. He ordered the other Cobras not to touch me. They held me so I couldn't interfere with them as they beat the crap out of Papo. Flaco warned me that if I didn't want to get killed I should stop hanging around with Papo and the Spanish Lords. Then they disappeared.

I helped Papo back to the 'hood. He was very upset that he had been beaten up while not a finger was laid on me. He blamed me for what had happened and walked away from me. After the Chi-West incident I had learned to expect Papo to act like a jerk whenever it was convenient. I no longer cared if he was mad at me.

17

Officer Friendly

I saw Maria driving by and called for her to stop. I asked her if she was still going to register me for school. She explained that the events of the other evening wouldn't affect our friendship and that I was still welcome at her house. But, she continued, none of the other guys who frequented her house were welcome anymore. I didn't bother asking why she felt that way; I kind of understood her feelings. I reminded her of the Clemente registration deadline. She assured me that she would be ready and then drove away.

As I headed to the bus stop to go by Jenny's house, someone beeped a horn at me. I didn't recognize the car so I ignored it. The car pulled over next to me and I realized it was Morena with a couple of her friends. I jumped into the car, gave Morena the usual kiss on the cheek, and asked her to drop me off at Jenny's house. Morena introduced me to her two friends. She told them that I was her favorite little brother. Her friends were also Latin Queens. Their names were China and Giggles. China appeared to be half Asian, but she was actually half Mexican and half Puerto Rican. She was cute and seemed shy—another of the many beautiful girls who for some reason chose to hang out with gang members. I couldn't keep myself from staring at her. Morena noticed and began trying to play cupid. Morena's other friend, Giggles, was a heavyset girl with long hair and a very funny laugh.

We drove down by the lakefront to Montrose Harbor, where all the Kings went to party. The girls had a cooler full of beer and wine in the trunk of the car. We each took something to drink and then went and sat on the rocks. The night was falling fast. From where we were sitting we could see the Chicago skyline—a very beautiful sight. I was talking to China, trying to get to know her better. The alcohol in our heads and the beautiful, romantic, scenic background took control of us. We simultaneously kissed each other as if to make sure that the other wouldn't have a chance to move away.

Soon the Montrose Harbor rock area was full of Kings and Queens. Everybody was drinking and smoking and just plain getting rowdy. We were having a really good time until the police came by and tried to throw us out.

Some of the guys were very drunk and became hostile. They threw cans and bottles at the police cars. Within seconds the whole area was filled with police. China and I just sat there holding each other, watching as the police arrested people who didn't want to leave the park and beating those who didn't want to get arrested.

Morena came over and told us to get in the car so we could get the hell out of there. We did just as she said. She started the car and reversed out of the parking lot. She turned and headed toward the lakefront exit. I watched in horror as the police beat on the people they were arresting. It didn't matter whether they were male or female—everyone received the same treatment. I heard someone yell "Stop that car," and suddenly a police officer jumped in front of us. One officer came to the window, pointed at me, and said, "That's the little jackass who threw the bottle at us." I yelled, "Bullshit, you have the wrong person!" They didn't care. They opened the door, reached in, and pulled me out by my hair. I could hear China screaming and crying. I glanced over and saw Morena being held while a policewoman hit her repeatedly. The policewoman kept telling her to cool out and leave but how the hell could she obey those orders while being held and beaten? I tried to get the officers to let go of my hair and got kneed in the abdomen. I fell to the ground, buckled over in pain. I heard one officer say to another to put me back in the car because I was a minor. Again I was grabbed by the hair. I was lifted to my feet. I got angry and resisted. This just earned me another blow to my abdomen. They threw me in the car and told Morena to pull out before we all got arrested.

I sat there trying to fight off the pain and wondering what we had done wrong to deserve this kind of treatment. We drove by a sign that said "PARK CLOSES AT 11:00 P.M." I realized that it was after 2:00 A.M. already, but I don't think that sign gave the police the right to use physical violence against us.

Morena cursed the police all the way back to Maplewood Park. When we got there we got a couple cans of spray paint and went on a vandalism spree. We must have driven around for three hours vandalizing stop signs, the National Guard building, schools, and anything we knew would upset city officials. That was our own way of getting back at the police for what they had done to us. It was a stupid idea, but it made us feel a whole lot better. Morena took us to an apartment that was used like a clubhouse for the Latin Kings of Kedzie Boulevard and Armitage Avenue. The place was empty. All the Kedzie and Armitage Kings who hadn't been arrested at the lake were outside on the street throwing bricks and bottles at any police car that happened to pass by. I was tired. I laid down on a sofa and tried to get some sleep. As I drifted off to sleep, I came to the conclusion that the police were definitely an enemy of Latinos.

18

China

I WOKE UP with China lying next to me. I looked around and saw several bodies, including Morena's, sleeping on the floor and on the other sofas. I lay there waiting for Morena to wake up so that she could drive me back by Maria's. I stared at China as if I was in some kind of trance. Even with her hair messed up and her clothes wrinkled and dirty she was still very attractive. I still couldn't figure out how she fit into this type of lifestyle. There were a lot of beautiful girls who hung out with gangs but none of them were like China. She didn't smoke, would rarely drink, and considered marijuana a dangerous drug. I kept thinking about all the things we had talked about at the lake the night before. China told me about her dreams of going to college and becoming a teacher. I remembered that she hadn't wanted to drink but Morena had talked her into it. I began to realize that the friendliness and affection she had shown me were because of the alcohol and not because she liked me. I wondered how she would react when she woke up and found herself curled up against me. I decided to kiss her before she woke up because I probably would never get the chance again. I kissed her and her eyes opened. She smiled at me, kissed me on the cheek, and hugged me hard.

China got up and complained about having a headache. She said, "What the hell am I doing here? My stepfather is going to kill me!" and then went into the bathroom. Her voice and the sound of the bathroom door closing woke up several people but nobody actually got up. I looked around again and laughed to myself about how much the Kings' clubhouse looked like a mission for the homeless. Everyone looked like a zombie. I heard whining noises coming from the bathroom and went over there. China was sitting on the edge of the bathtub crying, with her head in her hands. She didn't even notice I was there until I closed the door behind me. She looked up at me and asked to be left alone. I told her that I would as soon as I washed my face, but I had no intention of leaving her alone.

I washed my face and rinsed out my mouth, then asked if she had a comb or brush. China reached into her back pocket and gave me her comb. I asked her what was wrong, not expecting her to actually tell me anything. She got up, fixed her hair, and asked me to go for a walk with her. We walked to Humboldt Park. We looked at the vandalism that we had created the night before on the walls of the National Guard building. (It didn't dawn on me at that time that the damage we did was to our own neighborhood.) China began calling me Lil Loco because, according to her, I had a crazy personality.

She started to tell me about why she had been crying. China's father was Mexican; her mother was Puerto Rican. They divorced when she was about five years old. Her mother had an affair with a friend of her father. That guy was now her stepfather. The same thing that happened to me in my family was now happening to China. She told me about how her stepfather used to be so sweet to her and her mother until a kid of his own was born. After that he became abusive to her and her mother. Listening to China brought back vivid memories of how Pedro used to abuse me.

China told me that when she began to mature into a young lady her stepfather began touching her private parts whenever he got the chance. She told her mother about it, only to have the accusation dismissed. Her mother claimed it was all in her head. As China's body continued to develop, her stepfather's advances became more aggressive. He would try to force her to tongue kiss him. He would go out of his way to get her mother out of the house so that he could make his unwanted advances without fear of interruption. He would go into a silent rage when China begged her mother to take her along and her mother agreed.

China's tears were now rolling down her cheeks. She cried hysterically as she told me that she had to sleep with well-fastened clothes because of the time when she was sleeping and felt someone touching her legs. She awoke to find her stepfather kneeling naked over her and trying to pull down her panties. She began screaming as he tried to rape her. When he heard her mother coming, he jumped up and started saying things like, "If you didn't want it, why did you tease me?" China believed that her mother knew in her heart what was going on but pretended to believe her stepfather anyway. She began treating China badly. China's mother suddenly started making comments like "Get your own man" and "Maybe if you didn't act like such a bitch you would get respect." China told me that her mother didn't care if she didn't come home but her stepfather would get pissed. He knew that as long as China stayed out of the house he would not have the opportunity to rape her. The fact that several Latin Kings had confronted him and warned him to leave China alone didn't make him too happy either.

The more she told me, the more tears I shed. China asked me why I was crying and wiped my eyes. I told her about Pedro and how my mother had turned her back on me as well. She asked me where I lived. I told her the truth—I lived wherever I could find a welcome. I explained my situation at Hector's and the experience with the Spanish Lords. We spent almost all day walking around the park, talking about our lives and about how fate had brought us together. China and I decided to continue seeing each other. In the back of my mind I thought about Jenny but at that moment I really didn't care. I knew that as long as I could climb up her window she would be there, ready and waiting.

STORIES OF ABUSE while the other parent ignores the cries for help are all too common where I was raised. Mostly it was uneducated, unskilled, and scared mothers who ignored the abuse. The memories of my mother's ignorance were so vivid as I listened to China. That's what China and I and many other gangbangers had in common—these memories bonded us together. That's why gang members embrace each other's acts of violence. That's why they go to jail for one another. That's why gang members kill and die together. That bond relieves the pain of what is the truth.

We walked back to Kedzie and Armitage. From there I asked Morena to drive me back to Maria's apartment. When I got to Maria's she called me into the bedroom. Sex entered my mind immediately, but I was wrong. Maria handed me a bag full of new clothes and told me to try them on. All of them fit me perfectly. She reminded me that on the following day I would be enrolled in school. For a moment I thought Maria had changed her wild ways and had become a mother figure. I decided to test her. She was hanging my clothes in her bedroom closet. I walked up behind her, reached around, and squeezed her breast. Maria turned around and pushed me so hard that I fell over. She told me that she was sorry that she had taken advantage of my innocence when we first met. Then she begged me to please forgive and respect her. Maria began crying. All I could say was that I would respect her no matter what. She told me to go with her so that she could buy me some shoes to go with my clothes.

On our way to the store we sat in the car silently. I thought about what she had said. I couldn't see why she thought she had taken advantage of me. I had not yet realized that what happened between Maria and I, coupled with my cousin raping me, were part of the reason for my constant thoughts about and desire for sex. I thought it was natural for a male, regardless of his age, to accept sexual advances from females, young or old, and treat women as sex objects.

Lucy and her friends were rarely home anymore. Maria was treating me as if I were her son. She requested that I spend more time at home. She said that she didn't want me getting into trouble, especially with school just around the corner. I realized that Maria was feeling very lonely and was using me to forget all her problems. I also knew that all that would change once she found herself another boyfriend.

SCHOOL WAS BACK in session and I couldn't wait to go back. Hector bought me all the school supplies I needed and put furniture on the second floor where my family once lived so that I could stay there. I thought he did this so that I could stay away from the junkies, but actually he often asked me to let them in so they could shoot up.

19

Back to the Hunting Grounds

THE MORNING OF the first day of school I met Jenny on the corner of Western Avenue and Potomac Street. She showed up with a bunch of her friends; we all walked together, then separated when we got to the school. Papo and Speedy were going around asking all of the new kids in school what gang they belonged to. I don't know what made me follow them around but I did. I therefore gave the impression that I was either a Spanish Lord or an Unknown. While school was in session I rarely left the neighborhood unless it was to visit Jenny or China. Papo had forgotten about the whipping he received from the Cobras, and we became close friends again. I began representing (flashing gang signs) for the Lords even though I wasn't a member. When I went by Jenny's or China's I would represent the Kings. I did it for the fun of it. I didn't really think it was anything serious.

Jenny and I became inseparable during school. After school I would walk her home, go back to the 'hood, play baseball or get high, then go back to her house at night for our usual sex session. We rarely talked about anything meaningful. Our conversations revolved mostly around sex, how it felt, what we should try next. With China it was different. We did kiss but that's as far as it went. Mostly we talked about what we wanted and what we didn't want. We shared our dreams and expressed sympathy for each other's unfortunate positions in life. I looked forward to seeing Jenny at school and when I was horny, but when I wanted a friend I went to China. In fact, when I had sex with Jenny I would often pretend that it was China or somebody else. The kisses China and I shared soon became deeper and more passionate. I began to have the same sexual thoughts about her that I had about Jenny. Yet somehow I gained a respect for China that kept me from following through on those feelings.

At school my involvement with Papo and Speedy was affecting my grades. I was constantly cutting class to get high. The nickname China gave me, Lil Loco, began appearing on the school walls and in the surrounding area.

One day we were coming out of the cafeteria and Speedy spotted a rival gang sign on some guy's folder. We followed him into the stairway area where Speedy approached him. The guy said that he was a Latin Disciple. I didn't know the Latin Disciples were at war with the Kings. Since the Unknowns were united with the Kings, they were at war with them as well. I asked him if he knew Chico. A look of relief appeared on his face as if he was among friends. He said that Chico was his chief. When he said that, Papo and Speedy began beating him. The guy pulled out his pencil and tried to stab me with it. I retaliated. I kicked him in the abdomen three times as he bent over trying to guard himself from Speedy's and Papo's blows. I kicked him again in the throat area. He began to choke and fell to the floor, gasping for air. Papo and Speedy backed off. I kept beating on him and ended up pushing him down the stairs. I wanted to go after him, and continue beating on him, but Speedy pulled me away and out of there. We went outside to the restaurant across the street from the school. A few minutes later an ambulance arrived and carried the guy out. From the restaurant we could see detectives walking around, asking questions. I was getting pretty scared, but one of Speedy's boys assured me that there were guys walking around making sure nobody talked. Papo, Speedy, and I decided that it was in our best interest to leave the school area. I suggested we go and hang out at Kedzie and Armitage. Papo and Speedy agreed.

My seriousness about school and education took a turn for the worse. School wasn't the same. It ceased being a place I adored where the desire for knowledge engulfed me. Instead, it became a place to win a popularity contest. I had become a full-time hoodlum, only I didn't consider myself lost because I wasn't an actual member of a gang. Clemente High School was nothing more than a hunting ground and its students were my prey. How unfortunate for all of us.

WE GOT TO Kedzie and Armitage and saluted the usual group of Kings and Queens that hung out there. China was across the street with Morena and a couple of other girls. I had hoped to see China there. China's problems at home had made it hard for her to concentrate in school, so she had just about stopped going. She saw me and immediately came toward us. Speedy saw her crossing the street and said that he was going to get her and for us to watch. I was going to make sure he stayed away from her but then decided to just watch and see how she would react. Speedy walked up to her with all the confidence in the world and introduced himself. China told him her name, pointed at me, and said, "and that's my boyfriend, King Lil Loco." I laughed at Speedy and walked away with China.

China and I went on our usual walk to Humboldt Park and spent most of the day there. I hung around by Kedzie and Armitage until dawn. Papo and Speedy had gone back to the Lords' 'hood before I got back from the park. China had been staying with a friend and had no intention of going home. For some reason I got it in my mind that maybe China and I would go farther than just kissing now that she wasn't living at home. I asked her if she wanted me to stay with her. She said no. Her friends' parents were church people and she didn't want them to see us together. I pursued sexual activity with China but not as aggressively as I had with Jenny. China was in the mood for conversation and became very upset when she noticed that I was paying attention to her body instead of her words. She pushed me away from her, told me she would see me when I wasn't thinking with my dick, and then walked away. I thought about stopping her but decided not to. She was right; at that moment I was thinking with my dick. I left Kedzie and Armitage and went by Jenny's. Jenny wouldn't care if I didn't listen to her talk. She *wanted* me to think and speak with my dick.

20

Betrayed into a Coma

It was a long walk through hostile territory to Jenny's house. I chanced it anyway. I made sure to avoid side streets and put the expression of a lost little boy on my face. I reached my destination without being touched, thank God. At Jenny's house I immediately climbed up to the window, knowing that she would be waiting and willing. Jenny, however, blocked my way. I thought that maybe her parents were up and she didn't want to take a chance, but that had never stopped her before. Something had to be wrong. I threatened to make all kinds of noise and tell her parents the truth if she didn't let me in. She looked at me with a scared, puzzled look on her face, then moved out of my way. Once I got in and approached her with a kiss she became the waiting and willing Jenny I'd known and come to expect.

Jenny had gotten used to me performing oral sex on her and had actually begun to expect it. This time, however, she completely refused. Even when I persisted and faked anger, she refused. This was not at all the Jenny I was accustomed to. I began wondering what was going on. After we had sex I asked about her sudden refusal of oral sex. Jenny put a serious look on her face and said that she had to confess something to me but that it was my own fault. Jenny confessed that Speedy had just left her room about fifteen minutes before I got there. She said that Speedy had told her all about China and me and that since I had decided to share myself with someone, so had she. I asked her if she had fucked Speedy. She said yes without hesitation. Angrily I asked her why she had slept with me right after having sex with Speedy. She said that I was a better lover. Maybe she thought that saying that would make me feel better. She was wrong. I felt betrayed, used, and I was angry as all hell. I began wondering how many other guys were climbing up to Jenny's window when I wasn't around. My pride was hurt and my male ego was shattered. I got dressed, slapped the shit out of her, and quickly climbed out the window. I would usually wait for the bus at the corner but this time I was so angry that I just kept walking up Western Avenue on my way to Hector's.

Jenny's unfaithfulness did not hurt me emotionally. I considered Jenny a piece of meat and nothing more—my personal piece of meat. Now I felt that she had violated my manhood and disrespected me. All that turmoil and we were barely fifteen years old! (The sex between Jenny and me and between Jenny and Speedy took place in her bedroom while her parents had no clue. Instead of slapping Jenny, I could have killed her and her parents would have had no idea what happened. For some reason, Jenny's parents did not have the slightest thought about what was going on in her life right there in their own home. Was it their ignorance or her conniving ways? Whatever it was, this scene is all too familiar in the 'hood.)

I kept thinking about how I was going to kill Speedy for being such a backstabbing bastard. If he had just made the move on Jenny without snitching on me, then I wouldn't have thought it was his fault. But no, no, he had to use me to get into my girlfriend's panties. What a punk! The fact that Jenny had sex with Speedy without even trying to find out if what he told her about China was true really drove me crazy. Maybe she had become a prick-loving bitch like Lucy and her friends. As far as I was concerned, Jenny had acted like a cheap bitch by having sex with me using the excuse that Speedy didn't satisfy her. What a fuckin' whore! (It never crossed my mind that I was out there getting laid by other girls without Jenny's knowledge. Why had sleeping with many partners made me a stud while it made Jenny a bitch?) I tried blocking Jenny out of my mind by thinking about China.

I suddenly realized that I was in the Gaylords' 'hood. I looked around and didn't see anybody except for a kid about my age throwing a ball under a viaduct. It was a white boy. I began walking at a faster pace, knowing I could handle the kid under the viaduct but not wanting to be seen by anybody else. The viaduct was located on Western Avenue and Bloomingdale Street; Western ran under it. As I got closer the guy saw me and stopped throwing the ball. When I got under the viaduct, he stepped in front of me. I tried going around him but he blocked my way. "What the fuck's wrong with you?" I asked. He said, "Hey, spic, don't you know where you're at?" Then he said, "You're a dead Puerto Rican!" and tried to hit me. I blocked his punch and punched him in the face. I pulled back and got ready to hit him again when I suddenly felt a sharp pain on the top of my head and then another. Everything went blurry and I fell to the ground. I covered my head and face with my arms and felt a blunt object pounding me. I felt pain on my lower back and on the back of my leg. I thought I had been stabbed. I started silently praying for mercy and then finally passed out.

I woke up in the hospital. Everything was blurry when I opened my eyes. I could see figures standing on each side of me, but I couldn't make out who they were. When my eyes focused I could see Maria, Morena, and China. Doctors and nurses came running in and started to perform various tests on me. I heard one of them turn around and tell Maria that her son would be all right. China held my hand tightly and kissed it. I could see tears of joy running down her face. I heard Morena telling someone on the phone that I had finally woken up. I looked at China and tried to ask her what Morena was talking about, but I had a hose stuck down my throat that prevented me from talking. I also had hoses up my nostrils and in one of my ears. I had an IV needle stuck in one arm and one giving me blood in the other arm. I must have looked like Frankenstein. I was in bad shape. Morena bent over me and kissed me on the forehead. She said, "Hey, sleeping beauty, you've been out for nine days. My kisses finally woke you up." Maria told me that I was lucky to be alive. Then she went on nagging about how she had told me to stay home. Visiting hours were over and a nurse came in to escort Maria and the girls out. The room became dark and lonely. I began feeling pain all over my body, especially in my head. Every time I fell asleep, nightmares would kick in. I saw myself standing in a pool of blood. I was looking at myself lying in it. I woke up screaming violently. The IV needle came loose and I pulled the hoses from my nose and mouth. It hurt like hell when I did that; they were all the way down my throat. The nurses came running in and stuck a needle in my arm. That's the last thing I remembered until the following morning.

I awoke to the sound of voices in the room. China, Morena, and a couple of Kings were there waiting for me to wake up. The Kings had come to give me a card that everyone had signed. They also told me that they would get revenge for what was done to me. Morena and the Kings left, but China stayed there with me. She was there by my side every day until I got out of the hospital. I loved her for that. The nurses had tied me down to the bed the night before so that I couldn't pull the hoses out anymore. I couldn't even move my head. China waited on me hand and foot. She read the card and told me the name of each and every person who had signed it. She bought several *Mad* magazines. She would read them and show me the pictures. China said that I resembled the Alfred E. Neuman character on the cover of *Mad* magazine.

After I got out of the hospital I stayed at Maria's. It took me about two months to fully recover from my injuries. It took me another month to actually start consistently hanging out on the streets again. I had not gotten stabbed; I was beaten with a blunt object. My head was gashed open in several places. By covering myself with my arms, I had saved my own life. One would think that I had learned my lesson about gangbanging, but in truth my reaction was completely opposite.

Nine days of unconsciousness in a coma caused by hate and ignorance. I almost died at fourteen. At an age when I should have been experiencing the joys of being a teenager I was desperately trying to survive. I was lost with no safer days in sight. Those who came to my side and supported me were lost themselves. Although they meant well, they came talking only about revenge. It was the only encouragement I came to know.

21

Madness

I WAS TOLD that the Latin Kings had shot a couple of Gaylords for what they did to me, but I didn't care; I still wanted to get revenge myself. The attitude that I must do something to prove my worth was turning me into an animal. I felt like I had to defend my pride and my honor. Maria and China nursed me back to full health. I was ready to go out and face the world for the first time in about three months. When I was jumped by the Gaylords it was summer; now that I was ready to hit the streets again it was already winter.

I was told that Papo had been arrested for the incident at Clemente High School during those three months I had been in seclusion. Hector had been raided twice in one week and was arrested both times. As always he made bail rather quickly. But after his second arrest Hector moved out of the neighborhood and left everything, including me, behind. The building where we had lived was now abandoned. I had no idea where he was and I didn't care to find out. His place had been a haven for junkies and homeless people. I was told that junkies would walk out of the building carrying Hector's furniture to sell. I didn't care. Maria had already told me that I could consider her home my home. I was also told that Jenny was having sex with anyone who approached her. Somehow I wasn't surprised. I did not want to see or even hear about Jenny.

I decided not to go back to school until it got warm outside. In the meantime I was spending a lot of time with China. Maria gave China the OK to come and stay with me in her house. Maria became more motherly than I had ever imagined her to be. I made sexual advances toward her several times when we were alone but she refused, even when she was drunk. Instead she would scold me and start crying and apologizing about having molested me. I stopped coming on to her so she could stop that song and dance—it was getting old. I came to realize that I would never again make love to Maria, but in my heart I was really thankful for the things she had taught me. She made me a man and I was especially thankful that she cared enough to give me the food and shelter I needed to survive.

China and I converted the closed-in back porch into our bedroom and used an electric heater to keep it warm. Lucy and Myra were hardly ever home any more. They would stay out for days, sometimes weeks, at a time. Maria had told them that if they had one guy living with them it was fine but that her house would no longer serve as a hotel for them. The other girl, Yolanda, had moved out while I was in the hospital. She met a sincere man. She was smart enough to recognize this and became faithful to him. That move paid off for her—he asked her to live with him and they were planning to marry the next summer.

Although China and I slept together, we didn't have sex. I tried and tried to make love to her but she had too much respect for herself. She kept telling me that she made a promise to herself, her father, and to God that she would still be a virgin when she married. She wasn't about to break that promise for anyone, not even me. I respected her wishes but then again I didn't have any other choice. Even though I knew China would refuse, I kept trying. She still considered me her boyfriend and didn't deny me anything but sex. The sexual tension became so great that I started making stupid remarks like, "Don't be a prick teaser." China kept her cool and said that I was teasing myself. She told me how far she would go but I wouldn't listen. She was right, as always. I began going by Jenny's again—she was still waiting and willing—only now I wasn't the only one that was climbing up to her window.

Jenny acted like she was so happy to see me but I knew that she was only happy because she had someone to fuck. Same old Jenny. She wasted no time getting me in the mood. When Jenny and I first began making love to each other, I felt the need to make sure she was satisfied, but now I didn't really care what she felt. Jenny tried hard to make sure it lasted but I gave her the wham-bam-thank-you-ma'am treatment, then got dressed. As I got dressed, she would tell me how I wasn't as good as before and how she missed the old me. All I said was be patient—someone else would be knocking on her window shortly. By the look on her face I knew she was hurt by what I said but I didn't care. I meant it to hurt her. She actually told me that, no matter what happened, I was still her number one. That bitch had some nerve thinking those little words were going to change anything. Nevertheless, I kept going to her to relieve my sexual frustrations, and she never turned me down. I became bored with the same old routine every day. First I would get myself horny as hell with China and then I would go and get off with Jenny.

THERE WERE ABOUT two months of school left so I decided to go back. I told Maria to call the school. They said I could report to class on the following Monday. On Saturday a couple of Kings from Kedzie and Armitage came by Maria's house to talk to me. They were the same guys who visited at the hospital. They came by to see if I was all right and to tell me that they had made a hit on the Gaylords in my name. I said I wanted my own revenge, but I didn't really mean it. I was acting tough, trying to enhance my reputation as a bad ass. The Kings did the unexpected: They volunteered to drive and help me get my revenge. I swallowed a gallon of saliva trying to hide my fear and nervousness. I agreed to meet them at Tuley later on that night. As soon as they left I became panicky. My body trembled with fear. I ran downstairs and tried to catch them to say I had changed my mind, but they were gone.

China noticed my fear and knew right away what was wrong. She tried to talk some sense into me. She said it would be stupid for me to go with the Kings. She reminded me about our dreams for the future and how I could get killed or go to jail. All I could think about was being thought of as a coward; my macho pride was more important than anything else. I didn't want the Latin Kings to turn on me like the Lords had. I had to act. I spent the rest of the day pacing back and forth, nervous as hell. China kept lecturing me; I kept ignoring her. I searched every corner of the house looking for marijuana, but to no avail. I had to get high. It was the only way I could calm my nerves. Against China's protest I went outside.

I went by Tuley and found Snake, Rican, and Speedy. They were drinking jungle juice (Bacardi) and smoking weed. I joined them. When I took a hit from a joint, I felt relief. I began talking about what I was going to do to the Gaylords. After a while I was pretty high and I was anxious for the Kings to arrive. Rican had a piece of pipe about a foot and a half long in his car. The pipe was completely wrapped in duct tape. It was heavy and solid. I asked Rican to let me borrow it. He agreed to lend it to me but only if I promised to bring it back with Gaylord blood on it.

Snake and Speedy had gone to get another bottle of jungle juice. When they returned, Snake began teasing me about Speedy having sex with Jenny while I was still her boyfriend. I had completely forgotten about that until then. I had come to realize that Jenny was addicted to sex, so it was going to happen sooner or later. With that in mind I tried to ignore Snake's comments. I laughed off the insults Snake was throwing at me.

Then Speedy joined the onslaught. He started bragging about Jenny's pussy being his and how he was fucking the shit out of her every day. My anger was becoming evident, but I controlled myself by thinking of Jenny as nothing but a horny bitch. At that very moment the Kings arrived to pick me up. Speedy kept teasing me. He said I wasn't man enough for Jenny. I realized that ignoring him and laughing at him was just making Speedy talk more shit. I advised him to stop the bullshit and began walking toward the car. The asshole didn't stop. The last thing I heard him say was that if I was a man Jenny would still be mine. I turned around, rushed him, and began beating him with the pipe Rican had lent me. Rican, Snake, and the Kings pulled me away from him. His face and head were bleeding. I had no remorse for what I had done. I grabbed the bottle of Bacardi, took a long drink, and walked toward the car, anxious to get on our way. Before I left, I warned Speedy that the next time he fucked with me I would kill him. I went to hit him again but Rican stepped in the way. My heart was beating so fast that it felt like it would pop out of my chest. "Come on, brother, let's go," one of the

Kings said as he pulled me toward him. I got in the car with the Kings and began our search-and-destroy mission against the Gaylords.

The two Kings with me were named Lalo and Paco. Lalo was driving, I was riding shotgun, and Paco was in the back seat. Lalo was a tall, slim guy with push-backed hair. He always had this evil look on his face, as if he was some kind of psycho. Lalo spoke very little but when he did talk all he did was curse. Paco had a medium build with long, stringy hair that he kept in a ponytail. He had a birthmark on the upper left side of his face that made him look mean, but he was a comedian and was always making jokes. Paco was the total opposite of Lalo. He talked a lot and was very articulate. The only time Paco cursed was when he told a joke or described something that made him angry. Both Paco and Lalo were in their twenties. Both had been Latin Kings since their early teens. They asked me about the incident with Speedy. When I told them about it, they laughed and then told me that they would have done the same. They also advised me to have a talk with the Unknowns about it. They told me to tell the Unknowns that I was a King, and they would be fair to me because of the unification between the two gangs. Lalo said he would go with me and verify that I was a King. I didn't think all that was necessary because I knew almost all of the Unknowns personally, but Lalo insisted.

On our way to the Gaylords' 'hood we passed under the viaduct where I had been beaten senseless. Immediately after the viaduct we turned west on Bloomingdale Street and headed toward Campbell Street. By experience we knew that we would run into some Gaylords long before we reached the intersection of Moffat and Campbell Streets where they hung out. We spotted four guys crossing Bloomingdale headed south. I recognized one of them as the guy who had stopped me under the viaduct. I told Lalo to follow them. He sped up and turned south on Campbell even though it was a one-way street going north. The Gaylords had stopped under the viaduct and were too busy spray painting the walls to notice us. Lalo handed me a gun. Papo and I jumped out of the car and cornered them under the bridge. Papo also had a gun and was going to start blasting right away, but I stopped him. I walked up to the guy who set me up and asked him if he recognized me. He began to cry and beg for mercy. He found none. "Don't kill me, man, I'm not a Gaylord," the guy said. "Fuckin' pussy, don't you remember me, motherfucker?" I yelled at the top of my lungs while standing only inches away from him. "I'm sorry, man, I'm sorry," he said as I got ready to swing the pipe. "Gaylord killer," I yelled as I began beating the shit out of him with the piece of pipe. I completely forgot I had a gun in my other hand. I became oblivious to the other Gaylords who were there or anything else, for that matter.

The Gaylord put his hand in front of his head in an attempt to protect himself. I heard the bone break when I hit it. I had lost my mind. The more blood I saw, the harder I hit him. Suddenly I heard gunshots. I snapped out of my crazy spell and noticed that Papo had shot one of the other Gaylords and was getting in position to shoot another one. The guy was standing too close to me so Papo hesitated. He must have been so scared that he couldn't move, because he had the chance to run but didn't. I stepped out of Papo's way and he shot him. The guy fell toward me and I busted his head with the pipe.

Papo and I ran toward the car. Papo jumped into the driver's seat. We reversed to go back down Bloomingdale and saw Lalo repeatedly stabbing the last of the Gaylords present. We drove toward Lalo and he jumped in the car. He stuck his head out the window and yelled, "King Love!" as we sped away. Lalo and Papo dropped me off at Western and North Avenue and told me to walk home from there. I had a better idea. I spotted the bus coming up Western and decided to sneak on. I still had the gun Lalo gave me in my possession. Papo had told me to leave the pipe in the car so they could get rid of it. I snuck on the bus and rode it to Potomac Street. I felt no fear. In fact I felt brave and proud—indestructible. I had gotten my revenge, the Latin Kings were my allies, and, most important, I had taken a big step toward building the tough-guy reputation I so desired.

As I got off the bus I noticed the Spanish Lords standing on the corner yelling out their gang slogan. I crossed the street and joined them. They were yelling at the Cobras who were standing on Artesian and Potomac Streets exchanging hostilities with the Lords. I went by Crazy One and asked him to give me some of the wine he was drinking. I drank about half of the bottle in one swallow. I gave Crazy One back the wine and asked him to walk with me toward the Cobras. As we crossed the street I turned around and lifted my shirt so the Lords could see I had a gun and therefore would not follow us. When the Cobras saw us coming, they spread out in a hostile manner. Crazy One was yelling at them to get out of the Lords' 'hood. The Cobras yelled obscenities as they threw bottles and rocks at us. I pulled out the gun and ran toward them. When they noticed I had a gun, they started running west toward their 'hood. There was one guy who had a Cobra sweater under his leather jacket. As he ran he slipped on some ice and fell. By the time he was getting back up, I was standing above him with the gun held to his head.

I demanded he give me the sweater. He took it off and gave it to me. I told him to leave before Crazy One began beating the shit out of him. Crazy One and I walked back to the other Lords, congratulating each other. I gave the sweater to Rican and told him that the sweater should be enough of a payment for losing his pipe. He took it and told me that I should have killed the Cobra. It seemed like the only one satisfied was Crazy One. All the others were talking about how I should have pulled the trigger. I was high but I wasn't that high. I ignored them and walked to Maria's apartment. My opinion of the Lords began to deteriorate quickly after that. I made up my mind never to join them. I thought I might become a King or even an Unknown but never a Lord.

THINGS WERE HAPPENING fast. In one night I had a confrontation with Speedy, the Gaylords, and the Cobras. I was digging my own grave because I wanted to be accepted. I wanted to be looked up to. The only way I knew of achieving that status among the gang members was to commit as many violent acts as possible. That's how it worked. Do unto others, then do unto someone else. Finally those around me stopped thinking of me as a coward.

Maria's apartment was now my official home. Hector never came looking for me or sent anyone to ask about me. I really didn't care. I had a new family that cared for me now. Morena showed up and told me to stay in the house. Rumor was that one of the Gaylords had given the police a pretty good description of me. Morena told me that if I didn't have any police record the police would probably pick up anyone that fit my description. All I had to do was stay out of sight.

I got scared. I wasn't high at that point so my thoughts were clear. I saw myself going to jail and being beaten and raped. I smoked a joint and it calmed my nerves. Whenever I got high I became lost in a kingdom of macho trips. I would brag about my actions and advertise my desire to repeat those acts. Sober, however, I was nervous and paranoid, like a puppy trying to hide from thunder.

China saw right through my mask. She was there when Morena told me about the police and saw how worried I was. She got some hair clippers and gave me an army-style haircut and then started bitching at me. China said she didn't want a hard-core gangbanger for a boyfriend. She also said that she had decided to make love to me but now that was an impossibility. I knew this wasn't really true. She often used that type of psychology with me, but it didn't work anymore. China had hopes that going back to school would change my attitude. She said she would leave me if I didn't change.

22

Rosie

MONDAY WAS HERE and it was time for me to go back to school. I walked out of the house looking like an innocent little schoolboy. On my way there I spotted the police questioning a couple of guys and got somewhat nervous. I walked right by them and didn't even get a second look. I even turned back around and asked them what time it was and then went on my way. I realized I was safe.

When I got to school I found out that they had put me in a different homeroom. My class schedule was changed to fit in some tutoring so that I could try to make up for the time I had missed. I was sitting in class surrounded by a bunch of strangers when the most beautiful, sexy, delicious-looking girl I had ever seen walked into the room. Her name was Rosalinda; they called her Rosie. She was Miss Popularity and she knew it. Rosie was just as stuck up and conceited as she was hot. I said hi, but she walked by me as if I wasn't even there.

Rosie had a friend named Sheena. She was one of the few African American students in school. Sheena was a very attractive girl. She was the product of a Puerto Rican father and an African American mother.

From the very first day I saw Rosie I became infatuated with her looks and style. I approached her many times and tried to start a conversation, but she either ignored me or said something like, "I don't speak to nobodies." Sheena, however, was friendly. She would tell me not to feel bad because Rosie had a boyfriend anyway. When Rosie saw her talking to me, she advised her it would ruin her reputation because I wasn't in their circle of friends. I didn't care. The more Rosie turned me down, the more I went after her. I began to get the idea that Sheena was interested in me. I should have been proud to have Sheena interested in me, but I was too busy chasing Rosie to even think about her.

In the meantime China got in contact with her father and decided to move in with him. She came to visit a couple of times, but when she saw I was getting deeper and deeper into gang activities she stopped coming around. Just like that, China was gone. The last words she said to me were, "There's more to life than hanging on the corner and getting high, so don't be stupid." I'll never forget them. I don't know if it had to do with my age or whether China wasn't as important to me as I had thought, but I didn't do a thing to keep her from leaving. In fact, I was kind of relieved that she left because it opened the door for me to have a relationship with Rosie. Maybe if she would have become sexually active with me I would have reacted differently. I don't know.

23

Convenient Agreement

I BEGAN STUDYING hard (in part to impress Rosie) and soon my grades were respectable. But I still hung around with the Spanish Lords and the Latin Kings. Getting high became a bigger and bigger part of my life. The Unknowns showed up at Maria's apartment wanting to talk to me about the incident with Speedy. I agreed to go by their 'hood and get the problem settled. After they left the house, I headed to Kedzie and Armitage looking for Lalo. I wanted Lalo to tell the Unknowns that I was a member of the Latin Kings as he had said he would. I found Lalo standing on the corner with Morena and some other members of the Kings and Queens. I told Lalo about the Unknowns and he agreed to go with me. We left Kedzie and Armitage in Lalo's car. Morena came along. We stopped at Maplewood Park and got high for a little while before we left. I had been kind of scared about fighting Speedy. Well, not so much fighting him. I was really scared I would get my ass whipped. He was older and slightly bigger than me, which made me nervous. But after a couple of joints and several beers I was ready to go.

When we got to the Unknowns' 'hood on Leavitt and Schiller Streets they were out there waiting. They saw me and started teasing me about how they thought they'd have to come looking for me. "This King brother ain't no punk," Lalo defended me. Speedy popped up out of nowhere and started talking shit about me not belonging to the Kings, but he was quickly told to shut up by his leader.

The leader of the Unknowns was called J.J. He was a big, stocky guy with blond hair and blue eyes. Those who didn't know him swore that

J.J. was a white boy, but he was actually Puerto Rican. J.J. informed Speedy that Lalo was a well-known King; therefore, his word was to be respected. Lalo and J.J. stood there complimenting each other and the relationship between their respective gangs. (Apparently the Unknowns were started by the Kings in order to direct some of the heat the police were putting on them elsewhere. That move made it easier for the Kings to continue their drug-selling business. The letters *U K* stood for Undercover Kings, or, as they called themselves, Unknowns.) After what seemed like an eternity of ass kissing, we went inside the Unknowns' clubhouse and got ready to settle the conflict between Speedy and me.

Speedy told his version of the fight between us. He made it sound like I hit him because he took Jenny from me. He didn't mention that he had teased me until I snapped. I looked around the room and noticed that everyone there except J.J., Lalo, and myself had sarcastic grins on their faces. I guess they found the fact that we were fighting over a girl funny. Meanwhile, I couldn't sit still. I would sit down and then stand back up and walk around the room, never taking my eyes off Speedy. Speedy kept elaborating on his argument that I was angry because Jenny left me for him.

Finally it was my turn to talk. I began by admitting being angry about Speedy having sex with Jenny but also pointed out that the reason I snapped was because of the teasing. Chuckles and giggles were heard throughout the room when I said that. Only J.J. looked around seriously and stopped the Unknowns from busting out in laughter. I took a step toward Speedy and said, "Punk, don't be using my name to get pussy!" J.J. stepped between us. J.J. and Lalo warned us about going at each other before a decision was made and then left the room to make a decision. While they were gone everybody was quiet. I lit up a joint and sat on the floor by myself on one side of the room, while Speedy and the rest of the Unknowns looked at me from the other side. It seemed like something very serious was about to happen. I felt like an outsider being left to relax before I was victimized. My only hope was Lalo.

J.J. and Lalo came back and instructed Speedy and me to stand up in the middle of the room. J.J. preached that it was a shame that we let a girl break up our friendship. He continued talking about how the relationship between the Unknowns and the Kings had always been a good one. Therefore it was decided that the problem should remain only between the two of us. "If you two want to hurt each other over a bitch, so be it," J.J. declared. If we wanted it, a one-on-one fight was to take place between Speedy and me. Regardless of who won, we were to let the argument end there. I quickly agreed with their decision. So did Speedy. We decided to fight.

We went out the back door of the clubhouse, which led into the alley. Outside, a circle was formed around us and we went at it. Speedy had the reputation of being a good fighter so I was pretty scared. However, the fear of getting a reputation as a punk took over me and I attacked him. It turned out Speedy wasn't much of a fighter after all. The first punch I threw landed right on his nose. He put his hand over it and noticed the blood gushing out. While he was busy nursing his nose I hit him a few more times in the face. Speedy went into a rage. Tears began flowing out of his eyes in buckets and he began yelling, "I'll kill you! I'll kill you!" One of the Unknowns standing close to Speedy had a baseball bat. Speedy snatched the bat and charged me. He swung wildly and hit me above my left eye. J.J. ordered him to drop the bat. When he didn't, the other Unknowns stopped him. The Unknowns charged Speedy, held him, and took the bat away from him. J.J. then told his boys that "Speedy had acted like a pussy." He grabbed Speedy by the neck, told him that he was no longer an Unknown, and then ordered his boys to whip Speedy's ass. Speedy had opened a big gash above my eye, and I was bleeding like crazy. The left side of my face and neck were completely covered with blood. Yet, as bad as the cut was, it was nothing compared to the beating Speedy was getting. There were at least ten guys beating him with no mercy. The guys who were beating him were the same ones who were cheering for him to hurt me just a few minutes before. I stepped toward them with the intention of stopping them, but before I could do anything significant Lalo grabbed me and led me away from the scene.

A gang's loyalty to its members is very tenuous. If a member is not righteous in the eyes of the leaders, he may as well be a rival. This is probably the reason why so many gangs exist in so little territory. The falling out between Speedy and me was sudden and unexpected. Jenny could have been the cause of it, but I think that it had more to do with a lack of respect and true friendship. The incident increased my popularity and fame as a fighter.

Lalo dropped me off two blocks away at the emergency room of St. Elizabeth Hospital and told me that he would send Morena to pick me up later. "*Amor*, brother," Lalo said as he drove away. It took fifteen stitches to close the cut over my eye—three inside and twelve outside.

While I was in the hospital, I just couldn't stop thinking about how Speedy was beaten by his own so-called friends. I rationalized that Speedy must have done other things that made the Unknowns react the way they did. I didn't understand that gang members could turn on one of their own within seconds.

After I got stitched up, I met Morena in the hospital lobby. She drove me to Maria's and then went to pick up the prescription for pain pills that the doctor had given me. When Morena came back, I had already cleaned up and changed my clothes. Morena asked me to take a ride with her. The Latin Kings wanted to have a word with me.

We drove to Maplewood Park where Lalo and several other Kings were waiting for me to arrive. The Kings told me they were impressed by the bravery I had shown in the incident with Speedy and the incident with the Gaylords. As they talked I became lost in my own lonely thoughts. The fact was that my so-called bravery with Speedy was fear more than anything else and, had it not been for the booze and marijuana in my head, the Gaylord incident would never have taken place. The Kings explained that I would have to become a member of their gang. If I didn't, they would have to deal with the fact that Lalo lied to the Unknowns about my membership.

Lalo took me for a walk and explained in detail what would happen to him if I didn't comply with the wishes of the other Kings. He told me that the Kings would give him a head-to-toe violation, which meant that three other members would be chosen to beat him from head to toe for three minutes. Lalo also told me what I would have to go through to become a member of the Kings. He said that usually an incoming member would have to prove himself to even be considered becoming a member. Since I had joined the Kings in their retaliation against the Gaylords, I wouldn't have to go through the proving phase. Lalo told me that I would have to take an initiation violation that consisted of two chosen Kings beating me for three minutes. Unlike the head-to-toe violation, they would not be allowed to hit me in the face, groin, or basically anywhere where I could be seriously hurt. This was supposed to prove my toughness. After listening to Lalo, I decided to become a member of the Latin Kings from Kedzie and Armitage—not because I wanted to, but because I was too scared to say no.

We walked back to Maplewood Park and announced the news to the others. They all seemed happy to hear the news. Morena was especially happy. She said that we would have to go celebrate.

Morena, Lalo, and I left Maplewood Park and went to Kedzie and Armitage. When we got there, Lalo told the Kings about my decision. Lalo was not the leader of that section, but he was a high-ranking officer. After a brief conversation with the leader, a date was set for me to be formally initiated. The leader of the Kings from Kedzie and Armitage was a guy called Loco; the nickname alone described his personality. He was not big or strong, but he was a homicidal maniac. I sat on the hood of a car with several other Kings as I watched Lalo and Loco discuss my future. Loco kept glancing my way and looking me up and down while he talked to Lalo. After a couple of minutes Morena was called over too. She came back and told me that an initiation date was set.

24

My Girl

MORENA AND I drove to a liquor store where she picked up some beer. Then we drove to her basement apartment, located across the street from Maplewood Park. Her apartment was basically empty. All she had was a big waterbed, a stove, and a refrigerator. But at least it was clean. Morena pulled out about an ounce bag of marijuana from under her pillow, gave it to me with a pack of strawberry-flavored rolling papers, and told me to roll some joints. We sat there drinking, smoking, and talking trash for a couple of hours. Then the conversation turned to the subject of what it meant to be a Latin King.

Morena excused herself and told me to make myself at home. She came back about half an hour later. Morena had bathed and changed into some shorts and a T-shirt. She looked pretty sexy. She apologized for taking so long and explained that she felt kind of muggy so she had decided to clean herself up. Morena brought a notebook with her. The cover of that notebook had the words *Nation Literature* written on it. The notebook contained the laws, prayers, and purpose of the Latin Kings. I always thought of the Latin Kings as just a big street gang, but there was obviously more to its history than that. Morena told me that the Latin Kings were formed a long time ago when Puerto Ricans first started coming to Chicago. In those times, she explained, Puerto Ricans were being victimized by whites and blacks. They formed the Latin Kings as a way to protect themselves and began fighting back. As time went by, the Latin Kings became well known and were feared throughout the city. The Puerto Rican community was so supportive of the Latin Kings that they allowed them to have a float in the annual Puerto Rican parade. But these things were all in the past. Now Puerto Ricans were labeled as very violent and criminally minded people because of the actions of the Latin Kings. I understood why such a gang would be formed by an ethnic group to protect its members, but I did not understand why now this gang was fighting other gangs of the same race. I asked Morena about it. She simply said that those other gangs were *crusaos* (traitors). They were gangs started by guys who were once members of the Latin Kings. They wanted to be chiefs without first being nobodies.

Morena went on explaining the contents of the notebook. She explained that laws were made to keep discipline among the Kings and Queens. There were laws written in the notebook that I never saw anybody following or respecting—like the one that said honor your parents or the strict laws concerning too much drug use. I just couldn't see how being in a street gang, staying out at all times of the night, taking a chance on going to jail, or getting killed was honoring your parents. I did notice that the members who were acting this way often came from a family situation similar to mine. There were others, however, who had both parents at home but did nothing to honor and respect them. I also found it kind of funny reading laws regarding drug use while sitting there with a joint in my mouth and a whole bag of weed waiting to be smoked. Morena explained that what the drug laws meant was that you should be able to control your high. They also meant that becoming a junkie would not be tolerated. In other words, the drug laws were basically about the use of highly addictive drugs like heroin, cocaine, and PCP. It was the most hypocritical shit I had ever heard! Morena read the different prayers that all gang members had to memorize. There was one in particular that had to be memorized one week after the initiation took place. Failure to do so would result in discipline.

I believe Morena's intention was to prepare me for what I was about to get into. What she did, however, was confuse me more than I had been to begin with. Finally she put the notebook away and made me promise not to tell anybody that she had shown it to me before I was a member. I assured her that I would keep it between the two of us.

We continued smoking and drinking and soon the conversation became sexual in nature. We joked and laughed about each other's sexual experiences. I had initially had sexual thoughts about Morena, but from the beginning she treated me like her little brother. I respected her more than any other girl. Nevertheless we were high, on her bed, and talking about sex. I decided to make a move on her. The fantasies I once had about Morena were suddenly coming true. We were graduating from best friends to lovers. I was making love to my best friend—how fortunate I felt. Morena lay there with her eyes closed and let me do anything I wanted to. I took full advantage of her willingness.

The next morning we woke up in each other's arms. The first thing that came to my mind was how envious all the other guys would be when I told them that Morena was my lady. Morena woke up and looked at me with an expression that said, "What the hell are you doing here?" Then she noticed we were both naked. She got up raging mad about what had happened between us the night before. She began cursing and accusing me of taking advantage of her intoxication. I was shocked at her sudden reaction. I tried talking to her, but she wouldn't listen to me. When she finally did calm down, I tried to explain that what happened between us was mutual and that I did not take advantage of her. I should have kept my mouth shut. Those words just made her flip out again. "You're just a fuckin' little kid," she screamed. Morena lifted a corner of the waterbed and pulled out a gun. She put it to my head and said, "You little raping bastard, I ought to kill you. If you ever tell anyone about this I will kill you." She pulled my hair and pressed the gun against my cheekbone. She pushed me and I fell on the bed. She put a T-shirt on and left the room, mumbling obscenities. I got dressed and left for Maria's apartment.

Maybe Morena was too high to notice what was happening. Maybe she was regretful. Maybe I wasn't that good. Whatever the reason was, her anger was real. The drugs and alcohol clouded our judgment to a point where we had different interpretations of our actions. In Morena's mind, I had taken advantage of her while she slept. In my mind, Morena had been a willing participant. The only thing we agreed on was that our relationship was threatened. I never had the desire to brag about having sex with Morena or even mention it. What happened that night is one of those things one completely blocks out as if it never happened. That morning I learned that sex could put a strain on a friendship. I still block out that night—to me it never happened.

I got to Maria's, took a shower, and sat down to watch television. The incident with Morena was still fresh in my mind. I had been pretty confused about life as a gang member, but now I was completely lost. I didn't know what to expect. Maria was not home. When she arrived she immediately started nagging me about my swollen eye. "*Stupido,*" ("Stupid") she said, "how can you be such a *pendejo*?" After cleaning and dressing the wound from my fight with Speedy, she told me about her new boyfriend. He was a nice guy, she said, which really surprised me because Maria rarely had anything good to say about men. She planned on introducing me as her son. Maria had this glowing look on her face and a big smile. At first I thought that the guy was just another lover in Maria's life, but something told me that this guy might just be someone special. Maria told me that her daughter Lucy was pregnant and had moved in with the baby's father and his parents. She expressed hope that maybe Lucy would finally get her life together once she became a mother.

That afternoon Morena came by to talk to me. I didn't know how to react to her visit, so I threw myself on her mercy, hoping that she had left her gun at home. Luckily, Morena had completely calmed down. We talked about the night before and she apologized for reacting the way she did. Morena explained the she became angry because she knew that the beautiful friendship we shared would never be the same again. I assured her that nothing had changed between us and that we could go on being friends like before. Deep down, however, I knew she was right. Although I was saying the things that I knew she wanted to hear, my mind was on her body, how sexy she was, and how good it felt to make love to her. Morena and I used to be able to sit and talk for hours without worrying about offending each other. Now I found myself looking for the right words to say. I was mostly undressing her with my eyes, wanting to kiss her, hold her, and ultimately make love to her again. Morena knew what was going through my mind. She looked at me and began laughing. Then she got up and kissed me passionately. After that kiss I thought for sure she would be mine. Morena grabbed my face, looked me straight in the eye, and said, "I hope you enjoyed that kiss. It's the last." She told me that we would not be able to hang out together anymore. "I should have dotted your other eye," she said as she started down the stairs. Morena ignored my calls. She didn't even turn back to wave good-bye. Just like that, it seemed our friendship was gone. I thought about it for a while and realized that I was regretting ever making love to Morena. I couldn't believe it, but I was actually feeling bad about having sex with a beautiful girl. Finally the weekend had come to an end and it was time to go back to school.

25

Prove Myself Worthy

THAT MONDAY I expected to be confronted by Speedy at school, but he was nowhere to be seen. Once again I went about chasing Rosie, but she still ignored me. She was now making fun out of the fact that I had a swollen left eye. Sheena in turn gave me her attention and had some nice words of sympathy. That week went by rather quickly. I went through the same old routine of going to school, going by Kedzie and Armitage, and then going home. I still had not heard from Hector, nor did I want to.

Friday came along and I was invited to a party the Kings were having on Cortland and Whipple Streets. This was the territory of a different Latin Kings section. I got home from school, changed clothes, and headed to the party. I got to the apartment where the party was being held early, but most of the Kings from Kedzie and Armitage were already there. They were all outside huddled in several different places getting high. I walked over to where most of the kids my age were hanging out. Loco called me over to an older group and gave me a joint. I lit it up and passed it back to him. He told me to smoke it by myself. Loco asked me if I was ready for my initiation on that upcoming Sunday. I told him that I was. He shook my hand and told me that he wanted me to go on a mission with him and some other Kings later on that night. Like an idiot with a death wish I quickly agreed. I walked away from Loco and went back to hang around with the guys my age. I didn't show it, but inside I was scared as hell about the mission. I decided to get so drunk that Loco would change his mind about taking me along with them. I began drinking beer and then wine, then more beer, coupled with joint after joint. I got drunk all right, but now I was looking forward to going on that mission.

The party was great. There were so many people there that we could hardly move. The deejay kept playing the Funkedelic song "One Nation Under a Groove," which the Kings had adopted as their anthem. There was marijuana and cocaine being passed around and it seemed like every guy there had claimed a girl for the night. I met a girl named Blanca. She was a Queen from Cortland and Whipple. She was short, with dirty blonde hair, blue eyes, and very light skin.

Blanca and I danced and then decided to get out of the crowded apartment where the party was going on. We went out into the hallway and then downstairs to the first floor. We talked and smoked weed for a little while and then began kissing and touching each other like two dogs in heat. We were really getting carried away. Had it not been for the people who kept coming in and out of the party we probably would have had sex right there in the hallway. Soon the hallway was crowded with people, mostly couples making out.

I heard Loco coming down the stairs and realized that it was time to go on the long-awaited mission. Blanca promised me that she would be there when I got back. I figured that if she did stay there she would do it with some other guy. If she didn't, I could probably get it on with some other Queen. After all, the Queens were there—waiting and willing. I loved it. Loco walked past me with two other guys and motioned for me to follow. I bragged to Blanca about what I was going to do and then kissed her deeply. She seemed impressed by my machismo and asked me to shoot a rival gang member for her. *"Amor de Rey"* ("King love"), Blanca said as I walked down the steps.

Me, Loco, and two other Kings got in a car and drove out of the neighborhood. The two other Kings were Cat and Pito. Cat was a King from Cortland and Whipple. He had a slim build with an ugly scar on his neck and face. This was the result of a confrontation with rival gang members. Pito was from Kedzie and Armitage. He was a lot like my old friend Julio: brown skinned, pushed-back hair, and a deep Latin accent. Pito gave me a can of gold spray paint and Loco began explaining to me what the mission was all about. We were headed to a rival gang's 'hood.

They called themselves the Imperial Gangsters. Their 'hood was on Palmer Boulevard and Drake Street, about a mile and a half from Kedzie and Armitage. The plan was for me to get out of the car about a block away from their 'hood and walk toward their territory. The guys were going to try to make the Gangsters chase them. When they did, my job was to spray paint the letters *A L K N* (Almighty Latin King Nation) over a mural they had painted of their slogan.

I got out of the car half a block from Armitage and Drake. As soon as I got to the corner of Armitage and Drake, I spotted the emblem. It consisted of a pink crown with the letter *I* on one side and *G* on the other, painted on a black background. The words *KING KILLERS* were also written in big, pink letters right next to the emblem. I stood on the corner and panicked when I saw all the Gangsters that were out there. I thought about turning back, but all the alcohol I had consumed gave me the sudden courage to go ahead with the mission. Loco and the other guys drove slowly past the Gangsters and made themselves known as Kings. The Gangsters immediately reacted by chasing the car down the street. I ran up to the wall and began spray painting. The Gangsters were so occupied with the King brothers that they didn't realize what I was doing. I went crazy with the spray paint. I completely covered the words *KING KILLERS* and then put the name *Lil Loco* on the wall with a five-point crown above the name. From that day on, I would be called Lil Loco.

When the Gangsters started yelling obscenities at me, it was my cue to take off running toward Armitage. Loco and the boys were supposed to pick me up two blocks away from Drake Street on Kimball Avenue. When I got to Kimball the guys were waiting for me. I got really brave and told them to go on without me—I was going to make it back to the 'hood on foot. I felt indestructible. The Kings followed me closely in the car. I painted the letters *L K* and wrote *Lil Loco* on buildings all along Armitage. On one of my stops I decided to paint a crown. I stood there taking my own sweet time spray painting the wall when I was confronted by two guys. I recognized both of them from school. I had seen Rosie hanging around with them. One of them held up the Gangsters' hand sign. The other one held up the Disciples' hand sign. I sprayed paint at the Gangsters' faces and made them chase me toward the car where

Loco and the others waited. When I got next to the car I stopped, turned around, and threw the spray paint can at the guy who made the Disciple sign. He ducked and tackled me to the ground. Then the other guy came over to help him. They would have liked to beat me to a pulp, but instead they just set themselves up for a beating.

Loco, Pito, and Cat jumped out of the car with baseball bats and began hitting home runs with my attackers' heads. The guy who flashed the Gangster sign ran out into the street screaming and holding his bleeding head. He never saw the van coming down the street. The van hit him so hard that he landed back on the sidewalk. We immediately stopped beating on the Disciple, jumped into the car, and drove away as a crowd gathered. Loco and I got out of the car on Kedzie and Armitage while Cat and Pito drove away to get rid of the car. We went inside the Kings' clubhouse and went about celebrating the success of the mission. Loco found it amusing that I had decided to call myself Lil Loco. He figured that I named myself after him, but I picked that name because that's what China called me and it was the first name that came to my mind while I was painting. After about fifteen minutes we heard police sirens speeding by and then an ambulance. We glanced out the window and saw detectives pulling over anybody and everybody who looked like a gang member. They were asking for a "Lil Loco." Loco and I looked at each other and began laughing. Then we went back to smoking weed and drinking wine. I wasn't worried that the police were looking for me or that a human being might have been killed because of my actions. No, I was worried about getting high and getting laid.

26

Rape

ABOUT AN HOUR had passed when we heard a knock on the door. It was Morena and Blanca. Blanca and I quickly continued where we left off before my mission. Loco and Morena got up and went into another room.

I couldn't believe how easy it was to get laid with girls that were in gangs or hung around with them. It seemed like the more violent and criminally active a guy was, the easier it was to get whatever girl you wanted.

Blanca took off her top but refused to take off her pants. That didn't stop me. I kept trying to completely undress her, but to no avail. After wrestling with her for a while I got mad, called her a prick-teasing bitch, and told her to get up and get out. Blanca was looking for her bra while I was calling her every name in the book. Morena came out of the other room and yelled at me to stop disrespecting Blanca. I yelled back that if the bitch didn't intend to give it up she should not have teased me. Morena saw that Blanca was half-naked and told her that if she was woman enough to tease, she better be woman enough to please. If not, she was going to be dealt with for disrespecting me. Enticing me with promises of sex and then not following through was disrespectful and would not be tolerated. Morena went back in the room with Loco while Blanca just sat there staring at me with tears rolling down her face. I felt sorry for her but didn't have any intention of letting her off the hook. I began undressing her. She whined and whispered, "Please don't. I'm still a virgin." If I had been sober, I probably would have had pity for her and left her alone. The fact that I was high, combined with my arousal, made me take advantage of the situation. I took Blanca's virginity as she lay there crying and begging me not to. After it was all over, she got up crying and went to the bathroom. She returned, looking for her clothes. I grabbed her, laid her down, and had sex with her again. I was becoming an animal with no consideration for anyone's feelings. What happened between Blanca and me was rape.

The next morning Blanca wouldn't even look at me. I kissed her on the cheek and cupped her breast. She didn't pull back or complain but all along she lay there with no emotion whatsoever. I was sober now and I cared about what she was feeling. I realized it was a little too late, but I tried to talk to her anyway. It took a while but she finally opened up and said what was on her mind. I thought that now that it was all over Blanca would accept it, but I was wrong. She belittled me as best she could. "You're not a man," she said in a soft, stern voice. "Real men don't do shit like that."

After she finished I felt like a total asshole. I apologized and even shed some tears but it was too late. I tried to make her feel better by asking her to be my girlfriend. She said no but then changed her mind. I guess she figured since I was her first lover she might as well try to like me. I was taking the blame for everything that had happened, but she finally admitted that she also was at fault. Blanca confessed that the drinking and smoking had affected her judgment. She said she wasn't really a virgin but that she never had any intention of letting things go so far. She vowed never to drink or use drugs again. She knew that if she had not been intoxicated the whole incident would never have taken place. I didn't like Blanca, I didn't find her attractive, I didn't even want her as a friend, but I asked her to be my girlfriend because I felt sorry for her. What we had was emotionless sex fueled by the need to conquer.

At noon, members of the Kings began arriving at the clubhouse. Pito came in with a couple of Queens. One of them attracted my attention. It became pretty obvious that the feeling was mutual because of the way we just stared at each other. I tried to ignore the girl to show respect for Blanca; after all, I was her boyfriend. The girl was called Cubana. She had caramel-colored skin, long, black hair, and the biggest brown eyes

I had ever seen. She had a beautiful body, but it was her eyes that caught my attention. The weed I was smoking began to take effect, and although I was very aware of Blanca's presence, I could not keep myself from staring at Cubana. Cubana did nothing to avoid our eyes meeting, even though she saw Blanca kiss me several times. As soon as Blanca walked away from me, Cubana came over to where I was and started a conversation. She asked me why I was staring at her and if I liked what I saw. "Yes," I answered. By this time I was pretty high. Blanca came back and sat next to us, but I ignored her. Blanca finally stepped between us, called me an asshole, and walked out. Cubana laughed at Blanca and said, "I guess you're single now."

I spent most of the day talking to Cubana and trying to get to know her. I found out that she had been a runaway since she was thirteen. When I asked why she left her home, she refused to talk about it and became very upset when I kept pushing the subject. Throughout our conversation Cubana made it a point to emphasize that just because she was a runaway did not mean she was easy. She said she was still a virgin and she planned on staying that way. I thought to myself, "Yeah right, that's what Blanca said." She began telling me a story about how she stabbed a guy who was once her so-called boyfriend when he got carried away and tried to take advantage of her. "He swore he was going to get a piece," Cubana said matter-of-factly, "until he felt that blade in him." I knew she was trying to get a message across but I ignored it— words didn't mean a thing to me. I just reached out and kissed her, she kissed me back, and then warned me to be careful and respect her or I would live to regret it.

More Kings began arriving at the clubhouse. They kept telling me that the police were looking for me and that the Gangster that was hit by the van died. The seriousness of the fact that I was being sought by the police for what would probably be a murder charge did not set in. I actually found it funny. I was pretty high and too busy impressing Cubana with my tough attitude to realize the seriousness of my situation. It seemed as if I was becoming coldhearted. I even suggested that we throw a party to celebrate the death of a rival gang member. "The pleasure was all mine," I exclaimed. "I can't wait to do it again." Cubana was very impressed.

Night set in and I still had not left the clubhouse. I was high as a kite playing puppy love games with Cubana. The clubhouse was full of Kings and Queens. There were a lot of them there that I had never seen before, but I met them all that night. At about 1:00 A.M. Cubana and I were sitting by the window smoking a joint when we heard a commotion outside. We looked out and saw a couple of Kings running across Armitage headed north up Kedzie. We heard somebody yell out "Gangster," and about four gunshots went off. Loco was in another room at the time. When he heard the shots, he came running out with a gun in his hand. I took the gun from him and went outside. Once outside I looked down Kedzie and saw the two Kings ducking behind a car. I also saw three Gangsters. Two of them were pointing their guns in the direction of the Kings. I crossed Armitage toward the Gangsters, making sure I wasn't noticed. I peeked out from behind the building on the corner to see where the Gangsters were. The two Gangsters doing the shooting were standing in the middle of the sidewalk, while the other one stood in between two parked cars. I jumped out from behind the building and opened fire. I didn't aim at any particular target. I didn't even know how many bullets I had. I just pulled the trigger. The two Kings took advantage of the attention I attracted and ran for safety. Pito showed up with a shotgun. I got out of his way and he opened fire. I heard one of the Gangsters scream out in pain and then two shots went off in retaliation. It seemed as if we were in some kind of movie, only this was real. Nobody ran away. We just kept shooting at each other with no mercy. All of a sudden somebody yelled, "*la Hada, la Hada*" ("the police, the police"). Then, and only then, did the shooting stop and everyone retreated. Pito and I ran back into the clubhouse before the police saw us.

Looking out from a window we could see the cops searching every place a human could hide. We also saw them put the Gangster who had been shot inside an ambulance. The paramedics were also attending to an innocent bystander who got hit by a stray bullet. Gang crime detectives stopped a couple of Kings who showed up at Armitage and Kedzie.

After searching them and roughing them up a little they handcuffed them, put them in their squad car, and drove away. After that, everything was quiet. The only people to be seen were some police officers who kept cruising the area and a couple of drunks. Inside the clubhouse everybody settled down in whatever corner they could find and decided to spend the night there. Cubana and I lay down on the sofa and the next thing I knew it was Sunday morning.

Pulling the trigger was becoming second nature to me. I didn't know how to load or unload guns and had no idea that they came in different sizes. All I knew was how to point and pull the trigger. Pulling the trigger was not only a way of enhancing my image; it also improved my chances of getting girls. Girls loved me. They gave me attention, affection, and sex because I pulled the trigger without hesitation.

27

Crowned

I woke up at about ten o'clock and noticed that most of the people who had slept over had gotten up and left. Cubana was also gone. I was sober now and all at once the facts of the past two nights hit me like a ton of bricks. I was suddenly worried about going to jail for murder. I wondered if anybody had seen me shooting at the Gangsters the night before. My nerves were jumpy and I was even afraid to look out the window. All I could think about was being with my mother in Puerto Rico. Anything seemed better than what I feared my future would be like as a King. How could I be so stupid? There was no way I was going to join the Kings. Now sober, I did not like the lifestyle that came with being a gang member. I heard a knock on the door and was scared to get up and open it. I just sat there and waited for one of the other guys to do it. I began imagining that the cops were on the other side of the door. I visualized the police charging in, slamming me to the floor, and handcuffing me. To my relief, when the door was opened, Cubana walked in.

Cubana had cleaned up and changed clothes. She gave me some food she had picked up on the way over and joked and played around with me as I ate. She had a happy-go-lucky personality. It was wonderful, but I really wasn't in the mood. Cubana noticed my seriousness and asked me what was wrong. I couldn't find the words. I had too many crazy thoughts in my mind to talk about anything. Cubana kept trying to cheer me up, but I was just too depressed. The vision of the police finding me, beating me up, and then taking me to jail kept appearing over and over in my mind. I became angry with myself for not staying in Puerto Rico with my family. I wanted to take off running and never stop but I was too scared to even move from where I was sitting. Cubana kept prying until I finally told her what was on my mind. I dug my face into her neck and whispered, "*La hada*, they're going to get me." Cubana started laughing and was ready to blurt out my fears but I held her real tight before she could. "Don't, please don't, don't say nothing," I whispered in her ear. She looked me straight in the eye as I shed a tear. Cubana kissed me softly on the lips, and said, "*Perdóname, Loquito*" ("I'm sorry, Lil Loco").

Soon the place began to fill up with Kings. Today was the meeting when I would officially become a member. Again, joints were being passed around. At first I turned them down, but eventually I started smoking also. I was hoping that with some weed in my head the crazy thoughts would stop. It worked. I became relaxed. Now I was trying to figure out how to get myself out of my impending initiation.

Before I came up with an answer for myself, the meeting started. All the Queens excused themselves and left. They would have their own meeting at a separate location and then join ours later. All the Kings stood up and bowed their heads as Pito said a prayer. The prayer Pito recited was known as the universal prayer of the Latin Kings; it was mandatory for all Kings to memorize it. "*Amor*," Pito said when he finished the prayer. He then pounded his right fist upon his heart, brought it up, kissed it, and formed it into the Kings' sign as he held it up in the air. (The Kings' hand sign consists of the index finger, little finger, and thumb held up while the other two fingers are folded. It is the same sign used to symbolize "I love you" in sign language.) Everybody in the room did exactly as Pito had done. I wasn't allowed to; I was not yet a King. In fact I wasn't even supposed to be there for the prayer. My actions of the previous night earned me the right to be there. Also, Loco was completely sure that I would become a King that day, so he gave the OK for me to be there from the beginning of the meeting. After the prayer my membership was announced. Any protest against me becoming a King had to be made at that time. Lalo spoke favorably about me. Pito and Loco did the same. I was hoping that someone would protest so that my initiation could be put off for another day, but that never happened. It was unanimous. I was welcomed into the gang. I stood there like an idiot with no desire to be a King but no courage to say so. The one chance I had to prove that I was not a coward by speaking up and saying no passed me by. Because of my cowardice I was about to be initiated into the biggest and most violent Latino gang in Chicago.

Pito led me into a separate room. The room was empty except for a couple of mattresses that were lying on the floor. We picked up the mattresses and stood them up against the wall. Pito left the room and returned with three other guys; he also had a stopwatch in his hand. The three guys he brought would have the honor of making me a King by beating me for three minutes. They were Peewee Latin Kings who were all around my age. I was instructed to stand against the wall. The other three guys surrounded me. There was one on each side of me and one in front of me. I was scared as hell. I wanted to back out at the last minute but I was petrified of the consequences I would have to face if I did. Finally I braced myself and told Pito that I was ready. Pito gave the guys the go ahead and they immediately began pounding on me. They hit me on my legs, arms, chest, and stomach. At first it hurt like hell but after a while they got tired and their punches began to lose force. The guys had this expression on their faces like they enjoyed what they were doing. After the three minutes had elapsed, Pito told them to stop. I was officially a Latin King.

The guys who had done the initiation honors embraced me one at a time and said, "*Amor*, Brother." I was glad the initiation was finally over. Now I had to be macho and hide my pain. I could hardly lift my arms because of the swelling in my shoulders. The muscle in one of my legs was so sore that I had to walk with a limp. We went back into the room where the meeting was taking place. I was greeted with applause, a lot of handshakes, and a hug from Loco. He announced that from that day on I should be referred to as King Lil Loco. I was given a notebook containing the laws and prayers of the Latin Kings. It was exactly like the one Morena had shown me. I was then told which prayer I had to memorize by the next meeting. Failure to do so would result in disciplinary action. Lalo congratulated me and gave me a joint. It wasn't customary to get high while a meeting was taking place, but they were making an exception for me. I sat on a windowsill, lit up the joint, and watched as the meeting continued.

THAT DAY I became part of something, part of the "in" crowd. I had proven my worth on the battlefield and through initiation. I had earned the right to wear the colors, hold up the hand sign, and be an ambassador of the Latin Kings. With that honor came public labels. I was now officially a bum, junkie, drug user, dealer, criminal, thief, stupid, violent, good-for-nothing, two-timing snake in the grass. The Latin Kings became my new family. They praised me for doing things I had gotten beaten for by my previous family. An Almighty Latin King, that's what I was. I wore an imaginary crown coveted by many and I ruled an imagery kingdom. I had no idea what I had gotten myself into. Maybe I didn't want to know.

The weekly dues were collected. Every member had to donate five dollars a week, which was used for the purchase of guns, large amounts of drugs, and bond money for members who got arrested. Surprisingly, some of the money was also used for members who were incarcerated for crimes they committed for the benefit of the gang. Many of those guys were actually doing time for the actions of others. After the money was collected, the treasurer, a guy called Chico, counted the money and announced that the total amount of money in the treasury was now fifteen thousand dollars. Lalo, who was the chief enforcer of the gang, made a request for money to be used for the purchase of guns that were being offered to the gang by a member of the South Side Latin Kings. According to Lalo, the guns were being brought from out of state and were brand-new. They included .357 magnums, 9-millimeter automatics, automatic rifles with eye scopes, and riot or pump shotguns. Ammunition for all the weapons was also being supplied. Lalo was asking for approval to use five thousand dollars to make that purchase.

Pito was the vice president, second in command under Loco. He asked for approval of another five thousand dollars for the purchase of twenty pounds of marijuana. He explained that the marijuana would be sold in ounces, half-ounces, and nickel bags. He thought the money used for the purchase could easily be doubled.

Loco then took over the meeting. He started by announcing that the total sum of money given by Chico did not include the cocaine and heroin profits that had not been collected. He estimated the profits to be between fifteen and twenty thousand dollars. As he talked, I began to realize that there was more to being a King than just standing on the corner representing.

Loco continued explaining that any members who wanted to make some money could sell drugs. Those who wanted to do this had to understand that they were responsible for all the drugs they were given and all the money they collected. The only excuse that would be accepted for lost profits was getting busted by the cops and this had to be proven. Loco called to our attention that a lot of older Kings were getting involved in using heroin. He reminded us of the Kings' law against using that drug. He told us that anyone using heroin and calling himself a King should be beaten without question. He also warned us that most of these guys were pretty crazy and wouldn't care about killing one of us for their drug. Great, I thought, not only am I in danger of being killed by rival gang members, I also have to watch out for some of our own.

The subject returned to the money needed for the purchase of guns and drugs. Everybody was to vote by raising their left hand above their heads showing the Kings' hand sign. The vote was unanimous. The guns and drugs would be purchased and an extra pound of marijuana would be bought for the personal use of the Latin Kings. With those issues settled it was time to move on to other business.

I gave my undivided attention to everything that was said. I never knew how highly organized gang life was and how much it was run like a legitimate business. Until then I had thought being a gang member was all about partying, getting high, and fighting with other gangs. This new knowledge of gang life intrigued me but also left me with an eerie feeling.

The next item on the agenda was to hear charges that were being brought against four members. Three of them were being charged with rape and one King was being charged with stealing money from the gang. Everybody was asked to leave the room except for those who formed the committee—Loco, Pito, Lalo, Diego, Paco, and Gordo—who would decide their guilt or innocence. Loco asked me to stay and serve as some kind of usher so that I could see for myself the seriousness of violating the laws of the Kings. The committee decided to hear the member accused of stealing first. I was instructed to walk the three guys charged with rape to the door. They were to wait outside until it was their turn to be tried.

The guy charged with stealing, Slim, was a skinny kid who couldn't have been any more than thirteen years old. He looked pale and nervous and it seemed like he was ready to cry. Slim had been given fifteen quarter bags of cocaine to sell. He was to keep seventy-five out of the three hundred and seventy-five dollars he was responsible for, but none of the money ever showed up. Lalo asked Slim about the whereabouts of the money. Slim replied that a junkie stuck him up. When asked if he recognized the guy, Slim said no. Lalo asked him if he used cocaine. Slim answered no. He was then reminded of the fact that he was responsible for the money. Slim said that he was aware of that but it wasn't his fault that he got stuck up. Diego asked him if he was sure he didn't have a cocaine habit. Slim said he was sure. Diego accused him of snorting the cocaine with a local prostitute who sold her body for the purpose of supporting her coke habit. Diego explained that for a dime of coke the prostitute had told him what had happened to the coke for which Slim was responsible. According to Diego the prostitute had "eaten Slim's mind up" with the prospect of sex in exchange for coke. They ended up in the prostitute's apartment snorting coke and having sex. Slim finally broke down and admitted his guilt to the charges being brought against him. It was now a matter of punishing him. I was instructed to take Slim into the room where I had been initiated while the punishment was decided.

Inside the room I couldn't help but notice the look of horror on Slim's face. It seemed like he could sense his punishment. I asked him about the night with the prostitute. He told me that she was an attractive girl. She grabbed his crotch and promised him oral sex in return for a bag of coke. He agreed and planned to pay for it out of his cut of the money. They went to her apartment. She quickly undressed and told him to do the same. They snorted some coke and started having sex. She did a lot more with him than what she had originally offered, Slim explained, but he had no plans of giving her more coke. The next thing he knew he woke up on her bed. She was gone and so was the cocaine. Slim said that the prostitute claimed he gave it to her, but he didn't remember doing that. I began scolding him and telling him he was a stupid fool for getting himself into that situation. "They're gonna kill me, man, they're gonna kill me," Slim said as he busted out crying. The door opened suddenly and we were called out. It was time for Slim to be sentenced.

We walked out of the room together. Slim stood in front of the committee. I sat on the window ledge and waited to hear what had been decided. Slim was asked if he wanted to remain a King. He did. He was then given two choices. One was to get violated out of the gang and the other was to take a one-minute head-to-toe violation. Slim asked for time to make up his mind. His request was denied. He was then advised that if he planned to continue using cocaine he was better off quitting the gang. "You're snorting, but you can't handle it and that will not be tolerated," Pito told Slim. Slim decided to get violated out of the gang. I guess he must have been really hooked on coke to make a decision like that, but then again his other choice wasn't any better. Loco gave me the names of three guys who were going to have the honor of beating Slim out of the gang and told me to go get them. The guys were part of the Peewee faction of the Latin Kings. Crazy Tony, Cisco, and Spade were all about the same age and height as Slim, but they were much heavier and stronger. They seemed very anxious and enthusiastic about carrying out the order they were given. Paco got up, grabbed the stopwatch, and took all the guys into the beating room. I was instructed to go get the other guys who were charged with rape.

As a member of the Latin Kings, phrases like "I will die for you" were readily used. It was part of the lingo, a way of letting a member know they belonged. Brothers, that's what we were, brothers. Slim, however, was not given any brotherly treatment. He was not given any advice or offered any help. No importance was given to his addiction. The answer to his problem was an ass whipping. There was no way Slim could get out of the clubhouse that day without being hurt.

ACE, JIMBO, AND Lucky were part of the Juniors faction of the Latin Kings. They had been members of the gang for a while. They were charged with the rape of a Queen. Although rape of a Queen was one of the most serious charges one could face as a member of the Kings, these guys came in joking and laughing and noticeably confident of their innocence. They stood before the committee and were told to wait until Paco was through dealing with Slim. From the beating room you could hear Slim screaming and begging for mercy. You could also hear the guys doing the beating taunting him while they punished him. I sat wondering if Blanca would charge me with rape. I became nervous. I began thinking that the reason that I was asked to play usher was so that I could be dealt with also.

Finally the screaming stopped and Paco walked out of the room and made a comment about how weak Slim was and that he took the beating like a pussy. Crazy Tony, Cisco, and Spade came out of the room with smiles on their faces as if they had just won some big contest. They described Slim as a pussy, a punk, and a sissy, among other things. Slim had collapsed from the beating. Loco immediately ordered those who had beat Slim to pick him up and carry him outside. When they carried Slim out, he had this look of horror on his face. It was pretty obvious that Slim had been seriously hurt. He was having trouble breathing and couldn't even walk on his own. I felt sorry for him but I made sure not to show it. I didn't want to be thought of as soft. I walked them to the door, locked the door behind them, and went back to my place on the window ledge.

Not a minute had passed when I heard screams outside. I looked out the window and saw Slim lying on the concrete being beaten by just about all of the Peewee Kings. I called what was happening to Loco's attention. Loco said that since Slim was not part of the gang anymore he was on his own. He then asked me if I had any problems with that. Although I did, I answered no. Out of the corner of my eye I could see Slim being kicked and hit with bats and bottles while he laid there on the street unable to defend himself. The regrets I had about joining the Kings were growing stronger by the minute, but I knew that if I changed my mind now I would get the same treatment as Slim. I began mentally kicking myself for not giving life in Puerto Rico more of a chance. I wondered how my family was and wished that I could turn back time so that I could be with them again.

My daydreams were interrupted by Lalo's voice calling out my name. I was told to get away from the window and to go stand by the door. The charges against the three Junior Kings were about to be heard. The guys' confident attitude had not changed a bit. They stood before the committee with big smiles on their faces. Loco asked them if they knew the serious nature of the charges. Ace replied, "The bitch didn't have to be raped. She gives it up to everybody." They began laughing simultaneously but were soon quieted by the reminder that the girl who was accusing them had plenty of witnesses against them. Loco told them to have a seat and keep quiet until it was their turn to talk. I was then told to call in Dimples and her witnesses. Dimples was a Queen from Cortland and Whipple. She had the reputation of being a wild child who was easy to lay. Her witnesses included Morena, Cubana, and two other Queens from Cortland and Whipple who I had never met. A couple of Kings from that same section were also present to speak on her behalf. Loco asked Dimples if she knew the seriousness of the charges she was making against Ace, Jimbo, and Lucky. He also asked her if she knew what the consequences would be if they found her to be lying. Dimples said that she knew what she was getting into and that she also knew what had happened to her.

Dimples began giving her account of what had happened. She came to Kedzie and Armitage looking for Morena. She ran into Ace, who told her that Morena had just left the 'hood and then invited her to smoke some weed. They walked back toward Cortland and Whipple together. They stopped and sat down on the steps of an abandoned building located on Homer and Albany Streets about three blocks from Cortland and Whipple. Dimples admitted that she had always had a crush on Ace so she didn't mind when he started making advances toward her. They began kissing and touching and decided to go inside the building where there were mattresses laying in just about every room. That particular building was used for everything from partying, to a hideout, to a hotel. They were about to enter the building when Jimbo, Lucky, and the two

Kings from Cortland and Whipple called out to them. After hanging out with them for a few minutes Ace and Dimples proceeded inside.

Dimples and Ace immediately began getting sexually intimate while the other guys were outside getting high. After a few minutes, Lucky walked in on Ace and Dimples as they were having sex. Meanwhile Morena, Cubana, and the other two Queens had arrived and were outside talking to the guys. Tears were now running down Dimples's face. She began sobbing and stuttering as she talked. She explained that Ace noticed that Lucky was watching them and asked him if he wanted to be next. Dimples protested and tried to push Ace off her but he held her down. Lucky kneeled over her and put his hand over her mouth so she couldn't scream. She started squirming and fighting with them. Ace got angry, punched her in the stomach, and then continued having sex with her. After the pain in her stomach had gone away she began fighting with them again. This is when Jimbo walked in. He asked what was going on. Lucky told him to help him hold Dimples down. Jimbo hesitated but did as Ace told him when asked a second time. Dimples bit the hand Lucky had over her mouth. He went crazy and started beating her savagely. Lucky choked her and threatened to kill her if she screamed. Ace got off her and helped hold Dimples down while Lucky penetrated her. She pleaded for Ace to help her but all he did was say, "Shut up, bitch. This is a dream come true for you." After Lucky got off her, Jimbo penetrated her. While Jimbo was on top of her, Ace was telling Lucky that he wanted to fuck Dimples in the ass. Dimples made one last attempt to get away from them. She somehow freed her mouth and began screaming at the top of her lungs. Those who were outside heard her and quickly ran inside. They saw what was going on and came to her aid. Ace, Lucky, and Jimbo just stood there fixing their clothes and grinning from ear to ear as if nothing had happened. They said that Dimples asked for it but then couldn't handle it. Morena flipped out and had to be restrained when she repeatedly tried to attack Ace, Lucky, and Jimbo. Cubana and the other Queens consoled Dimples and helped her get dressed.

Dimples began crying uncontrollably as she told her story. Her words became hard to understand. She was obviously traumatized by what had happened. Throughout her story members of the committee sat there with blank expressions on their faces. Ace, Jimbo, and Lucky, on the other hand, made disbelieving faces in response to every accusation.

Dimples was asked to sit down. Morena was called to speak before the committee. Morena had an angry expression on her face. She began by saying that she didn't know what went on before she went into the building but that if Dimples volunteered her body the guys wouldn't have had to beat her. She looked at the guys being accused as if she was ready to commit murder. She screamed, "These ain't no Kings. They're fuckin' pussies!" She went at them. Loco jumped out from behind the table and grabbed her just as she got ready to hit Ace. "I'm cool, I'm cool," Morena said as Loco took her toward the door. "Ace and Lucky were holding her when we went in; Jimbo was getting off her," Morena said. Loco turned to Dimples's other witnesses and asked them to corroborate Morena's claim. Loco asked the girls one at a time and they all agreed with Morena. Loco finally released Morena. She sat on a window ledge with her face in her hands mumbling something.

The two King brothers serving as Dimples's witnesses were called before the committee. The point was made to them that they were from the same King section as Dimples. They were asked if they knew Dimples personally or just as a Queen sister. The first one to answer was a short, stocky guy with a cranky voice, named Mario. He said that he had known Dimples for a long time and that he thought of her as a bitch because of her many sexual partners. Mario said that he was only there because Dimples was a Queen sister and therefore should not be subjected to abuse. He confirmed what Morena had said and then turned to the accused and said, "You all fucked up, man, fucked up." The other King was a tall Cuban guy named Dice, who looked African American. "These brothers tripped out," Dice said. "She's a Queen. They shouldn't do that." Then he sat down.

Dimples was asked if she had anything else to add but she said no. "I have something to say," Morena said. Loco immediately went to her to make sure she wouldn't go off again. "Don't hold me, I'm all right," Morena told Loco. "These so-called brothers raped a Queen. She may be a bitch but she is still a Queen," Morena exclaimed. "Dimples has

thrown down for the nation many times and she has earned her crown."
She was reminding those present of the violent acts Dimples had committed in the name of the Latin Kings and Queens. "If these punks are
not dealt with properly, the message that it's OK to disrespect a Queen
will be out," Morena claimed. "I'll kill one of these motherfuckers if
they disrespect me. We're Queens and Kings, leaders, not followers!"
Morena screamed. She walked back to the window ledge and sat down.
The whole room was quiet. It seemed as if everybody was afraid to even
breathe. Morena had a reputation of becoming violent when pushed.
Knowing that, Loco sat next to her as the proceedings continued.

Ace, Lucky, and Jimbo were called up. Ace stood up by himself and
said that he would talk for all of them. Ace explained that when he and
Dimples were having sex she kept saying that she had thought he would
be better and that she was going to need more after they were finished.
Dimples jumped up and called him a liar and was quickly restrained by
Mario and Dice. Ace went on. He said that when Dimples saw Lucky in
the room she said, "If you like what you see, come and get some." Ace
supposedly thought Dimples was only teasing and even tried to cover up
her nakedness. She pushed him away and called Lucky to her. "Lucky
wasted no time in agreeing to the invitation," Ace said. "He dropped his
pants, told me to get out of the way, and went at it." Ace explained that
he got mad and punched Dimples in the stomach and then in the eye.
After he hit her, she kept teasing him about not being man enough for
her and that he should take sex lessons from Lucky. At that moment
Jimbo walked in and decided that he wanted to take a turn. But Dimples refused until Lucky talked her into it. Once Jimbo had fucked her,
she said, "Damn, Ace, even Jimbo is better than you." Ace said that he
lost his temper and began whipping her and that's why she started
screaming. He ended by saying, "She didn't get raped. She was just disappointed that there were only three of us and not more." Lucky and
Jimbo were asked if they wanted to add anything. Lucky said no. Jimbo
said that if she had not invited him he would not have touched her and
that he only did it because he was high.

The accusations were finally over and everybody was asked to leave
the room until a decision was made. I walked everyone to the door and

took advantage of the opportunity to talk to Cubana. We agreed on getting together after the meeting. As soon as I closed the door, the guys on the committee busted out laughing. I looked at them, wondering what they found so funny, but knew better than to question them. Lalo asked Loco what they were going to do. Loco was too busy laughing to answer. Paco said that everyone knew Dimples was a "horny bitch," and that she probably did give it up to all three brothers.

Loco got up and pounded on the table in a very serious manner. It was hard to believe that this was the same guy who had just been holding his side in pain from laughter. Loco told everyone that even though Dimples was considered a bitch, she was still a Queen, and it seemed pretty obvious to him that she was telling the truth. "Did you hear the bullshit those brothers made up? They ought to be violated for not thinking up a better lie," Loco said. He said that if justice was not served regardless of the fact that the accused brothers were down for the nation, it would be like giving the go ahead for other brothers to disrespect the Queens whenever they felt like it.

Gordo commented on the fact that Dimples was known more for her sex life than anything else. Finding the brothers guilty would be taking the respect they had earned and giving it to Dimples. The decision was made to find the guys guilty only to keep the Cortland and Whipple section happy and to ensure respect for other Latin Queens. A private meeting with the Juniors and Seniors would be called to let that be known. There would be no discipline for the brothers.

I realized that there was a favoritism game going on between the leaders of the Kedzie and Armitage Latin Kings. I wondered if I was one of the favorite sons of the Latin Kings. After all, I was the only one outside the Seniors and Juniors that knew about the secret decision. The accused and the accusers were called back in to hear the decision. When it was heard, Dimples's sadness disappeared in an instant. Ace, Lucky, and Jimbo quickly protested. The only thing they were told was to stay after the meeting had been adjourned for their discipline. I went to the door and called everybody in. The subjects that were spoken about were again mentioned. I was again given a welcome into the Latin Kings Nation. Lalo said a prayer and the meeting was officially adjourned.

"*Amor de Rey,*" everybody said simultaneously as they placed their right fists upon their hearts and threw up the Latin Kings' hand sign. This time I joined them. I was now allowed. I was now a King.

I tried to hurry outside to meet Cubana, but I was called back by Loco. He took me into the beating room and advised me not to say anything regarding the secret decision. He told me that the whipping Slim got would be considered a slap on the wrist compared to what would happen to me if I said anything to anybody. I assured him I could be trusted. Loco gave me a plastic bag with about half an ounce of weed inside and then I was on my way. The sounds of the Kings pounding their right fists over their hearts echoed as I walked out. I was part of a family now, a family that was willing to kill or die for me.

28

Violence Rules

MORENA AND CUBANA were waiting for me outside with Lil Chino from the Spanish Lords. We got in his van and drove toward the Spanish Lords' 'hood on Western Avenue and Potomac Street. We arrived just in time to see a little commotion on Potomac. On the way there we had been drinking, so by the time we arrived I was beginning to feel the effects. I got out of the van and realized that the commotion was between the Lords and the Cobras. Papo saw us, walked over, and told us what was happening. He said that the Cobras had come by the neighborhood representing and spray painting the walls. My reaction was to ask for a gun. "We have to kill one of them pussies for what they did," I said. Papo got a gun and we walked toward the Cobras. The Cobras didn't notice us coming. Papo hid in the alley between Artesian and Campbell Streets. I kept walking straight toward them. The Cobras noticed me but hesitated to come after me. I continued to taunt them until they thought I was by myself. Finally they came at me. When Papo saw me run past him he jumped out of the alley and opened fire on the Cobras. Two Cobras were shot. I could hear screams of pain as I ran back to the safety of the Lords' 'hood. I heard them shout "We're gonna get you, you motherfucker!"

I got in the van. Papo headed in a different direction. Lil Chino drove me, Morena, and Cubana by Maria's apartment. They dropped me off and headed for Kedzie and Armitage. Lil Chino was wary that the Cobras might have seen me get into his van. He wanted to put the van in a garage just in case the police came looking for it. I went upstairs, but there was nobody in Maria's place. I had to let myself in through the back porch window. Maria always left that window unlocked for me.

About two hours later, Papo arrived with Lil Chino and Morena. I was relieved to see them, especially since they brought beer and weed with them. I felt edgy. I knew getting high would calm me down. We began getting high while we laughed about how the two Cobras were crying out and screaming in pain. Lil Chino, Papo, and Morena took turns complimenting me on my craziness. They said I was a real down brother. "He has to be," Morena said. "That's Lil Loco from the Almighty Latin Kings." I felt indestructible, proud, like a real tough guy. After all, I was Lil Loco, a Latin King, down for my nation and proud of it.

I was informed that one of the guys that got shot was a Latin Disciple so we should be expecting retaliation from them. The Latin Disciples were a pretty big gang, more to be reckoned with than the Cobras. An all-out gang war was inevitable; we just didn't know it. That night we heard gunshots echo in the air. The gunshots came from the direction of the Unknowns' 'hood. We went there and found out that the Cobras had killed an Unknown. The dead Unknown was called Scarface. He was one of their leaders.

A big war had just begun between the Cobras and the Unknowns. I didn't know it then, but the Kings would also become part of the war because of their unification with the Unknowns. The stage was set for one of the bloodiest months I had ever witnessed in the city of Chicago.

The area was flooded with police. We started walking back toward Maria's before the police stopped us. About a block and a half from Maria's place a squad car shined their spotlight on us. Morena, Papo, and I stopped immediately. Lil Chino was carrying a weapon, so he took off running. The police couldn't catch him, so they took their anger out on Papo and me. An officer grabbed Papo by the hair and throat and demanded that he tell them where Lil Chino was going. Papo was trying to talk, but the officer was squeezing his throat so hard that he began to choke. The officer kept screaming questions at Papo, expecting him to answer while at the same time preventing him from doing so. "Let him go, he hasn't done anything," Morena screamed at the officer. The officer turned around and said, "Shut up, you little bitch, before we whip your ass too!" It was now my turn to get into the act. I immediately rose to Morena's defense.

"She ain't no bitch, motherfucker. Leave us alone. We have nothing to do with this," I barked at the officer. He walked up to me and punched me in the stomach. When he hit me, I buckled over, holding my midsection in pain. When I did that, he punched me in the back and I fell to the ground. Then he repeatedly kicked me and kept telling me, "So, you wanna be a hero, you little faggot spic! Fuckin' pork chops infest our city with roaches, then want to get tough too." He repeatedly kicked me. They took Papo into custody and left me there lying on the ground. Morena had been handcuffed and was being held, face down, against a car. "Leave him alone, leave him alone," I heard Morena scream. "Shut the fuck up, bitch," I heard a police officer scream at Morena. I was in too much pain to do anything other than cover my face just in case the officer decided to kick me there, too. "Take that one—he's a Spanish Lord and they hang out with the Unknowns," I heard an officer say, referring to Papo. That same officer grabbed me by the hair, lifted my head, took a good look at me, and said, "This one is new. I've never seen him before. I think that one is a Queen." "Just take him [Papo], leave these two."

The officer let my hair go and walked away. The officer who had been kicking me kicked me once more as he told me, "I'll be watching you." The voices, the sound of police radios, the flashing lights, and the abuse finally disappeared. I was still lying on the sidewalk, in pain and afraid to move. "Are you OK?" Morena asked as she helped me up. "Keep your mouth shut when you get stopped by the cops," she advised. "Fuck them pigs, they don't scare me," was my response.

The police officers I had met in school as "officer friendly," the ones I used to look up to as heroes, were now my most feared enemies. The prospect of running into rival gang members did not faze me, but just the sight of a police officer sent chills down my spine. I could defend myself against gangbangers. I couldn't do anything against the police. I had always been aware of the dangers of being a police officer. What I hadn't known about was the abuse inflicted on unarmed individuals without a shred of evidence when the cops assumed they had done something wrong. I now understood why people in the community felt so alienated.

How can you trust someone who frightens you? The fact that the police beat me didn't linger in my mind as much as the racial slurs they used.

A couple of days had gone by since Scarface was killed. The Unknowns were letting the heat die down so they could retaliate. Finally, the following weekend, they did retaliate. Three Unknowns drove into the Cobras' 'hood and opened fire on a group of people. One person was wounded and one was killed. As it turned out, neither of the guys hit was a Cobra—they were both Disciples. The war was about to get out of control. A couple of nights later the Disciples drove into the Spanish Lords' 'hood and opened fire on two guys they thought were Lords. The guys they shot at were Latin Kings from California and North Avenues. So the violence spread. The Kings did not get hit, but it was enough to warrant retaliation by the Latin Kings.

I was at Maria's when Loco came by and told me about the Kings from California and North getting shot. I was sober, so my reaction was very low-key and not reactionary. Scared and confused, I went with him to Kedzie and Armitage for an emergency meeting. I was scared as all hell. I knew I would have to go on a mission to retaliate against the Disciples. I didn't want to go, but I was too scared to say so. On the way to Kedzie and Armitage we picked up some wine and began drinking. By the time we got to the meeting, I had drunk half a bottle of wine. Sitting at the club, waiting for the meeting to begin, the wine began to take effect. Suddenly I was Lil Loco again, Mr. Macho Latin King. "We gotta kill one of these punks," I said to nobody in particular. "We're Latin Kings, we're almighty. They can't get away with that shit," I said as I looked for more wine. "Want to kill a D, Lil Loco?" Loco asked me matter-of-factly. "Fuck yeah, give me a piece. I'll kill me a Disciple." Loco pointed at me, called to Paco, and walked away. Paco walked toward the door, looked at me, and said, "Come on."

We left the clubhouse, got in a car, and headed for North and California. As we approached California, Paco pulled over and parked. "Get in the back seat," Paco told me as he looked around. About a minute or so later, some guy approached the car and got in. "This is King Indio from North and California," Paco said as they gave each other the customary handshake. "King Lil Loco is one of our new boys," Paco told Indio as he started the car and drove off. Indio, in his mid-twenties, was a black Puerto Rican with a mid-size afro and a goatee. Indio was tall, with a slim build and a very serious demeanor and he spoke perfect English. Indio turned around, shook my hand, and said, "So you're the one who's going to pull the trigger?" "Fuck yeah," I said. Indio chuckled, then looked at Paco kind of strangely. "He's a down little brother," Paco assured Indio as we drove toward the Disciples' 'hood.

On the way there I explained to the guys that I knew the Disciples' neighborhood like the back of my hand, so I would be able to set the Disciples up for an ambush. In fact I had become nervous about what would happen if I shot at the Disciples but didn't hit anybody. The ambush idea was my way of trying to get out of being the triggerman. I still was all for shooting a Disciple, I just didn't want to be the one who did it. Paco and Indio agreed to my idea of an ambush.

We drove up Hirsch Street until we reached Rockwell Street. There were about twenty Disciples hanging out in the Von Humboldt School playground. The guys dropped me off and proceeded to an alley on Hirsch between Rockwell and Maplewood Streets. The plan was to make the Disciples chase me to the alley where Loco and Paco would be waiting for them. When I walked into the schoolyard, I noticed my old friend Speedy hanging out with the Disciples. I looked around, decided exactly where I was going to run, and began yelling, "King love, Disciple killer, Almighty!" The Disciples immediately came after me. I ran across the street, went south on Rockwell, and turned east on Hirsch. All the while I kept yelling "King Love!" so that the brothers would know I was coming. I passed the alley and kept running east toward Western. When I got to Maplewood I heard gunshots go off and then the screeching of car tires as the brothers drove away. I kept running until I reached Maria's place back in the Lords' 'hood. When it was all over, one Disciple was dead and three were wounded. Our mission was accomplished.

At Maria's I became uneasy. I wanted some weed or beer, so I could get into the frame of mind that allowed me to forget the horrors I was involved in. I kept wondering what Speedy was doing hanging out with the Disciples and why he didn't react to my presence. I was beginning to panic. I was paranoid. I needed to get high. Reluctantly I left the house looking for a high.

29

Madman

I WENT BY Tuley and found it deserted. The Lords were getting hit hard by the Cobras and Disciples and were keeping a low profile. They had begun hanging out near LeMoyne and Claremont Streets, rather than by Tuley. I went by Papo's house but he wasn't home. His brothers were there watching the Cubs' game. It had been a long time since I had watched a baseball game, let alone a Cubs' game. I sat down and began to feel very uneasy because of the contrast between the lifestyles of those watching the game and mine. To get rid of this unease, I wanted to get high. I asked Heraldo, Papo's brother, to let me use his bike. After much deliberation he finally agreed. I took off on the bike and headed toward Kedzie and Armitage. By the time I got to North Avenue, however, my destination became Jenny's house. It had been a long time since I had seen her. I wondered if she would welcome me as she once did. I couldn't think of any reason why she would turn me away. I went there with the confidence that Jenny would be ready and willing to give me sex. I rode the bike down Western Avenue, past Bloomingdale Street, toward Jenny's house. I rode over the spot where I had been beat into a coma by the Gaylords. They weren't a threat anymore. The Gaylords had just about disappeared with the growth of the Puerto Rican community and the Latino gangs. However, I kept a lookout for Puerto Rican gang members. You never knew if you could trust the guy who looked like you, sitting next to you, who could be a member of a rival gang. They posed a worse threat than the Gaylords ever did.

Thoughts of violence became thoughts of sex as I approached Jenny's house. When I reached my destination, I climbed up to Jenny's window like I always had before. I peeked inside carefully to make sure I wasn't seen. The window was open and Jenny was sitting on her bed watching television. "Hey, *mi amor*, how are you doing?" I whispered. Jenny jumped up, startled, and told me I had scared her. "What the hell are you doing here anyway?" she asked. "I wanted to see you," I responded as I climbed into her room. "Wait, you can't come in, get out of here," Jenny said. "I came to visit you and this is how you treat me?" I said as I sat on the windowsill inside the bedroom. "I thought I would always be your only one," I told Jenny. "You got some nerve," Jenny responded angrily. "You slapped me, remember?" I wanted sex. I changed the subject quickly before I lost control.

"Hey, where's Lisa and Lil Man?" I asked Jenny. "Lisa is living with this guy, she doesn't stay here anymore," Jenny said as she sat on the edge of the bed across from me. "Lil Man is locked up for shooting some Gaylord." "Wow, that's too bad," I responded as I walked toward Jenny. I couldn't care less about Lil Man or Lisa; my intentions were to get Jenny to receive me like before. I wanted her to forget about our last meeting and become the passionate, sex-loving girl I came to see.

"Stay away from me, please, or leave," Jenny said as I sat next to her. "I missed you babe, I really have," I said as I tried to kiss her. Jenny turned away and said, "If you must know, I'm pregnant. You better leave." "Yeah, right," I said in laughter as I tried to kiss her again. Jenny put her hand on my face, pushed me away, and said, "There'll be no sex, so please leave now." I became upset by Jenny's rejection. I grabbed her and threw her on the bed. I got on top of her, put my hand on her crotch, and began squeezing. "You know you want me, come on, let's fuck like before," I told Jenny as I forcefully fondled her body. "Get off me, you motherfucker!" Jenny yelled. "Get out of here, get away from me!" Jenny continued screaming. I heard footsteps coming toward the room. I rapidly got up and headed for the window. I jumped out and got on the bike as fast as I could. I heard Jenny sobbing, and her father asking, "*¿Que paso? ¿Que paso?*" ("What happened? What happened?") I rode the bike out of the gangway and into the street. I heard Jenny's father yell, "*¡Hijo de la gran puta, te voy a matar!*" ("Son of a bitch, I'm going to kill you!") as I rode away. I peddled as fast as I could nonstop until I reached Kedzie and Armitage. The fact that I was riding through dangerous 'hoods didn't even cross my mind. At Kedzie and Armitage everybody was surprised to see me. I immediately looked for something to get me high. Many words were said to me, but I didn't hear any of them. I did not begin to pay attention to anybody until I had downed two beers and smoked about three joints. Jenny, her father, the violence I had been involved in, it was all forgotten for the time being. It all became just another day.

Jenny's rejection surprised me. No doubt she had become pregnant right in her own room while her parents paid attention to who knows what. It never dawned on me that the baby she was carrying could be mine. This was the last time I saw Jenny.

LALO ADVISED ME that the police were looking for me. Apparently the Disciples had given them my name and description. I figured Speedy must have been the one who set me out (snitched on me). I told Lalo about seeing Speedy hanging out with the Disciples. Lalo said he wasn't surprised because Speedy had cousins who were Disciples. Lalo offered to drive me to Maria's apartment so I could get off the street. I accepted the ride, but when I saw Cubana on my way to the car I changed my mind. Cubana crossed the street to where I was and gave me a hug and a kiss. "Hey, Cubana, let me talk to this brother for a minute," Lalo said. Cubana told me not to leave without saying good-bye, kissed me on the cheek, and walked away. "Get in the car," Lalo told me. "I don't want to leave yet," I said. "I'll be all right, man. I'm a King, remember?" Lalo was angry. "Get in the fuckin' car. I ain't taking you nowhere, just get in." Lalo and I got in his car and drove off. He gave me a clear plastic bag half full of weed and told me to roll a joint. I rolled a joint, then another, and another. Not a word was said. Finally Lalo pulled into an alley and told me to light up a joint. It seemed like we had driven a long way but we were actually only about a half-mile from Kedzie and Armitage. I lit up a joint, passed it to Lalo, and continued to roll joints.

"Don't roll no more," Lalo said. "I'm taking some with me," I answered, and continued rolling. "Look at you, man, you can't even function without that shit," Lalo told me. He took the bag from me, gave me the six or seven joints I had rolled, then began preaching.

"Listen up, little bro," Lalo began. "If you need this shit to feel good then you don't need it." "I don't need it," I answered, "I like it." "Let me drive you home, man. Cubana will always be here waiting for you," Lalo said. "It ain't Cubana," I snapped, "I just don't feel like going home." "Look, you little motherfucker," Lalo continued, "*la hada* is looking for you and you are willing to risk it for a piece of pussy."

"You're wrong, brother," I answered, "I'm risking it for a damn good piece of pussy." Lalo laughed, then said, "You think you're bad and know everything. See how many good pieces of pussy you're going to get if you're locked up." Lalo turned the car on and drove back to Kedzie and Armitage. I got out of the car and walked directly over to Cubana. "*Amor*, my brother, I love you too," I yelled at Lalo as he got ready to go into the clubhouse.

Cubana and I took a walk to Humboldt Park. I told her about what had happened with the Disciples. She seemed so impressed by how "brave" I was. Her reaction made me feel good. We sat on the grass and smoked some weed. I told her about my other violent encounters. I even made some stuff up that never happened. It seemed like the more I told her about the violence I was involved in, the more passionate she became. It was dark and we were rolling around in the grass like two dogs in heat, oblivious to anything or anybody around us. Ultimately we ended up having sex right there in the park.

Until that day, I thought Cubana was different from the other girls who hung around the Latin Kings. But she turned out to be the same. She wasn't a virgin as she had claimed, and although she wasn't too into drugs and alcohol, violent guys were her weakness. This encounter strengthened my view of all women being bitches. I began to believe that all it took to get a woman into bed was lies. As far as I was concerned, women had to admire and please me. I, on the other hand, didn't even have to respect them. To me Cubana became just what she had been that night: a wild hump in the grass. Our conversations died. My thoughts about her became purely sexual. Humboldt Park became kind of a hotel for us. Each and every time we happened to be there at night we had sex. Cubana did one thing, however, that nobody else could do—she made me smile.

SURPRISINGLY, THE WAR that was underway among all the gangs cooled down for the summer because of police activity. The war didn't cool down soon enough, however; fourteen people died and half were reported to be innocent bystanders. Chicago's mayor at the time, Jane Byrne, was on television almost daily expressing disgust over the gang violence in the city, threatening to have anyone who resembled a gang member congregating on a corner arrested. The mayor didn't want young Latino men hanging out on any corner. (Yet I'm sure young white men could congregate anywhere they wanted without being arrested.) The mayor even had gang members paint over their own graffiti while police monitored them. A member of the Insane Unknowns was deported to Puerto Rico for being a menace to the city of Chicago. That happened after the chief of the Spanish Cobras was gunned down with his baby in his arms. Within weeks, however, the gang situation was back to normal and flourishing. Worst of all, a hatred had been born between a group of gangs that would wreak havoc on the Puerto Rican neighborhoods for years to come.

30

Losing Maplewood Park

SUMMER VACATION ENDED and it was time to go back to school. I was a sophomore now. I didn't know how recognizable I'd become as a Latin King during the summer. Rosie (the girl of my dreams) and I were in their gang same homeroom again. For some reason that really bothered her. It was a tradition for the Kings who went to Clemente to show up wearing their gang colors on the first day of school. I wore black Converse All-Stars with gold laces, black baggy pants, and a Pittsburgh Pirates T-shirt—black and gold from head to toe. I thought I was impressive and cool, but Rosie didn't think so. "Hi, Rosie," I said. "Stay the hell away from me," she responded as she walked off. The King brothers and everybody else who heard her laughed and teased me. Normally I would have looked for a rock to crawl under, but I had smoked a joint on my way to school so I was able to laugh it off. "Before the year is over you'll be mine," I yelled at Rosie. "Fuck you," she responded.

I tried to stay high even while I was at school. Being high gave me confidence to continue my relentless pursuit of Rosie, regardless of what she said or did. When I wasn't high I was too timid to even look at her, much less talk to her. I didn't like that, so I made sure I smoked a joint on my way to school every day. I was more interested in being popular than making good grades. After school I would hang out with the Kings on Kedzie and Armitage, have sex with Cubana, spray paint the Kings insignia, or fight. There were also a few instances when I was present at major confrontations between the Disciples and the Latin Kings of Maplewood Park. Many kids who lived around Maplewood Park went to school at Von Humboldt. The Disciples took advantage of that fact and began recruiting these kids. Soon there were just as many Disciples living around Maplewood Park as there were Kings, only the Kings didn't know of this disadvantage. Nor did they care. Suddenly the Maplewood Park Kings' membership became depleted due to incarceration. The cops were somehow finding out where guns and drugs were stashed and who had stashed them. The homes of the leaders of the Maplewood Park Latin Kings began to get raided on a consistent basis. The Maplewood Park Kings became weak. That's when the Disciples made their move.

The Disciples began to make their presence known after a second raid on the Kings' leaders. That raid landed three of the main heads of that section in jail for possession of drugs and firearms. Latin Kings from all sections took the initiative to protect that 'hood from being taken over. Meanwhile the Latin Disciples began moving more of their boys into the neighborhood. The few Latin Kings and Queens who still lived there, including Morena, moved out. Those who stayed became Latin Disciples. Still, Latin Kings from other areas tried desperately to keep Maplewood Park a Latin Kings' section. This included the Kings from Kedzie and Armitage. Although the leaders of the Maplewood Park Latin Kings got penitentiary time, three others who were locked up with them were released. They returned to the only home they knew only to find they now lived in hostile territory. Two of those Kings were brothers whose family still lived across the street from Maplewood Park. Their father had been one of the original Latin Kings and was doing time for murder. The brothers were called Jawbreaker and Maddog. They were both in their early twenties and had been Kings all their lives. Jawbreaker was the older of the two. He was an alcoholic with a very violent temper. Jawbreaker had tattoos all over his body, mostly gang related. He had been in and out of jail and was on parole for an aggravated assault charge. Maddog was more down to earth. He didn't drink a lot, but he loved to smoke weed. Maddog had also been in and out of jail several times. He had beaten two murder charges because the witnesses against him never showed up in court. The brothers were determined to take Maplewood Park back for the Latin Kings.

From the day they were released and returned home, they made their presence known in Maplewood Park. Kings from other sections were also out there with them. The Disciples were not intimidated. They grouped up in numbers to show their force and made it a habit to be there at all times of the day and night. A deadly confrontation was unavoidable. One Friday night the situation exploded.

I went by Kedzie and Armitage looking for Cubana. The brothers there told me that she had gone with Morena and Loco to Maplewood Park. I knew walking into that area was dangerous, so I asked Lalo to drive me there. Lalo gave another King brother the keys to his car so he could take me. The King brother was called Dino. Dino was tall and well built with long black hair and dark brown eyes. He was very handsome and had the reputation of being a ladies' man. Dino acted cool and was soft-spoken, just like a mama's boy. However, in reality Dino was a master con artist and a stickup man. Dino gave me a gun and advised me to start shooting at the first sign of trouble. The gun was just like the one I took from Loco the night I shot at the Gangsters. It was black metal, square, flat, and kind of heavy. "It's ready to shoot, just take off the safety," Dino said. I looked at the gun, wondering where the hell the safety was and what I was supposed to do with it. "Do you have a joint?" I asked Dino. "Give me the piece, man," Dino said as he took the gun from me, clicked a little lever on it, and handed it back. "Don't worry about getting high now, we're almost there," Dino said. When we got to Maplewood Park, the hostilities had already begun. Jawbreaker, Maddog, Loco, Morena, Cubana, and several other Kings and Queens were outside exchanging obscenities with a crowd of Disciples. Dino drove past the hostile mobs and went through the alley behind Maddog and Jawbreaker's house.

We parked the car in the alley and walked to the front. We did the customary hand shaking. I kissed Cubana and then began looking to get high. I was scared as shit. I desperately wanted to just leave that scene. I went there to get Cubana, but she didn't want to leave. She was interested in seeing and being a part of what was going to happen. Finally I went inside the house, where I found beer on a table. Jawbreaker and

Maddog's mother, little sister, and Jawbreaker's two sons were in a bedroom watching television as if nothing was happening. I sat inside the house, drank two beers like I was drinking water, then went back outside. The hostilities were getting more serious as it grew darker. Loco noticed some Disciples pulling guns from hiding places and said, "It's time to get busy." One by one we all went in the house. "*Quedate en el cuarto y Ciera la puerta*" ("Stay in the room and close the door"), Maddog told his mother. "*No dejes que los niños salip de el cuarto*" ("Don't let the kids come out of the room"). Jawbreaker kept bringing out guns from a back room and handing them out to the Kings and Queens. I still had Dino's gun. I pulled it out, ready to use it. I was on my fourth beer now and I was feeling brave and macho. I sat on the floor along the wall just beside the window. Loco sat next to me and told me not to get too crazy. "Stay down and out of sight," Loco said. "Take care of Cubanita." Cubana sat next to me, kissed me, and held my hand tightly. She was obviously scared. I had to be brave and strong for both of us. Then all hell broke loose.

"Those fuckers are spreading out, man. They're up to something," Dino said as he peaked out the window. Chants of "Di-sci-ple" and "King Kill-er" were heard from outside. "*Llama la policia, llama la policia*" ("Call the police, call the police"), Jawbreaker's mother yelled as she peered out the bedroom door, barely revealing her head. "*Cierra la puerta y acuéstate con los niños en el piso*" ("Close the door and lay down on the floor with the kids"), Jawbreaker shouted at her. The crash of glass breaking was heard as a brick came flying in through the front window. "Motherfucker, King love," Maddog shouted as he began shooting at the Disciples with a shotgun. Shots were fired back and forth. A Queen got hit in the arm; she screamed in pain and threw herself on the floor next to Cubana and me. I had not yet fired a shot, nor had I attempted to. I was scared. Even though I was high, I was still scared stiff. The shooting only went on for about two minutes, but it seemed like hours. From the bedroom the screams of Jawbreaker's mother and her grandchildren could be heard. "King love, Almighty," Maddog shouted while he shot repeatedly in the direction of the Disciples. "Oh shit, I'm hit, I'm hit," one of the Kings screamed as he fell to the floor holding his face. "Aah, help me, help me." He lay screaming while bullets kept flying all around him. He had been shot in the eye and was bleeding profusely. The shooting stopped. Sirens could be heard in the distance. "Let's get the fuck out of here," Dino advised Loco. "Come on, Lil Loco, let's go, let's go," Dino shouted.

I grabbed Cubana by the hand and pulled her with me as I ducked my way through the house to the back door. Along the way I stepped over the King who was shot and slipped on his blood. Jawbreaker's mother was crying hysterically as Maddog tried to comfort her. Mostly everybody was just scrambling to get out of the house before the police arrived. Everybody was able to get out except for Jawbreaker, Maddog, and those who were shot. The King and Queen survived their gunshot wounds. The King brother did, however, lose his eye. They were both incarcerated after being released from the hospital. Three Disciples were shot during that battle and one of them died. Jawbreaker and Maddog were charged with these shootings and were sentenced to time in the penitentiary. Cubana, Morena, Dino, and I got out unscratched. Loco had a cut on his left cheek and several on his right arm from the flying glass.

The Disciples continued to hang out at Maplewood Park. The increased police activity following this battle kept the Latin Kings from doing anything to retaliate. As a result, the Latin Disciples gained sole control of Maplewood Park. Walking to Kedzie and Armitage, up North Avenue, or even riding the bus that way became dangerous. I couldn't go to Kedzie and Armitage as frequently as I wanted to unless I got a ride from someone or was high enough not to care. That slowed down my gang activity somewhat, but not completely.

Jawbreaker and Maddog's family was the first one I met where gang-banging was a family affair. Their father was a King and the sons and daughters were all Kings and Queens. This kind of family existed in every neighborhood I ever hung around in. The members of these families are usually violent, promiscuous, drug users, and eager to get everybody else involved in their actions. Sadly, this type of family still exits in many neighborhoods.

Since I couldn't get to Kedzie and Armitage as frequently as I wanted to, I started hanging out with the Spanish Lords. At this time the Spanish

Cobras were making a big move on the Lords and were making their presence known on a daily basis. In turn, the Spanish Lords began to hang out on LeMoyne and Claremont Streets exclusively. In essence, they were relinquishing Tuley to the Cobras. Clemente High School was still dominated by Latin Kings and their associates. In fact, the only thing that kept the Cobras from completely moving into the Tuley area was the presence of the Kings at Clemente.

Gang-related violence escalated at Clemente because of the ongoing wars. King brothers, including myself, were worried about the gang affiliations of others more than we were about our studies. We walked around school looking for any sign that would set someone apart as a member of a rival gang. Everything from the color of their clothing to the marks on their notebooks was immediately questioned. Those who didn't have the appropriate answers to our questions were usually beaten. The real impact of our actions was a lack of education within the Puerto Rican community.

31

My Rosie

MY POPULARITY AT Clemente grew—not because I was an academic standout or a jock but because I was a Latin King. I enjoyed the way crowds in the hallways would part when I walked through. No matter how long the cafeteria line was, I could be first if I wanted to. I could sit in the stairway, smoke a joint, and be warned of any authority figure coming. It never crossed my mind that it was others' fear that made me popular. I never bothered to consider the consequences. I rarely attended classes anymore. I went to school for the sole purpose of gangbanging.

The one class I did attended everyday was homeroom. That's where I could confront Rosie without her being able to walk away. Rosie was not impressed by my popularity. She still avoided me. But Sheena became more friendly. Sheena would give me invitations to parties and volunteered to be my tutor if I needed one. She was one of the top students at Clemente and was involved in many activities. I kept asking Rosie out on dates and she kept turning me down.

One day, however, everything changed. Rosie came to class and, instead of avoiding me as usual, she sat next to me. It was a Monday after a weekend of gang activity against the Disciples. I didn't have rolling papers to smoke my customary joint before class so I was in my normal state of mind when Rosie approached me. She asked how my weekend went. I just stared at her, swallowing saliva, surprised she was even talking to me. I didn't know what to say to her. I just sat there staring at her like a fool. Rosie took the initiative and did all the talking. She told me that her friend Sheena never stopped talking about me and because of that she realized how cute I really was. I was speechless. At first I thought she was going to try to set me up with Sheena. Rosie said that she wanted to see more of me and she was sorry for being so rude. She promised it would never happen again. We met each other after school and she wanted me to walk her home. She told me she lived at Rockwell and Potomac Streets. I explained that I couldn't walk her home because she lived in Disciples' territory. She kept insisting. "If you really like me you would walk me home," Rosie said. I pointed out that if she really liked me she wouldn't ask me to endanger my life. She was upset and disappointed, but said she understood. We kissed and she went on her way. Her kiss was more cold than passionate, but I figured it was better than none at all.

The relationship between Rosie and me flourished. At school we became inseparable and after school our passion took over. Within two weeks we became sexually active. Rosie said having sex with me was her way of showing that she would die for me. She wanted me to know that I was the most important person in her life. Making love to me was her way of telling me. We made love everyday. We talked about having a family and a successful future together. Still, Rosie would become very upset when it was time for her to go home and I wouldn't walk her home. She knew that was out of the question, yet she kept insisting.

My life began to revolve around that girl. I stopped going by Kedzie and Armitage to hang out during the week. I only went on weekends, when I couldn't see Rosie, and for the mandatory meetings. I used schoolwork as my excuse for not hanging out. I avoided Cubana. I didn't want to do anything that would jeopardize my relationship with Rosie. Rosie made me feel special, like a true King. I started thinking of ways to walk her home without being noticed by the Cobras or Disciples. I knew I would be in danger, but I thought that Rosie was well worth it. Rosie would assure me that nothing would happen because her brother was a Disciple and she had talked to him. He promised to cover for me as long as I went inside her house once I got to Rockwell and Potomac. Rosie told me her birthday was on the upcoming Tuesday, so it would be celebrated the Saturday before with a party at her house. She thought that would be the perfect time for me to meet her family. I couldn't agree more. That Friday, the day before the party, we went to the movies and then to Maria's apartment. It was the first time Rosie was with me at night. She would usually go home just before nightfall. Maria had gone out, so we had the apartment all to ourselves. After smoking a joint Rosie became very seductive. She told me over and over how much she loved me and how she couldn't wait for her parents to meet me. She said she wanted to have my baby and be with me forever. I felt so good, so wanted. We made love with more passion than ever before. I was in love. When it was time for Rosie to go home, I told her I would walk with her all the way this time. She preferred that I wait until the following day so that her brother could be aware I was coming.

As usual I walked her to Western Avenue and Potomac. On the way there we talked about our future: where we would live, how many kids we would have, and what we would name them. Before Rosie went home she made me promise that I would go to her birthday party. She made it clear that if I did not go, our relationship would have to end. After she said that, we kissed passionately and went our separate ways.

I immediately started making plans to go to Kedzie and Armitage on Sunday and quit the Kings. I would use school as the reason. I knew I would have to take an ass whipping to get out, but Rosie was worth it. Our future together was much more important to me than being a Latin King. On Fridays I would usually go to Kedzie and Armitage, get high, and get rowdy with my King brothers. Not this Friday. I went back to Maria's apartment and fell asleep thinking about Rosie, our wedding, our future family, and how much fun her party was going to be. It was going to be a night to remember. I would meet her parents and assure myself a permanent place in their family. I had to be on my best behavior. In my mind I repeatedly went over what I would say and how I would say it. Rosie was the girl of my dreams and she was giving me the opportunity to make my dreams come true. I had to make the most of it.

FROM THE MOMENT I got up Saturday morning I began preparing for the party. I pressed my best shirt, my best slacks, and shined my shoes until they looked like mirrors. I asked Maria for a few dollars and got a haircut. I was determined to make a good impression on Rosie's family. After the haircut I went back to Maria's and sat around impatiently waiting for nightfall. I planned to leave for the party at about 8:00 P.M. I began getting dressed at 5:00 P.M. I was in the bathroom doing and undoing my hair, looking for that perfect hairstyle, when Maria knocked on the door and said someone was here to see me. I went out into the hallway and found Sheena standing there reading all the graffiti on the walls. Her eyes were red and her face was flushed as if she had been crying. I was surprised to see her. I invited her in. She said she couldn't stay long because her mother was outside waiting for her.

Inside Sheena looked deep into my eyes and began to cry uncontrollably. She was trying to say something, but because of her crying I could not make out what she was saying. Maria gave her some tissue and looked at me as if to say "what did you do to her," but remained silent. Suddenly Sheena reached out, grabbed my arms, and said, "Please don't go to the party. It's a setup." I pushed her away and yelled, "What the hell are you talking about!" "Rosie does not love you, she does not even like you. She's with you because you are a King. She's setting you up to be killed."

I freaked out. I did not believe her. I told Sheena that Rosie and I were in love and she was just jealous. Sheena told me that Rosie's real boyfriend was a Disciple and that she was setting me up to prove her devotion to him. She said that Rosie having sex with me was not part of the plan but that she did it to convince me that she cared for me in order to get me to go by Rockwell and Potomac. Everything Sheena said sounded logical, but I didn't believe it. Maybe I just didn't want to believe it. I became upset at the accusations against Rosie and lashed out in anger. I had to defend Rosie; after all she was the sweetest, most beautiful, and most passionate girl I had ever met.

I told Sheena to shut up and get the hell out of Maria's place. Maria came to Sheena's defense. "Listen to her, you dummy, she just may be telling the truth," Maria said. I yelled, "She likes me and wants to break Rosie and me up. That's why she is doing this." Sheena grabbed me again and told me that Rosie didn't care about me, that she wanted me dead. She kept begging, "Please don't go to the party, please don't." I pushed

Sheena away, grabbed her by the arm, escorted her to the hallway, then shut the door on her crying face. I stood by the door for a minute listening to Sheena going down the steps crying. Maria told me I was stupid and that I shouldn't go to whatever party Sheena was talking about. "You're a Latin King, *pendejo*, why are you going to Rockwell and Potomac?" I didn't listen. I walked into the bathroom and continued getting ready. "I'm calling Morena and Cubana. Maybe they can talk some sense into your *pendejo* head," Maria said. I opened the door to the bathroom and yelled, "You better not call them," then slammed the door closed. It didn't matter what anybody said. Nobody knew Rosie like I did. Everything was going to be OK. Rosie and I were victims of circumstance. Because of the idiotic gang wars it seemed like we lived in different worlds when we really lived just blocks away from each other. We had decided not to let other peoples' problems interfere with our love. It was now up to me. I had to make the next move—I could not miss that party.

I continued to fix myself up. I was determined to show up at Rosie's party looking handsome and well-mannered. About five minutes later there was a knock on the door. The first thing that came to my mind was that Sheena had told somebody about the party and this person had come to stop me from going. I opened the door to tell whoever it was that Sheena was lying. It was Sheena and her mother who were knocking. Sheena was still crying and hanging on to her mother's arm. Sheena's mother was a big burly woman. Her skin was dark, her lips were big and full, and her hair was in an afro. The only feature Sheena had gotten from her mother was her big brown eyes. She asked to speak to my mother. I told her I didn't have one. In a very compassionate way, Sheena's mother explained to me that her daughter was not lying. She begged for me to listen to her because she was trying to save my life. This woman's demeanor mesmerized me. She was very soft-spoken, yet her words seemed loud with attention-deserving authority.

I didn't want to hear what she was saying. As far as I was concerned, it was all bullshit. I blocked out Sheena's mother's words by thinking about how late they were all making me. I told Sheena's mother that her daughter was only acting this way because she liked me and was very jealous of my relationship with Rosie. Her soft-spoken ways disappeared in an instant. "Listen, don't you flatter yourself thinking my daughter has the hots for you," Sheena's mother said angrily. "My daughter is trying to save your life! You want to die? Fine. See you at your funeral!" She turned around, held Sheena by the shoulders, and told her to just forget about me. Her exact words were, "Let's go home. You tried your best to save him. Now let's go get ready for his funeral."

Finally they're leaving, I thought to myself. Wait until I tell Rosie about this. Sheena, however, was persistent. She didn't want to go. She kept crying and begging me to believe her while her mother tried to lead her away. Sheena got loose from her mother, ran to me, and hugged me tightly around the neck. Damn, she's going to wrinkle my shirt, I thought. Sheena held on to me for dear life. "We can drive you by Rockwell and Potomac so you can see for yourself. Rosie is outside," Sheena said. "We can drive him, right, ma? We can drive him." She still held on to me. Her mother hesitated at first but agreed, mainly to satisfy her daughter. Sheena's mother made it clear that I was to keep my head down and out of sight. "I don't want to become a victim of stupidity," Sheena's mother said, "so you better stay down." I agreed to the offer. "I need a ride to get me past the Cobras anyway, so thank you," I said. I believed Rosie's brother would help me with the Disciples, but I still had to get past the Cobras. I knew Rosie would prove Sheena wrong by keeping her promise.

We got in Sheena's mother's car and went west on Potomac. I sat in the back seat, crouched down to avoid being seen not only by the Cobras and Disciples but also by the Lords. Sheena talked to me without looking at me. She said she could not believe that I thought she was lying to me. I responded by telling her that she was a beautiful girl but that my heart belonged to Rosie. Her mother immediately jumped on my case. She did not appreciate that I thought her daughter was simply trying to break Rosie and me up. I told her that she could get mad if she wanted to, but it didn't change the facts. She commented about how Puerto Rican men were all stuck in some macho bullshit that made no sense at all. I told her to look at her daughter and see how fine she was because of her Puerto Rican father. "I bet you didn't complain about Puerto Rican macho bullshit when you were making your daughter," I said with a smart-alecky tone. I hit a nerve with that comment. Sheena's mother lost control and began yelling obscenities at me. Sheena interrupted her to tell me to look up and see Rosie. "There she is, there she is. Now do you believe me?" Sheena said. I eased my head up in order to look out the window. Rockwell and Potomac had not changed much since I stopped hanging around there on my way to school. Gloria's candy store was still there and it was still the main hangout. To the right of the entrance to the store was a doorway used to get to the upstairs apartments. There was Rosie, hugging and kissing a guy with a Disciple sweater on. She was showing him the same kind of passion she showed me when we made love. She was wearing cut-off jean shorts and was wet from playing in the open fire hydrant on the corner. He had his hands all over her ass and she was enjoying it. I felt like a fool. I began to realize that I was the party Rosie was throwing.

Sheena's words echoed through my head. "She doesn't love you, she doesn't even like you, she's setting you up to be killed." I wanted to jump out and grab Rosie by the neck. The only thing that stopped me was the fact that there were about forty or fifty Disciples out there. It took about five seconds to pass Rockwell and Potomac, but it seemed like an eternity. I ducked down again and sat there lost in my own little angry world. Sheena and her mother were talking to me, but I didn't hear them. I asked Sheena's mother to drop me off at California and North Avenues. She wanted to take me to wherever my destination was, but I insisted she drop me off at California and North Avenues. I apologized to Sheena and her mother for doubting them, for being sarcastic—all of it—and got out of the car. Sheena got out with me. She said she was sorry and hugged me. I apologized to her again and told her I had to go and do some thinking. She gave me her phone number and told me to call her if I needed someone to talk to. She got in the car and they drove off. I stood there like a statue until I couldn't see their car any more and began walking toward Kedzie and Armitage.

ROSIE OPENED MY eyes to the seriousness and dangers of gangbanging. Until that day, even with the gunplay I had experienced, gangbanging was nothing more than a game to me. But from this point on, however, things were going to be different. I used Rosie as my reason to become more ruthless, more careless. No one and nothing mattered but me. Rosie was, I think, the last person I ever trusted.

At least I got a piece of pussy, I reasoned with myself, only to get depressed when I realized I wouldn't be getting it anymore. I was definitely experiencing an emotional overload and I didn't know how to handle it. I couldn't count on my King and Queen brothers and sisters. They would probably laugh at me or maybe discipline me. I didn't need either. I grabbed bottles and shattered them against walls. I represented to any and all cars that carried passengers that looked like gang members. I hung my head down, lost in sadness, fighting tears, destroying myself from within. I desperately needed to get high. It was the only way to get Rosie off my mind.

32

Down Brother

WHEN I ARRIVED at Kedzie and Armitage, Loco and about five other King brothers were standing on the corner. I forced on a happy face and greeted everyone with the usual handshake. I began asking for weed, liquor, anything that would help me escape reality. About a half hour later I was feeling the effects of marijuana and wine and was well on my way to getting completely wasted. Several brothers told me that Cubana had been asking for me. My face lit up when I heard that. To hell with Rosie, I thought. Cubana was just as beautiful and she was a Queen. I would be safe with her. However, I did not go looking for her. I sat there getting high. It was Saturday and I knew that sooner or later she would come to Kedzie and Armitage.

An hour passed and I was high as a kite. In my mind I killed Rosie over and over again. I became angry and uncontrollable. I was yelling obscenities at anybody who looked my way. King brothers looked at me and whispered things. They were not used to seeing me uncontrollably high. "What the fuck you looking at, shit," I yelled at them. They looked at me and did their best to ignore me. I threw a bottle of wine at a car because the passenger looked my way. I wanted to go gangbanging. I wanted to hurt someone, to make them feel the kind of pain I felt. A little blue Toyota with three guys who looked like gang members was stopped behind two other cars waiting for the light at Kedzie and Armitage to change. I yelled at the brothers, "Check these punks out," and walked toward the car. I walked up to the car and yelled, "What you all be about?" The passengers ignored me. I got closer. "King love, motherfuckers, what you all be about, pussies," I yelled at them. They still ignored me. The light changed and they began moving forward. I picked up an empty beer bottle and threw it at them. I hit the passenger in the face. I could see blood gushing out of the side of his face as they sped away.

Immediately the Kings began mobilizing in case there was some kind of retaliation. There were Kings on all four corners of Kedzie and Armitage. All of them had some kind of weapon nearby. There were at least six guns hidden in different strategic points. I was standing by the wall where the King emblem was painted, a couple of feet from the clubhouse entrance. I could see dried pink paint on the sidewalk. The Gangsters had driven by and thrown baby food bottles filled with paint at the wall just a few days before. The emblem had already been retouched and pink paint lay only on the sidewalk.

The King emblem on Kedzie and Armitage was nothing fancy but it stood out big time. It was painted on the southwest corner of Kedzie and Armitage on a store wall. It was about ten feet high and twenty feet wide. It consisted of a black background with a five-point crown right in the center with the letter *L* on the left and a *K* on the right written in old English-style lettering with gold paint. I stood right in the center yelling like a madman. "I'm a King, *amor de Rey*, King love, King love, King love!" I was yelling at the top of my lungs. Loco came down from the clubhouse and stood next to me. "*Hey, mi panita, calmate, vente vamos arriba*" ("Hey, little partner, calm down, come on let's go upstairs"), Loco said. I spread my arms out like a cross against the wall and yelled, "*Amor de Rey, hasta la muerte*" ("King love until death"). I pounded my right fist upon my chest violently and then threw up the Kings' sign. "*Amor*," I heard several brothers yell my way as I walked off with Loco.

We went up to the clubhouse. I sat on a sofa, leaned back, and closed my eyes. I was hoping Morena would show up so she could give me a ride to Maria's place. I don't know how long I was waiting, but I decided I wanted to change into some street clothes. When they didn't show up, I decided to walk home. It would be a long walk, so I got up to ask Loco for a pistol just in case; but Loco was nowhere to be found. The whole clubhouse was empty. "Loco, Loco," I shouted as I knocked on doors. "In here, come in here," I heard a voice say from way in the back. I walked toward the back of the apartment clubhouse and into the kitchen. As many times as I had been there I had never been to the back part of the apartment. In fact, the door leading to the kitchen was usually kept closed. "*Aqui*, brother, *aqui*" ("In here, brother, in here"). I heard the voice again, this time closer. I came to a door in the kitchen next to a refrigerator and tried to open it, but it was locked. I knocked and waited for an answer. "*Esperate, bro*" ("Wait, brother"), someone said. Several minutes passed and no one answered the door so I knocked again. Paco opened the door and said, "What's up, man? We're busy. Come back later." I heard Loco ask, "Who is it?" "It's Lil Loco," Paco answered. "Let the little brother in. I need to talk to him anyway," was Loco's response. Paco let me in and closed the door behind him. The room was big. It may have been the master bedroom. Until then I didn't even know that that room was there. It had a big table with eight chairs and a couple of couches. I stood at the entrance looking at those present and wondering what was going on and whether I wanted to stay or not. I was still fuming and daydreaming about Rosie. I just stood there until Paco yelled at me to close the door.

Loco, Lucky, and Tita, Loco's sister, sat at one end of the table. At the other end was an older white man counting money. Tita was like a bookkeeper for the Kings. She was counting cocaine and marijuana bags and then tossing them into their respective shopping bags. They would later be distributed to the Kings to sell on the streets. Loco noticed I was nervous and asked me what was up. I said, "That white boy is a narc." They all started laughing. Loco said, "Don't worry about him. That's Officer James, he's an honorary Latin King." Officer James was a big man, about six feet four inches tall, three hundred pounds, with brown hair, brown eyes, and a missing bottom front tooth. He said, "So you're Lil Loco. Boy, if those Cobras ever get their hands on you . . . I'm cool, little man. I don't bust Kings," Officer James said. At that moment he got up, stuck the money he was counting in his pocket, and got ready to leave. Loco escorted him to a door in the kitchen that led to the alley behind the building. They discussed some kind of deal for guns on the way there. Before he left, Officer James assured Loco that the guns would be delivered. "Just get the money ready," he said. Loco locked the door behind Officer James and came back into the room. He looked at me and asked, "What the hell were you screaming about out there? You made officer James nervous; he's our *chota*" (snitch), Paco said. "He's a fuckin' *hada*, man," I replied. "Yeah," Tita said, "only he works for the nation, not for the city." "Officer James gets paid to look out for us," Loco explained. "He tells us what his buddies are up to so we can avoid them." "He does a damn good job too. Maybe we should give him a raise," Paco said, and everybody laughed. It didn't make any sense to me.

"I got a surprise for you, little brother," Loco said. He went out of the room and came back with a shoebox. He sat next to me and handed me the box. Inside were two guns with two boxes of bullets. "Are these for me?" I asked. He said they were. "*Balla, bro, balla*" ("cool, man, cool"), I said as I grabbed one of the guns and looked it over. He told me that I should keep one stashed around Kedzie and Armitage and carry the other one with me. The guns were very shiny, a nickel-plated .25-caliber automatic and a chrome .38 special. I figured out how to load and unload the .38 special rather quickly. I had handled this type of gun before. It was exactly like the one I stole from Pedro. The .25 I just looked at, puzzled as to how to use it. I had seen and fired similar weapons before, but all I ever did was pull the trigger. Lucky asked me if I knew how to use an automatic. Loco answered for me, saying, "Of course he does, don't you, Lil Loco." I just sat there quiet, loading the .38, hoping they would teach me how to use the .25. The .25 was smaller, more compact, and easier to conceal, I thought to myself. Once I learned how to use it I could easily carry it around. Lucky picked up the .25 and showed me how to remove the clip. Now that I knew what a clip looked like, I noticed that there were two extra ones in the box. Lucky then showed me how to load the bullets into the clip. I took one of the clips from the box and began loading it just like Lucky was doing. It wasn't that easy at first; the spring inside the clip caught me by surprise and a bullet sprang straight up in the air. After I got the hang of loading the clip, Lucky taught me how to load it into the gun. He put the clip in the gun, then gave it to me and told me to take it out and then put it back in. That was easy. I did it about three times and then gave the gun back to Lucky. He then pulled the chamber back and let me look inside over the top of the gun so I could see the bullet going into firing position.

Lucky took out the clip, pulled the chamber again, and the bullet flew out of the top of the gun. He put the gun and the clip on the table and said, "OK, it's your turn now." It wasn't so hard. I got it right the first time. Lucky took me out on the back porch and had me fire the gun up into the air so that I could see its action. I thought I was so cool. I couldn't wait to let Cubana see my gun. I even thought about taking it to school and using it on Rosie. Lucky was a good teacher. He taught me how to clean the guns and how to carry them so they wouldn't be noticed or fall out. He advised me to carry the .25 in my waistband and to put the loaded extra clips in my socks held to my leg with a rubber band. I did just what he told me to. I put the .38 in my pocket, the bullets in a bag, and began giving farewell salutes to Lucky and Loco. Loco walked with me to the door and gave me a paper bag with fifty nickel bags of marijuana inside. He told me to sell them and keep two dollars out of every bag I sold for myself. He advised me that I should stash the guns and the weed while I was hanging out in front on Kedzie and Armitage. The Kings and Queens would send customers my way once they knew I was selling nickels.

The gifts and trust I was being awarded were a show of appreciation for the acts of violence I had committed for the Kings. It was a show of total acceptance on the part of the junior and senior factions of the Latin Kings.

IT WAS RARE for a Peewee Latin King to receive the special treatment I was offered. I became a favorite choice of older Kings to take along on hits. As a result, the name Lil Loco became well known within King sections throughout the city. Unfortunately, it also became well known by rival gangs.

"You're a down brother. That's why they gave you those," Morena said when I told her about the guns. "They'll probably make you chief of the Peewees next," Morena said. I asked Morena to look out for me while I stashed my merchandise. Morena whistled and yelled, "*Pongan ojo, pongan ojo*" ("Keep an eye out, keep an eye out"). I threw the bag of marijuana nickels in a garbage can that stood on the southeast corner of Kedzie and Armitage. It made it easy for me to grab the merchandise to sell and they weren't in plain sight so no one could take them. I hid the .38 at the trunk of a tree on the northwest side of Kedzie and Armitage about a quarter of a block up Kedzie. The Gangsters would usually show up around that area, so that was a good strategic point. I wrapped the .25 in a page of a newspaper and hid it under a parked car on Armitage on the inside of the front tire about two car lengths from the intersection.

Cubana and Morena hung out with me until I sold all the nickel bags. I couldn't believe how quickly they sold. When I turned in the money Loco offered to give me fifty more but I declined only because I wanted to go home and change clothes. He did, however, give me three bags for my own use. I picked up my guns and Morena gave me a ride to Maria's apartment. It was about 3:00 A.M. by this time, so I decided to stay home. Morena came upstairs to smoke some weed before she left, but we never got to smoke the weed—we rolled up the joints but fell asleep before we could smoke them.

A knock on the door woke me up Sunday morning. It was Sheena. I asked her to come in and excused myself to the bathroom. By the time I came out Morena had already introduced herself to Sheena and got the whole story about Rosie from her. Morena laughed at me, called me pussy whipped, then excused herself. Before she left Morena reminded me of the meeting and said she would pick me up. I went into the hallway with Morena and pleaded for her not to tell anybody about Rosie, especially not Cubana. All Morena said was, "I won't tell Cubana," as she walked down the stairs. That wasn't too reassuring. If she told the Kings, they were certain to call for a violation on me. I would just have to wait and see what happened.

I went back inside and sat down, trying hard not to make eye contact with Sheena. I couldn't avoid it. I sat there staring into Sheena's eyes, unable to say a word. I was nervous and very embarrassed. I wanted to smoke a joint so I could become the me that everyone else liked but I couldn't do it—not while Sheena was there. She finally broke the silence and asked me if I was all right. I told her I was and proceeded to apologize to her for acting like a fool. She was such an angel. She said she understood and forgave me. She suggested that I quit gangbanging before it was too late.

God, I wish I had listened to her. I wish I were as brave as I thought I was and made the right decision to quit the Kings. I couldn't; I didn't. I was a coward hiding behind the influence of drugs and alcohol. I was too scared to face the world as the person I really was. Being a King gave me a role to play, friends, a lifestyle—everything I wanted. I couldn't walk away from the life.

Sheena's mother beeped the horn for her to come out. Sheena gave me a kiss on the cheek and walked out. As soon as the door closed behind her, I lit up a joint. I walked around the house and noticed I was alone. Maria had not been there all night. I sat on the sofa, watched television, smoked weed, thought about Rosie, about the Kings, and about the crimes I had participated in. I fell asleep and had the first of what would came to be a series of nightmares that invaded my sleep for a long time.

In this particular nightmare I kept seeing the bullet enter and exit the girl who was with the Chi-West the night we went to retrieve the Spanish Lord's sweater. Her blood splattered over and over again. I woke up sweating, nervous, scared of the world around me, scared of myself. I didn't even want to look out the window. I tried to go back to sleep, only to have the nightmare continue. I fought to stay awake, only to find myself afraid to keep my eyes open. It was broad daylight, the sun was shining through the windows, yet everything seemed gray and dismal to me. I rubbed my eyes, trying to focus my vision, but it didn't work. I began to see shapes in shadows and imagined someone or something was out there waiting to get me. I heard the door creak as it was opened and freaked out. It was the police coming to arrest me or a rival gang coming to kill me. But it was neither—it was Maria. I was so happy to see her. My vision suddenly cleared, everything became light, no danger existed whatsoever. My heart, which had been pounding, slowed down to normal. "Give me some of what you had, boy, I need to feel that good," Maria said.

Maria had a friend with her. They both went into the kitchen. "¿*Comó está Rosie?*" ("How is Rosie?") Maria asked. I finally got up from the sofa and began straightening myself out. "I guess you were right about Rosie," Maria said. "You're not a *pendejo* after all." I kept quiet. I didn't want her to know I had been a *pendejo*. She never would have let me hear the end of it. It was better if she didn't know. "Come here, *papito* ("daddy"), I want you to meet my friend," Maria called out to me. Her friend was a short, stocky woman. She had long black hair and two gold front teeth. She also had a crown tattooed on her upper right arm. Her name was Sonia. "Call me Soni," she said. I asked her if she was a Queen. That was a mistake. She began preaching about when it meant something to be a Queen or a King. She went on about it not being right that the Puerto Ricans were killing each other but still had the nerve to call themselves Latin Kings and Queens. The more she talked, the deeper her Puerto Rican accent became. Finally she just spoke Spanish. "*Una raza divida no sobrevive*" ("A race divided will not survive"), Soni said. "*Quien va a siembrar la cemilla de nuestra cultura si estamos muertos?*" ("Who is going to plant the seed of our culture if we're all dead?") "*Calmate hija, no es para tanto* ("Calm down, girl, it's not that serious"), Maria said. Soni took the beer Maria offered her and sat down.

"You know something," Soni began again in a calm voice, "it was once an honor to be a Latin King or Queen. We helped our people by fighting those that were victimizing us. We didn't rip our people off, didn't feed them poison. We did nothing to hurt our people's chances to succeed. What Maria did to you, she should be ashamed," Soni added as she turned toward Maria. "It's OK," I said. "I liked it, I want more," I defended Maria. "*Tu no sabes nada*" ("You don't know anything"), Soni said. "Maria abused you. You're a little boy. Because of what she did your life will never be normal." Maria was now crying. "I was drunk, I was drunk," Maria said. I walked out of the kitchen, went to the living room, and lit up a joint. I sat there thinking about the things Soni said. Deep down I agreed with everything, but I was too much of a coward to let my feelings be known.

I was fifteen. I was given guns so that I could kill and maim and drugs so that I could learn the profitable business of dealing. All these things were happening at a time when I felt so much hatred for everything around me. Self-destruction was inevitable, but no one cared. I didn't care either. Soni's words were actually the only ones I had heard that made any kind of sense up to that point. Ironically, they were the ones I dismissed as bullshit the quickest.

Morena showed up to take me to the meeting. I reluctantly went with her. I really didn't want to go but I knew I had to. The consequences were too dangerous if I decided to quit the Kings. I asked her to stop somewhere and get some beer. She did. I drank it and felt better. At the meeting we went through the same routine. A prayer was said, the welcome of new members was announced, then on to the business at hand. Three new members would be initiated that day: two Juniors and a Peewee. It was announced that the guns and drugs that had been mentioned in a previous meeting had been purchased. Five thousand dollars was put aside to pay a lawyer for a brother named Weasel. Weasel was being charged with the death of the Gangster who was hit by the van. He didn't even take part in that incident! He was just the first King the police saw when they arrived on the scene. I was relieved.

That was basically the law of the street. It didn't matter if you did it or not; if you were part of the gang you were guilty until proven innocent. It was announced that those of us who had been given guns were personally responsible for them. I checked my waistband to make sure the .25 was still there. There was an announcement of a hit that was going to take place against a gang called the OAs. The Orchestra Albany was a small gang that hung out on Albany Street and Kedzie Boulevard. Apparently they had chased the brother of one of the Kings when he got off the subway train at Milwaukee. Those who would take part in the hit would be notified in due time.

Then I was offered the position of president of the Peewee Latin Kings of Kedzie and Armitage. A lot of murmuring broke out throughout the room when that announcement was made. Loco got up and said if anybody had a problem with me accepting that position they should say so. "He ain't been a King for that long," someone said. "He doesn't even hang out with us," said another. "Lil Loco is a down brother. He has earned the respect to ride with Juniors," Loco proclaimed. "That is why we chose him for the position. It's up to you, Lil Loco," Loco said as he turned to me. "Whatever you decide will be respected by all." "I'll think about it," I said in a tough voice while I glanced across the room.

I thought about the advantages of being president of the Peewee Latin Kings. I would be a big honcho and the Peewees would have to obey my orders. I could accept the position just to shut the mouths of those who spoke against me. Cubana, I knew, would be very impressed. Getting sex partners would become just that much easier. On the other hand, I would have to hang out with the Peewees more often. That meant being a constant companion to guys who didn't want to follow my lead. I decided not to alienate my fellow Peewees and declined the offer. I would wait until the meeting was over and tell Loco of my decision. Loco, however, asked for my decision just before the meeting ended. "No," I said, "the brothers are right, I don't hang out with them." Nothing else was said, as if nobody was surprised by my decision. The meeting was adjourned.

After the meeting I went looking for Morena to get a ride back home. I felt exhausted and wanted to get some sleep. The Queens had not finished yet. I sat by myself on the sidewalk to the side of the Latin Kings' emblem. Finally Morena showed up with Blanca. Cubana was nowhere to be seen. When I asked Morena for her, all she said was "You'll see her soon enough. If you want a ride, come on." Morena, Blanca, and I got in the car, and we were on our way. Blanca was very quiet. She didn't say a word to me the whole way to Maria's apartment, even when I flirted with her. When we got to Maria's I asked her if she wanted to stay over. She said, "You're Cubana's man now," and turned away. I went upstairs and helped myself to some food. About a half hour later Cubana showed up with one of the new brothers who had been initiated that day. His name was Felipe. His nickname was Daffy, as in Daffy Duck. He didn't look like a duck but he did a good Daffy Duck impression.

Daffy was Cuban. He had olive skin and slicked-back black hair. He was tall and skinny and loved to fight. He trained at the Von Humboldt Park gym with other members of the park's boxing team. Daffy was a Junior Latin King. He was nineteen years old and obviously had nothing better to do with his life. I hugged Cubana and gave her a deep, passionate kiss. I wanted Daffy to realize that Cubana was my lady. I shook Daffy's hand and demonstrated the fist upon the heart salute. I gave him a joint and told him to sit down. Cubana whispered in my ear that they needed to talk to me in private. Maria and Sonia were still there, but they were getting high snorting coke so they pretty much ignored us.

I led Cubana and Daffy into my room on the back porch and closed the door. Cubana and I sat on the bed and Daffy sat in the lone chair and began telling me why he was there. Loco had made the decision that Daffy was to make the hit on the OAs. I was to accompany him. The hit was to take place on Wednesday of the upcoming week. We were to decide how to carry out the mission and get it done by ourselves. I didn't like the idea, but since Cubana seemed highly excited by the fact that I, her boyfriend, was chosen for the hit, I sat there and acted macho. I told Daffy to meet me on the corner of Potomac and Claremont Streets at 5:00 P.M. the following Wednesday. I would let him know then how we were going to carry out the assigned mission. Daffy left. Cubana stayed behind. She said she wanted to spend the night.

I HAD REACHED the goal I so desired. I was looked to as a leader, not a follower. Not only was I chosen to be president of the Peewee Latin Kings, I was also entrusted to lead a Junior Latin King into battle. No one had ever empowered me with so much responsibility before. I had come a long way from the scared puppy who cowered at the thought of shooting another human being. No longer did I feel the necessity to run and hide under a bed. In my mind and heart I felt that I had done well. I had done what I had to do. All those around me thought the same.

Again I began having nightmares. The Chi-West girl appeared again, getting shot over and over. This time the Gaylords and the Gangster who got hit by the van appeared also. The girl would get shot, the Gaylord begged for mercy, the Gangster flew and bounced off cars. All three fell in a bloody mess. I would snap out of it only to fall right back to sleep and continue the whole thing all over again. "Please don't kill me, please don't kill me," the Gaylord pleaded as I snapped out of the nightmare for the last time. It was daylight Monday morning—time to smoke a joint and go to school.

33

Poor Rosie

I GOT UP feeling hung over. I lay there in bed looking at Cubana and suddenly realized I had to go to school. I got up, showered, and dressed as quickly as I could. I grabbed my books and headed for school. When I got outside, Morena was there waiting for me. Queen Dimples from Cortland and Whipple was with her. I got in the car and told Morena to drop me off at school. Morena insisted we wait for Cubana. When Cubana finally came down, we headed for Clemente High School. We drove down Potomac Street toward Western Avenue. On the way there, Morena demanded that I point Rosie out to her. Morena, Dimples, and Cubana were going to kick her ass and possibly kill her. I was sober, so instead of being glad, I cared. I didn't want anything to happen to Rosie. I was still mad at her but I didn't want to be responsible for her death. I lit up a joint and tried to play it cool. I didn't say a word. Cubana threatened not to see me anymore if I didn't point out Rosie. Morena added that she would bring up the whole incident at the next meeting. I thought about the beating Slim got for trading coke for sex and I put myself in his place. It was either going to be Rosie or me that got hurt. I decided it wasn't going to be me.

Rosie always waited for me by the fire station on Western and Potomac. This day was no different, but Rosie got tired of waiting for me and was already walking to school. Sheena was with her. Morena saw Sheena and asked me if the other girl was Rosie. "Yes," I answered in a low voice. I made sure they knew that Sheena wasn't a gangbanger and that she saved my life. Morena ordered Cubana and Dimples not to touch

Sheena. We pulled into the parking lot across the street from Clemente field on the same side where they were walking. I got out of the car and sat on the hood. My eyes were watery, knowing the fate that awaited Rosie. Rosie and Sheena saw me and walked toward me. Morena got out of the car, walked behind two other parked cars, and came up behind them. Cubana and Dimples got out of the car and stood on either side of me. A look of terror came over Sheena's face as if she knew what was going to happen. Rosie acted like nothing had happened over the weekend. She said, "I'm mad at you. Why didn't you go to my party?" I got off the car and said, "You stupid bitch," and grabbed Sheena. I saw Dimples punch Rosie in the face with brass knuckles and Morena attack her from behind. I didn't want to see anymore. I just held on to Sheena and led her away. I held my hand over her mouth so that she wouldn't say anything that would give her away as being the one who told me about Rosie. Sheena cried and cried. I heard a car horn being blown and heard Morena yell, "Pull out, *la hada, la hada.*" Then I heard police sirens. I kissed Sheena on the cheek, apologized, and took off running through Clemente field. I heard someone yell "Stop." I didn't know who was yelling or who they were yelling at. I kept running, scared as hell. I ran up the alley behind Tuley, through a gangway, across Bell Street, through another gangway, into an alley, and hid inside a garbage can. I stayed there for about four hours. I was too afraid to come out any sooner. I snuck over to Maria's apartment. Morena was there waiting for me. She took me to Kedzie and Armitage so I could chill out at the clubhouse. Rosie knew where I lived, so the police would surely go by Maria's looking for me. I was safer at the clubhouse. I would never again set foot in Clemente High School.

THE NEXT COUPLE of weeks went by without incident. I slept in the Kings' clubhouse because the police were asking for me around Tuley. Apparently Rosie had told them I set her up. Although I didn't show it, I was constantly paranoid and afraid of being caught. The police told one of the Spanish Lords that they were going to drop me off on Rockwell Street and Potomac in Disciples' territory if they caught me. I called Sheena a couple of times when I was sober. She told me Rosie had been stabbed eight times that day, mostly in her face and chest. Rosie was still in the hospital recovering from the attack. She had undergone two reconstructive surgeries and she still required more. I felt like an asshole but learned to live with the fact because this was the same girl who tried to get me killed.

The hit on the Orchestra Albany took place without me. I was too hot. My name began appearing on the walls in rival gang turf. *Lil Loco will die* was being written everywhere. I became well known by name only. A few times I was being talked about while I was sitting right in front of the speaker and they didn't even realize it.

I had not been by Maria's for three weeks. In my absence she got a new live-in boyfriend. He was a black guy. He was tall and skinny and wore his hair in an afro. He loved to wear expensive jewelry. He was also a drug dealer. One night I decided to go to Maria's and had Paco and Tito drive me. They parked in front of Maria's and stayed in the car while I went upstairs. They were going to wait for me so we could go to a Kings' Nation party together. While I was in the house, Maria's boyfriend came staggering in. He was bleeding from the face and neck. He said two guys in a blue car stuck him up and took his jewelry, money, and drugs. Maria had looked out the window when I was dropped off. She knew as well as I did that Paco and Tito did it. Maria went off. She told me to take my stuff and leave. She didn't want me in her house any more. I tried to reason with her but she was relentless. She had her mind made up—I was out of there.

I looked out the window and noticed the guys had taken off. I silently cursed Paco and Tito for pulling that stunt. In the meantime Maria was putting my clothes in a plastic garbage bag. She was serious. I took my stuff and went outside. I sat in front of Maria's building smoking a joint and hoping Maria would come down and take me back. It never happened. About thirty minutes later Morena showed up and picked me up. Morena knew what the guys had done, but she didn't know the consequences. When I told her Maria had kicked me out, she stood quiet and told me that as long as I was a King I would always have a place to stay. From that point on I slept wherever I could. I would be invited into the homes of King brothers and sisters—sometimes other members of the family didn't even know I was there. I slept in hallways, on rooftops, in cars, but mostly in the clubhouse. My relationship with Maria ended that day, thanks to the Latin Kings, my friends and brothers.

34

Juni

As MY DRUG use progressed, so did my violence. However, I still played baseball every chance I got. I was still pretty good at it. Once in a while I would go by Western Avenue and Potomac Street and play baseball with the Western Boys. The Western Boys knew about my gang activity, so they were reluctant to let me play with them. They made me promise not to represent while I was with them and to walk away if a rival gang spotted me.

The Western Boys had a new member. His name was Junior but everybody called him Juni. Juni was a puny kid with hazel eyes and brown hair. He had moved to Chicago from New York. Juni was fun to be around. He always made jokes and tried to make people laugh. He was a good kid. His parents were very nice people too. They never objected to me coming over for dinner or sleeping over. They cared for and loved Juni a hell of a lot. I could feel the love in their house. It made me wish that my own family had been as close and caring.

Juni heard about me from the other Western Boys. He told me he wanted to be a King. He bugged me until I gave him details of my gang war stories. I didn't encourage him to be like me but I didn't discourage him either. His first cigarette, his first beer, his first joint—he had them all with me. He learned how to represent the Kings' hand sign and the Kings' handshake by watching me.

The Western Boys set up a baseball game against a team led by some members of the Clemente baseball team. Juni was very excited about this game—it was all he talked about. He was planning on trying out for the baseball team when he became a freshman at Clemente the following year. The game was set for early Saturday morning. We met the Friday before to practice.

We practiced until mid-afternoon and then everybody went home—everybody except for me, that is. I didn't have a home. I walked Juni to his house on Claremont Street, across the street from Tuley. From there I headed to a restaurant right on the corner of Western and North Avenue called Taco Loco. I had some money on me so I decided to eat there and then call Morena or someone else from Kedzie and Armitage to pick me up. I was crossing LeMoyne Street one block before North when I heard footsteps walking up behind me fast. I reached for my .25 but realized I didn't have it. Thank god I didn't need it; it was Juni running behind me. Juni had told his parents he was going to play by Tuley and came after me instead. At Taco Loco I ordered food for both of us and began feeding quarters into the pinball machine. By the time we realized what time it was, night had fallen. I told Juni I would walk him home. I knew he would be in trouble, but Juni was sure that as long as his parents realized he was with me everything would be all right.

We walked down North toward Claremont and then proceeded up Claremont toward Tuley. As we walked a carload of guys drove by and yelled "King love." I didn't recognize the car or the guys so I didn't respond. Juni on the other hand returned the greeting and then looked at me waiting for my approval. "Those are your boys, Lil Loco, *Amor de Rey,* man, *Amor de Rey,*" Juni said. I didn't say anything to him. I just kept walking and talked about the baseball game. I became worried about the car that had passed. I looked back and sure enough it was coming again. By this time we were almost by St. Aloysious Church on Claremont and LeMoyne. I became truly worried but didn't want to do anything that made me look like a punk in front of Juni. What if there were Latin Kings in that car? How foolish would I look ducking and hiding from my own boys? No, I had to play it cool and show no fear.

The church had a cement canopy over the Claremont entrance; cement slabs held it up. I began to lead Juni toward it so that we could hide. Just before we got behind the cement slabs, "King love" was yelled again. Juni turned around and walked away from me. I reached out to grab him but missed. He walked by the side of the street and yelled, "King love." "Don't, Juni, don't. Come back, come back," I yelled as I ran toward him. Before I got to him I heard two booms like cannons going off. I heard Juni scream as I threw myself to the concrete. Then I heard a car screech as it sped away. When I lifted my head, Juni lay there bleeding to death. He was shot twice in the chest. I picked his head up and cradled it, screaming my head off. "Help, help, somebody call an ambulance!" I screamed. Juni was gasping for air, trying to talk, muttering something about how his mom was going to be mad at him. "Don't, Juni, don't die," was all I could say. His last words were "Tell the guys I won't be playing tomorrow." I sat there with him in my arms. He was dead and it was my fault. All I could do was scream obscenities about rival gangs. "Fuckin' *crusaos* are gonna die, all of them are gonna die," I screamed with hatred in my voice. But it was much too late for that—Juni was dead.

About twenty minutes passed before the police finally arrived, but still no ambulance. A crowd of people gathered. The police began asking the usual "what happened" questions. As usual, everybody denied seeing or hearing anything. As always, everybody said, "We just got here." A police officer told me to let Juni go and stand up. I began screaming, "He's dead, he's dead." The officer grabbed me by the hair and said, "I told you to let him go," as he pulled me upward. The officer pulled me up, slammed me to the concrete, and handcuffed me. By this time there were police all over the place. Detectives from the gang crime division put me in their car and began asking me questions. They asked me who did it. Before I could answer they asked me what gang Juni and I were in. I looked out the window where Juni still lay on the ground. Juni's parents were now on the scene. I could hear his mother screaming in terror. "*Mi hijo, mi hijo, diosito ¿por qué me quitaste a mi hijo?*" ("My son, my son, dear God, why did you take my son"), she screamed at the top of her lungs. His father stood there with a blank look on his face staring directly at me. I told the police about the car passing by representing the Kings and that Juni represented back. I clarified that Juni was not a gang member, but that I was a Latin King. One detective said, "You got your friend killed. I bet you really feel like a man now."

The other said, "You better think about this. Next time it may be you." After assuring themselves that I could not give any better description of the car or its passengers, they took me out of the car and took off the handcuffs. After giving me several warnings about continuing with gang activity the detectives let me go.

The paramedics finally showed up after Juni had laid there for forty-five minutes. I looked on from across the street as the police pulled Juni's mother away so that the paramedics could take his body. My clothes were drenched in his blood. Juni's mother looked my way and noticed the blood. She ran over to me screaming and swinging her arms at me. "*Hijo de la gran puta, que le hisiste a mi hijo*" ("Son of a bitch, what did you do to my son"), she screamed as she repeatedly slapped my face. I just stood there looking at the ground and feeling guilty about Juni's death. The punishment I was receiving was well deserved. Juni's father grabbed his wife and took her away. He came back and looked at me with a real hard expression on his face and said, "We're not supposed to kill each other. That's not what the Kings are about." Juni's father was never a King but he saw them form and grow when they were a group devoted to the Puerto Rican struggle. "We'll get revenge," I said. Juni's father grabbed me by my shirt and lifted me off the ground. "Don't you go killing somebody in the name of my son," he said. "If you didn't care enough to keep him alive, don't act like you care now that he's dead." Juni's father released me. I fell to the ground and he walked away angrily.

I had this numb feeling inside. I wished I had a joint or a beer so I could forget what had just happened. Juni was taken away. His parents went with the police and all the onlookers went back to whatever it was they were doing. Life went on.

When the Kings saw me coming, they freaked out. They thought I had been shot because of the blood on my clothes. I went to the clubhouse and told everybody what had happened. I had my other clothes there so I cleaned up, changed, and began getting high to numb the pain.

I began asking for Morena. She had my pistols and I wanted to go get revenge for what happened to Juni. Morena finally did show up and gave me the .25, but Loco had already talked me into cooling out for the night. He explained that the police would be expecting some kind of retaliation. He said I should wait until the next night, Saturday. I didn't sleep all night. Every time I closed my eyes I saw Juni dying in my arms.

Saturday morning Cubana came by and brought me breakfast. I pretended to be mad at her for not being around all night. I could have used her comfort. Cubana had regained her title as my confidante. I told her everything. After talking to Cubana for a little while, I finally fell asleep. Again Juni was in my dreams. I saw him covered with blood. Then I saw the bullet enter and exit the Chi-West girl. Then I saw myself covered with blood. Bullets entered Juni and he fell, calling to me. I stood there doing nothing. I woke up screaming and cursing. I drank a bottle of wine like it was water. Cubana tried to calm me, but I pushed her away. I grabbed my gun and went outside. I ran all the way to Morena's house. She had moved from Maplewood Park and lived across the street from Humboldt Park on Kedzie. She lived about a mile away from the clubhouse. I went there to get my other gun. I wanted to kill somebody. I decided the only way to get Juni out my dreams was to avenge his death. Morena questioned me about why I wanted the gun. I told her about what happened to Juni. "I'm going to kill one of those fucking Cobras." (Juni was killed in Spanish Lords' territory and since the Cobras were their rivals it was logical to think they had done it.) "Now give me the fuckin' gun!" Morena gave me the gun and told me to wait while she put her shoes on so she could come with me. As soon as she went into her bedroom I took off running.

I ran to Kedzie and North Avenue and got on the bus. I blamed the Cobras for pulling the trigger that killed Juni. It had to be them. I got off the bus on Campbell Street and walked southbound toward the Cobras' 'hood. When I got to Hirsch Street, Lucky and Cubana pulled up in front of me in a car. Morena came running behind me. They were able to talk me into waiting until later that night when more Cobras would be out. I went to Morena's apartment and stayed there all day smoking weed and watching television. Cubana was there with me for a while but left when I rudely rejected her romantic advances. I was in no mood for any kind of affection. I didn't want to eat, I didn't want to talk, all I wanted to do was get high. I wanted time to fly by so I could go out and shoot a Cobra.

By nightfall I was highly intoxicated and anxious to commit an act of violence. Lucky tried to talk me into letting someone else do the hit. I refused. When he said that I would have to go alone, I started walking toward the Cobras' 'hood. He realized I was serious and told me to get in the car. Lucky drove by Cortland and Whipple and picked up Queen Loca. Along the way Lucky explained to her what was going on. Loca had no problem with it; she was actually excited about it. Loca was about twenty-five years old. She was a short, dark-skinned Puerto Rican girl with a New York accent. She got her nickname because of her itchy trigger finger and because she would fight just about anybody, man or woman. Loca had some martial arts training and was good at it. She was the first hard-core girl gangbanger I met who was a parent. She had two little boys. Their father, a King, was serving an eighty-year prison term for murder.

We drove up Humboldt Boulevard to Division Street, then headed east. After some debate we decided to hit the Disciples on Rockwell and Potomac Streets instead of the Cobras. We drove up Division to Rockwell and went north toward Potomac. The plan was for Loca and me to open fire when Lucky turned west onto Potomac from Rockwell. I had my .38 with me. Lucky handed Loca a .45 automatic. Loca was very proficient with guns. She pulled out the clip, checked the chamber, then put the clip back in and held the gun in a ready position. We opened all the windows and got ready to shoot. As we got closer, we noticed there were a lot of Disciples hanging out on all four corners. There was also a lot of traffic due to the heavy drug sales going on out there. "Look at all those motherfuckers," Loca said as she rolled down her window. When we got to the corner, Loca began shooting before Lucky made the turn. I began shooting also. Lucky made the turn at a rapid speed. The Disciples were shooting back. The back windshield shattered as we sped away down Potomac. Lucky crossed California Avenue and drove right through the park until we got to the parkway. We drove across Sacramento Avenue and ditched the car. Lucky told us to get rid of the guns, then began running toward Kedzie. Loca grabbed me by the arm and took me with her toward Augusta Avenue. I looked back toward the car and noticed three bullet holes on the driver's side. I could only imagine what the passenger side looked like, since that's where most of the retaliatory gunshots had come from. We had to get off the streets fast.

35

Loca

ON KEDZIE AND Augusta Avenues there was another Latin King section. Loca took me across Augusta and through a gangway. We crossed an alley and went through a fence that led into the backyard of a three-story building. We went to the second floor and knocked on the door. A tall, slim, white lady opened the door and let us in. The white lady's name was Kaye. Her apartment was a party house for the Latin Kings. There were about seven guys and girls inside getting high. Kaye had three kids. All were present in the same room where the drugs were being used. Loca scolded Kaye about having her kids in the room, but she did nothing about it. Loca got some drugs from the people who were there and took me into the kitchen. We got high and shared personal stories. I told her how I ended up on the streets and what led to the hit we had just come from. She told me about her life as a Queen and assured me that I made a good decision when I became a King. Loca complimented me on my desire to kill a Cobra to avenge a friend. "You're a good brother," she said. "There aren't many like you anymore." Her words made me feel proud, like a man. I was glad I had become a King.

After about three hours of getting high Loca wanted to take a walk to the Augusta Pool, a Chicago Park District facility that was closed at night. Augusta Pool was located about a block and a half west of Kedzie on Augusta and Sacramento Avenues. As we walked, she told me about a gang called the Dragons that was formed on the other side of the Boulevard by a couple of ex-Kings. They were rivals, Loca said, "King killers." She told me that the two guys were once very prominent in the

Augusta and Kedzie King section. They had raped a Queen and were punished with a head-to-toe violation that left them both hospitalized. They got revenge by sticking up the head of the Augusta Kings for drugs, guns, and money. They started the Latin Dragons, a gang aligned against the Kings, as a way to protect themselves. Loca advised me to be careful while we were at the pool since the Dragons just might show up. About a half a block from the pool I pulled open a sewer cover and dumped the guns that were used in the hit. I still had the .25.

A big hole was cut in the chain-link fence that surrounded the pool so people could go swimming after hours. Although it was illegal to swim there at night, the police rarely did anything about it. We went in through the hole in the fence. There was nobody there. Loca jumped in while I stood there looking across the street for Dragons. Loca pushed me into the pool. She jumped in after me and began dunking my head underwater. The .25 slipped out of my pants and sank to the bottom of the pool. Loca dived to the bottom of the pool and got the gun. Her T-shirt lifted up to her shoulders when she came back up. She didn't have a bra on and her breasts were exposed. I stared. "Boy, what are you looking at? You've never seen tits before?" Loca laughed. She put the gun at the edge of the pool and then proceeded to try to dunk me under the water.

We were having a good time until we were interrupted by music from a radio. We looked to see four guys and two girls climbing in through the hole in the fence. I swam to the edge where the gun was and took it before they could see it. Loca got close to me and whispered, "Let's get out of here. Those are Dragons." "Let's pop them," I whispered. "The gun may not work. It may jam," Loca answered. We left in a hurry without even looking toward them. As we left, the Dragons called out to Loca to stay and play with them. We hurried back to Kaye's house, looking back every chance we got to make sure they weren't following us. At Kaye's, Loca told the Kings that the Dragons were at the pool. They all began to mobilize. I was going to go with them but Loca stopped me. She used Kaye's phone to call somebody at Cortland and Whipple so we could be picked up. About fifteen minutes passed when we heard a car horn. It was our ride back to the 'hood. When we got to the car we heard about eight gunshots coming from the direction of the pool. Screams could also be heard coming from that direction. We then saw a couple of guys running toward us. We got in the car and drove away before the police arrived. All four guys at the pool were shot; two died. Whether they were Dragons or not I don't know, but the fighting between the Kings and the Dragons did intensify after that incident.

We went to Loca's apartment on the corner of Cortland and Humboldt Boulevard in an apartment complex they called *la tumba* (the tomb) because several people had been killed in front of or inside that building. Surprisingly, Loca did not allow the Kings to come and party at her apartment. Her place was very clean and tidy with expensive-looking furniture. Loca's sister Delia was there babysitting for her. Delia was thirteen years old and pregnant. I wanted to go get high and find Cubana. Loca wouldn't let me go outside. She advised me to stay there. "*La hada* will be looking to pick up any brother in sight," Loca said. Loca gave me some weed and a pack of rolling papers. She pointed out a room where I could go get high. "Don't worry about Cubana," Loca said. "She lives here. That's her room."

I went into Cubana's room and laid on the bed looking at all the decorations she had on the wall. She had a lot of drawings that were sent to her from brothers that were in prison. Most were King/Queen related, but there were also many that had romantic themes. I was reading one that proclaimed true love toward Cubana when she walked in. She became upset about me being there and asked me to leave. Loca stepped in and told Cubana that she had told me to go into her room. "I don't care," Cubana said, "he shouldn't be in here." She led me out of her room and locked the door. I stood there wondering what the hell had gotten into her.

Someone came and picked Delia up. Loca prepared the sofa for me and told me to sleep there. Loca retreated into her bedroom and the apartment became dark and quiet. I was sleepy as all hell but I was afraid to close my eyes because of the nightmares I was having. Fatigue took control and I fell asleep.

The nightmares returned. I saw Juni getting shot over and over again and the Chi-West girl screaming for mercy as the bullets entered and exited her. I woke up in a deep sweat. My heart was pounding and I was scared out of my mind. I got up and went to the bathroom. I saw Juni's bloody face in the mirror when I turned on the light. I was so fuckin' startled I pissed all over the bathroom floor. I cleaned up the mess I made and went back to the sofa.

I found Cubana sitting there waiting for me. We talked about the drawings on her wall. She confessed to having a boyfriend in jail. He was a King brother named Jibaro. He had been locked up for ten years and had about fifty to go. She met him through Loca when they went to visit the father of her kids. Cubana was eighteen years old, Jibaro was thirty-something. Cubana was his mule. (A mule is a female who sneaks drugs in for prisoners, usually in her vagina.) I figured she was having sex with him too but she denied it. It didn't matter. We went in her room and had sex. That's all that mattered to me. She could be the girlfriend of every guy in jail for all I cared. As long as she had sex with me, it was all right.

Cubana said that she never told me about being a mule because she loved me and didn't want me to think less of her. Cubana was one of many Queens used for this purpose. It is their pleasure and honor to even be considered for the task. Being a mule was one of the ways Queens earned rank within the gang.

Cubana had a good reason to keep that part of her life from me. From that day forward I didn't trust her as much any more. She became like another Jenny—someone to have sex with when there was no one else available. I stopped sharing my inner thoughts with her.

Loca became like Maria. She would let me sleep at her place and always made sure I had something to eat. Her two little boys, Angel, eight years old, and Tony, six years old, got very attached to me. They were very well behaved and polite, which surprised me. Loca warned me not to represent or even mention the Latin Kings around them. I found her request kind of odd since she was a Queen. I obeyed her nevertheless, not wanting to lose my newfound shelter.

36

Morena, R.I.P.

On Sunday I went to the meeting. It was the same routine there: the purchase of more guns and drugs was announced and the meeting was adjourned. Before I left, Pito talked to me about making myself too hot. He said that the brothers preferred that I cool out for a while to avoid getting arrested. I thought maybe they really cared. I don't think they realized that it was the drugs and alcohol that made me into the person they loved so much. I was too weak, too scared, too much of a coward to live the life of a gangbanger without getting high. Every time we got together for the meetings you could look into the eyes of many of the Kings and realize that more than half of them were just as scared as I was.

I followed the instructions of my leaders. I didn't see much action for the rest of the summer. I went to the park a lot and hung out with Loca, her kids, and Cubana.

Toward the end of summer tragedy struck big time—Morena was killed. She was standing on the corner of Kedzie and Armitage a few feet away from the Latin Kings' emblem when a carload of Imperial Gangsters drove by and shot her. Morena was shot in the chest and face with a sawed-off shotgun. She died right there on the street. The night it happened I was at the lakefront hanging out with Cubana, Loca, and her kids. I felt so guilty. I just knew that if I had been with her Morena would still be alive. At her funeral I kneeled at her coffin until they closed the funeral home. I thought about how we met, how she saved me at the Chi-West shooting and didn't reject me for not pulling the trigger, how she was the sister I always wanted, and how I couldn't imagine not having her around anymore. I felt numb. Yet I didn't make it to her burial—I was busy getting ready to make a hit on the Gangsters. I went on a shooting spree to avenge Morena's death. For four days straight beginning the day of her burial I went out shooting at the Gangsters. For the first hit I just took the bus to Palmer Boulevard and Drake and began shooting in the direction of the Gangsters as soon as I got off. I don't know if anybody got hit; I didn't care. I just shot and ran back to Kedzie and Armitage. The next two hits were drive-bys done with other brothers. The last hit I did by myself. That hit was the beginning of the end of my tenure as a Kedzie and Armitage Latin King.

Exactly one month after Morena was killed I was with Cubana at Loca's apartment. As always I was smoking a joint and looking forward to having sex with Cubana. We started kissing, then began making love. This time it was different. I imagined it was Morena I was making love to. I smelled Morena's sweet scent, heard her voice, and saw her face when I opened my eyes. It was like I was reliving the night Morena and I made love. I freaked out. I stood up, crying, and got dressed. Cubana yelled, "What's wrong? What's wrong?" I grabbed the .38 I was now carrying (I got rid of the .25 after the second hit on the Gangsters) and hit the streets. It was about two in the morning. I walked toward Kedzie and Armitage and ran into a King everyone called Duce from Cortland and Whipple. For some unknown reason Duce did not get along with me, but he was willing to help me steal a car to make the hit. I needed his help; I knew nothing about hot-wiring cars. I didn't trust Duce, but I thought to hell with it. It was something I had to do.

Duce and I walked down Albany Street toward North Avenue. I was a lookout while he broke into and then hot-wired a car parked near Bloomingdale Street. He reversed the car onto Bloomingdale and I got in. We headed toward Central Park and Armitage. The Gangsters had grown and spread their 'hood out. They had hangouts on side streets along Central Park. The streets were almost deserted. We were becoming impatient because we couldn't find anyone to kill. Just before we got to Armitage two guys came out of a gangway and began walking north toward us. "Gangster," I shouted as we drove by them. "Imperial," the guys shouted as they flagged us to come back. "Them punks think we're Gangsters," Duce said. "Let's go, let's go," I told Duce, "these pussies are mine." "There's no traffic," Duce said, "I'm going to reverse so they'll be on your side." "*Balla bro, balla*. Let's go!" As Duce reversed, I could see the two Gangsters walk onto the street getting ready to be picked up. I was jumping with anticipation. I couldn't wait to see them lying on the concrete bleeding to death. Duce stopped the car inches before we reached the Gangsters. The Gangsters stepped forward to get in the car, not knowing who we were. I opened my door and began shooting.

"King love, motherfucker," I screamed as I repeatedly pulled the trigger. Both Gangsters fell to the ground bleeding from gunshot wounds. "This is for Morena, motherfuckers! *Amor de Rey!*" I stood over them emptying the gun. When I didn't have any more bullets I kicked the Gangster closest to me. "Come on, let's go! Get in the car," I heard Duce yell. I got in the car and held on as Duce quickly drove off. I was elated. "That's for you, Morena, that's for you," I yelled as I looked up to the sky. Duce in the meantime was driving through red lights, barely avoiding getting into accidents. I didn't care if he killed us. I was too busy being happy about what we had just done. Duce parked the car on Bloomingdale, between Kimball Avenue and Kedzie. We ran from there. On our way back to the 'hood I cleaned my fingerprints off the gun and tossed it up the viaduct that ran along Bloomingdale. Once we got to Cortland and Whipple, Duce went his way and I went mine. Back at Loca's I explained to Cubana why I had run off and what I had done. Cubana expressed her approval and then made love to me. This time I smelled Cubana, I felt Cubana, I made love to Cubana. Morena was resting in peace.

Gang members believe that a dead comrade will not rest in peace unless their death is avenged. A gang's honor and reputation are at stake if every action taken against them is not met with a worthy act of retaliation. Most of the anger in the hearts of gang members stems from the memory of dead comrades. It is this anger that binds members and keeps the gang like a family. Those same memories are transplanted into the hearts of new members in order to continue building hatred. New members seek to avenge the deaths of people they never knew until they have their own fresh memory to go on. Memories of a dead comrade fan the flames of gang warfare. It is, and always will be, the hardest thing to extinguish.

The King brothers came down on me hard because of that hit on the Gangsters. Dino was picked up and charged with the crime. One Gangster died; the other was left crippled. A special meeting was called to talk to me about my actions. Only the committee members and myself would be present. Loco picked me up at Loca's and began scolding me from the moment I got in the car. I sat there quietly. I didn't even pay attention. I blocked him out. I got out of the car at Kedzie and Armitage to a sea of staring eyes. It seemed as if something very bad was in store for me. I became nervous, so I did what I always did whenever I got nervous or scared—I lit up a joint. We went up the stairs to the clubhouse. Not a word was spoken. Inside the guys who formed the committee were waiting for us to arrive. "What's up, Lil Loco? "*Estas caliente*" ("You're hot"), Paco said. "Put out that joint, Lil Loco, and have a seat," Loco said in an angry voice. I sat on the sofa near the window, took one last, long puff off the joint, then ashed it out.

"We told your ass to chill out," Loco began, "but you had to fuck up anyway, right? What do you think we should do, Lil Loco? Tell me, huh, what should we do?"

"Morena was my girl," I said. "I had to do it. Violate me if you want to. If any one of mine gets taken out, I'll do it again."

"It's not what you did, it's how you did it!" Loco screamed. "You have to let us know when you're going to pull shit like that."

"Dino is locked up now. He may never get out," Paco said, "all because you didn't let us know."

"We ain't going to violate you, you're a down little brother," Loco said. "But we are warning you, you don't move unless we say so."

"Fuck that, I'm a King, a leader," I responded.

"If you move without us, you get a head to toe," Paco warned me.

"Think about it," Loco said. "Get out of here before we kick your ass." I sat there momentarily, feeling confused. I thought it was a good thing to take out a rival gang member. Brothers were picked up and charged for other people's crimes all the time. What difference did Dino getting picked up make? I got up and left without saying a word.

At Loca's, she explained that the brothers were acting this way because Officer James was coming down on them. I was making it too hot for him to come around and deal with the Kings. That was the true reason behind the warning. It had nothing to do with Dino—it was a business move. That meeting was the first time I saw that money was becoming more important to the Kings than brotherhood. Had Officer James not put pressure on the Kings that meeting would never have taken place. I still wonder why Officer James didn't pick me up and arrest me. Maybe money changed hands, maybe he didn't really know if I did it or not. I guess locking Dino up was satisfactory. I was still a minor, so not much could be done to me. Dino, on the other hand, took a deal from the state, pleaded guilty, and got a twenty-year sentence for a crime he didn't commit. It was one of those things that just shouldn't happen but instead was routine.

Latin Kings from all sections went on a killing spree to avenge Morena's death. As far as I was concerned I had already done that. Still, I joined the brothers when they asked me to. I had become a hard-core gangbanger whether I was high or sober. I was thinking more, but at the same time I was caring less. Morena's death was a turning point in my life.

The Latin Disciples had grown into a very strong and dangerous street gang. They were united with the Spanish Cobras, who hung out a few blocks from their territory on Maplewood and Potomac. The newly formed Latin Jivers, who also hung out a few blocks from the Disciples on the opposite side, had also united with the Disciples. Together they formed the most dangerous opposition to the Latin Kings. It was my idea that we should hit that area as a message that the Latin Kings weren't afraid of nobody. Since I knew my way around Rockwell and Potomac Streets I would call attention to myself and lead whoever chased me into an ambush. The hit was planned for a Tuesday night. We were hoping a smaller crowd of Disciples would be hanging out that night. We were right.

Daffy stole a van the night before and stashed it so we could use it for the hit. Queen Loca drove the van while another Queen named Rubia rode shotgun. Ace, Daffy, Lalo, and I sat in the back of the van. It didn't have any side windows so we couldn't be seen. We went from Western Avenue down Potomac toward Rockwell. On her way to the 'hood, Rubia drove through the Rockwell and Potomac intersection and she reported that she saw only about six or seven Disciples on the corner. That was an ideal number. (There would usually be close to a hundred people on all four corners.) We parked half a block past Rockwell and I got out. I walked up Potomac toward Rockwell. I was about six houses from the corner when the door of a house I had just passed opened. I turned around and saw my old friend Speedy. I looked him right in the eyes. He didn't hesitate at all before he shouted out, "That's King Lil Loco! Get him!" I ran through the gangway of the house I was in front of and headed for the alley. "D love, King Killer," I heard someone shout behind me. I hit the alley and ran west toward California Avenue. If I could reach the park two blocks away I knew I would be all right. Ahead of me I saw more Disciples entering the alley and running toward me. I took a detour over a wooden fence. "Go to the front," I heard someone yell. Instead of running to the front of that house, I jumped the fence again from the side and into the gangway of the house next to it. I heard a vehicle screeching in the alley and Rubia yelling, "King, Queen Love." Then gunshots went off. I knew the guys would come back around down Potomac, so I headed toward the front. I ran through the gangway and right into the barrel of a shotgun held by my old friend Julio. We looked each other in the eyes and said each others' names simultaneously. It was the first time I had heard my real name in a long time. "So you're Lil Loco," Julio said. "I could kill you right now, man." Julio still spoke with that deep accent. He had grown tall and muscular. We were the same age but I looked like a baby next to him. I just stared into his eyes. I didn't dare move or talk. I heard the van coming down Potomac. "Shit, I'm dead," were my only thoughts. Julio pointed the shotgun up in the air and told me to leave before we were seen together. "I owe you one, *mi hermano* (my brother), I owe you one," I told Julio as I took off running. I heard the shotgun go off as I reached the front of the house. Julio must have shot up into the air. The blast from the shotgun made the Disciples chasing the van pause long enough for me to run to it and get in. So Julio saved me again. About three bullets hit the van as I got in. A fourth hit me in the lower front part of my right leg near my foot. The bullet just skinned me but it bled and hurt like hell. We drove out of that neighborhood at a blazing speed. When Loca made the turn onto California, the van nearly tipped over. Back in the 'hood, Loca and Lalo helped me inside Loca's apartment. Daffy drove off to get rid of the van. Everyone else scattered every which way to get off the streets before the police came looking for people to arrest. My lower leg and foot swelled up something ugly for about a week. All the Kings were so proud of me. My first battle scar—it was cause for celebration. Cubana gave me lots of special attention. I loved the feeling. I was brave, macho, indestructible. I was a leader, not a follower.

37

NRA? Lucky's Death

Toward the end of the summer I witnessed a gun purchase. Two white men from somewhere in southern Illinois were coming up to sell us some guns. Some brothers in prison set up the deal. Loco, Lalo, and I met the two white men at a bar on North Avenue across the street from Humboldt Park. They were both big, burly men who looked like bikers. Loco and one of the men sat at a table. Lalo and the other man sat at the bar. I went to the pool table and began playing with the cue ball. Loco got up and called me. He whispered something to Lalo and then headed outside. The white man who was talking to Loco followed him and so did I. Outside all three of us went to the parking lot on the side of the bar to a blue Cadillac. Loco told me to look out for the cops while he took care of business. The white man opened the trunk and Loco looked inside. After about five minutes Loco walked away from the Cadillac to the car we had arrived in. The white man called to me, saying, "Hey, little man, come check these out." I walked over and looked in the trunk. There were two wooden boxes full of guns and rifles. There were about twenty of what the white man told me were M-1s, the kind used by the Army National Guard. That rifle used the biggest bullets I had ever seen. The white man laughed at my reaction when I saw the M-1 bullets. He reached into one of the boxes, pulled out a .357 Magnum, and gave it to me. He said that it was a strong gun with not much kick so I ought to be able to handle it. It was a gift from him to me. The gun was a little bigger than the .38 I had but weighed about the same. The bullets were also bigger. I couldn't wait to shoot it.

I stuck the gun inside the front of my pants and left it there. A feeling of strength came over me. "Kill yourself one of them Dis-ci-ples, one shot will do it," the white man said. Loco parked our car next to the Cadillac and with help from the white man moved the boxes from one car to the other. Loco gave the white man a gym bag and they both sat down in the back seat of the Cadillac. I sat on the front hood of the car. I looked inside and saw them counting money. I noticed a sticker on the windshield of the Cadillac with the initials *NRA* in the middle, and the words *National Rifle Association* in a circle along the borders. So that's where all those guns come from, I thought. I wanted to join that group when I grew up. About fifteen minutes passed. Loco got out of the car and told me to go get Lalo, and we were off.

I really never thought about that whole incident until much later on in life. I wonder if those white men would have sold us those guns if we lived in their city or if we were still fighting only white gangs.

We took the guns to a part of the city called Bucktown, where Lucky now lived. Bucktown also had a Latin Kings section. Lucky, like most of the other leaders of the Kings, moved out of the old neighborhood to stay safe. The leaders would commute to the 'hood for meetings or when something serious was going down. Mostly they stayed off the streets of the 'hood and let the foot soldiers do whatever they needed to protect it. Lucky was an exception. Moving away did not stop him from hanging out. He began running around Bucktown with some older Kings.

About that same time Lucky began changing. He became skinny and didn't bother much with personal hygiene. The rumor was out that he was shooting up dope and was going to get kicked out of the Kings. Lucky had been a King for a long time and could get mighty crazy when pushed. Loco and the other brothers decided against giving Lucky a violation. They would, however, ask him not to represent the crown anymore.

Lucky showed up drunk to one of the meetings saying something about not being trusted. Apparently the Kings had moved everything they had stashed at Lucky's. He was upset. When Lucky was told not to represent he went off. "Fuck you, pussy motherfuckers, none of you can take my crown," Lucky screamed as he threw the Kings' hand sign up in the air. "Don't fuck around, Lucky," Loco said, "don't fuck around and leave!" "Fuck you, Loco, Mr. Chief, you ain't shit!" Lucky yelled.

"Beat the shit out of this punk," Loco ordered. Four of the Junior Kings grabbed Lucky and threw him down the stairs. Lucky could be heard yelling outside about his plan for vengeance. "Watch your backs, motherfuckers, watch your backs!" shouted Lucky. "Y'all don't scare me. *Amor de Rey.* Once a King, always a King!"

"If that punk comes to the 'hood, move out on him quick," Loco ordered.

Three days later Lucky went to the new location where the Kings had their guns and stuck up the brothers who were in charge of them. Lucky took most of the guns and sold them for drugs. The Saturday of that same week Lucky was out in the middle of the street, strung out, swearing at the Bucktown Latin Kings. Nobody said anything to him— they just looked his way and did nothing. Suddenly there was a boom and Lucky fell backward. He had been shot right in the forehead with an M-1. The bullet went through his head and blew out the back of it. The Latin Kings killed Lucky. Nobody went to his funeral: nobody was allowed to. Justice was served the Kings' way.

38

Crazy Ways

I BEGAN TO visit different Latin Kings' sections throughout the city and suburbs with older King brothers. The section I enjoyed the most was Chinatown. It was a totally new experience for me—a different culture, a different way of life, and still Latin King territory. The Kings of Chinatown, with many Chinese members, had heard of my fame as a gang member. They welcomed me and extended an invitation to return and party with them. I loved the oriental food, their mannerisms, and their women. Unlike the women that hung out with the Puerto Rican Kings, the oriental women weren't as quick to offer themselves. There was mystery. The ones that did were always spoken for when I came around. I had such a desire to experience sex with an oriental woman that I began looking for ways to get to Chinatown. Then I met Cindy.

Cindy was the sister of a Latin King. "Chinita," I called her. She was gorgeous, with a shy smile. Chinita was different from any other woman I had ever met. She knew right from the start that my intentions in befriending her were sexual. Unlike others, Cindy didn't threaten me into respecting her. She didn't even mention it. Instead, Cindy earned my respect by demonstrating the respect she had for herself to others and to me. Any inappropriate action, such as an attempt to touch her, would cause Cindy to walk off. Chinita became a very good friend of mine. I loved talking to her. Cindy got me interested in school again. I decided to try to enroll again the following year. She promised to help me earn respectable grades. "All you have to do," she said, "is have the desire."

I wish I had listened. As winter grew colder, my visits to Chinatown became fewer. Finally Cindy and I became phone friends.

Just before winter ended the gang wars flared up again. Innocent people were being killed because of the colors they wore or where they were standing. Anything that could be mistaken as gang affiliation could get a person killed. Two students standing at a bus stop on their way to school were shot to death because they were standing next to a gang insignia drawn on a wall. One of the students just happened to be wearing the same colors that belonged to the gang that was represented on the wall. The students had no gang affiliation.

A Latin King from the Beach and Spaulding Streets section was also killed. Plans for revenge were discussed at the weekly meetings. I didn't want to join anybody else's planned hit. I felt safer and more confident doing my own thing. Most of the time I was asked to be the triggerman anyway. Granted, it was mostly because of my big mouth, but still I was the one initiating the action so what difference did it make? While the Kings of Kedzie and Armitage were talking about waiting for warmer weather, I thought a wintertime hit would be more appropriate.

The last snow of the year was falling. It was a blizzard. It snowed so hard and so heavily that you could barely see five feet in front of you. Everything was hidden by the snow. To me it was perfect weather to make a hit. I had an Eskimo-style coat that winter. The hood on it nearly covered my whole face. I walked up Humboldt Boulevard, through the park, and down Division Avenue toward Western Avenue. There was nobody around. I carried a can of spray paint, a bottle of wine, and my .357 Magnum. As I approached Maplewood Street and Division, I saw about four people standing on the corner. As I got closer, I could see that there were five guys and they were Cobras. I clenched the gun inside my pocket, put my head down, and walked hurriedly like somebody wanting to get out of the cold. As I was crossing Maplewood toward the guys, I tried to pull out the gun, but it got stuck in my pocket. "*Bolsas, bolsas*" ("bags, bags"), one of them called out as I walked by. They were selling bags of weed. I walked right by them. They paid me no mind. Once I got past them I pulled out the gun and the spray paint. I started writing my name on the wall. I wrote *Lil Loco LKN* in big, bold letters.

Finally one of the Cobras noticed what I was doing and alerted the others. "Cobra" was the first thing they said. "King Love Almighty" was my response as I pointed the gun toward them and began shooting. There were screams. Whether they were from pain or fear I don't know. I didn't stick around to find out. I did hear retaliatory shots as I ran toward Western.

I went by the Lords' clubhouse only to find out it no longer existed. The Lords were now hanging out by Claremont Street and North. The Cobras had made them move. I went to Western and North and hopped the bus back to Kedzie and Armitage. I went straight to Loca's and fell asleep. Nobody came by to scold me about doing things on my own this time.

MEETINGS BECAME FEW and far between that winter. The clubhouse no longer existed. King brothers were getting locked up left and right. The Latin Kings began losing their organization and respect. Other gangs became stronger and bolder in their actions against the Kings. It became common to go out and find that a rival gang had vandalized the walls in our 'hood with their insignias. Officer James was no longer on the payroll and became a cop to be feared. He loved busting Kings. It was only because of the activities of brothers like myself with nothing better to do that the Latin Kings of Kedzie and Armitage remained a section to be reckoned with.

In summer the wars escalated and so did my involvement with the Kings. Again I was asked to be the leader of the Peewee Kings of Kedzie and Armitage. Again I declined the position. I was then promoted to the Juniors. I began making pretty good money selling weed and I started experimenting with other crimes as well. Burglary became my money-making crime of choice. Daffy was my partner in crime. He was very good at it. Daffy could climb like Spiderman and break doors open by pushing them with his legs. Every burglary we attempted was successful. Cubana's closet was full of electronics and jewelry. I gave a lot of stolen merchandise away as gifts to girls I wanted, but mostly I sold the stuff. I spent whatever money I made as quickly as I got it getting high. My life was just one big party. Promiscuous sex, heavy drugs and alcohol, dodging bullets—what more could a sixteen-year-old boy ask for? The more criminally active I was, the more popular I became with my peers.

The local news stations began reporting on the savagery of the Latino youth. Gang colors, hand signs, and graffiti were all covered on television. Most of the information reported was inconsistent or fabricated. Gangbangers avoided reporters and their cameras like the plague. Reporters didn't care. They would talk to any kid with colored shoelaces who was willing to be on television. The result was that kids ignorant of the ways of the gangs told stories they had heard as if they had firsthand experience. These kids ended up as targets for gang members at school as well as in their own neighborhoods. Without realizing it the news media had endangered the lives of these kids.

The media had a direct impact on kids deciding to join gangs. Actual gang members knew better than to display themselves for the world to see. The few who made that mistake were dealt with violently by their own gangs. The innocent kids who didn't know enough not to talk to reporters became the victims of gang media hype. Kids who otherwise shied away from gang activity were now looking to join a gang for protection.

An Imperial Gangster suspected of being the triggerman in Morena's murder was killed. His funeral was held at Caribe Funeral Home on Armitage near Central Park. This was a Gangster 'hood. The Kings were determined not to let him rest in peace. A meeting was called involving all the Latin King sections on the North Side and a plan was made to disrupt the funeral. All of us were told to make sure to be present on Kedzie and Armitage the day after the meeting. That was the day the wake was being held for the dead Gangster. Nobody knew what was going to happen. We were only told to show up.

That night I dreamt I was walking with Morena up Kedzie when she got shot. She fell on top of me and said, "It's your fault." I woke up screaming, "No, no, no!" Cubana held me, but I pushed her away violently. My body was shaking, my head hurt, and my vision was blurry. I saw Morena enter through the bedroom door. I jumped off the bed and hugged her legs. "I'm sorry, I'm sorry, please forgive me," I cried. I felt a hand run through my hair and a woman's voice said, "It's OK, it's

OK, come on, get up." It was Loca. She had come to see why I was screaming. Both Cubana and Loca looked at me with compassion. "You better lay off those drugs," Loca said, "they're fucking you up." "I dreamt about Morena," I told them. We all stood quietly for a moment. Then Loca left the room. I lay back down and fell asleep.

I got up early the next morning and went to Kedzie and Armitage. I started getting high while I waited for all the brothers to show up. By noon hundreds of Latin Kings had shown up and were headed toward Caribe Funeral Home. We went by car, bike, and on foot. The idea was to arrive there all at the same time from every direction. The Gangsters were caught by surprise. They could be seen running every which way as we approached the funeral home. We blocked off the road to both people and cars. Many King brothers had guns pulled out. They were watching the rooftops and guarding gangways against Gangsters. Several King brothers went inside the funeral home and carried the dead body out with them. The mother of the dead Gangster was screaming and begging for mercy. Her cries went unheard. The body was thrown in the middle of the street and repeatedly shot. Then everybody scattered. No one was arrested. It was time to celebrate our victory in avenging Morena's death so memorably.

We wanted to send out a message that the Kings should not be messed with. But this didn't happen. Action against the Kings not only continued, it escalated. As for me, I had another scene added to my nightmares. Night after night I saw myself being thrown on the street. I heard my mother screaming and I woke up just before I was shot.

39

Disciplined

THE PHILOSOPHY OF all gangs is that any innocent kid from another neighborhood who is killed by a stray bullet is probably a future member of a gang, so it's OK. But any innocent kid killed in *your* neighborhood is a tragedy that requires vengeance.

One day that summer three carloads of Kings drove around looking for any rival gang member. We decided to go by Von Humboldt School looking for Disciples. The school was on Hirsch and Rockwell. We knew most of them would be hanging out on Rockwell Street. We were hoping to find a small number of them at the schoolyard and beat them senseless. If there were a lot of them, we could do a drive-by shooting. We found about ten of them there, mostly Peewees playing baseball. We jumped out of the cars and rushed onto the playground. A couple of them got hit by baseball bats, but they all managed to get away except for one ten-year-old kid. He stood there making the Disciple sign with his fingers and yelling, "D Love." A King slapped him in the face, but he still stood there. What the hell was wrong with this kid—didn't he know that his life was in danger? Duce pulled out his gun and ran toward the kid. I ran with him. "King Love, DK," Duce yelled as he got ready to pull the trigger. The other brothers were heading back toward the car. Just before Duce pulled the trigger, I stepped in front of the gun.

Duce became furious. "Get the fuck out of the way," he yelled. "He's only a kid," I yelled back. I turned around and told the kid to run, but he didn't want to. "This is my 'hood. I don't have to run," the kid said.

"D Love, punk, kill me, I ain't scared, you're a punk," the kid taunted as I pleaded for him to run. Duce reached around me with the gun, but I pushed his hand away as the gun went off. The kid still stood there taunting. Finally I punched him in the nose, grabbed him by the neck, and told him, "Run, you little bastard, before you die." I let him go and he took off running.

At that moment I heard the brothers yelling, "they're coming, they're coming," and gunshots went off. The Disciples blocked the Hirsch exit of the schoolyard. I grabbed Duce and pulled him toward the fence on the North Side of the school in between the mobile classrooms. Duce let off two shots before he started running. I hoped that the hole in the fence that I climbed through years ago would still be there. It was. We jumped through and ran up the alley. All we had to do was run two blocks to the park for safety. When we got to the end of the alley the King brothers were coming down the road. We jumped into the car and got out of there in a hurry. "What the fuck is wrong with you? You're getting a violation!" Duce shouted at me. "He was a kid, man, a little kid," was my response. Duce called me a punk on the way back to the 'hood and kept talking about how I was going to be violated. I sat there quietly, lost in thought.

Back in the 'hood Duce went ballistic. He wanted to fight me because I didn't let him kill that little kid. We went at it. We busted each other up pretty good. Loco and Lalo finally split us up and an emergency meeting was called. The meeting was held at the clubhouse of the Cortland and Whipple Latin Kings. At the meeting I was clearly outnumbered. Everybody felt that I should have let Duce pull the trigger. It didn't matter how much I emphasized that it was a ten-year-old kid Duce was going to kill. The point was that he was a Disciple. The logic was that it was better for him to die a kid than for him to grow up and kill a King. I was found guilty as charged and would have to endure a three-minute violation. Duce's request for a head-to-toe violation was denied.

Ace, Pito, and another King named Joker were chosen to do the honors of beating me. They were all Juniors and they were all much bigger than me. Pito weighed about two hundred and fifty pounds and

Joker was into weightlifting. I was dead meat. I couldn't back out of the violation. If I did, it would be even worse. I remembered Slim and the beating he got. Now it was my turn. There was no beating room. I stood against the wall, crossed my arms over my chest, and prepared for the worst. All the other Kings sat and watched. I was scared. I closed my eyes and the beating began. It hurt like hell. The only thing that kept me from collapsing was the continuous punching from every direction. Those were the longest three minutes of my life. When the beating stopped I collapsed in pain.

The meeting was adjourned. Everybody walked out and left me lying there on the floor. I lay there for about thirty minutes before I found the strength to get up. I could barely walk and I couldn't lift my arms at all. Every little twitch hurt. Nobody helped me. I was left there in pain. Then Cubana came in and helped me get up off the floor. We walked outside. Loco, Lalo, and Pito were sitting on the hood of a car. Loco got up, asked me if I was all right, and gave me a joint the size of a hotdog. Pito got a bottle of Bacardi 151 rum and gave me half a cup. I drank it like water. I sat on the curb with Cubana and smoked the joint. Nothing else was said.

I was bedridden for about a week. Loca and Cubana were my only company during that time. I did a lot of drinking and smoking to relieve the pain. When I went back to the streets it was as if nothing had happened. Duce and I continued to have bad blood against each other. The kid I saved grew up to be a Latin Disciple. He was killed in a shootout at the lakefront about three years later.

I still don't know what made me protect that kid. Maybe it was because of the abuse I received when I was his age or maybe I genuinely cared. When I found out that same kid was killed some years later I regretted saving his life. I took a major ass whipping for that kid and he went and got himself killed anyway.

I DIDN'T TAKE part in any more hits for the rest of the summer. The only action I saw was the unexpected type. I began to despise hanging out with the Latin Kings. I no longer saw the gang as a brotherhood. Now it seemed that you were respected to the extent that someone needed your help, and if it would help them to get you hurt or killed they would do that too. I mostly hung out with Loca and Cubana and got high every day. I started experimenting with acid. My favorite was the purple microdot, a tiny pill that would rev you up to warp speed. My drug of choice, however, was still marijuana. I could do without any other drug, but I would do anything to make sure I had my daily supply of pot. Daffy and I continued doing burglaries. This was my main source of income.

The police began playing a big part in the continuing gang wars. There were some cops who would flat out tell us that if we stopped gang-banging they would come looking for us. We were feeding their children and paying for their houses. Any time it seemed like the fighting had cooled down, a gang member would be picked up and dropped off in the neighborhood of a rival gang. Twice I was dropped off in the Gangsters' 'hood—one time I got away, the other time I got my head busted. On both occasions the Kings retaliated by making a hit on the Gangsters.

Through Cubana I learned that the real leaders of the street gangs were in jail doing hard time. The main head of all the Latin Kings had been locked up since he was seventeen. He was serving an eighty-year sentence for murder. In his day he never fought Latino gangs—he killed Vicelords.

All the big deals for guns and drugs were done through a penitentiary connection. I met many guards who would come by the neighborhood and pick up drugs to take into the prison for the brothers. A few of them got killed for either burning the Kings out of merchandise or refusing to deliver them. As a mule Cubana knew all the leaders. She was constantly on the phone with them. She also became pregnant by one of them. When she told me she was pregnant I immediately denied any responsibility but then became upset when she said she knew it wasn't mine. When I was violated by the Kings, Cubana and I went a whole month and a half without having sex. It was during that time that she had become pregnant.

Cubana always had older King brothers come pick her up and take her to the penitentiary. Mostly it would be King brothers from the North Side. After the one brother who had been her ride got arrested, a South

Side King became her chauffeur. His name was Agila. He was Mexican, about six feet tall, kind of chubby, with long, black hair. He always had something smart to say about the South Side Kings being more together than the North Side Kings. He would make references to stories that all North Side Kings were becoming junkies and robbing from other King brothers. Those of us who met Agila did not like him. He knew it but he didn't care. He was a top-ranking King on the South Side and had to be respected. He took full advantage of his situation. Agila somehow found out that I was Cubana's boyfriend when she became pregnant and began teasing me about it. I ignored him but he persisted. He began questioning my manhood and made references to me being a faggot. "*Pinche puto* ("fuckin' bitch") can't even keep a girl from a locked-up brother," Agila would say. Both Cubana and I pleaded for him to stop. Agila was one arrogant son of a bitch. "What you gonna do, *pinche puto*, kick my ass?" Agila would say. I made it a point to avoid him altogether. Cubana would tell me when he was coming and I would go for a walk until they left.

One day the situation with Agila exploded. I had just finished getting high with some King brothers. I went to Loca's to pick up some weed I had there and Agila was outside. "Hey *puto*, let any of your boys get your girlfriend lately?" Agila said, laughing. "I told you about that shit, Agila," I responded. "Leave it alone already." "Fuck you, little punk faggot," was his response. I became angry and the drugs and alcohol in my body made it hard to keep control. Cubana was looking out the window. She noticed I was getting upset. She asked Agila to stop and come upstairs to wait for her. Agila declined. He began telling me to look at Cubana and see what I couldn't handle. "What a punk," he said, "a man in jail took his lady." That did it. I snapped. I knew I couldn't beat him up so I pulled out my .357. I thought he would run behind a car or something but he didn't. Instead he told me to go ahead and shoot.

I shot him in the knee at point-blank range. The bullet went right through. Then I pistol-whipped him until he was nearly unconscious. Cubana and Loca came running out, grabbed me, and tried to get me away from him. I put the gun against his other kneecap and pulled the trigger. "Who's the punk now, motherfucker?" I yelled at Agila. "No, Lil Loco, stop, they'll take you to jail," I heard one of Loca's little boys say. I snapped out of my rage and put the gun away. "Take your kid upstairs, Loca, before the police come," I told Loca. Loca made me promise not to do anything else, grabbed her little boy, and went inside. I looked at Agila lying there covered with blood and I spat on him. I grabbed Cubana by the neck, told her, "This was your fault, bitch," slapped her with the gun, then took off running.

I knew I would be in deep shit with the Kings, but I didn't know just how deep. I found Loco and told him what had happened. He told me that he would have done the same thing and assured me that he would back me up. That was the last day I saw Cubana for several years. She packed up and moved to the South Side somewhere. Agila needed over a hundred stitches to close up his head and face. His legs were amputated at the knee. A rumor spread that I was to be taken out for what I did to Agila. Loca called Cubana and confirmed that the rumor was true. The Latin Kings had put a hit on me.

Loca had become pretty attached to me. She treated me like her little brother. She didn't want me to get hurt so she took me to a friend's house on the Far North Side of the city. She said I could stay there while she tried to get the hit canceled. I asked her to get me some money so I could go to Puerto Rico. She declined. Loca was on my side but she was still a Latin Queen first and foremost.

Loca's friend lived on Lawrence Avenue and Kedzie. There was another Latin Kings section there. I was afraid to even look out the window, thinking that by now every King in the city was hunting for me. I was staying with a heavyset Puerto Rican lady with four kids. They called her Cuca. She was an alcoholic and a pothead and did all her drinking and drugs in front of her kids. Cuca didn't mind me staying there at all. She took full advantage of the fact that I could serve as a babysitter while she went out and partied. She was rarely home while I was there. When she was there, all she did was complain about how messy the apartment was, but she did nothing to clean it up. Cuca's kids had no discipline. They cursed at their mother and threw things all over the floor. They talked about getting high when they grew up and about joining the Kings and Queens. The oldest was a twelve-year-old girl who would come and go as she pleased. She wasn't a Queen, but she hung out with them. Twelve years old and she didn't even know how to read or write. She did, however, know how to pick the door locks when her mother locked her out.

I had to get out of there. I began calling Cindy to keep my sanity. She kept me up to date on the street situation. She told me Duce had agreed to carry out the hit and was out looking for me. He had been to Chinatown thinking I would be there with her. She also told me that Loco was going to visit the chief of all Kings to talk about me. Meanwhile, Cindy was improving her life. She was still hanging out, but only because she was desperately trying to get her brother away from the Kings. She had a car and came by a few times and drove me into the northern suburb of Evanston, by Northwestern University. She loved it there. Her dream was to graduate from Northwestern with a degree in computer science.

Loco visited the head of the Kings at Stateville penitentiary. It was agreed that I would go there with Loco and see him the following week. In the meantime the hit on me was postponed. Loco told me to stay where I was until we went to Stateville. He didn't trust Duce.

We went to visit our chief on a Wednesday. It was a long drive. I was nervous, especially when I saw that visitations were not held behind glass as I had seen in the movies. We sat at a table right across from each other. Our leader was called Tino. He was a big man with massive muscles. Tino was soft-spoken and talked very intelligently. He listened attentively as I explained my reasons for attacking Agila. Like Loco, Tino also agreed that he would have done the same. He told me he had heard a lot of good things about me and that I was a down brother. He told me not to worry about the hit, but that I would have to take a three-minute violation as discipline for what I had done. Tino said that I should go to a South Side Kings 'hood the next Sunday and take my punishment like a man. The South Side Kings would appoint three of their boys to do the honors. They would also contact Loco to tell him exactly where the violation would take place. He warned me that if I didn't show up, I might as well be dead. I thought about my first violation and seriously thought about not showing up. If I could only have raised the money to go to

Puerto Rico, I would have split in a second. Loco kept any of that from happening. He got the Kedzie and Lawrence Kings to watch over me.

Every day until Sunday those Kings came up to Cuca's and partied with me. I couldn't get away even if I had the money. I pictured the violation in my mind to the point where I almost felt the pain. I thought about Lucky and how he had been killed without warning. The same fate could be waiting for me and I wouldn't even know it. When I talked to Cindy, all she said was to go to the police, quit the Kings, and get back in school. I stopped calling her. Getting high wasn't relieving my mind like it used to. It just pumped me up to the point where I wanted to go out and do something crazy.

On orders from Loco, the Kedzie and Lawrence Latin Kings didn't let me leave the house. I ended up doing something beyond crazy. I began having sex with Cuca's twelve-year-old daughter. The little girl had come on to me several times, but I had turned her down. When it did finally happen it was I who approached her. I went into her bedroom, woke her up, carried her out to the living room where I slept, and had sex with her. I abused that little girl just as Maria had done to me. Yes, she was willing and not a virgin, but that didn't matter—it was still abuse. I was sixteen and Cuca's daughter was twelve. Some may rationalize that I was a kid in my own right and not responsible for my actions. Yes, the little girl had a promiscuous sex life, but I still should have known better. She was obviously a victim of an uncaring mother, just as I was. I didn't see it because there was no violence.

ON SUNDAY LOCO and Lalo came and picked me up early in the morning. We went to the clubhouse on Cortland and Whipple. The guys were giving me their full support. They wanted to prove to the South Side Kings that the North Siders were not pussies. I didn't care much about proving anything to anybody since I was going to be used as a punching bag. By noon I was already drunk and had popped two tabs of purple microdot acid. I was totally out of it. I was talking macho bullshit and acting like I welcomed the violation. At 1:00 P.M. we took off toward the South Side. Two carloads of brothers from both Kedzie and Armitage and Cortland and Whipple followed us. Just before we got to

Twenty-sixth Street we met up with two South Side Latin Queens. They got in the car and led us to Faragut High School.

We got out of the cars and walked into the schoolyard. Everybody was given the customary welcome salute except for me. I took offense to that and began talking crap about not needing their fucking salutes. I was a King in my heart and didn't need their approval. I sat against the school wall and lit up a joint. We had to wait until Agila got there. He was going to be the one who picked those who would beat me.

The acid I had taken began to take hold of me. I was messing around with everybody as if we were on some kind of picnic. The South Side Kings ignored me and gave me hard looks while I yelled, "Damn, if looks could kill, everybody here would get violated!" Most of the Queens were laughing at my antics. That was my cue to go flirt with them. The Queens were a little friendlier with me than the Kings were, but most of them walked away.

Although I was among my so-called brothers, I was alienated and in hostile territory. Everybody was there for the pleasure of seeing me get my ass whipped. I was fuckin' high and I didn't care. I made the situation worse. "North Side Latin Kings are the only Kings," I yelled. "Cool that brother out, man," a South Side Latin King told Loco. "Fuck, you all want to treat me like I'm a *crusao*! Fuck it, *amor de Rey* almighty!" I shouted. Most of the North Side brothers came over and stood by me. I no longer felt alienated or alone because my brothers were with me. The acid made me impatient. I kept talking shit. "Kedzie and Armitage Latin Kings," I shouted, as if those present didn't know where I was from. "Not another word," Loco warned me. "These are our brothers also. Give them respect." I lit up another joint and sat there.

Finally Agila arrived. He was in a wheelchair. Suddenly the only people at my side were Loco and Lalo. Everybody else just stared at me as Agila maneuvered his chair straight at me. "Look at me," Agila said. "Do you feel like a man now? 'Cause you're not going to be feeling like a man for long."

"Fuck you, man, you asked for it," was my reply. "I felt like a man before! You just had to fuck with me." I had to open my big mouth. Agila tried to jump at me and fell, adding insult to his injury. Loco grabbed me by the front of my shirt, pushed me against the wall, and yelled at me to shut up. I stood right there against the wall with a smart-alecky look on my face until two big guys walked up to me. These guys were men in their twenties or thirties and they were huge. They would be the ones that would violate me. I protested immediately. "These brothers will kill me, man," I said, laughing matter-of-factly. I was the only one who laughed. Everyone just stared. "All right," I said. "Come on with it! Fuck this shit! King Love Almighty."

Loco looked at his watch and signaled for the guys to start beating me. I don't know if it was the acid or if I had gotten used to this type of beating because of the last time it happened, but it wasn't that bad. One of the guys hit the wall and hurt his hand so he didn't do much damage. The other guy beat the shit out of me. When it was over I buckled over in pain and waved everybody away from me. I fell back against the wall and sat there absorbing the pain for about five minutes. I then pulled a joint out my pocket and lit it up. I took one long puff and yelled, "King love!" A couple of South Side Kings came over and helped me up. All was forgotten, but not for Agila. He promised to kill me and rolled his wheelchair away.

Where before I had been alienated, now I was the center of attention. South Side brothers confessed that they wished they had been the ones to pull the trigger on Agila. We stood there partying until almost sunset. I sat in the car in pain for most of that time. I met a lot of new people and gained more fame for the name Lil Loco. More importantly, I met some cute Queens who were interested in me. Names, addresses, and telephone numbers were exchanged. I looked at the South Side as new turf where I could hang out when I got too hot on the North Side.

Back on the North Side it was time for celebration. Just about all the Kedzie and Armitage Latin Kings were at the Cortland and Whipple club-house congratulating me. Some Kings and Queens from the South Side came down to party with us. I sat on a recliner licking my wounds, so to speak. I moved only to shake someone's hand or to bring a beer or joint to my mouth. I was in deep pain but refused to show it. I didn't want to ruin that moment of glory. A South Side Queen was keeping me company. Her name was Teresa. "Tere" was her nickname. She was a tiny girl and her hair was black with gold streaks in it. I loved her hair. It was long and straight and made her look so sexy. Tere was Mexican. She had been in the United States for five years. She spoke mostly Spanish, but I preferred for her to speak English because she had a cute accent. I asked Tere to be my girlfriend the same night I met her. She said yes. I really don't know why I asked so many girls to be my "girlfriend" when all I really wanted was sex. I guess it made it easier to get what I wanted. Tere was the first of a long line of relationships that lasted less than a week.

The morning after the violation I woke up in pain like I had never felt before. I couldn't move and began throwing up blood. Tere was there with me. She began screaming. I looked at her and passed out. I woke up in an ambulance on my way to the hospital. I had alcohol poisoning and had to have my stomach pumped out. The doctors found two fractured ribs along with many bruised and swollen areas of my body. They began to ask questions about the injuries. I blamed my drunkenness and told them I had no idea what had happened the night before. Doctors and police officers surrounded me at the hospital asking me questions. They asked me everything from who had given me the alcohol to what gang I was affiliated with. I kept my mouth shut. All I did was complain about the pain. Finally they gave up trying to get information from me. A doctor took my pulse and told me, "You came within seconds of dying, do you know that?" The room emptied and a nurse came in. She was going to wash me. The nurse was a very nice oriental lady. She showed me a lot of compassion as she cleaned me up. I felt so relaxed with her. By the time she finished washing me I had answered all the questions that the doctors and police had been asking.

I was mostly bragging. I told her about my family being in Puerto Rico and that I was all alone. About an hour later I heard her talking to the police about needing to call the Child and Family Welfare Department to take care of me. I was only sixteen, still a minor. I started screaming for a phone to call my mother. They repeated everything I had told the nurse and tried to make me believe that I would be better off with the CFW. I told them I had lied to them and that I wanted a phone to call my mother. They gave me a phone. I called Loca. When Loca answered, I screamed, "Mom, come get me, I'm in the hospital and they want to take me to a home!" Loca caught on to what was happening. Within the hour she was at the hospital to pick me up. She knew they were going to say she was too young to be my mother so she brought her next-door neighbor to claim she was my mother. It worked like a charm and within minutes I was on my way back to the 'hood. As before, I recovered from my injuries at Loca's. This time I recovered much more quickly. Within a week I was on the streets doing the same old thing.

40

No Lesson Learned

THE GANG SCENE got even more out of hand. More and more King brothers were getting killed or locked up. Our numbers were being depleted big time. The arrogance I had demonstrated because I was a King became fear. Many brothers and sisters started turning against the Kings for some reason or other. There was no one to trust anymore. I got lost in my own little violent world. I did drugs on a consistent basis. Alcohol was my water. I got a tattoo and thought it was so cool, so I got another one. I grew a tail of hair on the back of my head and dyed it gold. I continued to be a walking Latin King gang insignia—a walking target. I was getting shot at or doing the shooting almost daily. I became a trigger-happy idiot. I hung out just about anywhere there was a King section or a gang affiliated with the Kings. These were places where I could meet stupid girls who gave it up easy or places where I could sleep. I always carried a gun. Because of my gang activity I was given guns without question. I was now carrying a .25 automatic. Guns made me feel like a man, like I could do anything. They made me brave. I would go places and say things I wouldn't even dream of if I didn't carry a gun. I carried a gun twenty-four hours a day, seven days a week. I pulled out my gun whenever someone looked at me wrong. I shot at cars, buses, and trains. I harassed adults, teenagers, and sometimes hung out at elementary school yards to harass suspected rival gang members. I cared little about myself and even less about others. I had a gun and the streets were mine.

On my birthday that year I got drunk with some Spanish Lords on Oakley Street and North Avenue. I was seventeen, an adult by Illinois law.

I was in the middle of the street making a fool of myself. I was stopping traffic, making passes at women, and harassing men. A car passed by full of girls. They whistled at me, pulled over, and called me over to them. There were three of them, each one cuter than the next. All of them were dressed very sexy. They asked me to go for a ride with them. A Spanish Lord named Pietro asked them if he could go too; they agreed. We got in the car and off we went. We were so busy messing around with the girls that we didn't realize where they were taking us. The girls were being very seductive and easy. I was lost in the sensuality of one of the girls when I heard Pietro yell, "Oh shit, Cobras!" I pushed the girl off me and realized that we were being driven to our deaths. The girl who was driving took us to the side of Humboldt Park where the Cobras and Disciples hung out. The girl I was with grabbed me by my hair tail so that I couldn't get away. I punched her in the face repeatedly until she let go. Then I jumped out the window of the moving car. I hit the ground hard and twisted my ankle.

I got up and ran into the park behind some trees. Pietro was trying to wrestle the steering wheel from the driver while the other girl held him by the neck. He got the girl to lose control of the car and then turned it in the direction of the main street outside the park, which was California Avenue. He managed to get away from the other girl and push the driver out of the car. In the process he also fell out. The car rolled and crashed into some parked cars on California.

It was now a footrace for survival for Pietro and me. I had a head start but had paused to look for Pietro. I wasn't going to let him die by himself. Pietro ran up California behind some parked cars. I ran through the park trying hard to keep trees between myself and the Cobras. The Cobras had split up. They were chasing after us and shooting. We were able to make it to North Avenue. A couple more blocks and we would be in the Kings' 'hood. As Pietro crossed North Avenue from the park, he was shot in the leg. I was way up ahead of him but turned back to help. The Cobras were coming in for the kill. Many people were out there watching what was happening, but nobody did or said anything. With all the excitement that was going on I had forgotten I was packing the .25. Pietro didn't forget. He started yelling, "Shoot, shoot!" I pulled out the gun, took the safety off, and began blasting.

The Cobras scattered back into the park. I got to Pietro and helped him, then went after a Cobra that was trying to sneak up on us. I went at him behind a car and he shot at me, then turned and ran. When he turned around, he slipped and fell. I ran up to him. He pointed his gun at me and pulled the trigger, but he had no bullets left. I put my gun about five inches from his face and pulled the trigger as I yelled "King Love!" There was no bang; the gun jammed. I hit him in the face with the gun handle and ran like hell. Pietro had made it pretty far on his own, but he still wasn't safe. The Cobras stopped chasing us only because they heard police sirens. Pietro told me to run before the cops came, but I stayed with him. I ran into an empty lot and hid the gun under a rock before the cops could see me. I stopped the cops myself and put on an act.

I told the police that we were just walking home when a gang started chasing us and shot my friend. The police called an ambulance for Pietro, Then they searched us and asked us questions about the incident while we waited. We denied any gang affiliation. They asked me if I could identify the gang members who assaulted us. I said I could. More police officers started arriving on the scene. They put me in a car with gang crime unit detectives who drove me by the Cobras so I could identify the perpetrators. The gang crime division detectives recognized us immediately. "What are Kings doing by the Cobras?" one of them asked me. "We were set up by some bitches," I told them. They laughed as I told them the whole story. "You fuckin' spics will do anything for a piece of pussy, won't you?" one of the detectives said. He was black and his partner was white. I didn't like being called a spic, but what choice did I have? They drove me right to Maplewood and Division. The Cobras out there recognized me immediately. They started surrounding the car: they thought the detectives were going to drop me off there. The detectives called for backup and announced through a loudspeaker for the Cobras to get away from the car. Police arrived on the scene in bunches. In no time the Cobras were up against the wall being frisked. The police asked me if I recognized any of them. I told them that almost all of them had been there. Then I pointed out those who I knew to be main Cobras as the triggermen. They got cuffed and put in a paddy wagon. The detectives dropped me off near the 'hood. It was just another day.

A couple of days later the Cobras were at it again. At about 8:00 P.M. on a humid Chicago night, three brothers and a cousin were killed as they sat on the front steps of their house. They lived on North and Western Avenues, two houses from the northeast corner. They were in the Spanish Lords' 'hood. Of the four guys killed, only one had any kind of gang affiliation. The Cobras were mobilizing big time. Cobra sections began sprouting up all over the place. Other Latino gangs began expanding into different areas as well. New gangs were being formed. Almost all of the new turf was being occupied by rivals of the Latin Kings.

Gangs were becoming more organized and diversified. There were now many blacks and whites who were representing Latino gangs because there was strength in numbers and the racial makeup of the neighborhoods was changing. Female gangs grew in numbers also and they became more involved in violent crimes. People like myself—no family, violent, high all the time, on our own—were role models. Kids looked up to us and envied our lifestyle. Adults in the neighborhood contributed to the loss of a generation by turning their backs and never seeing anything. They complained about not having enough police to protect them but didn't bother to help those who did try to stop the violence. Both a retired police officer and a Chicago Transit Authority bus driver who lived in the neighborhood directly contributed to gang activity. They would buy guns, sell them to us for a profit, and then report them stolen. The retired cop provided us with a special radio that picked up the local police frequency. We almost always knew when the police were coming our way. Most of the neighborhood residents knew what these men were up to, but no one said anything. So many parents conveniently closed their eyes to their kids' gang involvement.

The summer was finally coming to an end. I was glad. In the winter the gangs cooled off. Although we didn't see much action, our membership doubled.

I became a popular target for cops that winter, mainly because I was always out there. I was still selling pot and now I was selling acid too. I never got caught with anything on me but I was still harassed on a consistent basis. On one occasion they made me strip half-naked outside. It was five degrees below zero that day. The cops laughed as I shivered in the cold.

On another occasion it was much worse. I had just come out of Loca's and was on my way to the store to buy milk for her. I saw the police talking to a couple of Kings up ahead of me, so I crossed the street to avoid them. They saw me and called me over. I ran. I don't know why I ran but I did. I ran back across the street and into the alley. I wanted to go through the back door of Loca's building, but it was locked. Before I could do anything else the police were in my face. They stuck a gun in my mouth and lifted me off the ground by my neck. They were asking me for a gun. I told them I didn't have one, but they persisted. They thought I ran and got rid of a gun before they caught up to me. I explained that I ran because I was afraid they would harass me. That comment made them mad.

One of the officers grabbed me by the neck with both hands, lifted me off the ground, and slammed me against the wall. "Listen you little motherfucker, you better tell me where you threw the gun or I'll show you what harassment really is," the officer said as he strangled me. The other officer told him to let me go. He did so, but kneed me in the groin in the process. I buckled over from the pain while the officer laughed at me. The other officer asked me if I was all right. I couldn't answer. I was holding my breath in pain. He said to his partner, "Let's go, he's clean." "Bullshit," was the reply, "this little son of a bitch is up to something."

The officer again searched me, but all he found in my pockets was the five dollars Loca had given me for milk. He grabbed me by the hair and yelled, "Where's the gun, asshole?" I looked the other officer straight in the eye, silently begging for mercy. It was obvious that he didn't agree with what was happening but had to go along with his partner. The first cop let go of my hair but kneed me in the groin again, this time with so much force that he lifted me off the ground. I collapsed. "You fuckin' bastard," the officer said as he got in the squad car and drove away.

I was carried to Loca's by some King brothers. I lay there for a week with a bag of ice on my groin. One of my testicles swelled to the size of a baseball. A friend of Loca's with a son my age lent me her welfare medical card so I could go see a neighborhood doctor. I was sent to a specialist who informed me that I might have problems with reproduction when I got older. He advised me to see a specialist like himself later on in life. I took pain pills and penicillin for two months. By the time I was fully recovered and able to walk normally again it was springtime.

What I went through that day was the big catch-22 of living in a gang-infested neighborhood. Gang members as well as non-gang members feel the need to run and hide when police are present. If they didn't, chances are they would be harassed, beaten, or arrested for a crime they didn't commit. Police tend to believe that kids in the ghetto are guilty unless proven innocent. That's why kids run and that's why police are the enemy.

41

Spread the Violence

DURING THE SUMMER I spent most of my days drunk, high, or both. I would party until I fell asleep and I slept all over—in hallways, in cars, on rooftops, and in abandoned buildings—anywhere I could lay my head. I began meeting a lot of the Kings who ran the gang's citywide operations. They liked me because of my violent nature. It was then that I realized the wars between gangs were not about colors or revenge but about drug turf. The Latin Kings was not just a street gang run by local thugs; they were a drug empire run by adults who were rarely seen. These people were getting rich while kids were being shot on street corners thinking they were fighting for some honorable cause. For the small amount of time I hung out with the head honchos, I earned the privilege of going to fewer meetings. I also earned the privilege of being a King wherever I stood, not just from Kedzie and Armitage. I was no longer regarded as a King from one territory and no section leader had control over me. I only took orders directly from the penitentiary leaders or their generals. I gained more respect from fellow members and gained status within the gang. That little experience didn't last for long. I was too hot with the police and that made the leaders uncomfortable. The head honchos stopped coming around to see me. In no time at all I was back to being a street soldier fighting, so some assholes who didn't even care about me could live well.

I started hanging around Kedzie and Armitage again and returned to hard-core gangbanging. I did, however, keep the respect and rank I had gained from hanging out with the leaders. I was thrust into a position of decision making and power. Unfortunately, I wasn't aware of this and therefore didn't take full advantage of the situation. I could have asserted myself as a committee member of the Latin Kings if I wanted to, but didn't. I was satisfied being a popular foot soldier.

On the Fourth of July some King brothers got together to drive up to the Wisconsin Dells for the holiday. There were four carloads of us. All of us were getting high along the way and some of us, including myself, were packing pistols. We got up there and started partying and having a good time. We had food and drinks and laid out blankets to relax while we waited for the fireworks display. Some of the brothers went walking around checking out the scene and looking for girls. They came running back saying they were being chased by Cobras. In no time at all there was a confrontation. A shootout broke out between the two gangs. Those who didn't have guns ran for the cars. Those of us who did continued shooting into a crowd of innocent, unsuspecting people. We ran for the cars and took off back to Chicago. Only two carloads made it back to the 'hood; the others were stopped by police before they could get out of the Dells. Stray bullets hit several bystanders, but only one gang member got hit. That incident did not do anything to help the Puerto Ricans' reputation as savages. Within fifteen minutes of arriving at Kedzie and Armitage, a carload of Gangsters drove by and opened fire on us. Ace got hit twice in the leg. His girlfriend got hit in the abdomen and died on the way to the hospital. This was the spark needed to make the summer a bloody one.

The following weekend a hit was made on the Gangsters at Fullerton and Kimball Avenues—one dead, one crippled for life. It didn't take long for the Gangsters to strike back. That same night they made a hit on the Kings at Beach and Spaulding Streets, but no one was shot. Two nights later they were at it again. On the northwest corner of North Avenue and Kimball was a restaurant called Donald Duk's Red Hots (known as Duk's), an all-night hamburger joint. At about 10:30 P.M. I was there eating and playing the arcade machines with some other King brothers. A car stopped at the corner and one of the Kings recognized the occupants as Gangsters. He went outside and threw a bottle at the car, shattering the rear windshield. He came back in laughing. We all joined him. Everybody relaxed and returned to what they were doing except for me. I had been on the street for too long not to expect some kind of retaliation. Most of the guys in the restaurant with me were seasoned gang members and should have known better. "They're punks, we're Kings," they said when I told them we should be alert. I knew the Gangsters would come back. I walked in and out of the restaurant three times and saw nothing. I became relaxed also—relaxed but aware. Someone yelled "Gangsters!" and gunshots shattered the restaurant window directly behind us. Everybody hit the floor. I touched my body to see if I had been hit. Other than a few scratches from flying glass I was OK. It was a miracle none of us got shot. I got up and ran before the police arrived.

In the weeks that followed, by order of the leaders in prison, the gangs in Chicago formed themselves into two organizations: the Peoples and the Folks. Peoples and Folks are just like the Cryps and Bloods of Los Angeles—a group of gangs united to help each other kill off another group of gangs. The Peoples were Latin Kings, Vicelords, Gaylords, and all gangs affiliated with them. They wore hats tilted to the left and crossed their arms with the right on top of the left as a representation. The Folks were Disciples, Cobras, and all their affiliates. They represented the same way, only in the opposite direction. A show of colors on clothing also became very popular. Kids as well as adults were being shot at, beaten up, and harassed in any way possible just because of the clothes they wore. The style of clothes didn't matter; it was the colors that counted.

The unification of the gangs that made up the Peoples and the Folks was really surprising. Gangs who had been rivals since the very beginning were now united in their hatred for the opposing alliance. In a way that unification was a sign that gangs could in theory let bygones be bygones and stop the killing altogether

The gangs continued to grow. New sections were being formed in the surrounding suburbs. Suburban kids driving new cars and spending lots of money on gang activity became common. Some of them even started their own sections around where they lived. It was then and only then that the gang problem got a lot of continuous media and political attention. It took the gangs spreading into the suburbs for people to realize that something had to be done. But it was too late. Gangbanging had become some sort of rite of passage. So-called well-bred, well-raised girls thought it was the coolest thing to have a gangbanger for a boyfriend. The expectation of living dangerously was a turn-on to them.

I started dating a suburbanite from Elgin. Her name was Stephanie and she was the first white girl I dated. In fact Stephanie and her friends were the first suburban white people I had any kind of friendly relationship with. Stephanie had beautiful blonde hair, blue eyes, and a great body. She was a spoiled little rich girl with a brand-new car and a purse full of credit cards. We became sexually active the first day we met. "I love Puerto Ricans," she would say. "You guys are so passionate and brave." Her parents were either never home or thought she was sleeping at a friend's house. She would take us to party at her house while her parents were away. We had sex in their bed many times. She would pull out her parents' sex toys and X-rated movies and make fun of them. "If my mother had married a Puerto Rican she wouldn't need one of these," Stephanie said, holding up a dildo. "Look what it says on the package—marital aids. Marital aids, my ass," she continued, "they're fuckin' dildos."

We had some wild parties at Stephanie's with wall-to-wall sex and drugs. Stephanie thought it was so cool to wake up at the Kings' clubhouse on the floor with a dozen or so other people. She tried so hard to be a part of the gang. She didn't have to do this. She chose to. She got a tattoo of a crown with my name in a ribbon on her buttock and she supplied me with money for drugs. Stephanie thought gangbanging was all fun and games. She hadn't actually been involved in any kind of gang activity. She was a party girl and nothing else.

We were driving on the lakefront one night with her friend and a King brother called Pepe. Pepe saw a carload of guys in the lane next to us and represented the King sign. The guys in the other car pulled out guns and began shooting at us. Stephanie's friend was shot in the shoulder and my face was cut by the flying glass. Pepe and Stephanie were unscratched. We directed Stephanie to the nearest hospital and once there Pepe and I split. Several days later I went to her house. As always her parents weren't home. "Why haven't you been to the 'hood?" I asked. "We almost got killed, that's why," Stephanie answered. "Oh, girl, that ain't nothing," I told her. "For you it's not," she said, "but my friend almost died." I asked her if she was still going to be my girlfriend. "Of course, you silly," she answered, "I love you." Stephanie grabbed my hand and led me to her parents' room. She put on an X-rated movie and invited me to do everything we saw on screen. We didn't even watch the movie but we sure had a good time. That was the last day I saw Stephanie.

42

Enemies Near

BACK IN THE 'hood the brothers were getting together to make a hit on the Cobras. The Cobras had started a new section on Cortland Street and California Avenue; that's where the hit was going to take place. After some deliberation it was decided that only four brothers should go. I was one of them. I went to Loca's, picked up my .357 Magnum, and got myself nice and high. California is only four blocks away from Humboldt Boulevard so I decided to walk. Because of the increased gang activity in the area the police were stopping any car they saw with too many guys in it. Walking was safer. A newly initiated King brother named Cano and I walked east on Cortland toward California. Cano was an older brother. He was about twenty-two and a lifelong gangbanger. Cano was an ex-Disciple and the brother of one of the main heads of the Latin Kings. Cano was one of those guys who jumped from gang to gang, depending on what neighborhood he lived in. He was tall and muscular with light brown hair and many tattoos. He had just gotten out of prison. He had been in the same penitentiary his brother was in. Because of that, he had all his Disciple tattoos covered with King tattoos. Cano was, however, a cool person to hang out with. He was totally loyal to whatever gang he happened to be representing at the time. I had given Cano the .357. He was to be the triggerman. It was his first hit as a King. I was to attract the Cobras' attention while Cano played target practice. Two other brothers were going to drive by just in case we needed to hop in a car.

Somehow the Cobras found out we were coming. We were by Yates Elementary School just across Richmond Street when all hell broke loose. The Cobras opened fire on us. We didn't know where the shooting was coming from. Cano returned fire wildly, not knowing where to aim. We got close to the parked cars and retreated in a hurry. The Cobras continued the onslaught. I felt a pain in my arm, fell to the pavement, and hit my head. Cano helped me up and we continued running. At that time the brothers came by in the car, shooting as they drove through. That gave us enough time to get across Humboldt to safety. I had been shot in my left forearm, and the bullet had gone right through. Apparently the brothers in the car had hit a Cobra because there were police and an ambulance by Yates School.

Loca drove me to the hospital, where I was treated and put in a room to wait for the police. When they left me alone, I sneaked out. The police would have asked how I had been shot, or they might have charged me with the shooting of the Cobra. While I was in the hospital the police had come to the 'hood and arrested anyone they saw on the street that even resembled a gang member. I got to Loca's and stayed there all night. Since I had left the hospital before the doctor could give me a prescription for pain, I had to drink and smoke weed constantly to relieve the pain in my arm. Loca did her best cleaning and dressing my wound. Still, I got one ugly infection. It took about five months for that wound to heal. I was lucky I didn't lose my arm. The only good thing that came from my wound was that it kept me from doing any serious gangbanging. I stayed around the neighborhood getting high all summer and by winter I was hungry for some action.

During that summer I learned how to drive a car and Daffy, my old burglary partner, was released from the county jail. He was in on possession of cocaine and unauthorized use of a weapon. He was released on two years' probation. Daffy and I went back into burglary and also got into armed robbery. Cano joined us. The robberies were so easy and profitable that we made them our moneymaking crime of choice. We stopped doing burglaries altogether. Cano thought up a robbery scheme that was foolproof. We would get a couple of Queens to dress up very sexy and drop them off at a bar. The Queens would then find the man with the most money and try to pick him up. They would usually target Mexicans who didn't speak any English. Usually these turned out to be illegal aliens who were reluctant to call the police. With promises of sex, a Queen could easily get a man to leave with her. She would walk him to a dark place where we would be waiting to stick him up. To make sure we weren't followed after the stickup, we made it a habit to take our victim's pants with us.

Daffy got greedy and began doing this twice, sometimes three times a night with different Queens. Cano and I would only go on party nights—Thursday, Friday, and Saturday. Daffy got caught. This time he got sentenced to three years in prison—not bad for armed robbery and violation of probation. Cano and I continued doing armed robberies and became really tight.

I had Peewee Kings selling weed for me. They practically volunteered to do so. Loca would collect the money and give them more supplies when I wasn't around. Loco and Lalo rarely came around anymore. When they did, they were the object of the other Kings' admiration. They had big, beautiful cars and gorgeous females. They wore expensive clothes and lots of jewelry. Apparently they, too, were now living off the blood and sweat of the brothers who walked the streets. I didn't like being a King anymore, especially a foot soldier. I detested it, but I was too scared to say so.

43

Disowned

I BEGAN CALLING Cindy again. It took a little doing but I was able to get her number. I really had nothing to say to her. All I could do was brag about the wars I had been in. I thought she would be impressed by my gang activity like all the other girls I knew. She reacted in exactly the opposite way of what I expected. Cindy scolded me and sometimes even hung up on me for bragging about my crimes. She cried when I told her about my run-in with the cops and being shot in the arm. She was really upset when I told her about the violations I'd received. "How could you let them do that to you?" she asked. "I thought you were tough." Cindy had graduated from high school and was accepted to Northwestern University. She was so happy and proud. I was secretly jealous. I asked to see her, but without hesitation she said no. I was used to Cindy's rejections, so it didn't faze me. It was what she said next that sticks in my head to this day.

Cindy told me that of all the guys she had ever met I was the one who came closest to being special to her. She didn't appreciate that I chose gangbanging and drugs over her and my own education. Her voice began changing as she held back tears. "Are you crazy? Do you think I'm stupid enough to meet with you and take a chance on getting shot? You don't even respect yourself so sure you're gonna respect me enough to leave your gun at home, yeah, right." By this time she was crying and a tear was even rolling down my cheek. But she wasn't finished. "Think about what you're doing. You're killing yourself and your friends, they are killing you too," Cindy said. "How many visitors did you have when you were in bed with swollen balls? How many of your so-called brothers were worried when you almost lost your arm? Don't be stupid. If they were really your brothers they wouldn't be giving you drugs, alcohol, and then a gun so you could prove yourself. If they were your friends or brothers you wouldn't have to prove yourself." Cindy noticed I was crying. She paused, calmed down, and said more.

"Listen, being poor should give you a stronger will to succeed, not an excuse to have pity for yourself, to fail. My parents, our family, are dirt poor. That's why I have to finish college so that I can be their way out." Cindy hit a nerve with that remark. I snapped at her, "Your mother didn't abuse and abandon you! You don't know what suffering really is. Wait until nobody loves you!" I screamed. Then I hung up on her.

What hurt most about Cindy's words was that she spoke the truth. For the first time in my life someone had taken the time and cared enough to tell me the truth. But I ignored it, classified it as bullshit, and took it as an attack against me. I thought I had control of everything around me, but I was the one being controlled.

That's the last time I talked to Cindy for about three years. But I never forgot the things she said that night. After the call I went and did the only things I knew would relieve my pain and anger. I got high and then I got violent.

I packed a .25, got on a bike, and headed for the Gangsters. I was so high I could barely steer the bike. Cano was the only one who came with me. The things Cindy said were pumping in my head and I kept getting angrier. By the time we got to Kimball and Armitage Avenues, the Gangsters knew we were coming. They drove a car right at me. I jumped off the bike just in time. I was OK, but the bike was a mess. About five Gangsters were running toward us while Cano helped me off the sidewalk. The Gangsters who had tried to run me over were now on foot coming from behind. We were surrounded. I pulled out the .25 and fired at the ones behind us because that was our route back to the 'hood. They ran and hid and the Gangsters who were coming at us began shooting. Cano dropped his bike and ran zigzag between parked cars with me. I returned fire one shot at a time to cover our running. I didn't want to waste all the bullets. The Gangsters stopped and opened fire all at the same time. Car windows were shattered and people screamed. We had just ducked between two cars, looking up momentarily when the shooting stopped to make sure they didn't charge us.

The shooting had stopped, but the screaming continued. We looked and saw the Gangsters running back toward their 'hood. Cano and I took off running down Armitage toward Kedzie. On the way we passed a lady who was on the ground screaming in pain from a gunshot wound. A girl, maybe her daughter, lay about three feet from her with a bullet hole in her head. I didn't even think about stopping and helping them. I was thinking about myself and myself only. By the time we got to Kedzie we could hear police sirens. Cano went one way; I went the other. I made it to the Cortland and Whipple clubhouse entrance without being seen. I went in and locked the door behind me.

In the clubhouse brothers and sisters from the Cortland and Whipple section became angry at me. They didn't appreciate the fact that I ran to their clubhouse knowing the police were after me. "They didn't see me. Nobody saw me," I said. Still they persisted in telling me not to do it again and reminded me that I was a King from Kedzie and Armitage, not from Cortland and Whipple. "I'm a King everywhere I stand," I said angrily. "Fuck you all!" I said as I walked out the door. I carefully made my way toward Loca's, ducking into shadows every time I heard a car coming. Cindy's words were echoing in my mind like crazy. She was right. I knew it but I didn't know what to do about it. I made it to Loca's safely, but no one answered the door. I slept in the hallway, or at least tried. Every time I nodded out, nightmares appeared. Blood, violence, death, people being shot—I saw these things whenever I closed my eyes. At eight in the morning Loca opened the door. I entered and went directly to sleep.

Later that afternoon Loco came by and bitched at me for doing the shooting and then running for the safety of the Cortland and Whipple clubhouse. I yelled at Loco about all the things Cindy had said. I began bad-mouthing the Latin Kings and the whole gangbanging idea. "What the fuck do you care, motherfucker, as long as your drugs are sold?" I screamed as I walked out into the hallway. "Get back in here, Lil Loco," Loco called out to me. "Fuck you, man, fuck you!" was my response.

Spectators to our confrontation were now gathering in the hallway. "Come inside," Loca said. "Fuck that shit," I responded. "That man don't care for nobody but himself." "*Callate*" ("Shut up"), Loca warned me. "He's never out here protecting the 'hood, he don't know what's going on," I said. Loco came running out of the apartment. He grabbed me and slammed me against the wall. He grabbed me by the neck and said, "Punk, we don't need you, you pussy-ass motherfucker!" Loco squeezed my neck harder and harder. I was gagging and fighting for air. I felt like I was passing out. "*Dejalo ya, dejalo ya*" ("leave him already"), Loca pleaded with Loco. At that moment Lalo, Pito, and several other brothers arrived on the scene. Lalo and Pito pulled Loco away. When Loco finally released me, I fell to the floor gasping for air. I passed out momentarily.

When I regained consciousness, Loco was still screaming at me. He was saying that I was no longer welcome at the Cortland and Whipple clubhouse or on Kedzie and Armitage for that matter. I was no longer to call myself a Latin King from Kedzie and Armitage. The main heads of the Kings had pretty much prohibited him or anybody else other than themselves from taking away my crown; still, he warned me not to hang around Kedzie and Armitage. He said actions were going to be taken to get me violated out of the Kings. I could have asked to be taken out of the Kings at that moment, but I didn't. I was still too much of a coward. I wasn't afraid to take a beating, but I didn't want to walk alone. I was afraid to be alone, not to belong. As long as I was a King I could hang out at various sections in and outside the city of Chicago.

Word about what I had said about the Kings spread throughout the neighborhood. Kedzie and Armitage was no longer my safe haven. Not knowing what else to do I went back to where all this craziness had begun—back to the Spanish Lords.

44

The Way It Is

THE CLEMENTE HIGH School/Tuley School area had gone through a transformation. The Cobras and Disciples were now the majority at Clemente High School. The Lords no longer hung out by Tuley—the Cobras did. Papo's family had moved away and he rarely came around. When he did, he called himself an ex-Lord. Kids who lived in areas where the Latin Kings, Spanish Lords, Insane Unknowns, or any gang united with them hung out were in danger if they attended Clemente High School. It didn't matter whether they were gang members or not. If a kid lived in those areas he was an enemy of the Cobras and Disciples. Most of the Spanish Lords who knew me had gone on to different things or were in jail. A couple of them had been killed.

I began hanging out with Flaco from the Unknowns. We became inseparable. Flaco was tall and skinny and he drank and smoked a lot. We had a lot in common, including being pretty much homeless. We stayed out all night most of the time. When we did sleep, it was usually in the apartment of a girl Flaco was seeing. Her name was Anita. She was an eighteen-year-old welfare mother. Anita was very voluptuous and sexy. I couldn't help but stare at her. She had two kids, a two-year-old boy and a newborn girl. The kids had different fathers. One had been killed and the other was doing thirty years in jail. Her apartment was a rathole. There were roaches everywhere and she didn't do much about cleaning.

Flaco and I lived on the edge. If rival gangs weren't shooting at us we were doing the shooting. We called it having fun. Most of the time we just shot at rivals as they drove by representing, but a couple of times we made some serious hits. On one of the first hits we did together, Pothead from the Lords joined us. Flaco and I debated whether we really trusted Pothead, but as he was the one supplying the weapons we had no choice.

It was a Friday night and the Cobras had been active since early that day. They were hanging out on Artesian Street between Potomac and Hirsch Streets, one block west of Western Avenue. Every so often they would let themselves be seen by sending a couple of their boys to LeMoyne Street and Western to taunt us. By nightfall we were sick of it and had thought out a plan. At about 11:00 P.M. we went into action. One at a time all three of us crossed Western between Hirsch and LeMoyne, being careful so that the Cobras wouldn't see us. We walked through a gangway into the alley. From there we walked in the shadows, across Hirsch, and down the alley toward Potomac. We heard the Cobras partying just before we got to Potomac. We went into a gangway where we had a clear view of the Cobras across the street. We ducked down in the darkness out of sight. The parked cars were our cover.

Flaco crawled to the end of the gangway to make sure there weren't any Cobras on our side of the street. He said there were people out all over the place so we would have to be quick. All three of us had guns. We counted to three and ran out of the gangway onto Artesian shooting simultaneously in the direction of the Cobras. There was a lot of screaming going on from all directions. I could hear one of the Cobras screaming, "I'm hit, I'm hit!" as we ran back through the gangway. We ran up the alley and through another gangway that led to Western. We crossed Western into another gangway and then up the alley to Hirsch. From there we ran toward the Unknowns' 'hood. Pothead got a ride from some girl to his house. Flaco and I hid out with one of the Unknowns until the next day.

The hit was a success. It was time to rejoice in the violence. We were so proud of ourselves! Our action made others treat us respectfully, welcoming us into their homes, feeding us, giving us all the beer and marijuana we wanted, and plenty of ego-boosting praise. Even an older Unknowns brother, a veteran of the gangbanging scene, complimented us. This was a big thing.

The Unknown was called Tarzan. He was a big, wild-looking guy in his late twenties. He was a career gangbanger. Tarzan was living with a short, chubby, Puerto Rican girl named Maria. Maria wasn't a gangbanger, but she did nothing to keep Tarzan from doing it or from teaching their three kids about it. They had two boys and one girl. The two boys were ten and eight years old and the girl was five. All three kids knew how to represent the Unknowns sign and also knew their handshake. Tarzan and Maria thought that was cute. When Maria asked them what they wanted to be when they grew up, the two boys said Unknowns and the girl said a Latin Queen. Tarzan bragged about how he had taught his boys to always hit first when faced with a confrontation. "And if they don't go down, hit them with something harder than your fist, ain't that right, boys?" Tarzan proclaimed. "Yeah, man, with a bat, right, Dad?" one of his kids answered. Tarzan laughed, Maria laughed, we all laughed. We got high in the same room with the kids. Tarzan would blow marijuana smoke in their faces and share his beer with them. Then we would all sit back and watch to see how they reacted.

Saturday morning Flaco and I walked to Anita's, smoking a joint on the way as if nothing had happened. In my mind the events of the night before were just a game. Nothing *had* happened. At Anita's we bragged about what we did and laughed about hearing a Cobra scream in pain. That's what we talked about all day. We couldn't go outside. *La hada* would be all over the place asking questions. By Saturday night two Lords had been picked up by the gang crime division for the crimes we committed.

The two Lords were charged for murder and attempted murder. Two Cobras were shot that night. One died on the scene and the other was in the hospital with two bullet wounds in his abdomen. Usually whoever was arrested for a crime would keep quiet about who really did it but this time it was different. One of the Lords who got arrested decided to save himself and pointed Pothead out as one of the triggermen. Pothead was offered less time if he named his partners in crime, but he didn't. He was advised by a public defender to take a plea bargain that the state was offering. Pothead pleaded guilty on both counts and was sentenced to fifty years with a chance for parole with good behavior after serving a minimum of twenty years.

The Lord who testified against Pothead was found dead at the lakefront about two days after he was released from jail. The rumor was that the police told the Lords which one of the two guys apprehended did the talking. The only thing important to Flaco and me was that we didn't even get questioned regarding the crimes. Two weeks later we were at it again.

The Cobras retaliated several times in revenge. They didn't kill anyone, but they shot a couple of Unknowns. Innocent bystanders, however, were not so lucky. On one of their hits a stray bullet fatally wounded a three-year-old boy. The kid was in a coma for a couple of weeks before he died. Instead of taking this as a sign that it was time to stop the killing, we used it as a reason to kill again. No way could we permit a child to be killed in our 'hood by our rivals without getting revenge.

IT WAS ABOUT this time that my luck with girls came to an end. My violent nature no longer got me any girl I wanted. Even the ugliest, easiest girls in the 'hood avoided me. It never crossed my mind that my hygiene needed attention. I didn't bathe or change clothes for weeks at a time. I spent most of my time drinking and getting high. I rarely ate full meals anymore—they were a luxury. Getting high made me forget about being hungry. I slept in the gutter most of the time—rooftops, benches, hallways, gangways, call them what you want, they're still the gutter. When winter came along I really suffered. I slept at Anita's most of the time but sometimes I knocked on the door and nobody opened. Then I had to sleep in the hallway or go hang out with the bums under the train tracks near Damen Avenue. The bums would get a fire going in a garbage can and they had liquor to keep warm inside. I was dead drunk and lost. I wanted to have sex so bad. My sexual urge coupled with the need for money, food, and shelter, led me to experiment with homosexuality at the age of seventeen.

I was desperate to get off the streets and out of the cold. An older gentleman picked me up one night as I was searching for somewhere to sleep. He pulled up next to me and invited me to get high. Without hesitation

I got in his car. He gave me a joint and let me smoke it by myself. As we drove around we talked about sports, women, and women as sport. His name was Freddy. He was a very light-skinned black man. He was about forty-five years old with a medium build and was a little overweight. He could speak Spanish. He invited me over to his apartment for a beer. I gladly agreed. I might just get a comfortable place to sleep, I thought. Freddy somehow knew I would agree. He pulled into a parking space in front of his apartment just as I asked him where he lived. I didn't even know where we were. I was too busy talking shit to notice what streets we had taken. "Let's go upstairs. I'll order some pizza to go with the beer," Freddy said as he led me into a multi-unit apartment building. I didn't recognize the area we were in, but I knew we were out of the 'hood. The streets were clean, there was no vandalism on the walls, and it was very quiet outside. I followed Freddy up to a third-floor apartment.

Freddy's apartment was very nicely furnished, clean, with pictures of kids he said were his all over the walls and shelves. Freddy went into a bedroom, came out with a T-shirt, and handed it to me. "Go take a shower and give me your clothes so I can wash them," Freddy said as he led me to the bathroom. He stood there while I got naked and took my clothes one piece at a time. "Man, you stink," Freddy said. "Wash yourself real good." I cleaned up and put the T-shirt on. Freddy was quickly there to escort me to the living room. He had prepared sandwiches while I was taking a shower.

As I ate Freddy asked me where I lived and where my family was. I didn't answer. "Someone should be taking care of you," Freddy said. "You're a beautiful kid. I bet you get a lot of girls, right?" "Hell, yeah," I responded. "Dirty and stinky as you are, I don't think so," Freddy said. "I bet you haven't had sex in a long time." He laughed and asked if I wanted to see an X-rated movie. I agreed. As we watched the movie we drank beer and smoked weed. Freddy kept saying, "Wow, look at that, I bet that makes you hard," about different scenes in the movie. "Oh, hell, yeah," I said, laughing.

"You don't have a hard-on. Let me see, I bet you don't," Freddy teased. I laughed and continued watching the movie. "I knew you weren't hard," Freddy said, "you don't even know what a pussy looks like."

"Hell yeah, I do," I said as I pulled the T-shirt up. "I'm so fuckin' horny, let me turn this shit off," said Freddy as he turned off the television. He sat next to me and asked me if I wanted twenty dollars. "Yes," I answered quickly. "You want to sleep here all the time?" Freddy asked. "You could be my roommate. Tomorrow I'll buy you some clothes. But you have to show me your dick again."

I looked at him, half laughing and half shocked. "Come on, let me see it," Freddy said as he reached for my T-shirt. I stared at him, not knowing what to do. I had never been approached sexually by a man before. I hadn't even thought about it. I felt the same motionless shock and fear I had felt the first time I went on a gang hit. Freddy grabbed my penis, bent down, and began performing oral sex on me. I watched him with no expression or thought. My sexual arousal took over. I did everything Freddy told me to do. I didn't consider myself a homosexual. I was just lost. That wouldn't be the last time I saw Freddy.

I began experimenting with masturbation after that night. My masturbatory fantasies were always about women. I vividly pictured all my past sexual experiences with women and fantasized about actresses I had seen on television. I guess that was my way of blocking out what was going on with Freddy. The slightest thought of sex made me go somewhere to masturbate. I did things like listen to Flaco and Anita having sex while pleasuring myself. I got myself off in hallways where anyone could walk in at any time and catch me. I felt like a sick individual, but I still did it.

I often sought out Freddy, or else he came looking for me. He provided me with food and shelter for most of the winter in exchange for sex, of course. Freddy was a closet homosexual. He asked me not to come around when he had visitors. He would give me money so that I could get a hotel room when he had a weekend guest. I used the money to get high and slept in hallways. Having sex with Freddy became natural and something to look forward to. There was no kissing, no caressing, no passion whatsoever. Just sex, raw sex. Freddy would perform oral sex on me, I would fuck him, and that was that. I was still very interested in females; they were the desire of my dreams, I just couldn't get any. I fantasized that Freddy was one of the women in the porn movies we watched while we had sex. It was the drugs and alcohol in my body, along with my need for food and shelter, that kept me there.

Even with Freddy's kindness, there were times when I thought I was going to die. On the nights when I couldn't stay at Freddy's I sat in hallways, crying because it was so cold. I ate very little and slept less. The stores in the neighborhood prohibited me from entering because of all the shoplifting I did. By summer I looked like a zombie. Most people thought I was shooting up heroin and avoided hanging out with me. Freddy moved away and stopped coming around looking for me. To this day the relationship I had with Freddy that winter haunts me.

45

Another Addiction

FLACO GOT ARRESTED for a shooting he didn't commit. In no time at all, Anita had another lover. I wasn't welcome at her home any more. With nowhere to sleep and no one to hang out with, I headed back toward Humboldt Park by Kedzie Boulevard and North Avenue. I made sure to stay away from Kedzie and Armitage. The park at least gave me soft ground to sleep on and I could attempt to hang out at Loca's again.

I found the park was there, but Loca wasn't. She had moved up north by Kedzie and Lawrence Avenue. Surprisingly, the Kings were glad to see me, or at least they acted that way. Cano took me to his apartment so I could shower and clean up. He even bought me some clothes. They were from a secondhand store, but they were a lot better than what I was wearing. Cano's apartment was in an attic. It was small but comfortable. He gave me a key and said that I could stay whenever I wanted, so I stayed there every night and most of the day. I rarely went out. I just sat in his apartment and watched television in a state of depression. When I did go out, it was usually to hustle for some weed or beer and then I'd go back to the apartment to get high. Cano never said anything to me. On the contrary, he was impressed by the fact that I was staying out of trouble. He was dealing cocaine and got me involved in the business. My job was mainly to look out for him while he made transactions to make sure he didn't get stuck up. Everything went smoothly except for one incident.

We drove to the city of Maywood, a suburb of Chicago, to deliver two kilos of cocaine. Cano told me that he had dealt with these Cuban brothers before but he didn't trust them. Cano told me these guys were former long-term prisoners in Cuba. Had Castro not kicked them out, they would still be in jail. Cano brought his girlfriend Candy along. Candy was a beautiful, tall, brunette white girl who was hooked on cocaine. Cano often told me that he knew she was only with him for the drugs, but he only wanted her for the sex so they were even. Candy was one of those women who dressed sexy regardless of where she was going or what she was going to do. A mirror was her best friend. She was a classic bimbo.

We got to Maywood early enough for Cano to show me where the deal was going to take place and what I was supposed to do. The deal would happen in the parking lot of a Jewel grocery store. Cano dropped me off a block away and drove off with Candy. I was to walk to the parking lot from there and hang out by the Jewel as if I was a neighborhood kid. Cano gave me a baseball glove and a rubber ball so I could keep myself busy. He also gave me a .357 Magnum just in case anything went down.

When I got to the parking lot, a van was parked next to Cano's car. I walked by close enough to notice that Candy was alone in the car counting money. I started throwing the ball against a wall about fifteen feet away from the car. From time to time I would let the ball roll in their direction so I could get a look at what was going on. One time the ball went farther than I wanted it to. It went under the van and rolled in front of Cano's car. When I walked past the back of the van to get the ball, I heard Cano saying *"No hagas eso, hombre"* ("Don't do that, man"). When I got to the side of the van I saw a guy getting into it with a black gym bag in his hand. I went to the side of the car and glanced at the van just long enough to see a gun being held to Cano. The Cubans saw me and yelled, *"Hey, vete para alla"* ("Hey, get away from here"). *"Mi bola esta abajo del carro"* ("My ball is under the car"), I said, and bent down as if to get the ball from under the car. I took the glove off my hand and grabbed my gun. As I did so, I heard the Cubans tell Candy to get in the van. I was scared of what was about to happen. I had not pulled a trigger in a long time and I was sober.

I didn't know what to do. I just knew I had to do something fast. My reputation was at stake. I held the gun tightly, thought about all the times I had used a gun, and came up shooting. I shot the guy holding the gun to Cano in the head and chest. The other Cuban began shooting at me and forgot about Cano. Cano took the gun from the guy I had wounded and shot the other one in the back. Candy was screaming and so were the people in the nearby area. We got in the car and drove off in a hurry. As we drove away, Cano noticed another car tailing us. At first we thought it was the police, but when we made a turn we could tell it wasn't. The car tailing us was apparently backing up the Cubans and was now chasing us. We raced down the street at about a hundred miles per hour dodging cars and driving through red lights. The car behind us was going just as fast, shooting at us. The chase went on for about two miles before the car chasing us crashed into a car that swerved to miss us. We got off the main road and drove through side streets until we got to the expressway and headed back to Chicago.

On the way back, Cano and I laughed about the whole incident. "Lil Loco is back, Lil Loco is back," I cheered for myself. Candy looked like she had seen a ghost. I don't know about Cano, but my bragging was more to hide my fear than anything else. Back in the 'hood Cano paid someone to get rid of the car and then reported it stolen about an hour later. I walked back to the apartment by myself. On the way there I dumped the gun in a sewer. I couldn't sleep that night without seeing bloodshed and horror in my sleep. I went two days without sleeping at all because of the fear I had of my nightmares.

Cano wasn't around for about four days. I thought he had been locked up. I didn't bother leaving the apartment. I just sat and smoked weed, scared as hell about every little noise I heard. My mind was messing with me big time. Marijuana started making me paranoid. Marijuana no longer had a tranquilizing effect on me, so I started drinking a whole lot more to make up for it. Drinking still made me act like a violent idiot but it was better than being paranoid. When Cano finally came back, he had a new car and another job for us to do. I was skeptical, but I needed the money. Cano was giving me five hundred or sometimes a thousand dollars just for going with him and watching his back. "Don't worry about the Cubans," Cano said. "Nobody cares if they're dead anyway." "I'm not worried, I'm a King," was my response. I didn't stop to realize that nobody would care if I died.

On this trip we were delivering three kilos of cocaine to the Latin Kings in Joliet. The delivery went without incident. We stayed in Joliet and partied all night. That night I heard that the cocaine was to be picked up by a Joliet State Penitentiary guard for the Kings doing time.

Cano gave me five hundred dollars and the keys to a Camaro Z28 he had purchased. I was making deliveries on my own now. I was pretty successful, mainly because I kept a low profile. I came out only to make my deliveries. Then I'd cool out for hours at a time before stepping out on the streets. Once in a while I would get drunk and go gangbanging with the Kings, but it wasn't the same anymore. The togetherness I felt when I first started hanging out was gone. Now it was common for a King to move to another neighborhood, join a rival gang, and then come by shooting at us a month or so later. At one time beating the right fist upon the heart meant "I will die for you"; now it was just a meaningless gang sign.

Female gang involvement also escalated. They once just set guys up. Now more and more often they were pulling the trigger. Drive-by shootings became more of a pastime than a planned hit. It was news when nobody got shot or killed. The demographics of the gangbangers also changed. When I first started gangbanging, most gang members came from abusive or broken homes. The new breed of gangbangers came from good homes with hard-working parents. We had members in the Latin Kings who were college students with damn good grades. Some members were professionals who worked behind the scenes providing alibis and money laundering. Cano told me these brothers had always existed; I was just meeting them for the first time. I got further and further away from the brothers who hung out on the street and became one of the ones who made money off of their blood. When I did hang out I didn't feel safe like I once had. I didn't trust any of them, and for good reason.

We were playing football at Humboldt Park one day when the Disciples came to the Humboldt Boulevard border and began taunting us. We stopped playing and headed for a confrontation with them. When we got about fifty feet from the Boulevard, we charged the Disciples. The Disciples retreated as we crossed the street, but then came back at us when we got to the other side. It was at that moment that I looked around and realized that only three of us had made it across the Boulevard. All of the other guys had turned around and gone back. The three of us tried to fight as best we could, but we just ended up taking a major ass whipping. I had a fat lip, a broken nose, and a black eye. In the past, cowardly actions by the Kings would not be tolerated, but this was no longer the case. Instead they made jokes about us getting whipped. The cowards received no discipline. I lost all my confidence in the Latin Kings. I no longer wanted to be a part of them. Still, I was too much of a coward to walk on my own without having the Kings to back me up.

Although I didn't hang out much anymore I still enjoyed the perks of being a King. I was able to get drugs and guns any time I wanted and the Queens were again interested in me. I still belonged to something— it wasn't anything good but it was something. I knew the streets and its ways better than I knew myself. I was oblivious to any other lifestyle but that of a gang member. As far I was concerned, illegal activity was the only way to make a living.

ON MY BIRTHDAY that year I experimented with cocaine like I had never done before. Now I was living the good life. I had money, a car, expensive clothes, and plenty of female attention. My birthday was a special event within my little circle of associates. Cano and Candy hosted a party in my honor at a local bar. They introduced me to a girl named Wanda. Wanda was a petite black girl. She was a beautiful girl with a mean coke habit. She was also my birthday present from Cano. The four of us went into a back room away from the party. We sat at a table snorting coke all night. The more we snorted, the more we wanted. After that night, coke became my drug of choice. I couldn't function without it. Since I always had a supply of coke for my personal use, Wanda became my constant companion. The sexual things that girl did were phenomenal. She often put coke on my penis so that I couldn't have an orgasm for a long time. When she first started doing that, I would end up in extreme pain from all the sex. After a while not only did I become used to it, I couldn't have sex without it. Wanda helped fulfill my fantasies of having sex with two girls and of watching two girls having sex with each other. She did all these things for coke. I manipulated her every move by becoming her sole coke supplier. The one time she went and got coke from someone else I tied her to the bed, had sex with her, and left her tied there all day and night. Wanda cried, not because she was tied up but because she needed cocaine. She didn't beg to be untied; she begged for a hit of coke. When I did untie her I beat her and threatened to kill her if she ever went behind my back again. After I beat her, I gave her some coke. Within a half hour she was smiling, cuddling up to me, and telling me how much she loved me.

I learned how easy it was to manipulate people who did coke and took full advantage of it. I had many girls that I treated just like Wanda. They all knew each other and didn't care. I demanded they do things that I saw drug dealers demand from girls in the movies. To come into my apartment they had to agree to disrobe and stay naked, or dress in sexy lingerie as soon as they got there. They had to be prepared to perform any sexual act I desired upon command. Failure to do so would result in the denial of cocaine and possibly an ass whipping. Several girls declined my offer but most readily agreed. Even those who had declined would have sex with me on a one-on-one basis in exchange for coke. The cocaine influence was a powerful one. I loved it. It got me accepted in places I had never dreamed of entering. I got just about every woman I desired and had many Kings willing to lose their lives for me. I was so busy manipulating others that I didn't realize I was also becoming a cocaine junkie.

Cano was also becoming a junkie, but his drug of choice was heroin. He was violating the rules of the Latin Kings by shooting the stuff up his veins. I told him that we couldn't hang out together unless he stopped. Cano relinquished the apartment to me and stopped coming around. Within a month he was arrested for possession of narcotics. I took over and supplied the customers he left behind. I was constantly surrounded by people who called themselves my friends and girls who said they loved me. My life became one big ongoing party.

I began supplying some of the Kings with quarter bags of cocaine so they could make money for themselves and for me. I used my money to buy guns for the Kings, bail some of them out of jail, and pay their lawyers. Most people in the neighborhood worshipped me because I gave money away and did nice things for people. I often bought hundreds of dollars worth of food and held big barbecues for the neighborhood. Even the adults got into the worshipping act. Many of them turned the other cheek when I had sex with their daughters, even those who were only thirteen or fourteen years old. Sometimes we had sex right in their homes while the parents prepared food for me to eat after I finished fucking their daughters. They knew that I would reward their hospitality with money, cars, anything they wanted.

One night we went uptown to the North Side near DePaul University. There were about five cars full of Kings and Queens. Everyone was high on some kind of drug. We went into an arcade and acted like we owned the place. We harassed and pushed people away from the games, then threatened them with death if they complained. They were outnumbered so they just left. We were there for about ten minutes when one of the Queens saw some guys take off pink and black wristbands and put them in their pockets. Pink and black are the colors of the Imperial Gangsters. Within seconds we had them surrounded. We asked them if they were Gangsters. They said no. I pulled out a gun and made them empty their pockets. When the Kings saw the pink and black wristbands, they began beating the guys. There were four of them and about fifteen of us. One Gangster got his head put through the glass screen of a video game. Two others were thrown out the plate glass window onto the street. The other one was stabbed repeatedly as he sat in a fetal position against an arcade machine. I stood there watching the whole thing happen, not lifting a finger to help the Kings or the Gangsters. On my word, everybody took off for the cars before the police could get there. There were at least a hundred onlookers, but nobody did a thing. They stepped out of our way as we walked calmly out of the arcade. "King love," someone yelled. "Almighty," someone responded. We ruled the city. We left the area undisturbed.

We headed for the lakefront and Montrose Avenue Beach. On the way there, we stopped at a liquor store to stock up on beer and wine. I paid for everything; I was expected to. At the lake I got drunk and wanted a Queen to have sex with me right there in the back seat of a car. She declined, saying that she wanted to go to a hotel. I got pissed and grabbed her by the neck. "Bitch, fuck me now," I demanded. Some King brothers saw what was going on and pulled me off her. I calmed down and snorted about half a gram of cocaine. I started walking toward Addison Avenue, where the Disciples hung out, and partied by the Addison Avenue lakefront rocks. I pulled out my gun and carried it in my hand. I was packing a .380 automatic that night. A couple of Kings caught up to me and asked me what I was going to do. I just kept walking. The Queen I was with also came to me and got in front of me. She started kissing and caressing me, and apologized for teasing me. I in turn apologized for grabbing her by the neck and asked her if she wanted to go to a hotel. She said yes. I pulled out a bag of cocaine and snorted another half a gram. I gave the coke to the Kings and told them to get a car and meet me on Addison. I wanted to shoot a Disciple. I continued walking toward Addison. One King came with me while the Queen and the other King went back.

As we got closer, we walked into the park area where it was darker. We walked in between trees and got about fifty feet from where the Disciples were partying. I wanted to start shooting right away, but the King brother with me talked me into waiting for the car to arrive. Within minutes the car arrived. We watched it go past, make a U-turn up ahead, and come back our way. I ran out into the clear, yelled, "Almighty Latin Kings love," and began firing. I unloaded the gun as people screamed and ran for cover. As soon as the gun was empty, I ran to the car. We heard police coming, so I got out of the car and ran toward the boat docks. Once there I threw the gun into the lake and kept walking as if I had nothing to do with the shooting. Police cars sped right by me as I walked calmly past the docks, across the park, and onto Addison. Once on Addison I flagged a cab and got a ride back to the 'hood. In the 'hood everyone was waiting. Most thought I had been arrested and had already started to get money together for my bail. I got my car and headed for a hotel with the willing Queen. I heard nothing about the shooting at the lakefront. As far as I know, no questions were asked and no one was arrested.

A King brother named Spanky became my right-hand man. Spanky was about six feet tall and weighed two hundred and fifty pounds.

Spanky came to me one day and asked if he could deal for me. He had a wife and two kids to care for and said he needed money fast. I trusted Spanky right away. He didn't get high, didn't drink, he didn't even smoke cigarettes. His wife was a small woman named Josie. She was a great cook. I hired Spanky to do the job I once did for Cano. On my suggestion, he also began dealing small amounts of cocaine on the side. Spanky had Josie sell the packages right from their apartment. They made a lot of money. He went from a man who had no car and a small, dirty, roach-infested apartment to renting a whole house and driving a brand-new car in about two months.

I became totally dependent on cocaine. I went from one hundred and eighty pounds to one hundred and fifteen pounds in a matter of months. Many of my drug connections refused to deal with me because of my habit. They dealt with Spanky instead. I was still making plenty of money, but I blew it as fast as I got it. Soon everybody began hanging around Spanky, and they only looked for me when they wanted to get high. I began gangbanging more often and became highly abusive to any female who tried to get close to me emotionally. I would slap them around in public and beat them in private, then expected them to understand why I did it. In no time at all, I was all alone again. The only kind of social life I had was gangbanging and getting high. The only money I made was from selling quarter bags of cocaine. I had to sell them myself. All the dealers were now working for Spanky. The roles reversed and Spanky was now supplying me. I still, however, had the bulk of the small-time customers because they knew me as the main supplier.

I had a pretty slick deal going on. It made it hard for the police to catch on to what I was doing or where I kept my supply. I never stayed in one place for very long and I cruised around on a bike whenever it was practical. Sometimes I would take a rubber ball and a baseball glove so I wouldn't draw any suspicion. I kept cocaine stashed in three or four different out-of-view places. I only sold to people I knew and who trusted me to walk away with their money knowing I would come back with their merchandise. When I did come back, I would walk away from the customer where they could see me and then I'd drop the merchandise on the ground.

I had never dealt with people addicted to cocaine on a consistent basis until I was forced to sell my own stuff. Although I was just as addicted as they were, I considered myself much better than them. After all, I had all the cocaine I wanted—they had to buy it from me. People would offer just about anything in exchange for cocaine. I would get televisions, VCRs, stereo equipment, clothes, jewelry, guns, and various other items in exchange for cocaine. Many people traded their government food stamps for coke. There were also a lot of very attractive (and not so attractive) women of all ages who offered their bodies to get their drugs. I turned down just about all of them. There were a few, however, who I found too attractive to resist.

One of those women was a twenty-six-year-old married woman who always got cocaine in return for sexual favors. She was a beautiful woman. Her name was Kelly. She was a tall, blonde, blue-eyed, very sexy all-American girl. Her husband was a paramedic. They were both hooked on cocaine. Sometimes he would come with her to buy the drugs, but mostly she came by herself. I was the one who initiated the conversation that led her to agree to give me sex in exchange for cocaine. Her only prerequisite was that I not tell her husband about our agreement. Kelley would usually perform oral sex on me right in her car. On several occasions, however, she came by and spent the night with me when her husband worked the graveyard shift.

On one of those nights Kelly and I went out to get something to eat at Duk's restaurant on North and Kimball Avenues. We had been having sex and doing coke for several hours and were pretty exhausted. As I pulled into the Duk's parking lot, I saw Wanda standing by a car in the parking lot. I sent Kelly in to get the food while I stood outside talking to Wanda. I tried to talk her into coming with us to get high (a threesome is what I really had in mind), but surprisingly she turned me down. She walked away from me and got in the car she had been standing by. At that same moment Kelly came out of the restaurant. I walked toward her, to help with the bags of food she was carrying. Just before I got to her, I heard a car screech. Someone yelled, "Cobra," then gunshots rang out. Instinctively I threw myself to the ground and Kelly fell by my side. I thought she had thrown herself also until I heard her scream in pain.

I watched the car speed away, then got up and helped Kelly. She had been shot in her right leg. I called an ambulance for her, warned her not to say she was with me, and then took off. I had a gun and some cocaine on me so I had to leave. I just wondered what lie she would tell her husband to justify her being in that neighborhood so late at night. She was back around a couple of weeks later with her husband buying coke. She called me to assure me that nobody knew we were together the night she got shot. She also said that we could continue our transactions when she was able to drive again. That day never came.

46

Close Call

My luck was running out. I began losing all my customers because I didn't have a regular supply of coke to sell. I was snorting and smoking more cocaine than I was selling. I began doing burglaries again to keep money in my pocket. Spanky had bought a house and distanced himself from me, as if I was his enemy. It didn't matter—I was in my own little world scheming on how to get more cocaine. I kept the loyalty of most of the local Kings by re-immersing myself in violent gang activity. But that wouldn't last long either. Again I began having nightmares night after night after night. I would see people getting killed over and over. The Cubans, the Chi-West, the Gaylords, the Cobras, the Disciples, and the Vicelords—they were all in my dreams. Every crime I had committed or been a witness to played back whenever I closed my eyes. So much blood and pain—Blanca screaming for me not to rape her, Slim being beaten by his so-called brothers . . . I became a nervous wreck. I became paranoid every time I was put in a position where I had to fight or argue. I cowered from confrontations. I was too scared to walk the streets. I went along with gang members and their ways so that my own people wouldn't beat me. I didn't do much. Mostly I just acted as a lookout for police. I relied on my past reputation to get respect.

A new gang who called themselves the Latin Lovers had formed. They were rivals of the Kings. I had only heard about them from brothers who had run-ins with them or had seen their graffiti. I didn't even know where they hung out or what their colors were. Turned out, the Latin

Lovers' 'hood was where Jenny used to live by Lyndale Street and Western Avenue. They actually hung out on Campbell and Lyndale Streets. Five of us drove to Fullerton and Campbell, where three of us, including myself, got out of the car. The plan was for us to walk up Campbell toward Lyndale and attract the Lovers' attention while the other two drove by shooting. The plan didn't work. The Lovers spotted us long before we got to Lyndale. Two carloads of them came from behind us and chased us toward Lyndale. As we ran, I could see a mob of guys coming toward us. All three of us ran through different gangways toward Western. We had to get across the street and then two blocks down where the Spanish Lords had a section before we were safe.

I ran through the gangway and into the alley. From there I had nowhere to go but run toward Lyndale. Two Lovers came into the front of the alley on Lyndale and blocked my exit. I slowed down to figure out where to run next and got hit with a brick in the back. The pain gave me momentum and courage to run toward the mouth of the alley. I didn't want to get trapped where no one could see what was happening. I thought that if I could get out in the open they wouldn't beat on me for too long. I ran toward the two guys with all the force I could muster. I heard gunshots as I neared the exit. One of the guys grabbed me and tried to tackle me. The other one hit me on the side of the head. I began to hear police sirens in the distance. I knew all I had to do was struggle just a little longer. I got away from the guy holding me and ran onto Lyndale. I turned toward Western so fast that I lost my balance and fell to the ground. When I tried to get up I was kicked in the back of the head and then in the ribs. I managed to get up but was knocked back to the ground by another kick in the back. When I lifted my head, there was a gun barrel staring me in the eyes about four inches away.

The guy holding the gun grabbed me by the hair and yelled, "Say King killer, punk, or you're dead." "Fuck you," was my reply. "Say King killer, punk," he repeated. It didn't matter what I said. He was going to kill me anyway so I screamed ,"King love!" at the top of my lungs. The guy pulled the gun back about six inches and pulled the trigger. I closed my eyes and prepared to die, but I didn't hear the boom of the gun. I opened my eyes and saw the guy struggling with the gun. I tried to get up, but he pushed me down. He pointed the gun at the side of my head and pulled the trigger again. "Click," was the sound I heard come from the gun. It had jammed. The police sirens grew louder and the Lovers took off running. I tried to get up but couldn't. Within seconds I was surrounded by police.

A police officer picked me up by the shirt and slammed me against a parked car. He searched me and then handcuffed me. I was relieved to see that it was a Latino cop who apprehended me. That joy didn't last for long. He held me against the car and began slapping me around while he asked what gang I belonged to. I wanted to tell him I was a King, but he would slap me every time I tried to talk. Finally, a couple of gang crime division detectives arrived on the scene and took me away. They put me in the car and began questioning me. I told them I was a King and that I wasn't from the area. I tried to make them believe that I had wandered into the Lovers' 'hood by mistake. I know they didn't believe me, but they were too busy trying to find out if I could identify those who had beaten me. I told them about the Lovers having a gun and that I knew who had it. They drove me to Lyndale and Campbell, and I simply pointed out anybody I saw who remotely resembled a gang member. I sat in the car as guys who were Lovers, and some that may or may have not been, were put into a paddy wagon. As I sat there, I envisioned being locked up and beaten by the detectives. It never happened. They took off the handcuffs and drove me back to Humboldt Park. On the way there they gave me all kinds of advice and offered to help me if I wanted to quit gangbanging. I got out of their car in a daze. It was the first time that a cop had tried to talk some sense into me. They were the first cops I had any encounter with since Officer Friendly who even remotely acted like they cared.

The other two guys I was with that night somehow managed to make it back to the car unscratched. They didn't come back for me; they didn't even attempt to. That night I learned what gangbanging is all about—if you don't save yourself, no one else will save you.

47

The Law

BACK IN THE 'hood everybody was talking about what happened and what didn't happen. Nobody was listening to me. I got high and then walked away. Nobody noticed me leaving. Nobody noticed me grimacing in pain and holding my ribs. I went and tried to sleep, only to again experience terror in my dreams. That night I saw a gun being put to my head hundreds of times and the trigger being pulled. Only in my dreams there was no "click." There was a boom and then blood spilled. I watched as my mother bled, then boom and Pedro would fall bleeding, boom again and one of sisters would fall, over and over, until I woke up screaming when it was my turn to fall.

After this incident, my true colors began to show. I became the coward I always knew I was but had been able to hide so well. I became a victim of my own way of life, but I couldn't step away. I was too scared. I sold my car and used the money to buy a quarter kilo of cocaine. I was determined to build my business back up. I didn't, however, stop using my own merchandise. Spanky sold me the cocaine and offered me one of his dealers. I turned him down, preferring to deal myself. I made plenty of money, but I was always broke. I kept blowing my profits partying and getting high. My life was spinning out of control.

Just when I thought things couldn't get any worse, they did. I got busted. I had about four ounces of cocaine left to sell. I was caught with three of them and about two thousand dollars. I also got caught with a nine-millimeter gun and an Uzi submachine gun. I had just purchased the guns from a junkie about three days before I was busted. The cops must have been watching me for a while, because they knew where everything was. They put me in their car and drove me straight to where the cocaine was hidden outside. Then they took me to my apartment and to get the guns. I was impressed by how much they knew about my operation. I was taken to the police station on California Avenue and Shakespeare Street and booked for possession with the intent to deliver. I didn't get charged with the guns and the money was never reported. I don't know what happened to that evidence, but I can guess.

I sat on a steel bench in a small cell listening to guys screaming profanities at each other and representing their respective gangs. At about three in the morning I got a cellmate. The guy was a Disciple called Fingers. He recognized me right away. He said he remembered me from when I attended Von Humboldt School. He said we used to hang out together. I didn't remember him; I didn't want to. He handed me a cigarette and said, "It's me, Jorge. Don't you remember me?" My old friend Jorge looked like a grown man, whereas I still looked like a little boy. He was tall and muscular with a beard and mustache. I was small, wimpy, and had not yet begun to shave. We were both eighteen. He was called Fingers because he was shot in the hand by Kings and lost two fingers. Ironically, the two fingers he lost were his ring finger and his middle finger on his right hand. Every time he lifted his right hand he was representing the King sign. Jorge and I didn't say much to each other. Mostly we just made fun of the guys that were screaming like idiots. We sat there smoking cigarettes, staring at each other.

In the morning Jorge was released on an I bond. (An I bond, or an individual recognizance bond, is a ticket to go home pending a future court date.) I was transferred to a station downtown and from there I was taken to Cook County Jail. At Cook County I was put in a cell along with about thirty other guys waiting to be taken in front of a judge. I sat in a corner with my knees up to my chest waiting for my name to be called. There were guys from many different gangs in that cell, some with clearly visible gang tattoos, yet nobody said anything to anybody. The guards brought us coffee and bologna sandwiches. Most of the inmates who didn't have gang affiliations had their coffee and sandwiches taken away from them. There was one phone in that cell for everyone to use. Only a few guys made phone calls before they went to see the judge. I didn't have anyone to call. At about eleven in the morning my name was called.

I was taken into another cell where there were two guys who had to be seen before me. A half-hour later I was in front of the judge hearing the charges against me. I was charged with possession of one hundred and fifty eight grams of cocaine with the intent to deliver. I closed my eyes and waited for the gun charges to be announced, but it never happened. I was asked if I had a lawyer. "No," I answered. I was then taken back into the cell where I waited for a court-appointed public defender to consult with me. I sat there for about forty-five minutes waiting patiently. Two black guys who were in the same holding cell were bragging about the crimes they were charged with, acting like it was common for them to be in jail.

Finally the public defender came in to see me. He was a short white man with a bald spot in the center of his head and he walked with a slight limp. He looked more like a librarian than a lawyer. The public defender got right to the point. He said we could get a deal from the state's attorney for a guilty plea. I would have to do six years in the penitentiary. He explained that with time off for good behavior I would only do three years of actual jail time. My other alternative was to plead not guilty and go to trial. If I did that and was found guilty, I could be given the maximum time for the crime, which was anywhere from fifteen to thirty years. Without even thinking about it, I decided to fight the charges. There was no way I was going to take three years of jail time without putting up a fight. "OK, suit yourself," the public defender said as he walked out.

I was taken back to the cell where all the rest of the inmates were. My name was called again at about four in the afternoon. This time I was taken directly in front of the judge. The public defender stood beside me and announced my plea of not guilty. The judge set my bond at fifty thousand dollars. I would have to come up with ten percent, or five thousand dollars, to be released. That was that. I was taken back to the crowded cell to await processing into the Cook County Jail population.

Back in the cell I made a collect call to Spanky, hoping he could bail me out. The call was not accepted. I sank into a corner lost in my horrible little world. For the first time in my life, I worried about my future.

I was going to jail. All the years of running around the streets like a madman and risking my life had never worried me as much as going to jail now did. I couldn't run, I couldn't hide. I had no gun, no drugs, nothing to cover my true cowardice. It was time to learn how to be for real.

I sat there motionless and scared of what would happen to me in jail. All the horror stories I'd heard about incarceration went through my head and made me tremble. I was falling asleep when a guard came by screaming, "Let's go, let's go, let's go, gentlemen, line up by the door two at a time." I got up and stood in line next to a South Side King brother. When we got to the door we were handcuffed together and put in a line that was slowly moving down a hallway. We were passed through a room where we had eye prints made. (Like fingerprinting, this was another way for the justice system to identify offenders. We had to put our face into a machine that scanned our eyes. Apparently this was better than fingerprinting.)

We were then taken into a long hallway where we were uncuffed and told to stand with our faces against the wall. Two guards came by searching each prisoner one at a time. After they searched all of us, we were asked to turn around. An African American guard announced himself as the man in charge and made it clear that everything would be cool as long as we did what we were told. "Gentlemen, take off your shoes and put them in front of you," he instructed. Two guards searched our shoes. His next command was to take off our clothes one piece at a time, beginning with our shirts. Guards came by and checked every piece of clothing thoroughly before we took off the next piece. This continued until we were naked. There was a strong smell of sweat and feet in that hallway. The smell was so strong one guard said, "This is the stinkiest group yet." Then came the body cavity search. We were told to face the wall, bend over, and touch our toes. "Gentlemen, when you feel a touch on your back reach behind you and spread your cheeks." Mumbles and snickers were heard throughout the hall. The guy next to me said, "Shit, they're gonna stick a finger up our ass." I didn't say a word. I was scared and nervous about the whole scene. I just did as I was told. To my relief, they were only looking for signs of anal sex, trying to weed out the homosexuals; no finger up my ass searching for drugs, thank God. After that we were told to put only our underwear on and pick up our clothes.

They marched us into an infirmary room. There we stood in line and waited as each prisoner had various tests done. The first test, I think, was for venereal disease. The test consisted of a nurse holding your penis and then shoving a long, thin, cotton-tipped stick into the opening at lightning speed. It didn't hurt that much then, but every time I urinated for the next three days it burned like hell. The rest of the tests were pretty normal. They took a blood sample and gave me a physical. They told us to get dressed and we were taken to holding cells that were already at full capacity. It looked like a zoo and we were the animals. There were guys sleeping on the floor while others yelled obscenities at the guards. Mostly everybody was sharing their crime stories. There was a small cell on the side of the bigger ones that housed transvestites. Profanities were being yelled back and fourth between that cell and the rest of the cells. I got together with a couple of other Latin Kings and talked with them all night long. By morning the cell was a little less crowded. About half the guys were given I bonds, including the two Kings. All I had to pass the time was the cigarettes they left me.

A big white guy tried to intimidate me so he could take my cigarettes but backed off when I told him I was a King. After coffee and more bologna sandwiches they began calling our names again. When my name was called, I hurried to the cell door thinking I was either going to get an I bond or someone had bailed me out. When I got to the door, the guard said "Division 6," and called out another name. I just stood there puzzled. Finally he looked at me and asked what I was waiting for. I told him my name. He pointed to a line of guys and said "Get your dumb ass over there." I heard laughter as I walked slowly toward the line headed for Division 6. Before we were taken away, about five more guys joined the line. Then we were on our way.

There were about thirty of us, all between the ages of seventeen and twenty-one, all of us walking with an attitude. They took us through several long hallways and into a supply room. As we walked past the supply room we were given sheets and pillows, a toothbrush, toothpaste, and bath soap. From there we were taken into Division 6 and separated into different cell houses. The cell house I was taken into was empty except for three guys lying on the floor on mattresses. There were two levels of cells, about twenty-four cells in all; each housed two inmates. I was told to sit at a table and wait. Within fifteen minutes I was called to the door and given a mattress. I laid it on the floor away from the other three and began putting the sheets on it. A guard watched over me while I did this. The other prisoners lying there gave me dirty looks. As soon as I was finished, the guard walked off and then there was a loud "clank" noise.

One by one the doors began to open and guys began coming out. "Turn on the television," "yo, put the game on," guys called out as they took their places at various tables. Some guys played cards, others played chess; mostly, it seemed, they just looked at me while I sat there like a lost puppy. I was recognized by one of my cocaine customers. "What's up, King," he said. He gave me a pack of cigarettes, pointed out his cell, and said that if I wanted to trade places to let him know. Two of the guys who had mattresses on the floor introduced themselves as Kings. They got some dominoes and we sat there on the floor playing as they told me about Division 6 and the cell house. They described Division 6 as a "gladiator school." Mainly young criminals were housed there. Ninety percent were gang members. The other ten percent joined gangs while there. Gang fights were common, so gang members stuck with their own.

There were two long tables in the area where we were sitting. It was called the day room. A television was suspended from the ceiling facing the tables. At meal times the tables were occupied only by gang members. Those who were not in gangs sat on the stairs or on the floor. The gangs also decided what was to be seen on television and who should have telephone privileges. There were two phones in the cell house—one controlled by the Folks, the other by the Peoples. Those who weren't gang members were called neutrons. They were mostly victims until they sided with one gang or the other. Neutrons had a tough time in Cook County Jail, I was told, because they had to pay the gangs for the privilege of using the phone and sometimes had food taken away from them. Those who did stand up for themselves ended up being beaten or stabbed. Most inmates had homemade weapons stashed away just in case fights broke out. One of the Kings gave me one my second week there when we were taken to the gym.

Confrontations were the norm. I was unfortunate to end up in a cell house where the majority of the inmates were incarcerated for gang-warfare-related charges. One-on-one fights in locked cells were a daily occurrence. Everybody has this badass attitude that made it very uncomfortable. Every single confrontation led to a fight. There was nowhere to run and nowhere to hide—you had to back up your words with violence. If you told somebody you were going to kick his ass, you had to do it right then and there. Failure to back up threats made one look like a punk, which in turn made the whole gang look bad. The result was a major ass whipping from your own gang, followed by an all-out free-for-all against the rival gang.

I WAS IN Cook County Jail for five weeks waiting on my next court date. To my surprise, I didn't get any withdrawal symptoms from not using coke. I guess my energy was focused elsewhere. While I was there, Loca came to visit. The first time she visited I was surprised when the guard called my name. I thought I had been bailed out. Instead I was taken to a room with about twelve booths. I was told to sit down in one of them and wait. Minutes later Loca came in and sat across from me. We were separated by glass. We talked to each other through the phone.

Loca had changed for the better since the last time I saw her. She had this glow about her that made me smile. Loca had heard about my dilemma from Spanky. She was upset that the Kings were not doing anything to bail me out. She took it upon herself to get money from older brothers to get me a lawyer. Those brothers considered me an asset in their drug business, an opinion based on my violent past. Loca also told me something that blew my mind. She said that there was a rumor that Spanky had set me up to get busted. The older Kings were investigating to find out if the rumor was true. If it was, Spanky was going to be killed.

I didn't believe Spanky would do such a thing. I told Loca that it was the carelessness brought on by my coke habit that had caused me to get busted. I asked her to tell the King brothers the truth so they could leave

Spanky alone. She said that if Spanky didn't set me up, then nothing would happen to him. Loca gave me a phone number to call and find out what was going on. She also gave me her phone number so that I could call and talk to her. She wasn't going to be able to visit me again. She assured me that she would be there on my next court date. I began asking her about her kids, but she didn't get a chance to tell me. A guard tapped me on the shoulder and told me the visit was over. I walked away from the booth looking straight into Loca's eyes, silently pleading for help. A tear rolled down her cheek. She got up and walked away.

I had this empty feeling when I went back into the cell house. I was blaming everybody for the predicament I was in—I blamed the Kings, Cano, and even Pedro for taking my mother away. I especially blamed my mother.

My vivid nightmares returned with a vengeance. I would wake up screaming. This was a much talked about event in the cell house. In a way this worked to my advantage. Everybody thought I was some kind of lunatic, a bomb waiting to explode.

I called Loca early the next morning and asked her to have some marijuana delivered to me. By nightfall I had a half-ounce of weed delivered, courtesy of one of the guards. I sold joints for items like cigarettes, soap, and toothpaste. I kept the Kings in my cell house supplied with anything they wanted.

Later I was "given the opportunity" to lock myself up in a cell with another inmate so that we could beat the shit out of each other. He didn't like the way I looked at him and decided he wanted to teach me some manners. It didn't matter who won or lost. It was the willingness to be a participant that earned you an aura of respect. However, if the fight resulted in a one-way bludgeoning, everybody would go at it. The administration would shut down the cell block floor for days when that happened. On several occasions the Kings decided to attack as soon as the lockdown was over. The guards transferred inmates from cell house to cell house in order to calm the hostilities. Because of that, the population of the cell house I was in changed to mostly older brothers. Things calmed down after that. There were eight other King brothers there with me. We pretty much controlled the cell house.

I called the number Loca had given me. I talked to a King brother named Deadeye. He was the brother who was shot in the eye when we had the shootout with the Disciples at Maplewood Park. We reminisced for a little while about old times and joked about his new nickname. He gave me the name of the lawyer who was going to represent me. (The Kings had hired a lawyer for me.) He told me that the lawyer was going to try to get my bond lowered so it would be easier to get me bailed out. Loca was going to be there with the money. Then our conversation turned to the topic of Spanky. I told him I had heard about the rumor and assured him it had to be a lie. "Spanky is a damn good brother," I told Deadeye. "He would never set a King brother up, especially not me." Deadeye was silent for a while and then said, "He did it, my man. He set you up." Before I could rebut his comment, he told me how they knew the truth. Deadeye explained that the lawyer hired to represent me got information from the police about how I was arrested. Spanky told the police my full name, nickname, where I lived, and where I kept my stash. He wanted to get rid of me so that he could be the only drug supplier in the neighborhood. I still couldn't believe it. I argued that the police could be making things up to get the Kings fighting against each other. All Deadeye said was, "You're a good brother, Lil Loco. We'll take care of it." At first I didn't know what he meant, but then I remembered what Loca had said—Spanky was going to be killed. Deadeye said good-bye before I could say another word. I was left to think about Spanky's fate. I didn't bother calling Loca. I spent the days until my court appearance high on weed. I didn't sleep or talk much. I just kept to myself, smoked, and waited.

48

Free?

THE COURT DATE arrived. I looked like shit from lack of sleep in anticipation of this day. At 7:00 A.M. the usual clank of the doors unlocking echoed through the cell house. All the inmates came out for breakfast. After breakfast everybody got locked back up except for those who had court dates. I was the only one with a court date from my cell house that day. I showered, got dressed, then sat at a table and chain-smoked until a guard came for me. Finally, the door leading into the cell house was opened and I was taken out into the hallway. A long line of inmates awaited me in the hallway, all bound for the same destination. We were marched through several long hallways into the courthouse. There we were separated into different holding cells depending on which judge we were going to see. I was there for about three hours, still chain-smoking, keeping to myself, scared to death. I heard my name being called but hesitated to move. The guard called out my name louder. Then I reacted and walked to the front of the cell. "That's me," I said. "For a minute there I thought you escaped," the guard joked. I was taken into another holding cell right behind the courtroom, where I waited for another hour or so. While I was there a tall white man with an expensive suit and very professional demeanor came in and called my name. He was the attorney the Kings had sent to represent me. He was a far cry from that short, sloppy, I-really-don't-care-looking public defender the state had appointed me. The lawyer cheered me up by asking, "Are you ready to go home today?"

The attorney filled me in on what was going to happen. He told me that the state wanted to make a deal where I would get three years in jail with a guilty plea. If I took the deal, he explained, I would do about a year and half with good behavior and then be released on parole. He then advised me that I could be facing a minimum fifteen years in prison if I went to trial and was found guilty. "I don't want to go to the penitentiary," I told him. He put his hand on my shoulder and assured me that if he had anything to do with it, I wouldn't even see the county jail again. The attorney then began advising me on the courtroom proceedings. He said he had gotten the state to agree to lower my bond from fifty thousand dollars to ten thousand dollars. I would have to come up with ten percent, or one thousand dollars, to get out. He told me that Loca was in the courtroom waiting with the bail money. I was elated. I was going home. The lawyer advised me to walk quietly and politely when my name was called and not to say a word. He would do all the talking. He shook my hand and walked out.

I sat down and started thinking about all kinds of things. I started questioning my need for freedom. I was going to be free, but I didn't have a home to go to. In jail I had a place to sleep, three meals a day, medical care, and recreation. The more I thought about it, the better the prospect of spending a couple of years in jail became. Hell, I thought, I could rid my body of that drug craving and devote myself to weight lifting or something. Education was also available in the penitentiary, so I could take advantage of that too. I wouldn't have to worry about being victimized by other inmates because I was a Latin King.

I came out of my daydream when someone called my name. I was escorted into the courtroom. I saw Loca immediately and smiled. I was taken in front of the judge, where the lawyer waited for me. I stood by his side while he pleaded my case to the judge. I didn't know what was said or what was decided until I was back in the holding cell. I just stood there daydreaming, confused about what I was going to do when I got out. Everthing did happen as my attorney predicted it would. The bond was lowered to ten thousand dollars and the attorney told the court that I was posting bail. As soon as Loca paid the bond, I would be released. Two hours later I was out on the street again.

Loca waited for me to be released and drove me back to the 'hood. She said I could stay with her for a while until I got myself together. Get myself together? How? I was uneducated, homeless, and unskilled. The only thing I knew how to do was gangbang. I asked Loca about Spanky. I thought maybe I could get some coke from him on credit and get my business going again. Loca told me that Spanky was in the hospital recovering from gunshot wounds. She said the Kings had shot him for setting me up. He was supposed to have been killed but somehow was able to survive after being shot four times. He had been shot twice in the abdomen, once in the buttocks, and once in the back. The shot to the back had shattered his lower spine. He lost the use of his lower body and the left side of his upper body. His intestines were useless and he had a bag to replace his digestive system. He would spend the rest of his life in a wheelchair. I couldn't help but cry when I heard of Spanky's fate. Loca, however, said he deserved it. She scolded me for shedding tears for a rat, especially one that ratted on me.

Loca had moved back to the Humboldt Park area and was living on Potomac and Spaulding Streets, three or four blocks from Beach Street. Cubana was at her house babysitting. She hugged me really hard when she saw me. I was quite surprised by her reaction. Cubana had already had her baby; it was a boy. She looked beautiful, even more so than before. Cubana was no longer seeing the guy in jail who fathered her child. He was seeing another Queen and had no time for her. Cubana had also become a welfare mother. Although she was young and able, for some reason she never bothered to even think about looking for or getting a job. Loca, on the other hand, was now working as a teller at a local currency exchange and had gotten off welfare. She did, however, deal small amounts of cocaine as a way to make extra money. Cubana had an apartment on the second floor of the building where Loca lived. I moved in with her. I don't know what Cubana felt about me, but I didn't love her. I almost didn't even like her. My relationship with her was one of convenience—I needed a place to stay, she provided it, and we became sexual partners again.

I used Cubana's apartment as a place to sell weed. Cubana sold Loca's cocaine from there too. I wasn't gangbanging much, but I was drinking heavily, smoking weed, and snorting coke on a daily basis. Although I lived with Cubana as her man, I was still very promiscuous.

I played Cubana dirty every chance I had and because of that we argued a lot. I became physically abusive with Cubana. She became very afraid of me. Every time she raised her voice to me I would slap her and grab her neck or worse. Once when she didn't want to have sex with me I pushed her down the stairs and locked her out of the apartment until the next day. I always said I was sorry and she always forgave me. I think she was too scared to do anything else. The abuse continued. The apartment became a Latin King hangout. Cubana didn't like the idea, but she did nothing about it. When she did complain, she got slapped.

It wasn't long before cocaine became my drug of choice again. I was spending all the money I made on my marijuana sales on cocaine. I was out at all times of the night and would get shot at by rival gangs on a weekly basis. The King brothers began referring to me as a moving target and only hung out with me at the apartment. While all of this was going on, I was still fighting the drug case in court. The lawyer was stalling to get a change of venue and a more favorable judge. In the meantime, I was running the streets like a wild man.

The Latin Kings began demanding that I show up at meetings, but I never did. Confrontations between the Kings and me became ugly in nature. I was threatened with violations if I didn't show up for meetings, but I still didn't go.

I began having sex with Loca. She had been like a mother to me for sometime and now we were lovers. This was the last straw for Cubana. She started seeing a King brother and I was no longer welcome in the apartment. It didn't matter. I didn't care. I moved in with Loca.

49

Older Woman

LOCA AND CUBANA stopped talking to each other and had a few confrontations in which Loca hit Cubana. Finally Cubana moved out. Loca and I became the talk of the neighborhood because of our age difference. I was eighteen and she was twenty-nine. Loca was very attractive and we got along very well together. I felt like I was loved and I felt I had to be faithful. While I was with Loca I didn't even think about other women. She pretty much supported me, but she also made me start doing things for myself. If I didn't comply with her requests, she said she would leave me. I enrolled in a GED class. Considering the fact that I was always high (mostly on coke), I did exceptionally well in the class. The fact that I was involved in some educational activity also looked good for the courts.

The attorney got my case changed to another judge. He called me one day and told me that if I could come up with two thousand dollars he could guarantee that my case would be dismissed by the new judge. Loca told me that the money was probably going to be used to buy the judge and immediately started calling people to raise the money. Within twenty-four hours she had the money. Several older brothers gave us the money. In return I had to make a hit on a King who had turned into a junkie. The next day we went downtown to the lawyer's office and gave him the money. He told me to consider my case dismissed and not to bother coming to court anymore.

From the attorney's office we went to Kedzie and Lawrence Avenues where we met some Kings. The Kings gave me a .357 Magnum to use for the hit I had promised to do. I was to locate an ex-King called Mago and blow away one of his kneecaps. I was not to kill him unless I had to. Mago had apparently burned a Latin King drug connection out of some dope. It wasn't a significant amount, but it was an act demanding disciplinary action.

Mago hung out in the Humboldt Park area. He was pretty well known and easy to find. That night I was told that Mago was at a local bar playing pool. I decided to get the hit over with as soon as possible. I went to the bar and saw Mago slouching down over a chair by the pool table. He had a beer in one hand and a cue stick in the other. I asked for change for the cigarette machine and then walked toward the back. I went around the pool table on the other side from Mago. I bought a pack of Newport cigarettes, then turned and walked toward Mago. I put the cigarettes in my pocket and went for the gun as I brought my hand back up. Mago was caught completely by surprise. I walked right up to him, put the gun three inches away from his left knee, and pulled the trigger. Mago fell to the floor screaming in pain as I ran out of the bar untouched. Outside I ran half a block and got into a car in which Loca was waiting for me. "You OK?" Loca asked. "Yeah," I responded. We drove home as if nothing had happened.

AT ABOUT THAT time the media's romance with gangbangers was rekindled yet again. Several Latin Queens were picked up by gang crime unit detectives and taken to the Oprah Winfrey show, where they were to be guests. The subject of that particular show was women in gangs. Apparently the police asked the Queens if they wanted to be on the show and they jumped at the chance to be on television. Two Latin Queens sat on stage at the Oprah Winfrey show bragging about their gang affiliation and criminal involvement. They wore their colors and flashed their hand signs to a supposedly shocked audience. One Queen made comments about what would happen if anybody walked into their 'hood wearing the wrong colors. She bragged about the crimes committed and the drugs sold by the Latin Kings and Queens. The other Queen just agreed with everything said. Little did they know that back in the 'hood their punishment was being discussed. The Queens thought they had done something honorable for their nation. After all, they presented the Kings' name, hand sign, colors, and actions to a national audience. The Kings, however, weren't at all pleased. The same evening the show aired the Kings decided to take action against the Queens.

The one Queen who did most of the talking was well known in the neighborhood. In fact her whole family was well known. Her home was once a party house for the Latin Kings. She now lived with some other Queens in an apartment on LeMoyne Street near the Beach and Spaulding Streets Latin Kings' section. That night the windows of their apartment were shattered by gunshots. There were small kids in the apartment, but nobody seemed to care about that. The only thing they cared about was the reputation of the Latin Kings. One by one the Queens that appeared on the show quickly disappeared from the neighborhood. They either left the city or left the state altogether. They were smart. Had they stayed around, further harassment was inevitable. I wonder if Oprah Winfrey realized the danger she put those young ladies in. I wonder if she even cared—probably not. Any gang crime detective could give accurate accounts of gang life without fear of retaliation, but I guess that wasn't good enough for television. I wonder how many tears Oprah Winfrey would have shed if one of those girls had been killed. Perhaps it would have been better if one had. Maybe the media would have been prevented from using gang members or wannabe gang members as freaks for their sideshows.

My relationship with Loca flourished. Loca became very motherly to me, kind of like Maria, only Loca was also my lover. The only thing that separated our relationship from that of a mother and child was our sex life. She took care of me so well. She bought my clothes, cooked my food, and made sure I had everything I needed for the GED classes. Within four months of enrolling in the GED classes I took the test and passed with flying colors. I often wonder how well I would have done if I hadn't been high all the time. I was high on the day I took the test, but I still passed.

The Kings stopped demanding I come to the meetings for a while, but then they changed and wanted me to attend. I got into a couple of fistfights with them because of that. I didn't want to hang out with the

Kings, but I was too much of a coward to ask for a violation out. I was still an active gangbanger whenever necessary, mostly when rival gang members came into the 'hood.

One night I went to Loca's job to walk her home. On the way home we joked and laughed like a couple of lovelorn kids. A car drove by slowly and suspiciously. I represented the Kings, sign at them. The car stopped and a guy got out and began shooting at us. We threw ourselves to the ground behind the parked cars. Loca screamed in pain. She had been hit. The sudden image of another person dying in my arms entered my mind as I scrambled to care for Loca. Thank God she had only been hit in the leg. I got in front of an oncoming car and forced the driver to take us to the hospital. I had witnessed too many occasions where the ambulance never showed up and I wasn't going to take a chance with Loca. The driver turned out to be a white man on his way to buy coke from Loca. He didn't mind driving us to the hospital as long as we sold him some coke. He drove us to the Norwegian Hospital emergency room, which was the closest hospital. I ran inside yelling for help. A crowd of hospital staff came to our aid. They took Loca out of the car, placed her in a wheelchair, and took her inside. I went back to the house to get Loca's insurance card and to get some coke for our chauffeur. We dropped off Loca's kids at a friend's house and then headed back to the hospital. I didn't have time to pick and choose bags of coke for our customer, so I brought the stash with me. I gave him a free bag of coke for his help and then stayed at the hospital. I waited patiently for news regarding Loca's condition.

I asked to see Loca and was told that I couldn't see her. The nurse walked me to the waiting room and promised to come get me when I was able to see her. In the waiting room I became impatient. I went into the bathroom and snorted some coke. I had a plastic sandwich bag with twenty grams of coke in it divided into individual gram bags. About every fifteen minutes I went into the bathroom and did more of the drug. I snorted two grams of coke within an hour and had started on a third. I was on my way to the bathroom for another snort when the nurse called me. I was now able to see Loca.

They still had her in the emergency room where they had taken a bullet out of her leg. Loca was still woozy from the anesthesia. Her pant leg had been ripped all the way up to the belt line and cut off. She had an IV needle stuck in one arm and a blood bag needle stuck in the other. She saw me and reached for my hand. I took her hand and asked her if she was OK. Loca rolled her eyes. The nurse tapped me on the back. I turned around quickly and became kind of dizzy. The nurse asked me for Loca's insurance card. I hesitated, then gave it to her on the second request. I turned back around and told Loca that I felt lightheaded and was going back to the waiting room to sit down. I don't know if she agreed or not. I just turned and headed for the waiting room. The room began spinning as I reached the door. I felt like I was going to fall and tried to hold onto the doorframe. I looked at the doctors and nurses staring at me and then everything went blank.

I opened my eyes to a crowd of people kneeling and standing over me. A doctor was putting down those electric shock things they use when your heart stops beating. He placed his hands over my heart and began pushing down repeatedly. "I'm only here to see my girlfriend," I said. I thought I had made it to the waiting room, fallen asleep, and somehow the coke had slipped out of my pocket. In my mind those standing over me were the police arresting me. "Worry about yourself right now," a doctor told me as they lifted me off the floor and put me on a rolling bed. I started to struggle. "Leave me alone. I want to go home," I said. The doctors and nurses held me down. I struggled harder. "Tie him down," I heard someone say. "No, I want to go home. Leave me alone," I screamed. A nurse got over me, pushed my chest down, and said, "You'll go home, but let us fix that nasty hole in your chin first." I calmed down immediately. "Do you feel any pain in your jaw?" a doctor asked. I shook my head no and wondered what the hell they were talking about. "Have you been doing any drugs tonight?" was the next question. Again I shook my head no. A doctor grabbed my chin and asked me if I felt any pain. "No," I said. He looked at the other doctor and said, "He's so fucking strung out he doesn't even know he has a big hole in his chin." "Sew him up, no anesthesia. We don't need a drug reaction," the other doctor responded as he walked away.

The nurse came over and told me she was going to put a cold towel over my forehead and eyes to make me feel better. "Tell me if you feel any pain, but don't pull away, just tell me," the doctor said. For the next half hour I felt him doing something to my chin but I didn't know exactly what. The towel the nurse had put over my forehead and eyes obstructed my sight. My hands and legs were still tied down. I just lay there not knowing what the hell was going on. Finally the towel was taken away from my face. A bright light shined right into my eyes and made me wince. The light was turned off and two doctors and three nurses stood over me, looking at me as if I was a freak. "I'm going to untie you now, just relax," one nurse said. I turned my head to one side and made eye contact with Loca as she lay on the bed next to me. What the hell had happened to me? "Do you feel any pain?" I was asked. "No." "Open your mouth slowly," I was instructed. "Do you feel any pain?" "No."

The room emptied except for a doctor, a nurse, Loca, and I. The doctor asked me what kind of drugs I had been doing. "None," I said. He turned to the nurse and asked her to get a mirror. The doctor began to untie me while he waited for the nurse. Within seconds the nurse returned, handed him a mirror, and walked off. The doctor handed me the mirror and told me to look at my chin. I put the mirror up to my face and saw a horrible-looking cut freshly stitched together. My chin was swollen and so was half of my bottom lip.

"You just fell flat on your face. It took fifteen stitches to close that cut and you feel no pain. Level with me. What drugs are you doing?" I didn't answer, I just looked over at Loca. "Your heart stopped beating. You almost died. If I don't know what caused it, I can't help you," the doctor said. "Cocaine," I said as I looked deep into Loca's eyes. "How much and when?" he asked. "I had two grams with me and I did them in the bathroom while I was waiting for her," I answered. "You just had a major overdose and you went into cardiac arrest," the doctor explained. "Had you not been here you would not have made it." He walked over to a nurse, said something to her, and walked out of the room. I got up from the bed and stood next to Loca. "You're crazy," she said. "I'm stupid," I answered.

I bent down and whispered that I had coke on me and was going to leave before any cops arrived. She nodded in agreement and kissed me on the cheek. "I'll come see you tomorrow," I said, and turned toward the door. As I was walking out the nurse came in and told me to wait. She had a bag in her hand. After getting some gauze she began pulling its contents out one item at a time. She pulled out some Tylenol with codeine and explained that I would be feeling excruciating pain in my jaw pretty soon. The Tylenol would help it. She then pulled out three little plastic containers that contained a clear liquid. She said that I should pour the liquid on some gauze and lightly wipe my wound clean and advised me not to get soap on the wound. She put everything back in the bag and handed it to me. I started walking away. The nurse walked with me and told me to follow her so that she could make an appointment for me to come back and get the stitches taken out. After that I went home. It was about 4:00 A.M. by then. I went to pick up Loca's kids, but they were sleeping. After answering a million questions about my ugly-looking, swollen jaw, I went home and went to sleep.

I woke up in pain. I felt my jaw throbbing and I could barely open my mouth. The Tylenol with codeine helped relieve the pain a little but not enough. I went out and got some weed to ease the pain. The Kings had already heard about me overdosing at the hospital. They also knew about Loca being shot but didn't give that as much importance as my overdosing. It seemed to me that the new hierarchy of Kings on the street had an ongoing desire to get me violated out of the gang. They didn't care about me endangering my life with a coke habit. No, they were upset because I had broken the rules by becoming a junkie.

Loca was in the hospital for about a week. I cared for her kids while she was there. I rarely left the house in that time, not because of the kids but because the Kings were constantly confronting me. They were coming to the house daily to remind me that I would have to show up at an upcoming meeting. "The brothers in the joint sent word for you to meet with the Beach and Spaulding Kings," they would say. "Bullshit," I thought to myself, while falsely smiling and agreeing to show up. Loca being in the hospital was my excuse to postpone what seemed to be the inevitable for another week. The Kings played a good game of deception. They came around asking about Loca's health, gave me weed, and asked if I needed anything. I knew damn well that they were just babysitting me until Loca got back. If the Kings were trying to scare me, they had succeeded.

50

Love Lost

I COULDN'T SLEEP. Bloody nightmares kept me awake. I replayed the beating I had witnessed Slim receive over and over in my mind. I knew the fate awaiting me but couldn't do anything about it. I thought about going to visit Loca and not coming back, but the Kings were one step ahead of me. They were always there waiting and willing to be my chauffeurs. They never let their deceit show.

A week and a half after Loca was shot, she was released from the hospital. I should have been happy, but I dreaded that day. It was a Tuesday; the deception stopped. The Latin Kings made their purpose known. A couple of Kings drove me to the hospital to pick up Loca. Nothing was said on the way there and only gangbanging bullshit was talked about on the way back. At the house they helped me take Loca inside and put her to bed. I walked to the door and met their true intentions. Four other Kings were standing outside the door on the steps. When I opened the door to let the others out I was ambushed. Four or five sets of hands simultaneously grabbed and immobilized me. A gun was pressed against my neck and the clip was pulled back. "Don't come out of the house," I was told. "Don't even look out the window. We'll come for you on Sunday. You can come to the meeting or you can die." The guy with the gun stepped back, put the gun away, and left. The Kings holding me pushed me inside and closed the door behind them. They sat on the stairs getting high, watching over me. I had not told Loca what was going on with the Kings while she was in the hospital. I didn't want to worry her. It was time she knew.

Loca became furious when I told her what was going to happen. She began calling older Kings to notify them of these actions. "You earned your respect a long time ago," Loca said. "They can't take nothing from you." In call after call Loca pleaded my case to anybody who would listen. The listeners were few. Those who did listen advised me to show up at the meeting. Apparently the Kings of Beach and Spaulding Streets had spread the rumor that I was shooting up heroin. Cocaine had become the drug of choice with most gangbangers, especially the older, career gang members who called themselves leaders. Saying that I overdosed on coke was not as bad as saying I was a heroin addict. That was still the great taboo in the Latin Kings' rulebook. Although most Kings were now addicted to one drug or another and most were also alcoholics, they still made a big deal about heroin use. Actually, they only condemned intravenous heroin use. There were many Kings who snorted heroin in a mix with cocaine (known as a speedball) on a consistent basis. The same Kings who continuously passed judgment on others were lost in the drug world themselves. In my case the judgment came out of convenience—I had defied them, so it was convenient for them to punish me as a way of getting back at me. They also wanted to show the younger generation of Kings that standing up for themselves against the gangs' elite members would not be tolerated. I was the odd man out. The loyalty I had earned had been diminished with the change of generations. I was fucked.

I talked myself into going to the meeting. I was scared, but I also didn't feel like being hunted in my own neighborhood. Loca and I spent many hours talking about the Kings' intentions. We felt that they just wanted to hurt me, plain and simple. We reminisced about our younger days as members of the Latin Kings and Queens—how together we were and how we genuinely cared about each other. Loca, being older than I, remembered the early days of the Latin Kings. They were the heros of the Latino people, giving up their lives and futures so that other Latinos could walk with dignity and respect. The Latin Kings were a respected Latino organization, especially in their own neighborhoods, where they protected their people from being victims and were always there to lend a helping hand. They earned the right to proudly display their colors on a float in the Puerto Rican parades. The Latin Kings represented the struggle for Latino equality. They represented a culture whose only desire was to flourish without losing its identity. Even when I joined the Kings, the togetherness and pride still existed, although it was slowly fading. Listening to Loca, I realized that I was one of those who had played a big part in transforming the Kings from heroes to cold-blooded murderers. I took part in the initial gun battles that lit the flame on a runaway fire that was now the main cause of the deterioration of Latino life in this city. Now the main victims of the Latin Kings were other Latinos. They harassed, hunted, drugged, and killed Latinos. More devastating, they prevented many young Latinos from getting an education. The Kings did all this while still calling themselves the Almighty Latin Kings Nation, a nation of leaders.

It was too late for me to start thinking straight. I had a meeting to go to that would decide my future with the Kings. I was so scared thinking about what would happen to me at the meeting that I decided to carry a gun. Loca repeatedly warned me to be careful as if she sensed something bad was going to happen.

The night before the meeting I couldn't sleep at all, not because the meeting was on my mind but because I was having those ugly nightmares again. But I saw myself being shot in place of those who I'd witnessed being shot. I saw myself being held by Juni as I bled to death. I woke up screaming to find Loca cradling my head and her kids looking at me as if I was crazy. After that I didn't want to fall asleep. I stayed up all night watching television and snorting coke. It was the first time I had snorted since the night I overdosed. The coke kept me awake and got me thinking about how I would shoot any King who tried to put a hand on me. I paced the floor. I unloaded and reloaded the gun over and over again. I planned my actions for the meeting. I went over what I would say, what I would do, how I would act, only to realize that when the moment presented itself I would do nothing. It didn't matter. I continued to fantasize about a violent confrontation where I would come out alive. I, Lil Loco, Almighty Latin King, would make the Kings heroes of the Latino people once again. The fantasizing helped me to metamorphose into the Lil Loco everyone knew and loved—a violent and uncaring criminal.

At noon on Sunday there was a knock at the door. Three Kings picked me up for the meeting. I had been waiting for them but didn't think they would come so early. I told them to wait a minute while I got a jacket and took that opportunity to get the gun. Loca kissed me deeply and told me to be careful. "Better them than you," she said as I walked out of the bedroom. The gun I was carrying was a nine-millimeter automatic. I pulled out the clip and checked the gun thoroughly. I wanted to make sure it wouldn't jam on me if I had to use it. I walked outside and headed to the meeting with the Kings. It was cold, raining, and dark— a classic black Sunday in Chicago. The Kings that walked with me were surprisingly friendly. It was all a ploy to get my guard down, I thought. We walked up Spaulding Street to LeMoyne Street, then into a gangway. We went in through a door in that gangway and into a basement. There were Kings standing and sitting all over the place. They had already begun to get high and drunk early. I was offered beer and weed but turned them down. Several of the Kings present knew me from my days at Kedzie and Armitage. A couple of them treated me as they always had; they shook my hand, hugged me, and asked what I was up to. The others sneered at me and turned away, not wanting to be associated with me in any way. I felt uncomfortable yet calm. I wanted to get this shit over with. I stared at those staring at me until they turned their faces away. I sat there planning my exit route, making sure not to show fear. Within fifteen minutes the leader of the Beach and Spaulding Latin Kings came in. It was time for the meeting to start.

Chico was a tall, muscular Puerto Rican with a taste for flashy jewelry. He was very well groomed and dressed in expensive clothing. Chico was very articulate and well educated. He was a college graduate. The man wasted no time in getting to the point of my presence. There were no prayers or business discussed as had been the custom before the main proceedings. These rituals were passé; the new generation of Latin Kings had more important things to do. Chico stood in the center of the room as the only person addressing the membership. There was no leadership or decision making by committee; Chico was it. "This brother here is Lil Loco, for those of you who don't know him." Chico said. "Lil Loco has been a brother for many years, only he's not so righteous anymore," he proclaimed matter-of-factly. "This brother is not from any section," Chico continued. "He's a King wherever he stands. We, the Latin Kings of Beach and Spaulding, have been designated by the Inca to deal with his breaking of our laws," Chico said as he turned my way. (The Inca is the head of all Latin Kings.) "The brother is becoming a junkie. He OD'd in the hospital when they shot Loca," he informed the others. "He will receive a three-minute head-to-toe violation or be violated out of the Nation," Chico said proudly. "It's his choice." Chico looked at me with a smirk on his face. He walked away from the center of the room, sat directly across from me, then stared at me. "What's it gonna be, Lil Loco?" Chico asked. It was as if he was enjoying what was going on. I had never met this man, let alone seen him, yet he was looking forward to seeing me get my ass kicked. I sat there shaking in my pants, not knowing what to say. I thought about my past and the reputation I had built as a violent person. I decided to play on that reputation for all it was worth.

"I ain't taking neither. Once a King, always a King, and nobody here can take my crown," I remained sitting calmly. Chico called my bluff. "Cooperate or by force, doesn't matter to me," he said. I got up and snapped out on Chico with words I couldn't even believe were coming out of my mouth. "You call yourself a brother, a King," I began. "Another brother stands before you with a problem and you solve it by having his ass whipped. What the hell is wrong with you? What happened to 'I will die for you?' What happened to '*Amor* to all Kings'? You're full of shit. Nobody in this room is going to put their hands on me," I said as I looked around the room. I watched the reactions to my words. Some brothers looked at me wide-eyed; others put their heads down. Most of them looked at Chico as if waiting for a command. "All you young brothers better think about your leader," I continued. "He cares about himself, not the Almighty Latin King Nation," I said in a last desperate attempt to win some comrades. My speech was finished. I brought my fist up to my heart, lifted the Kings' hand sign up in the air, and said "*Amor*," then headed for the door. Chico and various other brothers stood in my way and came at me. I felt myself being surrounded as Chico laughed out loud. I stepped back, pulled out the gun, and began pointing it every which way. Everybody stepped back as far away from me as possible. "You fucked up royally," Chico said. "I'm a real King," I responded. I opened the door, then turned around, looked Chico straight in the eyes, and told him, "If you come for me, make sure you kill me, because you know me and I'll be back if you don't." I walked out the door and took off running.

I got home and told Loca what had happened. Loca told me I was stupid, crazy, and I had put her family in jeopardy. She got on the phone and began calling the Kings that had the most rank and begged them not to take my actions out on her family. I sat in the living room and watched a football game with her oldest son while trying to keep my mind off Loca making phone call after phone call, begging for mercy. She came out of her room, still limping from the gunshot wounds, and began screaming at me. "Stay away from my kids! You're gonna get us killed! Get the fuck out of my house!" I got up, got my jacket, and headed for the door. Before I left I went back, gave Loca a big hug, and told her everything would be all right. Loca went into the bedroom. I headed back toward the door. Loca's boys were arguing about what channel to put the television on. Suddenly I heard a loud "boom, boom, boom," and then the windows came crashing down. I jumped toward the kids and fell on both of them as they cried in horror. Loca came out of the room screaming for her boys. "Get down," I screamed at Loca. Two more shots were fired, more glass went flying all over the place, and then there was silence.

The boys were whimpering and Loca was asking if they were all right. I crawled to the window, and saw the coast was clear. I went to the boys, picked them up one at a time, and took them into Loca's room. They were all right physically, thank God. Anthony, the oldest, had only a minor scratch on his leg. Mentally, they were scarred for life. Loca and I were OK. I had been hit in my back by four pellets from a sawed-off shotgun. The window, curtains, and the clothes I had on slowed down their velocity so they didn't do much damage. The paramedics were able to tweeze them out and clean and dress the wounds without having to hospitalize me. Loca's youngest son, Angel, was delirious. "I hate Kings," he said "Don't be a King anymore, Lil Loco, be a Cobra." "When I grow up I'm going to be a Cobra and kill Kings." I had no comment and neither did Loca. We just stared at each other blank-faced.

We spent the rest of the afternoon answering questions from the police. Mostly we told them that we didn't know who did it and that they must have shot at the wrong house. Uniformed cops, gang crime unit cops, and paramedics, all took turns giving us advice. "We could take your kids away," they told Loca. "You're going to get killed," they told me. None of them knew what was going on or could begin to understand. The city had the windows boarded up and had someone vacuum up the broken glass inside the apartment. They said they did it for the kids. They searched the apartment countless times but didn't find the gun or the drugs we had stashed. The cops were smart; they had a suspicion that the Kings had done the shooting. "Burned your boys, Lil Loco?" a detective asked. "We're going to keep a patrol car outside to make sure Lil Loco's brothers don't come looking for him," that same detective said as he walked out. For the rest of the night Loca and I comforted each other without saying a word. "I've got to move away from here," Loca finally said, then fell asleep. I stayed up all night with the gun in my hand reacting to every noise I heard. I paced the apartment back and forth. I was tempted to do some cocaine but decided against it. I never touched the drug again. My life was at a turning point. It was time to be a man.

51

Lesson Learned, Finally

LOCA'S FAMILY BEGAN coming around trying to help her find a different place to live. Among them was her sister-in-law, Luisa. She was the only one of Loca's relatives who got along with me. All the others denounced the older woman/younger man relationship Loca and I had. They blamed me for all that had happened to Loca. Luisa worked at a local university. She offered me a temporary job entering data for spring semester registration. I didn't know anything about computers but jumped at the opportunity anyway.

The Kings were still looking to teach me some kind of lesson. The older Kings came to the house and actually advised me not to worry about the younger brothers. The chiefs in the penitentiary also gave me their blessings as far as protecting myself was concerned. It was like the Latin Kings were divided against each other. King Tino, the Inca himself, talked to me on the phone and said that no one but him had the power to take my crown. I was surprised that the Kings had come to the point where they were trying to outrank each other. The brothers in the street were not as obedient to the brothers in jail as they once were. On the other hand, the brothers in jail seemed more interested in making money than they were in the well-being of the foot soldiers on the street. Still, the major gang moves and most of the big drug traffic were controlled from behind penitentiary walls.

Knowing these facts, I should have been relieved by their friendly gestures. The truth was that the guys in jail were not going to shield me from bullets and the older brothers on the street were too busy making money off the younger gang members to protect me. I had to deal with the problem at hand on my own. I had to stop being a coward.

Loca found an apartment on the Far North Side of the city. The apartment was in the territory of a gang called the Simon City Royals. They were King killers. The Royals didn't know me and I stayed inside the house all the time to make sure it remained that way. Still, I had to commute to the university every day. The Kings somehow found out where I was working and began cruising around the area. Luckily I was always able to see them before they saw me. I made sure to keep out of their sight.

At the university Luisa was so impressed with my work that she offered me a full-time position working for her. I became a totally different person because of the people around me at the university. I became obsessed with gaining a college degree. I got so involved in trying to get into the university that I completely forgot about the Kings. Loca started giving me a hard time about spending too much time at school. She continuously accused me of having a girlfriend my own age behind her back. I talked to Loca about my desire for an education, but she was too insecure to believe me.

Loca was still selling cocaine and soon the Kings began coming around. I advised Loca that the Royals were gonna see the Kings coming into her apartment and come after her. Loca didn't listen.

Loca asked me to move out the first chance I got. She told me I could be with her or go to college. I chose college, but I had nowhere to stay, so I slept on Loca's sofa. Every day she would tell me I had to move out. She began sleeping with the King who supplied her with the cocaine she sold.

Finally I met a guy at work that was looking for a roommate and I moved in with him. The guy was gay. I felt uncomfortable but didn't have the luxury of being choosy. The guy actually turned out to be pretty cool. His name was Alan. He was a suburban white boy who was disowned by his father when he came out of the closet. His parents were divorced and his mother lived in California with his sisters. Being all alone was the only thing we had in common. We respected each other's sexual orientations, and therefore were able to live together without conflict.

At school I ran into my old friend Cindy, who was on campus waiting for a friend. I had not heard from her for about three years. She had grown into a beautiful woman. She was so happy to see me in school but was disappointed to find out that I only worked there. Cindy had done so much for herself. For some reason she wasn't able to attend Northwestern University as she had dreamed. Cindy, however, was a strong-willed individual and instead of giving up she found an alternative. She drove a brand-new car, worked in a bank, and was one semester away from a degree in business from DePaul University. Cindy's dream of moving her family out of the ghetto had been fulfilled and she was very proud of it.

Cindy was still blunt about how she thought I was wasting my life. She asked me if I was still a King. I thought about lying to her but couldn't. I explained that I was still a King but was not hanging out anymore. Cindy snapped at me just as she had years before. She told me I was still a coward needing a gang to back me up if I somehow screwed up. Cindy asked me to please stay away from kids at school who were getting an education, so that they wouldn't get hit by a bullet aimed at me. I was angry that she didn't appreciate the changes I had made in my life. I wanted to lash back but just sat there fuming as she walked away. That was the last time I saw Cindy. That confrontation lit a desire in me to go face the Kings and let whatever was going to happen happen.

52

Crownless

I WAS DETERMINED to finish my business with the Latin Kings—no more hiding, no more waiting, it was time to act. I got on the train and headed for Beach and Spaulding Streets. I got off the train at Damen Avenue and boarded a bus on North Avenue that would leave me right at Humboldt Park on Albany Street. I saw Spanky in the park. He was in a wheelchair being pushed by his wife. Loca was also at the park. They were surprised to see me; so were the Kings who were out there. Spanky and I talked as if nothing had happened between us. As far as I was concerned, nothing did happen. I played with Loca's youngest son for a little while, then walked to where several Kings had huddled. "Where's Chico?" I asked. "Tell him I want out," I told them. "Chico is locked up," one of them said. "King DJ is in charge now." I didn't know DJ, but apparently he knew me. The Kings drove me to Beach and Spaulding where DJ was.

DJ shook my hand as if I was still part of the Kings and tried to talk me out of getting out. Somehow DJ knew about my antics when I hung out at Kedzie and Armitage years back. He said the Kings needed brothers like me.

DJ realized he wasn't going to be able to talk me into remaining a King and called two brothers over. All four of us walked into the alley to a garage. DJ whispered something to one of the Kings and he took off running up the alley. The worst thoughts began going through my mind. I felt certain they were going to waste me. DJ noticed my nervousness and offered me a cigarette. I had stopped smoking but took it anyway. I needed something to calm my nerves. As we waited, DJ informed me that there was no need for me to get initiated out of the Kings. He advised that I could retire, be a brother in reserve and be active only if necessary. I liked what he said and actually thought about taking his advice. Then I thought about Kings like Chico who weren't going to accept anything other than my violation out of the gang. Cindy's words began to ring in my mind as if she was standing in front me. My mind was made up—I wanted out.

Within minutes the alley was full of Kings. DJ sent several of them to look out for the police. He chose two guys my size to do the honor of violating me out of the Kings and asked me if I was ready. I hesitated but then nodded yes. I stood against the garage with my hands crossed over my chest and waited for the punishment. The beating Slim had gotten when I first joined the Kings flashed in my mind. I expected the same treatment but didn't care. I refused to go on being known as a Latin King. I no longer wanted to be a coward. The two Kings stood in front of me cracking their knuckles and waiting for DJ to give the sign to start hitting me. DJ walked up to me and shook my hand with the Kings handshake and, as he looked me straight in the eyes, told the guys not to hit me in the face. DJ was definitely different from any King I had recently met. The brother had this "I care" look about him that made me feel relaxed. He stepped back, looked at his watch, and gave the signal.

For three minutes I withstood punches to my upper body and legs. Fortunately it was nowhere near as painful as the violations I had previously received. Finally it was all over. I was no longer a King. DJ hugged me and everybody walked away. I was left alone in the alley to get over the pain of the violation. I was there for about ten minutes but it seemed like hours. I was still waiting for the Kings to shoot me or beat me into submission. It never happened.

I walked out of the alley and up Beach Street toward the park. There was laughter and whispers as I walked by, but nobody said anything loud enough for me to hear. I wasn't a King any more. Finally I had the courage to stand on my own two feet. "*Amor*, brother," I heard DJ shout as I made my way toward the park. "*Amor*," I replied.

I had been a Latin King for six years. Although the relationship had long ago soured I couldn't help but feel as if I had lost something. I felt as if I had lost my family. It kind of hurt to know there was no turning back. Somewhere deep inside, however, I knew I had done the right thing.

53

Tragedies Continue With or Without Me

SPANKY AND LOCA were still at the park. They were selling cocaine and marijuana. Cars would come up, make their purchase, and drive away. I told them I wasn't a King anymore and bid them farewell. They didn't believe me. They had expected my violation out to leave me hospitalized, just as I had. I noticed that Loca had one of her little boys stashing bags of cocaine in his socks and I felt disgusted. I wanted to grab her by the neck and curse her out, but I held back. I turned toward the bus stop and began walking away without saying a last word to anybody. I didn't intend to ever set foot in the Humboldt Park area again. "Once a King, always a King," Spanky yelled as I walked toward North Avenue to catch a bus.

I was crossing the Boulevard inside the park when I heard gunshots. They came from the direction where Loca and Spanky were selling their drugs. Instinctively, I ran back toward them while ducking behind parked cars. As I got closer I saw Loca on the ground bleeding and Spanky struggling on the sidewalk trying to hide behind a parked car. Loca's son ran screaming toward his mother and then two more gunshots went off. I saw a bullet hit Loca's little boy Angel in the back and exit through his front. "No, no, no," I screamed as I stood up and ran toward him, not caring if I got shot. I picked him up and cradled him. "Don't die, little man, don't die," I cried. It was too late; he had died instantly. Loca lay on the ground screaming, more about her son being killed than from the pain she was feeling from being shot in the shoulder. "Don't worry, little man, I'll get revenge for you," I said as I held the little dead body. The police arrived and then the ambulance about fifteen minutes later. Loca was rushed to a hospital and her little boy was taken to the morgue. Many questions were asked, but nobody saw anything, nobody knew anything—the same old story. I tried my best to cooperate with the police but unfortunately I didn't even know from which direction the shots were fired. Soon the cops were gone. The dealers continued dealing. Life went on as if nothing had happened.

I sat there on the grass, covered with blood, thinking of revenge.

WHEN I FIRST left the Latin Kings I dreamed of going to college and getting my degree. I have not been able to fulfill this dream yet because I've had to support myself. But I still haven't given up hope. The first step, quitting the Latin Kings, was almost the easiest. It's been uphill since then. For many years after I quit gangbanging and doing drugs I had horrible nightmares about the things I saw and did on the streets. The only way I was able to get my life completely together was to move out of Chicago.

Deep inside I can't help but blame my mother for the direction I took as a young man. But I have forgiven her. I'm sure something went drastically wrong in her childhood to make her act the way she did. I'm hoping the vicious cycle stops with me.

Memories about my days as a gang member remain very present in my mind. I shed tears every time I hear news of another victim falling to gang violence. After all these years the only solutions we are offered are to increase the size of the police force and to form committees to assign committees to watch over the committees. Gang-infested communities are still looking for officials to rescue them from their own children. I think it's time we take responsibility for our own neighborhoods and put a stop to the crying. If we don't do something to change the law of revenge that gangs live by, the killing will never stop. I thank God for giving me the courage not to avenge Loca's little boy Angel.

ALSo BY REyMUNDo sANCHEZ

Once a King, Always a King
The Unmaking of a Latin King

"Courageously honest."
—*Washington Post Book World*

"A sorrowful memoir . . . whose power lies in the naked honesty with which [Sanchez] chronicles his ultimate deliverance from the past."
—Jeff Evans, author of *Undoing Time: American Prisoners in Their Own Words*

"Sanchez's story of survival in the face of great odds rings true." —*Publishers Weekly*

304 pages, 6 × 9
Paper, $16.95 (CAN $18.95)
978-1-55652-553-7

Lady Q
The Rise and Fall of a Latin Queen
With Sonia Rodriguez

"An oftentimes painful, close-up look at the blow-by-blow evolution of a female gang leader . . . reveals the fear, despair, and longing inside a seeming heart of stone."
—Gini Sikes, author of *8 Ball Chicks: A Year in the Violent World of Girl Gangs*

"Gripping and uncensored, reveals one woman's struggle to find a sense of belonging and power, then ultimately herself."
—AMBERmag.com

288 pages, 6 × 9
Cloth, $24.95 (CAN $27.95)
978-1-55652-722-7

Distributed by IPG
www.ipgbook.com

www.chicagoreviewpress.com
 @ChiReviewPress

Available at your favorite bookstore, by calling (800) 888-4741, or at www.chicagoreviewpress.com